ROGERS

—— V. ——

ROGERS

A L E X A N D R A
P O S A D Z K I

ROGERS
— V. —
ROGERS

THE BATTLE FOR CONTROL OF
CANADA'S TELECOM EMPIRE

McCLELLAND & STEWART

Library and Archives Canada Cataloguing in Publication
Title: Rogers v. Rogers : the battle for control of Canada's telecom
     empire / Alexandra Posadzki.
Names: Posadzki, Alexandra, author.
Identifiers: Canadiana (print) 20230485561 | Canadiana (ebook)
     20230485626 |
ISBN 9780771003639 (hardcover) | ISBN 9780771003646 (EPUB)
Subjects: LCSH: Rogers Communications. | LCSH: Rogers, Edward
     (Edward Samuel), 1969- | LCSH: Telecommunication—Canada.
Classification: LCC HE7820.R63 P67 2024 | DDC 384.06/571—dc23

Jacket design by Andrew Roberts
Jacket art: Rogers Chair of the Board Edward Rogers attends
the company's AGM in Toronto on Thursday, April 18, 2019.
The Canadian Press/Chris Young
Typeset in Plantin Text LT by M&S, Toronto
Printed in Canada

McClelland & Stewart,
a division of Penguin Random House Canada Limited,
a Penguin Random House Company
www.penguinrandomhouse.ca

1 2 3 4 5   28 27 26 25 24

For my parents, Jacek and Małgosia,
and for Frédéric and Ludwig

"Time shall unfold what plighted cunning hides.
Who cover faults, at last shame them derides."

—William Shakespeare, *King Lear*

CONTENTS

ROGERS

—————— V. ——————

ROGERS

PROLOGUE

One Saturday in late spring of 2022, a dozen people gathered at 3 Frybrook Road, a palatial, white stucco home with pale green shutters and meticulously landscaped gardens in Toronto's upscale Forest Hill neighbourhood. The house was built in the 1920s in the style of a château from France's Normandy region, for the daughter-in-law of William Christie, the founder of Canada's largest biscuit manufacturer. In 1963, it was bought by an affluent couple—a British member of Parliament named John Roland Robinson and his wife, Maysie, the American-born heiress to the Woolworth department store fortune—as a wedding gift for their daughter, Loretta Anne Rogers. The present, which cost $168,000, came with one condition: that Loretta and her husband, Ted, never mortgage the house to finance his fledgling business—a promise that the couple broke not once, but multiple times. Fortunately for Loretta, the gamble paid off. Over the years, as the company she helped finance grew from a handful of radio stations into a cable and wireless juggernaut, Ted and Loretta renovated and expanded the home, knocking down an adjacent property to build a tennis court. Loretta continued to live at 3 Frybrook Road long after her joints were too brittle for tennis and her husband had succumbed to congestive heart failure.

Loretta was born in London in 1939, just prior to the Second World War, and she maintained her English sensibilities when it came to decor. The master bedroom in which her guests had convened on that sunny day in early June was furnished with a marble-topped dressing table, a crystal chandelier, and peach-coloured drapes that spilled down to the floor. Gathered amid the rosewood and mahogany furniture were Loretta's three daughters: Melinda, the slender, blue-eyed mother of four with cascading chocolate-brown locks; Martha, the round-faced, curly-haired naturopath who rarely left her mother's side; and Lisa, the stern-looking, blonde former triathlete who had flown more than 3,000 kilometres from her home in Victoria, B.C. for the occasion. Also in attendance were Loretta's niece Carolyn Robinson, her grandson Zachary, a man named Bob Reeves who worked for the family holding company, and two of the city's most renowned doctors—a family physician named Dr. Bernie Gosevitz and a cardiologist, Dr. Heather Ross. Finally, there was a small contingent of Loretta's closest girlfriends: Inta Kierans and Judith McMurray, who was accompanied by her own daughter.

Loretta, McMurray, and Kierans were a tightknit group that affectionately referred to themselves as "The Bitches." The nickname was spelled out in rhinestones on various items of jewellery—including pins, necklaces, and bracelets—that they owned. Perpetually sun-kissed, the three women shared a playful sense of humour and spent their golden years pursuing the adventures that had eluded them when their children were young. Well into their late seventies and early eighties, they strapped on snorkelling gear and dove into the depths of the ocean to swim with the massive, spotted whale sharks off the coast of Placencia, Belize.

Now, after decades of friendship and countless trips aboard

the navy-hulled, 154-foot *Loretta Anne* yacht, The Bitches had come to say goodbye. Loretta, the 83-year-old Rogers family matriarch, was dying.

She had been diagnosed just a few months earlier with a rare and aggressive form of cancer. Loretta was a heavy smoker. When she attended Blue Jays games at the stadium that her family owned, there was always a golf cart waiting for her at the bottom of the elevator so that she could zip away for a cigarette. Still, the diagnosis had surprised her children. If their mother were to get cancer, surely it would be in her lungs, they had assumed. Instead, the malignancy had originated in her gallbladder and spread rapidly to her liver.

Loretta's relatively brief battle with the illness marked the end of a difficult and painful period in her life. She had spent the better part of the COVID-19 pandemic fearfully hiding from the deadly respiratory virus circulating the globe. The health crisis had triggered a communications breakdown in her family, as lockdowns kept family members isolated from one another. Then, in the fall of 2021, the matriarch had found herself embroiled in a calamitous duel between her adult children regarding who should preside over the telecom and media empire she had co-founded with her late husband.

The dispute took a heavy toll on Loretta. It was exactly the kind of embarrassing public spectacle that Ted would have wanted to avoid. And although the conflict was behind her as she lay semiconscious in her bed, surrounded by family members and friends, the wounds were still raw.

One person was conspicuously absent during Loretta's final hours: her only son, Edward.

According to several family friends, Loretta and Edward had failed to repair the rift that had formed between them after Edward tried to fire Rogers Communications Inc.'s chief executive, Joe Natale.

Edward had stated publicly that he had lost confidence in Natale, pointing to the company's lagging share price. However, his plan to replace the chief executive with the company's chief financial officer, Tony Staffieri, was met with resistance from several of the board's independent directors, as well as his mother and two of his sisters, who were concerned about destabilizing the company at a very crucial moment. Edward's planned leadership change was exposed just as Rogers was trying to complete the biggest and boldest deal in its storied, sixty-year history: a $20 billion takeover of Calgary-based Shaw Communications Inc. If the two telecoms could win the blessing of federal regulators, the merger would combine the country's east and west cable networks, transforming Rogers into the truly national player its founder had envisioned.

Then there was the covertness of the whole operation, which appeared to have been underway for some time before the rest of the family caught wind of it, and the allegedly strange manner in which Natale had accidentally learned of Edward's plan—a plot that involved purging not only the CEO but also the majority of the company's senior leadership team. By the time the issue was brought before the full board, Edward had effectively fired Natale. All that remained was to approve a generous exit package and determine Staffieri's compensation.

To put it mildly, this sat poorly with several of the company's independent directors, who were rankled that the chairman had stripped them of what they felt was the board's most important duty: hiring and firing the CEO. Regardless, the company's ownership structure had enabled Edward to do so. Rogers Communications has two classes of shares, a structure that Ted had established to ensure that his family never lost control of the company. The widely held Class B shares came with no voting rights. The Class A shares, in contrast, gave their owners the ability to vote on major corporate decisions, such as the election of directors. The vast majority of those shares—97.5 per cent, to be precise—were held through an entity called the Rogers Control Trust. Edward was its chair.

Loretta initially backed her son's decision to replace Natale with Staffieri. But she later had a change of heart, siding with her daughters Melinda and Martha and four independent directors in a stunning counter-coup that dominated headlines for weeks, roped in almost every major law firm on Bay Street, and sent shock waves through the country's normally staid business community. In court documents, Loretta claimed that her son had misled her about the CEO's performance, and accused him of undermining his father's wishes. As the battle escalated, eventually landing in a Vancouver courtroom over a bizarre and unprecedented legal stalemate, it was Loretta who moved the motion to oust Edward as the chair of the Rogers board.

The feud had died down in recent months, but the embers were still hot enough that even Loretta's impending death couldn't reconcile the family. It wasn't the first time that Edward had treated Rogers like his own private fiefdom, according to his opponents, who described it as a pattern of behaviour that he had exhibited over many years. This time, however, he had apparently gone too far. According to several people close to Loretta, she had made it known leading up to her death that her son was not welcome at her bedside. During a private moment, with both Melinda and Martha out of the room, McMurray had asked Loretta if she wanted to say goodbye to her son, one person said. The answer, which McMurray relayed to the family, was no. If true, this would mean that their fractured relationship could never be mended.

Edward, however, did not feel that there were unresolved issues between him and his mother, and he didn't hold her accountable for opposing him in the very public family spat. Moreover, he was convinced that it was the people around Loretta who were barring him and his family from saying goodbye to her.

Lisa had sided with her brother during the conflict. Loretta was hurt that her eldest daughter had gone against her, but the transgression was apparently not severe enough to exclude her from her mother's farewell gathering. Over the course of more than three hours, as soft music played, Lisa and the other guests moved through the room, taking turns saying goodbye and holding the frail, silver-haired woman's hands.

"I'm taking you to Belize," Judith McMurray loudly proclaimed at one point. Loretta didn't answer, but McMurray was certain that her friend had heard her, as the rhythm of her breathing changed.

ONE

A HEAVY BURDEN

Edward Samuel Rogers Jr. met Loretta Anne Robinson at a party in Lyford Cay, a lush Caribbean oasis of crystalline waters, glittering sand, and colonial-style homes. The small community on the western tip of New Providence Island in the Bahamas was growing at the time, having been bought just two years earlier by Edward Plunket Taylor, a Canadian business tycoon and thoroughbred horse breeder who gradually transformed the tangle of mangroves and dirt roads into a luxurious, high-society enclave. Today, there are 450 homes on the cay, and prospective buyers are advised to apply for membership at the ultra-exclusive Lyford Cay Club before attempting to purchase one of them, in case they are rejected. Despite all the money flowing through the place—and there is *lots* of it, as the country's lax taxation rules have attracted high-net-worth residents such as automotive magnate Henry Ford II, the Bacardi family, and actor Sean Connery—it prides itself on its unflashy, Old World feel. In December 1957, when Rogers boarded a plane to go visit a Sigma Chi fraternity brother, construction was still underway on the Lyford Cay Club where, decades later, one of his daughters would be wed.

Tall and lanky with bright blue eyes, Rogers—who went by Ted—was staying in the Bahamas with Ian Henderson, a fellow student at the University of Toronto and the son of the Bahamian chief justice. When Henderson was invited to a party at the Robinsons' winter getaway a few doors down, Ted tagged along.

Ted was only twenty-four at the time, but he was already shouldering a heavy burden. A rail-thin child, he had been afflicted with health problems for most of his young life. As an infant he had suffered from celiac disease so severe that it caused him to lose most of the vision in his right eye. His father, Edward Samuel Rogers Sr., was a hard-driving inventor and entrepreneur who paid little attention to his son, opting instead to spend late nights tinkering with electronics in the basement of their Toronto home. Ted was only five years old when his mother, Velma, found her husband hunched over the sink in their blood-drenched bathroom, suffering from a ruptured aneurysm. He was rushed to Toronto General Hospital, where he underwent surgeries and received blood transfusions, but it was no use. Ted Rogers Sr., the inventor of the world's first plug-in radio and the founder of Toronto radio station CFRB, died on May 6, 1939. He was thirty-eight.

After her husband's death, Velma sank into alcoholism and, at the urging of her brother-in-law Elsworth, sold the family radio businesses, a move she spent the rest of her life regretting. To compensate for her misstep, Velma instilled in her son a dogged determination to regain what the family had lost.

Living up to the legacy of his father, a man who some had regarded as a genius, was a heavy cross for a young boy to bear, especially one with chronic health issues. At boarding school, Ted often fell asleep thinking about how he would get CFRB, the radio station whose call letters stood for Canada's First Rogers Batteryless, back under his family's control.

Ted didn't want to go to boarding school, but he was sent away at age seven on the advice of a pediatrician who believed that he needed a male influence in his life. After he spent a short and miserable stint at a school in Montebello, Quebec, Ted's grandmother convinced Velma to move him to Upper Canada College, an elite boys' school a short distance from the family's home in Toronto. His time at UCC featured regular canings from teachers and relentless bullying from his peers, who nicknamed him "Bones." These would have been traumatic incidents for any child, but especially for a boy who, prior to losing his father, had a nanny at his beck and call.

Ted hated life at UCC and desperately wanted to live at home. There was a glimmer of hope in 1941 when his mother remarried, but then his stepfather, John Webb Graham, was sent off to Europe to fight in the Second World War. Ted remained at UCC until he turned seventeen, seeing little of his baby sister, Ann, in the first few years of her life, even though he boarded only blocks away.

Despite his setbacks, Ted was undeterred. He took up boxing, eventually winning in his weight class, and also excelled at debating. From an early age he exhibited entrepreneurial instincts. In 1949, at the dawn of the television era, he rigged an antenna to the roof of his dormitory, connected it to a television, and charged the other boys admission. Although his high school grades were unimpressive, he was admitted to Trinity College at the University of Toronto, where he studied law and joined the Sigma Chi fraternity. He also became chairman of the National Progressive Conservative Student Federation, a position he used to help populist candidate John Diefenbaker win the Tory leadership. (Years later, after he had gotten into broadcasting, the gutsy Ted, panicking because he had only been given a ten-minute window with "Dief the Chief," would follow the prime minister into the bathroom to pitch him on something relating to business.)

Diefenbaker, a defence lawyer originally from small-town Ontario who campaigned on the promise of a more inclusive Canada, had just become prime minister when Ted found himself talking politics on the front steps of the Robinsons' Bahamian home.

His friend Henderson had gone inside, but Ted was enthralled by John "Jack" Roland Robinson, a Conservative British MP who had been knighted and would later become Baron Martonmere.

Like Ted's hero Diefenbaker, his future father-in-law was a populist. He pushed for paid holidays for workers and opposed government policies that hurt the poor. Nonetheless, his family lived a gilded lifestyle. His kids attended prestigious schools and bounced between family homes in Lyford Cay, Tucker's Town in Bermuda, and London. A picture taken in 1974 by Slim Aarons, an American photographer known for his images of jet-setting socialites in stunning locales, depicts Lord and Lady Martonmere in their Sunday best, strolling arm in arm alongside a Roman-shaped pool in the garden of their palatial Lyford Cay home, the Villa El Mirador.

Despite her family's wealth, Loretta's childhood was not an easy one. She was born in London on April 13, 1939, just before the war. When she was only a few months old, the government started evacuating millions of British children from towns and cities to keep them safe from German air raids, separating them from their parents, who stayed behind to work. Loretta and her older brother, Richard, were sent to live with the Woolworths in New York. Five years later, when the war had ended, the children waited at a train station to be reunited with their parents. Loretta, who had spent the most formative years of her childhood thousands of miles from home, had no idea what her mother looked like. Each time a woman walked past, she asked Richard, "Is that Mummy?"

Reintegrating the family after the war proved challenging. Although she had developed a close bond with her brother while overseas, Loretta clashed with her mother, who wanted her to be a proper lady. Maysie Robinson was an intimidating woman—a concert pianist and accomplished pilot who spoke fluent French and Italian. As a teenager, Loretta developed a rebellious streak. She smoked cigarettes, learned to sail, and eschewed the drab, conservative clothing that her mother wanted her to wear, in favour of bold, bright colours. While her mother followed a vegetarian diet, Loretta developed a taste for red meat.

"She could be stubborn," said Loretta's best friend, Judith McMurray. At Loretta's childhood home in England, there was a birch tree in the backyard. "If there was something she didn't want to do, she'd just take a book and go up the tree."

Ted and Jack Robinson had been chatting about politics for nearly half an hour when eighteen-year-old Loretta walked by, catching Ted's eye. Despite his establishment roots—the Rogers family were pacifist Quakers who had settled in Newmarket, Ontario, just after the American Revolution—Ted always considered himself somewhat of an outsider in high society. That helped him click with the rebellious Loretta, although she later teased him that he spent most of the night talking politics with her dad.

Ted remembered it differently. "We danced, and danced again," he wrote in his 2008 autobiography, *Relentless: The True Story of the Man Behind Rogers Communications*. The next thing he knew, everyone—including Ian Henderson—had gone home. Ted was left all alone to haul another partygoer, who was on the couch rapidly fading, out the door—but not before securing a dinner date with Loretta for the following evening. "I was intoxicated, but not with alcohol. It had been a fairy tale evening. That may sound corny, but that's how it felt."

Ted and Loretta spent much of their six-year courtship apart. Loretta attended Wellesley College, a prestigious private women's institution in Massachusetts, but she found the school's attitude too stuck-up. She transferred to the University of Miami, which was a better fit for the young sun-worshipper. A skilled painter who also excelled at math, she was told to choose one or the other but stubbornly refused and took courses in both.

Ted, meanwhile, attended Osgoode Hall Law School in Toronto. He wasn't particularly keen on joining the legal profession, but his mother insisted he have a plan B in case his business pursuits didn't pan out. Despite nearly flunking out of the program, he managed to talk his way into an articling position at Torys law firm, where he befriended John A. Tory, the son of the firm's founder. But his attention frequently wavered from his legal career, drifting instead to his entrepreneurial pursuits. Before law school, Ted had launched Rogers Music Services, a company that booked musicians to perform at school dances and other functions. The venture was so successful that he drew heat from the musicians' union for hiring non-members.

In 1959, standing between rows of books in the Torys library, Ted made a phone call that would alter the trajectory of his life. The federal government was planning to license Toronto's first private television station, and Ted wanted in. The problem was that he didn't have the capital for such a venture. While this may have been the end of the story for most people, Ted picked up the receiver and cold-called John Bassett.

Bassett—known as "Big John" on account of his towering, six-foot-four frame—was an intimidating, Ottawa-born newspaperman with a booming voice and a habit of slamming his fists on the table to punctuate a point. He was heading up a bid for the TV licence along with the Eaton family, of the now-defunct department store chain. When Ted read in the newspaper that another one of Bassett's partners, Roy Thomson, was pulling out of the bid in order to focus on his Scottish TV stations, he saw an opening.

At first, Bassett was skeptical of the unknown voice on the other end of the line. "Who the hell are you? I don't know you," he barked. But after a brief conversation—one where Ted name-dropped his business partner, the famous broadcaster Joel Aldred, as well as a number of Ottawa politicians he personally knew— Big John agreed to meet with him. In the end, Bassett's Baton

Broadcasting Ltd. gave Aldred Rogers Ltd. roughly a third of the CFTO bid.

On March 14, 1960, the Bassett-Eaton-Aldred-Rogers group appeared in front of the Board of Broadcast Governors, or BBG, in the Oak Room at Toronto's Union Station. Their bid faced stiff competition, including from the *Toronto Star* newspaper and CFRB, the radio station that had once belonged to Ted's dad. But in spite of a freak snowstorm that caused their elaborately planned video presentation to blow a circuit and plunge the hearing into darkness, they emerged victorious. The regulator awarded them the licence on March 24, giving them eight months to launch their station.

Almost immediately, things started to go wrong. Aldred, who had stepped into the CEO role, was clashing with Bassett, and the station's cost overruns were getting hefty. It wasn't long before Bassett gave Aldred the boot. Ted got to stay on but saw his ownership stake whittled down to 10 per cent.

At the same time, Ted was working furiously to get into radio, fuelled by the tremendous burden of his father's legacy in the sector. On September 30, 1960, Ted paid $85,000 to buy an FM radio station, CHFI-FM, from another entrepreneur, at a time when AM radio still reigned supreme. It was a risky bet, as few Canadians had FM receivers, but the sound quality produced by FM was indisputably superior.

Ted's early foray into radio was by no means glamorous. CHFI's studios were located in a three-storey building in Toronto's downtown core that was so infested with cockroaches that the company's chief financial officer quit because of the bugs crawling up his pant legs when he went to the bathroom.

Ted worked hard to popularize FM receivers, striking a deal with Canadian Westinghouse Company Ltd. to manufacture inexpensive sets bearing his station's call sign on the front in gold lettering. But he desperately needed a sister station in the more profitable AM market to subsidize the costs of the money-losing operation, and the AM dial was already crowded.

As he fought to secure an AM frequency, Ted faced attacks from CFRB. The station's owners even tried to sue Ted for copyright infringement when he changed his company's name to Rogers Broadcasting Ltd. in 1962. (CFRB's parent company, although operating as Standard Radio Ltd., had held on to the rights to the name Rogers Radio Broadcasting Company Ltd.) John Graham, who had taken on the role of mentor to his stepson, successfully argued that Ted had a right to operate a company under his family name.

As the battle for an AM station intensified, Ted passed his law school exams and was called to the bar, fulfilling his promise to his mother. Although she had gotten sober some ten years earlier, Velma now faced a battle against throat cancer that would span the better part of a decade. The news devastated Ted. "She was my rock, and this diagnosis would hit me hard," he wrote in his book.

Jack Robinson, meanwhile, was getting impatient with the ambitious young entrepreneur who had been dating his daughter for some time and had yet to ask for her hand in marriage. After receiving a stern lecture in a New York hotel room, Ted headed to Birks, Toronto's finest jewellery store, and—with a combination of debt and radio advertising time—purchased a three-carat ring. The couple was wed on September 25, 1963, an uncharacteristically sunny day by London standards, at St. Margaret's Church, Westminster. Toby Hull, Ted's childhood best friend and an insurance salesman, was his best man.

If Loretta had any delusions about married life curbing Ted's workaholic tendencies, they were quickly stamped out. Ted worked en route to the wedding, aboard the *Queen Elizabeth* that carried him across the Atlantic. Then, he cut their Kenya honeymoon in half, after just nine days, to attend a broadcast hearing in Ottawa.

The stakes were high. The new Liberal government had thrown a wrench into his AM licence ambitions, and without an AM station and the money it could generate, CHFI would not survive. "Without victory, the Rogers name in Canadian communications could have been extinguished forever," Ted later wrote. After a series of regulatory and logistical hurdles, he eventually secured his AM station, at the 680 spot on the dial. But his battle—to turn Rogers Communications Inc. into a $30 billion communications behemoth and build a legacy of his own, one rivalling his father's—was only just beginning.

Ted wanted to make it up to Loretta for cutting their honeymoon short. So in February 1967, the pair went on a six-week trip to the South Pacific, where Loretta could indulge her love of snorkelling. Loretta was obsessed with the ocean, which inspired many of her paintings. She loved the turquoise waters, bright corals, and tropical fish.

Meanwhile, Ted—being the kind of person who took his work with him everywhere he went—was getting bitten by the cable bug. Even while taking in some of the world's most beautiful sights with the woman he loved, the young entrepreneur was preoccupied with the future of cable television. In Australia, he met for several hours with media tycoon Rupert Murdoch to discuss the broadcasting business. (Murdoch wasn't yet an international success, but he was already a big deal in Australia, and Ted was grateful for his time.) In Fiji, he devoured a book about cable television, then heralded as the future of programming. By the time the couple got back to Toronto, Ted was dead set on entering the nascent cable industry.

He formed Rogers Cable TV Ltd. and bought a cable television licence from the federal transport department for $25. That was the easy part. The trickier part was securing the funds to pay the local phone company—in this case, Bell Canada—to string cables along its poles.

The first batch of funding came from Loretta, who, shortly after their wedding, convinced her father to advance her money from her inheritance to invest in her husband's business ventures. This made Loretta a business partner and earned her a seat on the company's board. When Ted got the idea of going into cable, it was Loretta who personally paid the $225,000 down payment for the first 600,000 metres of cable to be laid.

The next round of financing came from John Bassett. Ted offered Baton Broadcasting half of the company if it put up two-thirds of the funding. Bassett agreed.

For a while, things seemed to be going well. Having secured financing, the company got to work laying cable, signing up customers, and acquiring other local cable operations. But the partnership with Baton would later backfire, triggering the first of several near-death experiences that Rogers Cable would face.

In the meantime, Ted was encountering a different, more personal challenge. He and Loretta were having trouble conceiving. After unsuccessfully trying various fertility treatments, they decided to adopt. Born on October 9, 1967, Lisa Anne Rogers came into their lives. "My eyes welled up with happy tears as soon as I saw her," Ted later recalled. "She was so beautiful."

Although the baby brought the couple much joy, Ted wasn't ready to give up on conceiving a child, and he flew to Seattle for yet another procedure. This time, it worked; just days later, Loretta became pregnant with their first and only son. Edward Samuel Rogers III, the heir apparent to the Rogers family empire, was born on June 22, 1969. Melinda Mary Rogers followed a year and a half later, on January 27, 1971.

While the tides were turning in a positive direction at home, political storm clouds had begun gathering over Ted's radio and cable businesses. In response to lobbying from the *Toronto Star*, which felt that *Toronto Telegram* owner Baton had gotten too big, Pierre Trudeau's Liberal government set up a commission on media ownership concentration. On July 10, less than three weeks after Edward's birth, the telecom regulator announced that it would only renew Rogers Cable's licences if Baton exited the sector. Ted later described the news as "devastating, perhaps the darkest day of my business life."

Ted immediately started scrounging for the money to buy Baton's 50 per cent share of the company. He approached newspapers, real estate companies, a pension fund, and a movie theatre, all to no avail. Money was so tight during this period that, after covering payroll, Ted would place the company's unpaid bills into a hat and draw them until he ran out of funds. Loretta was a rock of support. The couple put a triple mortgage on their home, breaking their promise to her parents that they would never borrow against the house.

It was during this cash crunch that Philip Bridgman Lind joined the company. A notorious troublemaker and practical joker whose rebellious nature had earned him the nickname "Fidel" at boarding school, Lind was the oldest of four children born to Walter (Jed) Lind, a lawyer who had trained bomber pilots during the war, and Susie, a tough but loving woman with a green thumb. Phil's paternal grandfather, John Grieve Lind, had struck pay dirt in the Yukon during the Klondike Gold Rush, and had used the spoils to start a successful cement company in St. Marys, a small town in southwestern Ontario.

Lind was a teenager when he first met Ted at a national Tory convention, where they found themselves on opposite sides of the nuclear weapons issue that divided the party. Ted, then in his late twenties but still baby-faced, loyally supported Diefenbaker's anti-nuclear position. Lind, who belonged to the party's youth wing, was among the pro-nuclear contingent. Despite their ideological differences, Ted sent Lind, who was friends with his sister Ann, a congratulatory note when he later landed a job at the Progressive Conservative Party.

In October 1969, Ted hired Lind to work at his radio company, before putting him in charge of cable TV programming. Lind was a political junkie, having studied the subject in school—first at the University of British Columbia, where he fell in love with the West Coast, and then while completing his master's degree at the University of Rochester. His understanding of politics made him indispensable to the telecom as it navigated one regulatory quagmire after another. Over the years, he became one of Ted's closest advisers—his right-hand man, as Lind would later boast in his memoir, not so subtly titled *Right Hand Man: How Phil Lind Guided the Genius of Ted Rogers, Canada's Foremost Entrepreneur.*

On July 14, 1971, the day before the deadline for Baton to sell its Rogers stake, Ted's bankers at the Toronto Dominion Bank came through with a lifeline: a $2.3 million loan from the bank-owned venture capital company UNAS Investments Ltd. The UNAS loan carried a punishing 15 per cent interest rate and other tough terms, but it pulled the company back from the brink of bankruptcy.

After signing the papers, Ted and Loretta went to deliver the news to Velma. Despite her illness, she remained an active director of her son's company, with Ted often holding board meetings around her bed. Velma seemed pleased that night when she learned that Rogers Cable would survive at least another six months. She, however, would not be so fortunate. On November 5, 1971, Velma Melissa Rogers-Graham died in her home. She didn't live long enough to see her son's company flourish, nor to welcome her youngest grandchild, Martha Loretta Rogers, into the world on April 6, 1972.

Ted was a man racing against time. When his mother died, he was thirty-eight—the age at which his own father's life had been tragically cut short. He frequently told people, including his young son Edward, that he was going to die at an early age. "I've got to build this company before I hit this wall," he told fellow radio station owner Milton Maltz. "I've got to get this done before I hit that birthday because I don't know if I'm going to make it or not."

The one thing Ted would never get done was take back control of his father's radio station, CFRB. His family still owned some shares in CFRB's parent company, Standard Broadcasting Ltd. (formerly Standard Radio), and in his twenties, Ted was spending so much time at the station's studios that the owner had him barred from the premises and ordered all the pictures of his father taken down. The move only strengthened Ted's resolve. He made four attempts to buy the station, but his overtures were rejected. Finally, Loretta sat him down in their backyard and told him to let the dream go. "We have our own radio stations that you've built, with wonderful people working at them," she said. Ted took his wife's advice; a few years later, in 1975, he sold the last of the family's shares.

Starting in 1979, Ted made a series of acquisitions that would reshape the Canadian cable industry and secure his spot as the country's boldest communications entrepreneur. In the late 1970s, Canada's patchwork of small, family-owned cable systems started consolidating. "Eat or be eaten" became the industry's mantra. Loretta may have hoped this trend would lead to her hard-driving husband slowing down and spending more time with the family, but instead of taking his foot off the gas, Ted accelerated. While he had made great strides as a businessman, he wanted to secure his legacy for the next generation, to ensure that it couldn't be erased by his death. "Need new mountains to climb," he wrote in his day planner in 1977.

He found them, in the form of a pair of transformative deals. In 1979, after a bitter, eighteen-month battle, Rogers Cable acquired Canadian Cablesystems, the country's second-largest cable network. At the same time, Rogers made its stock market debut through a reverse takeover, a process through which a private company becomes publicly traded by acquiring a public company.

The following year, Rogers swallowed up another industry giant, Premier Cablesystems. The acquisitions vaulted Rogers Cable from sixth-largest cable company to the top spot, as its subscriber count grew from 200,000 to 1.3 million. The company's debt load also grew, from $2.5 million to $114 million, just as the economy headed for a period of runaway inflation.

But Ted still wasn't done. His ability to expand in Canada was limited; after closing two massive acquisitions, Rogers Cablesystems controlled almost a third of the Canadian cable market. So, on the advice of Lind and an executive named Colin Watson, the company ventured south of the border, where a cable gold rush was underway. In the early 1980s, Rogers snapped up dozens of local cable licences and picked up a majority stake in UA-Columbia Cablevision Inc., the tenth-largest cable company in the United States. Soon, Ted's face was gracing the cover of an American cable-industry trade magazine.

At the same time, Ted was planting the seeds of what would one day be the company's most profitable business line: wireless telephony. Ted was fascinated by cellular technology, which untethered callers from their landlines and could carry thousands of phone calls on the same airwaves simultaneously. But when he took the idea to his board in 1983, they shot it down; every director, including his wife, voted against the move. The company was in too much debt, interest rates were in the double digits, and the economy was in recession. Not to be deterred, Ted decided to invest his own money, entering into a three-way partnership with financier Marc Belzberg and Philippe de Gaspé Beaubien, the owner of broadcaster and publisher Telemedia Inc. And so Cantel was born.

The consortium won a national licence to use wireless airwaves on the electromagnetic spectrum to deliver cellular services, then set about building a national network. It was a costly and difficult project. Raising money was a problem, as Canadian investors were skeptical of Cantel's forecasts of explosive growth—predictions that, in hindsight, were extremely conservative. Cantel was forced to seek out an American investor, breaking its promises to Ottawa about Canadian ownership.

Also troubling was the state of the three-way partnership. From Ted's perspective, it was a Cerberus—a three-headed monster with no one in charge. The stress got so intense that, days before the carrier's July 1, 1985 launch, Ted suffered a silent heart attack.

Meanwhile, bankers were constantly nipping at the cable company's heels. Rogers had funded its U.S. expansion with bank loans, and interest rates were soaring. Michael Milken, the now-disgraced Wall Street wiz from Drexel Burnham Lambert who architected high-yield or "junk" bonds, helped Rogers raise US$181 million. Even so, money was tight.

The junk bonds also created a new problem. They attracted a slew of American investors. Although Ted controlled the company through his ownership of voting Class A shares, the majority of the company's equity was owned by non-Canadians, potentially putting the telecom offside in terms of foreign ownership rules. Worried that the broadcasting regulator, the Canadian Radio-television and Telecommunications Commission, might not renew the licence for CFMT-TV—the multicultural TV station that he had just acquired—Ted turned to Garfield Emerson for advice. Emerson, a lawyer who was married to Ted's cousin Melissa, was gaining prominence as an expert in the emerging field of corporate governance. On Emerson's advice, Ted barred Americans from selling Class A shares to non-Canadians, causing both classes of the company's stock to tumble. He then tried to buy back 8 million of the company's Class B shares from American owners, but the Ontario Securities Commission wouldn't permit such a targeted buyback. Ted was stuck.

Thankfully, Emerson came up with a solution. On October 20, 1987, the day after the massive stock market crash known as Black Monday, the newly renamed Rogers Communications Inc. was incorporated in British Columbia. The manoeuvre provided a tax benefit, while also addressing a technical aspect of the foreign ownership rules. But the B.C. incorporation would have unforeseen long-term consequences. More than three decades later, an unusual bit of B.C. corporate law would play a significant role in the fractious legal battle between the company's management and its controlling shareholder.

On a Sunday afternoon in April 1988, Ted summoned Lind and Watson to his home to share some difficult news. He had decided to sell the U.S. cable systems.

Both men had seen the writing on the wall. Rogers Communications was $1 billion in the hole after repatriating stock from its American investors, and Ted needed cash to invest in the wireless industry, which he could sense was on the verge of taking off. It was clear that he had already made up his mind. Still, Lind and Watson argued as persuasively as they could for remaining in the U.S. They had built so much so fast, and the American cable market was exploding. "Colin and I argued that many more opportunities would lie ahead if we didn't sell," Lind wrote in *Right Hand Man*. "Ted Rogers listened on that spring day, but that debt was hanging over the company like the sword of Damocles. And he knew it. So did we."

Then, Ted dropped another bomb: doctors had found an aneurysm along an artery just below his kidney. He needed surgery, and he didn't want to put it off. Ted most certainly knew how fatal a ruptured aneurysm could be.

The three-hour surgery was a success, but the recovery was more difficult than Ted had anticipated. He spent the better part of six weeks recuperating at his cottage on Tobin Island in Muskoka. Still, he managed to hold business meetings with senior staff and even briefly pop into the office a few times.

Meanwhile, a number of prospective buyers were kicking the tires of the U.S. cable operations. In February 1989, Rogers sold the business to Houston Industries Inc., the parent company of power utility Houston Lighting & Power, for US$1.37 billion—a US$1 billion profit. The money from the sale allowed Rogers Communications to buy out all of Cantel's owners, including the shares held by Rogers Telecommunications Ltd., Ted's family holding company.

Rogers Communications now had a horse in the wireless race. But Cantel was an insatiable money pit, eating up more than half of the company's capital expenditures in 1989 and 1990. By the end of 1990, the telecom's long-term debt had climbed to $1.9 billion, with its foray into wireless largely to blame.

Meanwhile, as one disastrous, three-way partnership dissolved, another was born. After buying out Cantel, Rogers was able to offer its customers both wireless and cable TV services. But Ted longed to be able to compete with Bell in landline telephony. So, in April 1989, Rogers bought a stake in CNCP Telecommunications, a telecom known as Unitel that was trying to open up the lucrative long-distance telephony market to competition.

Although the Canadian Radio-television and Telecommunications Commission did eventually open up the long-distance voice market, letting Unitel into the game, Ted once again found himself in a three-way partnership with no one in the driver's seat. Rogers and one of its partners, the American telecom AT&T, had ideas on how to turn the lagging business around, but felt that the third partner, the overly bureaucratic Canadian Pacific (or CP) railway firm, was standing in their way. The situation culminated in a vicious screaming match between Ted and CP's chairman and CEO, Bill Stinson. In the end, a consortium of banks took over Unitel, along with AT&T. Rogers lost $500 million on the venture, which Ted would later describe as "the worst business disaster of my life."

While the Unitel situation was playing out, Ted found himself grappling with another problem. Medical imaging had found blockages in several arteries at the base of his heart. As he prepared to undergo a quadruple heart bypass, Ted became contemplative. At his home, he sorted through personal items, put together a few family photo albums, and updated his family tree. It was time to get his estate in order.

TWO

FAST EDDIE

Toronto's most exclusive private club is housed within a three-storey, red-brick building that occupies the southeast corner of Wellington Street West and York Street. Built in 1889 by Frank Darling, the Canadian architect behind many of Toronto's landmark buildings, and his junior partner S. George Curry, the members-only clubhouse oozes understated elegance. But to JR Shaw, the western Canadian cable operator who had grown up playing hockey on frozen creeks and helping his parents on the family farm, it might as well have been Buckingham Palace.

JR had been summoned to the Toronto Club one evening in early 1994 by Ted. Although they were meeting on his turf, Ted was feeling somewhat uncomfortable. The two ageing cable titans were seated in an oak-panelled dining room at opposite ends of a very large table adorned with a white linen tablecloth. Ted felt strange negotiating across such a vast physical distance, but the matter before them was pressing.

While recovering from his quadruple heart bypass, Ted had taken some time to consider what to do next with his business. He had resolved to focus less on administrative tasks and more on strategic decision-making. Less than two years later, he found himself in the midst of a hostile takeover battle for cable and media conglomerate Maclean Hunter, whose Ontario cable systems neighboured his own. It was a delicate situation, as he was trying to avoid triggering a poison pill—a takeover defence that would flood the market with Maclean Hunter stock, making the deal significantly more expensive. The pill, or shareholders' rights protection plan, had been crafted by Garfield Emerson. Fortunately for Ted, the securities lawyer was now working for him, looking for ways to thwart the mechanism. But there was a problem: Maclean Hunter president Ron Osborne, who wanted to maximize shareholder value, had struck up talks with JR, trying to entice him into stepping into the role of the white knight and prying Maclean Hunter out of Ted's hands.

Ted liked JR. Virtually everyone did. The affable entrepreneur owed at least part of his success to the fact that people simply wanted to do business with him. He was born in Brigden, Ontario, a small agricultural community southeast of Sarnia, in 1934, making him a year younger than Ted. After completing a business degree at Michigan State University, JR moved his young family to Edmonton, where his dissatisfaction with his television choices prompted him to start a cable company just as the industry was taking off. He expanded his empire by befriending the families that owned nearby cable systems and persuading them to sell.

Ted needed to convince JR to back away from Maclean Hunter or he risked losing the deal. He proposed a truce. They could split up the cable properties, with Rogers picking up the eastern systems while Shaw snapped up those in the west.

The offer came as little surprise to JR. The night before, he had plotted out a similar plan over dinner with his two eldest children, Jim and Heather. The cable industry was continuing to consolidate, with smaller companies being gobbled up by larger rivals, and JR was determined to keep his company alive. But he also knew that if he went head-to-head with Ted and lost, he would get nothing. And he feared that if he made life difficult for the hot-tempered Toronto entrepreneur, he would have to contend with his wrath. In a sector that was shrinking to just a handful of players, JR saw the value of maintaining constructive relationships with his competitors. He agreed to the deal. Rogers would buy Maclean Hunter, then split the spoils with Shaw.

With the Shaws out of the way, Ted sealed the $3.1 billion takeover. He was now the owner of magazines such as *Maclean's* and *Chatelaine*, several dozen more radio and TV stations, and the *Sun* newspaper chain, as well as the cable operations. The deal ushered Rogers into a new era of convergence, where telecom companies—which controlled the "pipes" of cable, satellite, and wireless connections—were gobbling up content creators. It was also the start of a multi-generational bond between two families, one which was sealed over decades of funerals and elaborate practical jokes, and which split the country's cable systems into east and west.

Ted and Loretta's four children spent their summers in Muskoka, an idyllic region of Ontario carved into the rock formations of the Canadian Shield by retreating glaciers that left behind a tangle of rivers and some 1,600 lakes. One of those lakes is called Lake Rosseau, and in the middle of it sits Tobin Island, which houses the Rogers family cottage. Timeless and homey with a glass front, Ted had the cottage built next to his mother's when he was twenty-five years old. (Loretta, then nineteen, teased him for micromanaging the construction workers.)

For Melinda, one of the most highly anticipated aspects of these family excursions was not the destination but the journey itself. The kids would pile into an old Buick station wagon and brace themselves for a section of highway that dipped down before steeply climbing back up. When they got to "roller coaster road," Loretta would check to make sure there were no other cars around. Then, tightening her grip on the wheel and grinning wildly, she'd step on the gas, sending the car flying down the dip and back up, the kids laughing ecstatically while their stomachs dropped.

The children were close, particularly Edward, Melinda, and Martha. In the days prior to digital gadgets such as tablets and smartphones, the kids amused themselves by playing together outside. They would cover themselves in clay on the beach, or fill a canoe with water, allowing it to sink into the sand in a shallow part of the lake, creating a tub for them to play in. Sometimes they would flip the canoe over in the lake and hide from the grown-ups in the pocket that formed beneath it. They took up water sports, with Edward mastering tricks on the kneeboard while Lisa learned to waterski. Their dog, a Maltese sheepdog named, appropriately enough, Malta, chased them while they rode the zip line from their wooden playhouse, nipping at their butts.

In 1977, Ted and Loretta bought an oceanfront home in Lyford Cay, near Loretta's parents' place, for $177,000. It had been built after the First World War by a Wall Street financier, who owned it for half a century before his son inherited it upon his death. Loretta was a permissive mother who allowed her kids to fill a bathtub in the Nassau home with water, sand, and a couple of errant crabs that they had pulled out of the ocean. Their Toronto home, 3 Frybrook, was essentially a zoo. At various points in time, it housed mice, gerbils, guinea pigs, rabbits, dogs, budgies, a chicken, a rooster, and three ducks named Huey, Dewey, and Louie. (Loretta even allowed the chicken, the rooster, and the ducks to live in Melinda's bedroom for a period of time, before they were moved into hutches outside.)

The ducks were from a hatching program at Bishop Strachan, a private girls' school housed in a Collegiate Gothic structure. All three of Ted and Loretta's daughters attended the school on Lonsdale Road in Forest Hill, not far from their home. They all got good grades and made the dean's list. Loretta sat on the board and was a significant fundraiser for the institution, wrangling donations from friends such as Larry Tanenbaum, the construction magnate who lived across the street. Women's empowerment was important to her, and she loved how the school, whose mission was to create future leaders, boosted girls' confidence. It was through her involvement with the school that Loretta met Judith and Inta, fellow mothers of Bishop Strachan students who became her lifelong friends.

Like his father, Edward Samuel Rogers III studied at Upper Canada College. He was a shy, awkward boy with a stutter and big shoes to fill. At the time, it was typical for fathers to hand the keys to their business dynasties to their sons, and many believed that Ted was grooming his own son for the role. Edward was eight years old when he attended his first telecom regulatory hearing. He and his sister Lisa sat in the front row with Loretta while the Canadian Radio-television and Telecommunications Commission tried to resolve the contested Canadian Cablesystems takeover. The children's presence caught the attention of CRTC commissioner Charles Dalfen, who quipped to Ted, "Maybe, at the next one, you can bring your grandmother." The children were gone after the break.

As a teenager, Edward took a stab at entrepreneurship, starting a business called Rogers' Food Services that delivered food to people's cottages in Muskoka. Eventually, it drew the ire of a local grocer, who complained to the health ministry about improper refrigeration. Ted believed that the complaint was just a ruse to shut down his son's company, and he chewed out the man on Edward's behalf.

Business was certainly the way to earn Ted's attention. Although he had a childlike spirit and loved to play with the kids and all the animals in the house, he was also a workaholic who disappeared into his binders after dinner while Loretta entertained their guests. Sometimes, on weekends, he brought Edward to the office with him. Some family friends and former Rogers executives, playing armchair psychologist, speculated that the weight of Ted's expectations was responsible for Edward's stutter.

Ted later regretted not spending more time with the kids, particularly in the 1970s and early '80s, when they were very young. Of course, Rogers was facing huge challenges back then, "but, looking back, that's not good enough: I should have carved out more time for them," he wrote.

Loretta loved her children deeply and was always there for them when they needed her. But she wasn't the most hands-on mother, particularly when it came to organizing sports and other activities for her kids. This likely stemmed from the fact that she herself hadn't grown up in a traditional nuclear family. Much of the day-to-day childcare fell to the family's live-in butler. Ricardo, who was from Spain, became something of a second father to the kids. Tall, dark, and handsome, he spoke English fluently but sometimes slipped into Spanish when he was tired. Ricardo's duties included chauffeuring Ted around, preparing breakfast, and getting the kids out the door for school. He brought them musical instruments to play and tried to teach them how to dance.

Frybrook was a hub of after-school activity. The Rogers kids would host their friends in an upstairs playroom outfitted with a small kitchenette, a television, a couch, and a corded phone with three lines. They watched shows like *Fantasy Island*, *Mork & Mindy*, *Bewitched*, and *The Love Boat*. Sometimes they would get their hands on Loretta's cigarettes and break them, which made their mother furious. Eventually, they outgrew the playroom, and their hangouts moved downstairs to the family room and kitchen.

Lisa was told early in life that she was adopted, and according to her father she wasn't bothered by that. "She knows she is as loved and every bit as much of the family as anyone else," he wrote in his memoir. Still, she appeared to be somewhat of an outsider among her siblings. As teenagers, Edward, Melinda, and Martha all shared one big friend group, partying together at the cottage and the family home in the Bahamas. Lisa, however, tended to do her own thing, at least according to Melinda. "Lisa was older, so she had her own interests and friends," Melinda recalls.

At fifteen, Lisa went through a rebellious phase. She would stuff her bed to make it look like she was asleep under the covers, then slip out the window and down the side of the house. She and her friends would stay out half the night before she snuck back in, her parents none the wiser. That is, until Ted sat down at her bedside one night and figured out what was happening. She returned home to a note on her pillow that read, "When the real dummy gets home, come see me. Dad." Once, Ted enlisted the help of CFTR to try to locate his daughter. Hoping that the station was playing at whatever party she was at, he asked the announcer to read out a message: "Will Lisa Rogers please call home right now?" He earned props from Melinda and Martha, for embarrassing their sister just the right amount.

At one point, Lisa tracked down her birth parents. They had been young college students when she was born. "But she is a Rogers first and foremost," Ted wrote.

In 1855, six students at Miami University in Oxford, Ohio, split from the Delta Kappa Epsilon fraternity following a clash over the selection of a poet for the school's Erodelphian literary society. Joining forces with a seventh student who hadn't yet joined a fraternity, they decided to start one of their own. Its purpose, they wrote in the organization's constitution, was "to cultivate and maintain the high ideals of friendship, justice, and learning."

Like other fraternities, Sigma Chi had its own rituals, insignia, and colours (blue and gold). Its heraldry was heavily inspired by the Roman emperor Constantine. As their motto, they adopted the Latin phrase *"In hoc signo vinces."* According to a legend,

Constantine had seen the words—which translate to "In this sign thou shalt conquer"—on a cross in a vision the night before the Battle of the Milvian Bridge.

Becoming a member of Sigma Chi was something of a Rogers family tradition. Ted's stepfather John Graham had been a Sig, serving as chairman for the first fraternity-wide event held in Canada, the 1957 Grand Chapter. Ted was a Sig, too, and the relationships that he forged with his fraternity brothers served him well throughout his business career. For instance, in the 1980s, when Rogers was operating a cable business south of the border, Ted was able to secure a dinner meeting with the head of San Antonio's Frost Bank, who was a fraternity brother.

Ted liked Sigma Chi because he felt it was inclusive, not snobby like other fraternities. It was he and a group of his associates who suggested that a chapter be created at the University of Western Ontario, the school in London that all four of Ted's children would eventually attend. The Epsilon Omicron Chapter was installed at Western in 1957, the same year that the first Canadian Grand Chapter was held. Some three decades later, Edward followed his sister Lisa to the university and joined the chapter.

At Sigma Chi, Edward took on the role of treasurer. A portly man with hooded eyes and a thin smile, Edward had a quirky sense of humour and an unusual idiolect, including a habit of using antiquated terms like *fella*. Around the fraternity, his love of practical jokes earned him the nickname "Fast Eddie." (Edwin A. Goodman, one of the founding partners of Goodmans law firm, was also called "Fast Eddie," a moniker that he picked up during his time as an organizer for the Conservative Party.) Edward's signature move was making people's lips go numb by putting Orajel, a toothache ointment, on the rims of their beer bottles. His grades in university were not very good. "I probably enjoyed life too much," he said in a rare interview in 2008. But Sigma Chi was a memorable time in Edward's life. Through the fraternity, he met people who would become his lifelong friends. Years later, when he and fellow Sig Robert Hiscox founded a private real estate fund, they named it Constantine Enterprises in an homage to their fraternity deity.

Like her brother, Melinda majored in political science at Western. Martha studied for a year at Queen's University in Kingston, east of Toronto, before transferring to Western to be closer to her family and friends. She majored in western literature and civics. Although Melinda and Martha both joined the Pi Beta Phi sorority, neither of them really partook in any of the activities.

Edward, meanwhile, began an on-and-off courtship with a fellow political science major named Suzanne Kolev. They were eighteen when they met through a friend at the Wheat Sheaf Tavern, Toronto's oldest watering hole, which sits on the southwest corner of King and Bathurst. Frequented by truckers, cabbies, and bikers, it wasn't exactly the sort of place one would expect the scion of one of the country's most successful entrepreneurs to hang out, although its staff might have been willing to turn a blind eye to the fact that some of the patrons were not quite of legal drinking age.

Suzanne inhabited a very different world than the one that Edward had grown up in. She was born in Elliot Lake, a northern Ontario mining town, to Hungarian immigrants Suzanna and Miklos, who dressed her in clothing from Goodwill for the first ten years of her life. Her father was twenty-four when he died in a mining accident. As a student, Suzanne worked a variety of jobs, including waitressing at Kelseys and cleaning toilets at Muskoka's Clevelands House Resort. When Edward invited her to Sigma Chi's formal dance, she bought a dress from a local vintage shop for $20.

Their relationship was put on hold after university. Ted wanted his son to gain work experience somewhere other than Rogers, and he phoned up his old friend Ralph Roberts, the chairman of U.S. cable giant Comcast, and Ralph's son Brian, the company's president. He asked if they could give Edward a job. But not just any

job; he wanted them to give Edward "every lousy job they could."
When Edward phoned home from Towson, near Baltimore, six
weeks into his new job, he complained to his mother that he had
been forced to work every Saturday night. "Nobody else has had
to work every Saturday night," he told her. After getting off the
phone, Loretta confronted her husband. The job was good for
Edward, he said.

While the Rogers family name carried a lot of clout at Sigma
Chi—and in most places in Canada, for that matter—at Comcast,
Edward was an unknown. In some ways, this was a good thing.
Being the progeny of a man widely regarded as a business vision-
ary came with massive expectations. At Comcast, Edward had an
opportunity to learn the ropes of the cable industry, away from the
constant scrutiny of his exacting father. One long-time cable executive who worked at Comcast at the time described Edward as an
eager learner who didn't behave like a millionaire's son: "He didn't
act like a prima donna."

Edward eventually returned to Canada and started working at
Rogers in the mid-1990s, becoming a vice-president in Cantel's
paging division. The company was going through yet another
challenging period at the time. Cantel was racking up huge losses
while Rogers poured billions into the carrier's wireless network.
The telecom was also in the middle of what became known as the
"negative option billing" fiasco, having irritated its customers by
bundling new Canadian specialty channels with existing ones.
The idea was to increase the channels' penetration into homes in
order to prevent the industry regulator, with its mandate to promote Canadian programming, from demanding higher fees per
subscriber from the cable company. The problem was that customers were automatically billed for the new channels unless they
called to opt out. And because the new specialty channels were
bundled with existing channels, customers who cancelled the new
services could lose popular channels that they already had.

Rogers quickly reversed course and apologized for the error, but the damage to the Rogers brand had already been done. In Vancouver, where Rogers had a significant presence, livid customers had started throwing rocks at the company's red trucks. The incident rattled Ted so much that he resolved to change the company's name to Cantel, its cellphone brand. Lind felt it was a terrible idea. He knew how tirelessly Ted had worked to restore the lost legacy of the Rogers family name. Lind and Jan Innes, then the company's vice-president of communications, began compiling research and focus groups in order to stall for time. In the end, they were able to drag out the issue for so long that Ted had changed his mind.

Meanwhile, the telecom's debt load grew to over $5 billion. Rogers gained a reputation as a risky investment, causing its share price to sink. On Bay Street, Ted went from being heralded as the cable king to being derisively referred to as "debt-soaked Rogers." The moniker angered Ted, who did what any workaholic does when confronted by naysayers: he doubled down and worked even harder.

Ted was the embodiment of a hard-driving leadership style that is increasingly viewed by workers as archaic and toxic. His intensity and inexhaustible work ethic, likely the result of his traumatic childhood, strained his relationships with his employees, who would often wake up to find long missives from their demanding boss on their answering machines. He overwhelmed his staff with an endless barrage of memos. People who flocked to the company to work with the most exciting entrepreneur around found themselves having to contend with his explosive temper and obsessive micromanaging. Although he was brilliant and bursting with ideas, he was also impatient and perpetually dissatisfied, always feeling that success could be achieved more quickly. According to Lind, Ted was a bully, and he owed some of his business success to bullying others—whether they be employees, business partners, bankers, or suppliers—into doing what he wanted. His philosophy was that competition made people better, and he enjoyed pitting his employees against each other. While some thrived in this cut-throat environment, others felt that it created a poisonous culture rife with backstabbing and information-hoarding. Meetings often devolved into shouting matches, complete with name-calling.

Not everyone took a negative view of Ted's confrontational nature. According to Melinda, when her father tore into someone's work, there was usually a good reason for it. "He was either right, and you needed to change your viewpoint, or he was testing the strength of your idea." A few hours later, he would be clapping the person on the back and congratulating them on a productive meeting. He was so magnetic that most people forgave his outbursts and the discomfort they could cause.

He also managed not to bring his temper home with him. This was largely thanks to Loretta, who broke him of the habit shortly after their honeymoon. When Ted flew off the rails, Loretta would go into the bedroom and close the door, telling her husband that she would speak with him when he was prepared to be civilized. He would bring her flowers as an apology the next day. "At home, he was just Dad, and we'd never see his temper other than what you'd see from any typical dad," Melinda says. She recalls the time when she tore up the undercarriage and broke the roll bar of his red Mercedes convertible by gunning it on that hilly road to Muskoka. Ted was furious, but he didn't yell.

Although the pressure-cooker environment could be exciting for a while, many top executives eventually started burning out and heading for the exits. Among the most high-profile departures were Colin Watson, president and chief operating officer of cable TV, and Graham Savage, the company's chief financial officer, who left in 1996 after an argument with Ted about covenants on a junk bond issue became overly heated.

Savage's exit created an opportunity for Alan Horn, an accountant who was working for Ted's family company, Rogers Telecommunications Ltd., to move over to Rogers Communications.

Horn was a soft-spoken man with a thick Scottish accent, a dry sense of humour, and a mathematics degree from the University of Aberdeen. Tall and lanky like Ted, he made his first visit to Canada in 1978 for a three-week tour with his soccer team. The next year he returned for a two-year stint at Thorne Riddell, one of the predecessors to the Canadian arm of the accounting firm KPMG.

As the chief financial officer of Rogers, Horn worked closely with Ted, mirroring both his work ethic and his voracious appetite for information. Both men would read and absorb vast quantities of information pertaining to the company. Horn became integral in helping the company strengthen its balance sheet and transform its debt from junk bond to investment-grade status. Over time, his role expanded beyond a financial one. He became a close personal friend of Ted's, and a trusted confidant. Some people within the company came to view him as the closest proxy that there was to Ted himself. One of the roles that Ted carved out for Horn was to serve as a mentor to Edward, guiding him into his future role at the company after Ted's death. It was a request that Horn took to heart.

The late 1990s were difficult for Ted. He underwent multiple surgeries, including to remove skin cancers from his face, address his failing eyesight, and unblock a vein in his neck. Determined to turn Rogers Communications into an investment-grade company, he didn't let these procedures slow him down. One year, after having a ruptured aneurysm in his abdomen repaired, he announced a $600 million investment from Microsoft during a conference call he hosted via speakerphone while lying on his back.

Rogers was also entering the internet business. In 1995, it became the first North American provider of high-speed internet service, although two years later it made the ill-fated decision to switch over to a network called At Home founded by a Silicon Valley venture capitalist. The service was so bad that Rogers eventually switched back to its own network. Ted, who had personally invested in At Home's stock, lost millions.

Meanwhile, the Rogers share price was plummeting as investors soured on the North American cable industry. In 1998, it fell so low—hitting $4.80 per share—that Rogers was pulled from the Toronto Stock Exchange's benchmark indices because its market capitalization had fallen below the necessary thresholds. This came shortly after Ted suffered a major personal loss. On January 9, 1998, John Graham passed away. He was eighty-five years old.

Graham, who Ted considered to be his second father, had been a calming presence at the company, someone who valued the principles of tradition and honour. When Edward fathered a child with Suzanne out of wedlock in 1997—a girl named Chloé—Graham asked Edward if he was going to do the right thing and marry her, according to a source. But Edward and Suzanne weren't ready to tie the knot. If they were to get married, they wanted to marry for love, and not simply because they'd had a child.

Edward and Suzanne's relationship created tension within the family. Suzanne's flashy style—from her big, elaborately coiffed blonde locks to her penchant for over-the-top couture gowns—clashed with the strait-laced, conservative image of the Rogers family. There were rumours that the family feared their wealth was a factor in the relationship.

In any event, Melinda organized a christening for Chloé, writing the invitations by hand. She also created a nursery for her at 3 Frybrook Road. As young adults, Melinda felt that she and her brother were close, and could lean on each other for support.

Six months after Graham's death, Ted almost lost another significant presence in his life. It was Canada Day, 1998, and Phil Lind was getting ready to fly to Vancouver for a short fly-fishing excursion when his phone rang.

Fly-fishing was Lind's reprieve. He had learned it from his father in the early 1950s and passed the skill along to his own kids.

There was something so relaxing about wading into the cold water and casting a fly line.

But Lind wouldn't make it to Toronto Pearson International Airport that day. While he stood in the den of his Forest Hill apartment, discussing a snag in Rogers' acquisition of television channel Sportsnet, a strange sensation came over him, as if he were spinning inside of a tornado. Then, he fell to the ground.

Lind was rushed to Mount Sinai Hospital, where a neurologist told him to brace for the worst. A massive stroke had cut off the blood supply to his brain, paralyzing the right side of his body and leaving him struggling to speak. The neurologist told him that initial strokes were often followed by secondary ones—aftershocks that could be even worse than the first. In short, it was possible that Lind wouldn't make it through the weekend.

Still, the situation could have been much worse. Had his friend not stopped by for lunch that day, the 54-year-old likely would have died. A notorious womanizer, Lind was single and living alone at the time, having split from his wife Anne five years earlier. Fortunately, his friend had been there to call 911 while Lind lay on the ground, drifting in and out of consciousness.

The next day, Dr. Bernie Gosevitz, who was Lind's physician, briefed Rogers executives on the situation. Ted took the news badly, crying during the conference call. He asked two Rogers consultants—Missy Goerner and Alison Clayton—to stay by Lind's side over the following weeks and months.

The rehab process was arduous and took many months, but Lind's recovery defied expectations. Contrary to Dr. Gosevitz's prediction that he would never work again, Lind returned to the office less than a year later. Some people couldn't help but look at him differently. He was unable to use his right arm or leg and suffered from aphasia, a post-stroke complication that left him struggling to find the right words. Lind and Ted had always squabbled like an old married couple, but the stroke diminished Lind's ability to verbally spar with Ted, and their relationship changed as a result. Daily physiotherapy appointments cut into Lind's office time, and Ted began getting more involved in regulatory affairs, communicating directly with those who reported to Lind. Ted even tried to renegotiate Lind's contract on less favourable terms— an extraordinarily ruthless move considering how far Ted had gone to support him during his recovery. They remained close friends, but the stroke had markedly changed Lind both physically and mentally. Once outgoing and gregarious, he now faded into the background at parties. It would be incorrect, however, to assume that the stroke had softened him. In fact, he became a "bigger jerk than before," Colin Watson once joked.

At the turn of the millennium, the company's halls were becoming increasingly populated by Ted's friends and relatives. One family friend who began rising through the ranks was John H. Tory, the son of Ted's long-time ally, John A. Tory.

The younger Tory had known Ted and Loretta for most of his life. Initially, he'd thought of them as his parents' friends. But through the years, Tory had bonded with Ted over their shared interest in politics. Ted admitted he wanted to run for office, but he told the younger Tory that he was too consumed with building his business. In 1978, Tory married Barbara Hackett, who he'd met at York University where they'd both studied law, and over time the couple developed their own friendship with Ted and Loretta. Tory got to know Ted professionally as well, first as his lawyer and then as an executive at Rogers, where he was tasked with running the media division, then the all-important cable business.

Ted was a friendly and pleasant companion at the breakfast, lunch, or dinner table, but it was his wife who entertained their guests when he slipped away to work after meals. Loretta was a woman of few words—soft-spoken, even shy, according to some. She wasn't the type to yell over others during heated board meetings. But when she did speak, people listened. She was perceptive and insightful, and Ted often turned to her for business advice. "She had a mind like a steel trap," Dr. Bernie Gosevitz once said. She excelled at Sudoku puzzles and at card games, which she had a habit of winning 90 per cent of the time.

At Rogers, Loretta wielded her considerable influence subtly. Her calm stoicism balanced out Ted's excitable and mercurial nature. When he got carried away with an idea, it was Loretta who ensured that it got a sober second thought. People would often appeal to Loretta if they wanted to influence Ted. Nobody was quite sure how she did it, but somehow, during a quiet moment, she could nudge her intransigent husband in the right direction.

The company was Ted's passion, and he had always dreamed of his children becoming a part of it. Notwithstanding Edward's early stint at Comcast, their father encouraged them to take summer jobs at Rogers. They rode around in service trucks, peered up at cellphone towers, and climbed onto roofs. One summer, while inspecting a cell tower perched atop a Toronto skyscraper, Edward took a few ill-advised steps back to get a better view, coming within inches of falling a very long way to the pavement. This would be a very different story had he not stopped at the last second.

The first of the Rogers kids to join the family empire was the eldest, Lisa, who took on a role as a business development analyst. She even married a Rogers television executive named David Purdy. But Lisa wasn't passionate about the job, and her marriage to Purdy ended. Around 2005 she moved to Victoria, B.C., to find herself—"and, frankly, to get away from the pressures and complexities that come with being part of a family like ours," says Melinda.

Martha eschewed the industry entirely. She loved nature and the environment, and became obsessed with plants, believing them to hold the cures to humanity's ailments. It didn't make sense to her that health was a "genetic foregone conclusion." Although her father mused that she'd make a good lawyer, Martha decided to pursue naturopathy, earning a doctor of naturopathic medicine designation from the Canadian College of Naturopathic Medicine.

Out of the four Rogers offspring, Melinda was the most like Ted. "Poor girl," her father once joked self-deprecatingly. She was widely viewed as the brainiest of the bunch and had the paperwork to prove it: an MBA from one of the country's top business schools, the University of Toronto's Rotman School of Management.

Melinda joined the company in 2000, working on strategy, acquisitions, and partnerships. Unbeknownst to her, some people around the office started referring to her as "Ted in a skirt." (Asked about the nickname years later in an interview, she said she considers it a compliment.) Unlike her brother, whose focus on financials prompted their father to start calling him "Edward the Accountant," Melinda shared Ted's forward-looking view of the world. They both believed that Rogers had to focus on innovation in order to stay relevant and compete, not just in Canada but globally.

She inherited other aspects of her father's personality as well. They loved debating but could both be stubborn. Sometimes they'd become frustrated with each other. Neither of them viewed this conflict as inherently negative, however. What some perceived as stubbornness was, to Melinda, a sign of confidence in one's beliefs. "We respected each other greatly," she says.

Ted certainly didn't discourage his daughter's confrontational behaviour. Once, when she was a student at Bishop Strachan, Melinda told her dad that a science teacher was bullying one of her friends. Ted suggested that she take the matter to the principal. The next time that the teacher began attacking her friend, Melinda made a beeline for the door. "Fuck you," she told the teacher, when asked where she was going. She got in trouble, but Ted took her side.

By the time Melinda joined the company, Edward had already been appointed to the company's board and was steadily climbing the management ranks. In 2000, Ted moved his son over from

Cantel to Rogers Communications, making him a senior vice-president. He tasked Horn with overseeing him.

That year, an opportunity arose to swap roughly $4 billion worth of cable assets with Shaw. In exchange for 623,000 customers in British Columbia, Rogers could get Shaw's 600,000 subscribers in southern Ontario and New Brunswick. Roughly five years had passed since the rock-throwing incident in Vancouver, but Ted had never really let it go, and he was ready to pull out of the province.

Lind, who had deep ties to British Columbia dating back to his studies at UBC, felt otherwise. The Rogers cable systems in B.C.'s Lower Mainland were top-notch, and Lind believed that the systems they would be getting in return were mid-tier at best. Besides, Vancouver was a high-growth market, with tons of money pouring in, especially from Asia. He argued as persuasively as he could in favour of maintaining a footprint in western Canada, but Ted was hell-bent on consolidating around the Greater Toronto Area. It was one of their biggest-ever fights. In the end, Lind was overruled.

Ted and Edward met JR Shaw's eldest child, Jim, for dinner at a high-end French restaurant in Toronto called Scaramouche one Tuesday evening in March 2000. Jim was a brash business school dropout who had started at the bottom—literally, digging cable trenches—and worked his way through his father's company, before taking the reins near the end of 1998. He and Ted had very different management styles. The Shaws weren't micromanagers. They were delegators who strove to hire the best talent and provide leadership and guidance at a high level. Ted, on the other hand, was such a notorious control freak that he once showed Jim a report listing every Rogers employee who had recently been sick. When Jim asked Ted what he did with that information, he responded that he simply liked to know it. Jim respected Ted deeply, viewing him as something of a mentor, and for the most part he found his quirks charming. But Ted could be a psycho, Jim once told Ted. "I like the guy, and he knows he has this issue," Jim said. "There is no decision at Rogers too small for Ted to make."

Outspoken and aggressive, Jim was known for butting heads with the industry regulator, as well as for his raucous lifestyle. The adage "Work hard, play hard" might as well have been tattooed on him. Despite it being a Tuesday, he and Ted polished off three bottles of wine while they discussed the cable swap. Edward, who wasn't a big drinker, drank Coke while he urged Jim and his father to lower their voices.

By 2 a.m., they had a handshake deal. Rogers was exiting British Columbia, a province where the company's brand was still tarnished, while strengthening its dominant position in Ontario. As part of the cable swap, Rogers also acquired Shaw's stake in Cogeco, a Montreal-based cable company founded by Canadian engineer Henri Audet. Two decades later, the Audets would find themselves in Rogers' crosshairs.

THREE

THE WIRELESS WIZ

Many people were apprehensive when they were summoned to 3 Frybrook Road, and for good reason. The house had earned the nickname "the frying pan," on account of all the grilling that Rogers executives had endured there. But when Nadir Mohamed walked through Ted's front door on a Sunday in June 2000, it was a different kind of fear that gripped him. The polished and reserved 44-year-old Telus executive was confronted by a pair of large, unruly dogs.

Mohamed, who was terrified of dogs, tried to act calm as he petted the golden retrievers jumping up on him. It was his first time meeting Ted, and he wanted to make a good impression. He was being considered to replace Charlie Hoffman as the president of the telecom's wireless division. Hoffman, whose family lived in New Jersey, had grown tired of flying back and forth every weekend.

Ted immediately took a liking to Mohamed. He was polite and well mannered—a true gentleman. His family, originally from India, had migrated to East Africa during the colonial era. Although many of the Indians who made the move were brought over by the British as indentured labourers to build the Kenya-Uganda Railway, over time they formed an affluent merchant class. Mohamed was born in Tanzania in 1956. Like Ted, he attended a prestigious boarding school and grew up around entrepreneurial role models— including his grandmother, who ran a lumber yard. In 1971, when Mohamed was a teenager, his family fled to Vancouver amid a wave of anti-Indian hostility.

Although his parents wanted him to become a doctor, Mohamed opted to study commerce instead. In 1980, he earned his chartered accountant designation and joined BC Telephone, a regional monopoly in British Columbia that became BC Tel, before merging with Telus in 1998.

After chatting for several hours, Ted was ready to hire Mohamed, and he told Hoffman to write up the contract. But Mohamed wasn't quite ready to sign. He knew that Rogers was plagued by high levels of executive turnover, and was initially apprehensive about jumping ship from Telus.

Mohamed and Hoffman had been planning to visit the office following the meeting, and Ted decided to tag along. By that point, the telecom had moved to 333 Bloor Street East, a sprawling campus of green-domed buildings at the intersection of three major Toronto arteries—Bloor Street, Jarvis Street, and Mount Pleasant Road. Before they headed out, Ted emerged from the kitchen carrying three brown paper bags, each one containing a cheese sandwich. Mohamed was touched by how Ted, an industry legend, was treating him like family, and that warmth was part of what eventually persuaded him to come aboard. In August 2000, at the cusp of the wireless boom, Mohamed became president and chief operating officer of Rogers Wireless. He was promoted to wireless CEO less than a year later.

Nadir Mohamed joined Rogers while the telecom was in the midst of a protracted battle for Quebec's dominant cable company.

Groupe Vidéotron was founded and controlled by André Chagnon, a Montreal native who, like Ted, was hell-bent on challenging Bell's monopoly. Lacking sufficient scale, he enlisted the help of a Salomon Brothers investment banker named Robert Gemmell to help him sell the company. Gemmell knew Chagnon well. The banker had helped Vidéotron raise money in the high-yield bond market as it was reborn in the 1990s following Michael Milken's fall from grace. (Milken, the Drexel Burnham Lambert executive known as the "junk bond king" for his role in creating the market for high-yield securities, was charged with insider trading in the 1980s.) Gemmell introduced Chagnon to Ted and Alan Horn, who he had also done some work for. After weeks of intense negotiations, the two companies had a deal. Rogers would pay $5.6 billion for Vidéotron, creating a cable network that would allow them to better compete with their shared rival. The agreement was announced in February 2000.

But Ted and Chagnon had underestimated one important element: Quebec nationalism. One of Vidéotron's shareholders was the Caisse de dépôt et placement du Québec, a massive pension fund with a track record of defending Fortress Quebec. Although the Caisse owned less than 20 per cent of Vidéotron, a shareholder agreement stipulated that Chagnon needed its approval for the sale. And the pension giant was vehemently opposed to the idea of Vidéotron, which also owned a controlling stake in a French-language television network called TVA, falling into English-Canadian hands.

The sentiment was shared by Quebec's political leaders, who had a history of close cooperation with the province's business community. There was even a name for the phenomenon: "Quebec Inc." It referred to an alliance between the Quebec government and the province's largest and most influential companies. The premise of Quebec Inc. was that, by encouraging the growth of the francophone business class, the province could become an economic powerhouse that rivalled the might of Toronto's Bay Street.

Chagnon tried to sell the deal to the Caisse, but the pension fund's top brass had other ideas. They approached the chief executive of Quebecor Inc., a local printing and publishing powerhouse.

Quebecor was founded in 1950 by Pierre Péladeau, the son of a lumber merchant who left his family penniless after losing his fortune in the Great Depression. A moody intellectual who studied philosophy and law, Pierre bought his first newspaper with money that his mother had borrowed for a down payment on a home. His ability to parlay that $1,500 loan into a publishing empire turned him into a legend in Canadian business circles. But Pierre's life was not an easy one. He struggled with bipolar disorder and alcoholism and was a notorious philanderer, fathering seven children with three different women. The second of those children was Pierre Karl Péladeau.

Often referred to by his initials, PKP, Pierre Karl Péladeau was thirty-eight years old when he took over the company following his father's death. His ascension to the Quebecor throne hadn't always been a given. At fifteen, he was sent off to live with family friends in Montreal's north end after his mother, Raymonde Chopin, killed herself. She had struggled for years with depression, which Valium and electroshock therapy had failed to alleviate.

The loss turned PKP into a brooding teen intent on rebelling against his father, with whom he had a turbulent relationship. He espoused left-wing ideology and refused to take his dad's money, working as a dishwasher and waiter at a restaurant called Big Boy while attending one of the country's most prestigious private schools, Collège Jean-de-Brébeuf. At the Université du Québec à Montréal, where he studied philosophy, he became so enamoured with communism that he handed out leaflets for the party and even changed the C in his name—Pierre Carl—into a K in homage to Karl Marx.

But Marxism turned out to be a passing fancy for Pierre Karl, who eventually enrolled in law school and took a job at Quebecor in 1985. His conversion to capitalism was so total and complete that he was later denounced as a "catastrophe for workers" by Quebec's largest labour federation, facing widespread criticism for his hardball tactics during union negotiations.

Despite Pierre Karl's newfound alignment with his father's world view, their relationship continued to be a difficult one, the grudges seemingly more personal than political in nature. The older Péladeau toyed with his son as he worked his way up through the company, treating him as both a potential successor and a threat.

When PKP finally took the wheel after his father died in 1997, Quebecor was headed towards a massive iceberg. The growth of the internet was threatening to turn the printing and publishing industries into dinosaurs. It didn't take much prodding from the Caisse for Quebecor's new CEO to recognize the opportunity that Vidéotron provided.

The ensuing battle between Rogers and Quebecor, which lasted half a year, stoked long-simmering interprovincial tensions, with one former Quebec premier comparing the prospect of a Rogers takeover to Toronto buying Montreal. Eventually, Quebecor and the Caisse emerged victorious with a $5.3 billion all-cash offer.

Ted was eager to put the loss behind him. "They won. We lost. Next!" he proclaimed at a Canadian Club luncheon in Toronto, quoting American media mogul Barry Diller. But it wouldn't be the last time that Rogers Communications would go up against Fortress Quebec.

Ted didn't like losing, but a $241 million break fee helped to ease the pain. He immediately got to work spending it. While he had been fighting a losing battle for Vidéotron, Ted was also in talks to buy an 80 per cent stake in the Toronto Blue Jays, the city's Major League Baseball team. The deal, worth US$112 million, or about $175 million Canadian, was announced on September 1, 2000. (Rogers bought the remaining 20 per cent stake some four years later.)

Unlike Lind, Ted wasn't much of a sports fan. With Graham over in Europe during the war, he didn't have a father figure to take him to games when he was young. Shortly after buying the team, as he flew back to Toronto from a medical appointment at the Mayo Clinic, Ted turned to Dr. Gosevitz and asked him to explain the rules of the game. "Dr. G," as he was often called, was not only Ted and Loretta's physician, but also the chief medical officer of Rogers Communications and a close family friend. He drew a diamond on a sheet of paper and walked Ted through the sport. Luckily, Ted was a quick study. By the time he announced the deal at a press conference that evening, "you'd think he'd followed baseball his whole life," Dr. Gosevitz recalled.

Ted saw the branding opportunity that came with owning the team, as well as the SkyDome stadium, which Rogers bought for $25 million and renamed the Rogers Centre. The company then sank another $25 million into renovations. Despite it being a costly endeavour, Ted felt that owning the Jays was good for the city, providing a boost to civic pride and to local businesses. "We've lost money but we've gained great recognition for our company and our products," he said. As always, he had his eye on the big picture.

In 2002, Nadir Mohamed and Rogers wireless president Rob Bruce started keeping tabs on a cellphone carrier called Microcell Solutions Inc., which sold services under the brand name Fido. Although the carrier struggled to turn a profit, its culture was innovative and it used the same technology platform as Rogers: GSM. Other providers used a different technology, called CDMA.

Some Rogers directors and managers were opposed to the idea of acquiring Fido. They felt that wireless was a risky bet and that the telecom should focus on its cable business instead. But Ted could see the massive growth potential on the horizon, especially with BlackBerry devices gaining popularity. Mohamed and Bruce spent two years strategizing and producing projections that demonstrated the long-term benefits of the deal.

Then, on May 13, 2004, Telus stepped in with a hostile $1.1 billion bid for the carrier. That left Rogers in a bind. AT&T, which owned 33 per cent of Rogers Wireless and had several representatives on the Rogers Wireless board, could veto any takeover that cost more than $500 million. Despite Ted's attempts at persuasion, AT&T's top brass didn't think that buying Fido was such a smart move. In order to do the deal, Rogers would have to buy AT&T out—and the company was demanding what to Ted seemed to be an exorbitant price.

Thankfully for Rogers, Telus didn't move quickly enough. In September 2004, Rogers bought out AT&T for $1.8 billion cash, or $36.37 a share. Then it snapped up Fido, topping Telus's bid with a $1.4 billion offer, or $35 per share versus Telus's $29. It was one of the savviest business decisions of Ted's life, helping him achieve his goal of turning Rogers Communications into an investment-grade company with steady profits and dividends.

Rogers acquired Fido on the cusp of the wireless boom. Within three years, wireless surpassed cable as the company's main driver of both revenues and profits, transforming Rogers from a cable company with a cellphone division into a cellphone company with a cable division. Thanks to either incredible prescience or unbelievably good luck, GSM became the dominant technological standard across most of the world. That gave Rogers, the operator of the country's only GSM network, an edge over its competitors, Bell and Telus. When the iPhone arrived in Canada in 2008, Rogers had exclusive access to the device, which initially wasn't compatible with CDMA. "For a number of years, we had such a head start in the wireless space," one former executive recalls.

The wireless sector's explosive growth turned Mohamed into a rising star at the company. He and Ted may have seemed like an odd pair, but they had complementary strengths. Ted made bold moves, while Mohamed excelled at execution and incremental change. Some mused that Mohamed had usurped Edward in the role of Ted's favourite son.

Tensions began to build between those who worked in the staid cable division, with its reliable, low-single-digit returns, and those on the high-growth mobile phone side. "The wireless people walked around like they were God's gift to commerce, when the reality was that monkeys could have done it because Ted had made the right bet," one former executive said. Ted, always one to stoke the fires of competition, encouraged the cable and wireless folks to fight over capital and resources.

Mohamed's rapid rise through the company put him in direct competition with Edward, who made no secret of his wish to inherit his father's throne. "I'd like to have a shot at running it," he once said.

Edward didn't cross paths with his sister Melinda at the office very often. They worked in different areas of the business. Still, some executives began to sense growing tensions between the siblings, who were also seen as being in competition for the top job. Ted lauded his daughter as a "star," but criticized her for doing too many different things at once, a propensity that Ted had shared until John Graham straightened him out, teaching him how to focus and prioritize.

There had always been an expectation that Ted would one day hand the keys to the telecom empire to one of his kids. In the cable industry, it was customary to do so, and many of his friends had already passed the proverbial torches to their offspring, including the Shaws and the Roberts family, who owned Comcast. Although society had moved away from the custom of primogeniture, in which the eldest boy is the automatic successor, some still assumed that the job would go to Edward. In his final television interview before his death, Ted said that both Edward and Melinda "desperately" wanted it. But unlike her brother, Melinda never openly expressed interest in the CEO's chair, nor had she ever told her father anything to that effect. Some company sources speculated that gender norms may have played into the equation. Once, while Melinda was pregnant with her first child, Horn had told her—in the midst of a business discussion—that her job was to focus on what was below her waist.

Publicly, Melinda positioned her lack of interest in the job as ideological, espousing the belief that the family should focus on being owners, leaving the day-to-day operations to professional managers. That way, the CEO could be fired and replaced if they didn't perform. "You can't do that with a family member," she says.

Rather than coveting the CEO's chair, Melinda was drawn to working with smaller companies. In her role of overseeing strategy and venture investments, she became immersed in the innovation culture of Silicon Valley, where the idea that it was important to look towards the future permeated everything. This mentality resonated with Melinda. Rogers had become a behemoth, and she worried that implementing change would be as slow as turning around an oil tanker. In order to help the company become more agile, she created a consulting division, an incubation program that nurtured and invested in innovative startups, and a partnerships group.

It was also in the Valley that Melinda met venture capitalist Eric Hixon. They were set up by a Rogers director under the guise of a professional meeting. When Melinda, then in her early thirties, showed up at the restaurant forty-five minutes late—it was pouring rain and she couldn't get a cab—she was looking for a man who had been described to her as an obese, cigar-smoking Texan in his mid-fifties. Hixon, who was actually a tall, lean, outdoorsy tech geek, himself showed up thirty minutes late, expecting to be dining with a frumpy, out-of-shape old lady. Despite the deception, the pair ended up hitting it off. They had common ground: Hixon's family also owned a business, and he was familiar with the challenges of navigating a family dynasty.

Their relationship faced an early test when the accident-prone Melinda briefly landed in the hospital after crashing her toboggan into a tree, breaking several bones. Her parents blamed Hixon, although according to Melinda it wasn't his fault. They were married one summer in the Bahamas, hoping that the scorching temperatures would keep the throngs of her father's friends and business partners away. That turned out not to be the case, however. "Who the hell would want to go to Nassau in June, right? Everyone, apparently," Melinda recalled.

Edward, meanwhile, continued rising through the ranks. Ted had always made it clear to his son that he wouldn't get any special breaks. He'd have to work harder than everyone else, and he was paid below the market rate—in some instances, less than those who reported to him.

In 2003, Edward took over as the president and CEO of cable from John Tory, who stepped down in order to run for mayor of Toronto. Politics had always been Tory's passion. Although he lost the 2003 mayoral race, he would go on to become the leader of the Ontario Progressive Conservative Party, then mayor of Toronto in 2014. But his departure from Rogers appeared to be driven by another factor, as well. Ted had been planning to retire in May 2003, and Tory hoped to succeed him. When Ted announced that he was postponing his retirement, it became clear that the job wouldn't be vacant for a while.

Ted was initially apprehensive about giving his 33-year-old son the all-important cable job. During an emotional conversation, he told Edward that if he didn't hit his numbers, he'd have to remove him from the position. There would be no free ride for the founder's son. Ted loved Edward and didn't want to risk hurting him. But Edward was resolute, and told his dad that he thought he could do it.

The cable industry was steady and middling during Edward's tenure. Former employees who reported to Edward described him as personable with a great sense of humour. But he could also be frustratingly stubborn about how things should be done. "It felt like he had tunnel vision on certain things," one former executive said, citing Rogers Bank—a credit card loyalty rewards program that delivered only marginal benefits to the company—as one example. Edward had a solid grasp of the telecom industry, but many felt that he lacked his father's strategic vision. Then again, being the son of Ted Rogers meant being judged more harshly than others.

Ted was tough on his son at the office, according to people who saw them interact over the years. But Ted was tough on everyone, several of them noted. He simply didn't treat his son any differently. Over time, however, he confided in some of his friends that he had doubts about Edward's ability to run the company. Ted didn't think he was ready. In an interview with journalist Caroline Van Hasselt, he likened his son to a "good wine" that "needs some time to mature." He openly complained that "Edward the Accountant" was too financially conservative in his approach to business, and worried that he might miss the big opportunities. "I keep telling Edward, it's not just harvest time. You have to keep investing new money. You have to keep planting the seeds to make sure there's a harvest two or three years from now—or seven years from now."

In May 2005, Ted bypassed his son, promoting Mohamed to chief operating officer, a role that gave him oversight of both the cable and wireless divisions. Ted invited Mohamed's wife, Shabin, to the board meeting to commemorate the announcement—an unusual move, but one befitting a family enterprise. To many within the company, the subtext behind Mohamed's promotion was clear: Ted was grooming Mohamed to succeed him as CEO.

FOUR

RULE FROM THE GRAVE

T ed Rogers planned meticulously for his death. Losing his father early in life and watching his mother wind up with next to nothing had left an indelible mark on him. Determined not to repeat the same mistakes with his own family, he was thirty-five when he began laying the groundwork to ensure that the company remained in their hands long after he was gone.

Throughout his life, Ted was plagued by health problems—most notably heart failure—that left him acutely aware of his own mortality. He expected to suffer the same fate that his father had. Unlike his father, though, he received countless medical procedures over the years that allowed him to repeatedly cheat death, including when he collapsed in his home on August 14, 2003, the night of the infamous Ontario blackout, during a heated family dispute. A defibrillator roughly the size of a cigarette pack that had been implanted in his chest saved his life.

Ted had implemented a dual-class share structure when Rogers acquired Canadian Cablesystems in 1979. He argued that the structure, which kept him firmly in charge of the company, protected against the market's obsession with short-term financial results, allowing him to make the difficult decisions needed to build long-term value. Although dual-class structures had become controversial in the U.S., they remained common in Canada, employed by business families such as those that had founded Shaw, Quebecor, Bombardier, and Power Corp. Some institutional investors, including the Ontario Teachers' Pension Plan, complained, but they continued to own non-voting Rogers stock.

In 2002, Ted took his desire for control even further by introducing what was known as "super-voting" shares. Most owners of super-voting shares—a class of stock that carried multiple votes—restricted themselves to ten votes per share. Not Ted. His super-voting shares carried twenty-five votes apiece. This may have seemed unnecessary, considering that the subordinated Class B shares came with no votes at all. But Ted was preparing for a scenario where he might have to grant the Class B shareholders a vote to placate a takeover target, and issue new Class B stock to finance the deal. He'd seen such a scenario play out at Comcast. In 2005, he doubled the votes to fifty a piece, prompting one director to quip sarcastically, "Why not do 1,000?" He had arrived at the figure by calculating how many votes he would need in order to retain control if Rogers swallowed Cogeco, Shaw, and Vidéotron.

As Ted entered his seventies, succession became a frequent topic of discussion in relation to Rogers. Everyone wanted to know how the company would be run after its legendary founder was gone. In family enterprises, succession planning is notoriously difficult to get right. All families fight, and adding business into the mix creates an additional avenue for conflict, one that is both financially high-stakes and emotionally charged. For successful entrepreneurs, the companies that they build are more than just profit-making machines. They represent something far deeper—the living, breathing embodiment of their worth, of every struggle that they have overcome. Founders speak of their firms in what Gordon Pitts describes in his book *In the Blood: Battles to Succeed in*

Canada's Family Businesses as "mystical" terms, invoking words like *legacy* and *mission*. Family enterprises are typically governed not by sound management practices but by long-simmering emotions, writes Pitts, "and succession is the most emotional issue of all." Canada's Bronfman family created a multinational liquor empire, Seagram, but wound up selling it to Vivendi after a bitter succession battle and an ill-advised U-turn into the entertainment industry. New Brunswick's McCain family, which built the multinational frozen food producer McCain Foods Ltd., was ripped apart by a dispute over succession. Perhaps the most famous and dramatic example is that of the Guccis, the Italian family behind the massively successful luxury fashion house. When the last remaining heir, Maurizio Gucci, sold the company to investors in 1993, he was shot dead by a hitman hired by his ex-wife, Patrizia, who was afraid that if he remarried, her children would lose their birthright.

Not all dynastic families engage in full-blown warfare—or hire hitmen—but many of them see their companies languish as they are passed from one generation to the next. Wealth doesn't survive more than three generations, according to a Chinese proverb. Take, for instance, the Eatons, who, over the course of three generations, demolished the successful department store chain that Timothy Eaton had founded in the 1860s. The destruction of value by subsequent generations has been such a common occurrence in family enterprises that it has spawned the expression "From rags to riches to rags."

At Rogers, there were technically two successions to plan. The first involved designating a new CEO. The second issue, which was arguably even more critical, was to select the company's controlling shareholder.

Ted consulted Alan Horn, the elder John (A.) Tory, and other legal and financial advisers in crafting the structure that he hoped would keep the company in his family's control "for as many generations as the tax law allows." The plan was laid out in a pair of documents: a 39-page control trust will, and an accompanying 24-page document titled "Memorandum of Wishes." But in spite of his careful planning, the system that Ted devised was flawed, essentially giving his son carte blanche over the company and sowing discord within the family.

Ted worried that his family might try to split up the voting shares amongst themselves after he died. When other families had done so, it typically led to them eventually losing control of their companies. To prevent that from happening, Ted decided that the Class A shares would be held within family trusts, with dividend payments ensuring that his heirs could live comfortably without needing to sell stock. He believed that families that owned active businesses together were "more serious-minded and family-oriented," and that giving heirs the opportunity to work together generally led to more positives than negatives. "On the other hand, I have often seen wealthy families whose businesses were sold to be devoid of a unified purpose after a time," he wrote in his memorandum of wishes. "In many cases, the plentiful cash spoiled the families and robbed the young of initiative."

However, it was also important to Ted that one individual be put in charge of making decisions on the trust's behalf. His past experiences had taught him that decision-making by committee was slow and ineffective. The trusts that held the Class A stock would all be controlled by one entity, the Rogers Control Trust, which would be overseen by an advisory committee comprising fifteen members, including Loretta and the four kids, as well as Horn, Lind, and the younger Tory. (The advisory committee's composition seems to have changed slightly over the years. Although the version of Ted's will made public through court filings lists fifteen advisers, by the time the family was in conflict in the fall of 2021, the Rogers Control Trust had ten.) One person, the control trust chair, would be responsible for exercising voting control over the telecom giant—and duty-bound to consult "widely and earnestly" with other family members. Unlike the company's management, who would face market pressure to focus on short-term metrics such as quarterly financial results, the control trust chair was to take a longer-term focus.

In his will, Ted ranked his four kids in the order that he wanted them to be chair. He put Edward first, followed by Melinda, Lisa, and lastly, Martha. The ranking was based on a list of criteria, including their job experience. Edward had worked in the business longer—and in a larger variety of roles—than Melinda, who was to be the vice chair. Still, the decision was said to create tension between the siblings.

The chair of the trust didn't have unfettered powers. At least once a year, the advisers to the trust were to meet in order to review the chair's performance and that of the company. The chair was then supposed to leave the room while the committee discussed whether he or she should remain in the role for another year. The chair could be removed—and another person appointed to the role—by a two-thirds vote. Ted compared the system to the checks and balances between the U.S. president and the Senate and the House of Representatives. The president could veto any bill but should always consult Congress, which could override the veto with enough votes. It's unclear, however, whether those reviews of the chair's performance ever took place, as the inner workings of the control trust are private. While Edward's supporters say the terms laid out in Ted's will have always been "followed to the letter," his opponents believe the performance reviews have not been fulsome enough, in part because the advisers conducting them don't consult the independent directors or the company's management and therefore don't have a complete picture.

Many people believed that Ted had an uncanny ability to foresee the future, an impression he had created by investing in two emerging technologies—cable television and wireless telephony—when few others saw their potential. In his memorandum of wishes, Ted made another eerily prescient prediction: "Heaven forbid there arises a situation when the majority of the board of Rogers Communications Inc. are totally opposed to the interests of the Rogers family as represented by the Control Trust Chair." It was difficult to anticipate what might lead to this "worst of all options." It could involve a major acquisition or sale, or "the continuance of a CEO." If this were to happen, the chair must think hard about whether the issue was big enough to warrant risking "a very public spectacle." If it was of "bed-rock seriousness," the chair was to go through the "public gauntlet" of a shareholder meeting to replace the board.

In structuring the trust, Ted seemed to be acting out of a genuine desire to ensure the success of his company after his death, says Andrew Rogerson, a Canadian trust and estate lawyer. However, while the trustee was to be the Bank of Nova Scotia, the institution appeared to have been relegated to serving as an administrator for the advisory committee. "It jumps off the page that the 'advisory' committee are not so much advising but rather directing the trustees," Rogerson says, adding that the memorandum of wishes is "so tight as to effectively make the late Ted Rogers the director of everything." The whole thing, according to Rogerson, is "a charade—a sham trust," and trusts that are deemed to be shams can be set aside if challenged in court.

Ted made no secret of the fact that he wished to immortalize his grip over the family empire. "You can't rule from the grave," he once said in an interview, "but you can try." He made arrangements for his *actual* grave as well, detailing in his will and his memorandum of wishes how the maintenance of the Rogers family plot at Toronto's Mount Pleasant Cemetery—including gardening, stone repair, and the purchase of additional plots—was to be funded. "My father is buried there and I shall also be buried there," he wrote.

Unlike at Shaw, where JR had stepped aside and allowed his son Jim to step into the lead role, Ted remained unwilling to let go, even as he closed in on the last few years of his life. Edward urged him to slow down, to spend more time with his grandkids or even pursue a political appointment. But Ted didn't feel that his work at Rogers was done. He postponed his target retirement date four times, prompting the company to finally scrap the whole premise of him stepping down.

Ted was a man who placed an enormous value on being prepared. Yet in planning for his own succession, he made a glaring oversight. He never had an honest conversation with his son about the CEO role. "Dad didn't necessarily say what he wanted the kids to do. I think he hoped that it would naturally evolve," Melinda says. However, on multiple occasions, he and the board reassured investors that professional managers would run the company in his absence. "He felt that no family member would be a good CEO."

Rather than Ted designating a successor, it was determined that, after his death, a special committee would be formed to oversee an executive search. Horn, Edward, and Melinda would all be invited to join that committee, unless they were candidates for the job. In order to avoid prejudicing the outcome, no internal candidate was to serve as interim CEO. That role would be filled by Horn. But although Ted stopped short of formally naming a successor, he made no secret of the fact that he believed Mohamed was the obvious choice.

Ted's funeral took place inside a stunning Gothic Revival cathedral at the corner of Church Street and King Street East. If any doubt had remained regarding his success in restoring the Rogers name to prominence in Canadian society, the funeral would have eradicated it. It was a star-studded affair. Among the hundreds of mourners who piled into St. James Cathedral on a gloomy, overcast December day in 2008 were sitting prime minister Stephen Harper, Toronto mayor David Miller, two former prime ministers—Brian Mulroney and John Turner—and former Ontario premiers Mike Harris and David Peterson, the latter of whom sat on the Rogers board. Also in attendance were some of the country's wealthiest dynastic families, including the Westons, the Shaws, and the Péladeaus; titans of business such as Mike Lazaridis, the co-founder of BlackBerry maker Research In Motion; and even former Toronto Maple Leaf Tie Domi. Loretta, her blonde hair swept into an up-do and a string of white pearls adorning her neck, sat stoically in the front row. Her husband's death had crushed her, but her emotionally guarded British nature dictated that she remain composed.

Ted's passing had not come as a surprise. By the time he died of congestive heart failure, his health had been in serious decline for months. The family had even installed a cable car for him on Tobin Island, to ferry him from the cottage to the beach. Still, he had appeared reluctant to relinquish control. Roughly a month before his death, the company announced that he had been hospitalized for a pre-existing heart condition and was "temporarily" passing the reins to Horn. Mentally, he remained sharp and focused on the business right up until the very end. The night before he died, while watching the ten o'clock news on CBC, he pressed Edward about why Rogers' digital sales weren't higher that month. His deterioration had been painful for those close to him to observe, and it posed an existential question for the company. No decision at Rogers Communications was made without Ted's input; no one so much as sneezed without him knowing about it. The company was so synonymous with Ted that some wondered how it would survive without its exacting, micromanaging captain.

Ted's funeral was broadcast on a community TV channel, which allowed all of the company's thousands of employees to tune in. Horn delivered a eulogy, describing Ted as a dreamer who was "young at heart but wise in years." Melinda, who looked striking with her dark hair gathered into an elegant bun, spoke about receiving advice from her father during a private moment in the cable car.

The portrait that she and her sister Martha painted was of a man for whom business never came at the expense of family; who, despite his relentless work ethic, always managed to be home for dinner.

Then Edward took the stage. To some in the audience, the funeral was a graduation of sorts for Ted and Loretta's only son, presenting the opportunity for the heir apparent to finally step out from the massive shadow that his father had cast. Dressed in his usual suit and tie, his hair beginning to grey as he approached his fortieth birthday, Edward recounted his father's impressive business achievements, chronicling how he had built his empire through one bold takeover after another. He hadn't worked so hard and built so much only for his legacy to die with him, Edward said, invoking his father's famous catchphrase: "The best is yet to come." Then, he added, "With him gone, it is hard to think how this can now still be the case."

The funeral was followed by a reception at the Fairmont Royal York, a luxury hotel housed within a historic Châteauesque-style building on the southern edge of Toronto's financial district. Several mourners, including Melinda, spotted roughly half a dozen uninvited guests helping themselves to the food that had been laid out on tables both inside and just outside the large dining hall. They appeared to be homeless.

Melinda glanced at Loretta to see what she wanted to do.

"Melinda," her mother replied in a memorable act of generosity. "They're hungry."

In his memorandum of wishes, Ted listed three internal candidates for CEO: Mohamed, chief financial officer Bill Linton, and Edward. "It was common knowledge in the organization that it was on paper a three-way race, but in reality, a one-person race," recalls one former executive.

But Edward didn't seem to take the hint. Despite his father's apparent preference for Mohamed, he put his name forward. He'd worked hard for many years at the company, and becoming CEO felt to him like the natural next step. An executive search firm was brought in to evaluate the candidates while Horn served as interim CEO. Edward put together a dossier laying out his vision for the company and what he hoped to accomplish in the role.

At one point, he even tried to build his profile with the investment community over dinners with portfolio managers. The meetings were arranged by Dvai Ghose—then a telecom analyst at Canaccord Genuity—at the behest of Edward's personal adviser, Roger Rai. Ghose suggested hosting one large dinner with all of the investors, but Rai was opposed.

Instead, Ghose and Edward dined separately with roughly half a dozen of the managers. The meals took place not far from Rogers headquarters at the upscale Windsor Arms Hotel, where Edward would order steak with béarnaise sauce and a Diet Coke and then sit quietly, eating his meal, while the portfolio manager waited to see whether he would say anything about his leadership ambitions.

Some of the investors found these meals strange, on account of how little Edward said, and they reached out to the company for an explanation. This allegedly resulted in conflict and an internal investigation because, according to a former executive, the meetings contravened the company's own investor relations policy, which stated that at least one other company representative should have been present. On top of that, at least one of the meals took place during the so-called quiet period prior to the release of the company's quarterly financial results, the person said—although no one is alleging there was any material information exchanged. (One of Edward's supporters disputed the notion that the meetings caused internal issues, noting that "listening to investors, analysts, and bond holders is normal and healthy.")

In the meantime, Edward and Suzanne's family continued to grow. After living and parenting separately for several years,

Suzanne had given birth to their second child, Edward Samuel Rogers IV, in 2005. The following year they were married at the Carlu, an event space originally opened in 1930 by Timothy Eaton under the moniker "Eaton's Seventh Floor." Suzanne ordered custom handmade silk wedding invitations and wore a strapless dress with a 25-foot-long train, designed by Toronto's Ines Di Santo. In 2007, the couple had a third child, Jack Robinson Miklos Rogers.

In early 2009, after deliberating for several months, the selection committee settled on a chief executive. Edward's lobbying had apparently been in vain. At the end of March, the company announced that Nadir Mohamed would step into Ted's shoes, steering the company as it looked to find its footing in the wake of its founder's death.

Most of the company's employees reacted positively to the news. Mohamed was a known entity, and well liked around the organization. Both Melinda and Martha knew him well and trusted him. But Mohamed had some concerns about how he would manage the family members who worked within the organization, especially considering he had just defeated the founder's son for the top job. The contract that he negotiated ensured that he would be compensated generously to exit the company should he and the board disagree about its strategic direction.

Edward, meanwhile, accepted a role as executive vice-president of emerging business and corporate development, reporting directly to Mohamed. This put Mohamed in the unenviable position of being his boss's boss. Melinda would be reporting to him as well, in her role as senior vice-president of strategy. But at the same time, the Rogers offspring outranked the CEO—Edward as chair and Melinda as vice chair of the Rogers Control Trust, an entity with the authority to determine the composition of the telecom's board. It was a dynamic that many predicted would prove challenging, even for someone as smooth and thoughtful as Mohamed.

FIVE

TONY

Blue Mountain sits on a section of cliff known as the Niagara Escarpment, roughly two and a half hours northeast of Toronto. Although the scenic alpine resort is known primarily as Ontario's top destination for skiing, it also hosts corporate retreats and offsite meetings, providing a change of scenery for harried executives. In February 2010, less than a year into Mohamed's tenure, 200 or so Rogers vice-presidents convened in one of the resort's conference centres.

Mohamed was a steady hand for a company still reeling from the loss of its founder and chief executive. He shared Ted's operational focus, but also brought in some changes meant to ease the telecom's transition from a founder-led culture to a company run by professional managers. He streamlined the leadership ranks, putting in place stricter hierarchies. While Ted may have encouraged the cable and wireless divisions to scrap over the company's limited resources, Mohamed, a consensus-seeker, decided to tear down the walls between them. He reorganized the company, eliminating duplication by merging the cable and wireless divisions. The offsite meeting at Blue Mountain was one of the first times that all of the vice-presidents across the whole organization had been brought together. "That's reflective of Nadir's style and what he was trying to bring to the company—trying to bring people together and create collaboration," one former executive recalled. "Consensus building was certainly one of the top attributes that Nadir had."

But interdepartmental rifts that had existed for years couldn't simply be healed overnight. The integration was messy, with a number of the cable executives grumbling that their wireless colleagues had been handed the plum jobs. For instance, Rob Bruce, the wireless executive who had worked closely with Mohamed, was made president of communications, overseeing both wireless and cable operations. The restructuring also clashed with Edward's philosophy of the business, which he believed worked best when organized by product.

The speaker during dinner at Blue Mountain was John Furlong, the chief executive of the Vancouver Winter Olympics, which were taking place that month. Two years later, Furlong's legacy would be stained by allegations that he had abused First Nations students while working as a gym teacher at a Catholic day school in Burns Lake, B.C. in the late 1960s. But in the early months of 2010, he was a hero, and many of the Rogers executives found his speech inspiring. He spoke about teamwork and the values that the Olympic committee had embraced. His words resonated, particularly with those who felt that, despite Mohamed's reorganization, the Rogers corporate culture was still rampant with infighting and nepotism. "I thought, 'Great, we're finally going to get to the people part of this organization,'" one former executive later recalled.

Instead, Mohamed pivoted the session—and the remainder of the offsite—to focus on the financial headwinds facing the company. At the time, Bell was encroaching on Rogers' turf by launching a product called IPTV (Internet Protocol Television), which allowed it to deliver television services through the same fibre-optic cables it used for high-speed internet service. Rogers was facing heightened competition on the wireless front, as well. The company had become sluggish and complacent thanks to the advantages it enjoyed as the operator of the country's only GSM network. So when Bell and Telus launched a shared GSM network of their own in 2009, giving them access to the iPhone, Rogers was on the back foot. At the same time, its media division was grappling with an industry-wide meltdown in advertising revenue.

The best use of all the brainpower in the room, Mohamed told the executives, was to figure out how Rogers could remain financially sound and prepare for the looming storm clouds on the horizon. They broke out into groups and tried to brainstorm ways to cut costs throughout the organization. "That to me explained everything about where Nadir's priorities were," said the former executive, who felt that leadership cared more about the company's physical assets than its people. "We would spend gazillions of dollars upgrading our plant, and we wouldn't spend a dime on doughnuts for the technicians."

After being passed over for CEO, Bill Linton tendered his resignation. He told colleagues that it was time for him to do something different. A recruiter was hired to lead the search for a new CFO, and one of the candidates identified was an ambitious finance executive from Bell named Tony Staffieri.

Staffieri grew up in northwestern Toronto in a household preoccupied with business. His mother and father had both immigrated to Canada with their parents from small towns in Italy's Lazio region, which had been economically decimated by the two world wars. After meeting at a dance in the basement of St. Mary of the Angels, a Catholic church at the corner of Dufferin and Davenport, they wound up starting both a family and a business together. Staffieri, the oldest of three boys, spent his evenings and weekends helping his dad around the company, cleaning and packaging up the restaurant equipment that they manufactured. It wasn't the most gratifying work, and one of the strategies that he devised to get out of doing it was to fill his mornings and evenings with sports practice. He played virtually every sport he could, from track and field to football to volleyball, becoming team captain in most of them. Eventually, he told his dad that he needed a real job. The first one that he landed was washing dishes at Swiss Chalet, one of his father's biggest clients, for $2.65 an hour.

Staffieri was not a risk-taker. He settled on a career in accounting after filling out a questionnaire administered by his high school guidance counsellor. He wanted a good, stable job and accountant came up as a match. Growing up, Staffieri had watched his parents struggle while their lawyers and accountants occasionally showed up in their expensive cars and left after a few hours. That was the job he wanted, he'd thought to himself.

Staffieri was the first of his family to attend university, and he took his studies at York University's Schulich School of Business seriously. He graduated in 1986, earning his chartered accountant designation two years later. From there, he quickly climbed the ranks at accounting firm PricewaterhouseCoopers, becoming a partner when he was just thirty years old. By the time he left the firm in 1998 for a senior vice-president role at electronics maker Celestica, he was a senior partner in PwC's mergers and acquisitions tax division.

Celestica grew rapidly during Staffieri's tenure, from a single plant to fifty-six facilities around the world. Eventually, travelling between all of them started to take a toll on him. He had married his high school sweetheart, a fellow Italian Catholic named Concetta Chiappetta—or Connie for short—just before their twenty-fourth birthdays, and they'd had three kids. In order to spend more time at home with them, he took a job at the incumbent telephone company Bell.

Staffieri worked at Bell during its unsuccessful attempt at going private. He went from overseeing the finances of the division that serviced small and medium-sized businesses to a role as senior vice-president of finance operations for the whole company. When he was first asked whether he might be interested in replacing Linton as the CFO of Rogers, Staffieri rejected the overture. He liked his job and wasn't keen on the idea of going to work for the competition. But when the recruiter came back roughly six months later with a softer ask—would Staffieri at least consider speaking to a few people about the opportunity?—he agreed.

Those conversations wound up winning him over. Staffieri believed that Rogers had better assets than Bell did, and he was drawn by the fact that Rogers was a family company. He'd seen the structure work effectively at Celestica, a subsidiary of Onex Corp., which had a controlling shareholder. And the job presented an interesting challenge. Not only would it be a significant promotion, it would also be an opportunity to help a company reset its financial priorities amid heightened competition. Despite efforts by Bell to retain him, Staffieri had made up his mind.

Once at Rogers, Staffieri cleaned house, replacing several executives with his former Bell colleagues. Those who liked Staffieri found him personable, approachable, and genuine. One executive who worked with the new CFO described him as introverted but warm, the kind of person who took an active interest in others rather than talking about himself. If he got in the elevator with someone, he'd know their kids' names by the time the ride was over. "Tony is the man with no ego. He doesn't take up all the air in the room."

But his friendly manner belied a competitive, even ruthless, streak that may have dated back to playing sports in his youth. Staffieri was a man preoccupied with winning. This made him a good fit at Rogers, which had a hyper-competitive culture and strove to surpass its peers on key performance metrics such as wireless subscribers. Within the company, many people suspected that Staffieri had his eye on the CEO's chair. He was widely viewed as a competent executive, although not everyone was a fan of his almost fanatical fixation on controlling costs. Shortly after he came on board in 2012, the company announced that it was shedding more than 300 jobs. The cuts were "indicative of the operational focus" of the telecom's new CFO, RBC analyst Drew McReynolds said at the time.

Nadir Mohamed was a considerably more cautious leader than his predecessor had been. Unlike Ted, who was known for his bold, audacious takeovers, Mohamed made only one major acquisition during his five years at the company's helm.

In 2011, the Ontario Teachers' Pension Plan decided to sell its majority stake in Maple Leaf Sports & Entertainment (MLSE). The company owned the National Hockey League's Toronto Maple Leafs, the National Basketball Association's Toronto Raptors, the Toronto FC soccer club, and the Air Canada Centre, home to the Leafs and Raptors. The sale dragged on for much of the year, with Rogers and Bell eventually emerging as the top bidders.

Since Rogers already owned the Blue Jays, MLSE would give it control over virtually all of the city's most valuable professional sports teams. But both Mohamed and his counterpart at Bell, a six-foot-eight university basketball player named George Cope, were reluctant to shell out the $1.32 billion that the pension giant was demanding. In late 2011, the two former Telus executives cut a deal that would see their companies each acquire 37.5 per cent of MLSE. At the same time, Larry Tanenbaum, the businessman who lived across the street from Loretta and was MLSE's chairman, upped his stake from 20 to 25 per cent. Edward and Melinda were disappointed, according to an article in *Toronto Life* magazine. They had wanted Rogers to buy the entire stake.

Not long after the MLSE deal, Mohamed decided that, after four years, it was time to call it quits. He had grown tired of navigating Rogers' fraught corporate structure, according to several company insiders. The news of his imminent departure came as a shock to the industry. It seemed abrupt. Although Mohamed was to stay on for nearly a year, no successor had been lined up when the telecom announced in February 2013 that he was stepping down.

The dynamic within the Rogers family had shifted in the years following the patriarch's death. Martha and Loretta had begun spending more time together, bonding over cigarettes, card and computer games, and their shared love of nature. Alan Horn had taken Edward under his wing, fulfilling a promise he'd made to Ted that he would groom him to take over as the chair of the company's board. And Melinda had relocated full-time to Palo Alto, California, to run Rogers Venture Partners, a $150 million venture capital fund that sought out innovative early-stage companies in the telecom and media space. Mohamed felt it would be advantageous for Rogers to have boots on the ground in the Valley, to stay abreast of technological change. Melinda, who already had a house in California, flew down to open the fund while she was on maternity leave after prematurely delivering her third son, Charles.

Melinda's relocation might have given Mohamed a bit of breathing room, but Edward continued to be an ever-present force. He and Mohamed sometimes disagreed on business matters, sowing confusion among the rank and file about who was really in charge. Getting caught in between Edward and Mohamed became known as the "second most uncomfortable place to be," according to one former executive. (The most uncomfortable position was being caught between Edward and his father back when Ted was still alive, the same executive said.) Some employees were keenly aware of the impermanence of the CEO title and, driven by their own survival instincts, began to congregate around Edward instead of Mohamed.

There were rumours that Mohamed had given the board an ultimatum by presenting them with an organization chart that didn't have the name "Rogers" on it. In doing so, he had supposedly triggered the clause in his contract that allowed him to walk away with a substantial sum of money should he and the board find themselves with irreconcilable differences regarding the company's direction. According to two board sources, however, the clause was not triggered. Mohamed has never publicly confirmed whether or not it was, although in an interview with the *Globe and Mail* he characterized his departure as "absolutely categorically my choice." He left with a retirement package worth roughly $18.5 million.

Several retirement parties were held for Mohamed, both on and off the Rogers campus. But his real last hurrah was outmanoeuvring both Bell and the CBC to buy the NHL broadcasting rights in a blockbuster twelve-year, $5.2 billion deal. While Mohamed and his team were negotiating with the NHL, a recruitment firm called Spencer Stuart was working to secure a new chief executive. Edward, who had previously lobbied so hard for the job, didn't put his name forward a second time. By that point, he had resolved to focus on his role as an owner of Rogers Communications, a decision he'd arrived at with the help of Alan Horn. Chief executives came and went, with an average tenure of about five years. It was a demanding job, and many of them burned out. Rather than work in the business, Edward would rule his father's empire from a higher perch, as its controlling shareholder.

SIX

ROGERS 3.0

I n February 2015, throngs of Rogers employees descended upon a cavernous arena at the bottom of Bay Street that was owned by MLSE, the sports company that Rogers had bought a stake in several years earlier. Although the employees had been summoned to the venue, then known as the Air Canada Centre, for a corporate town hall, the thumping music and bright lights that assaulted their senses when they arrived were more in keeping with a rock concert. The star of the show was a tall, balding Brit with small, squinty eyes, a double chin, and a confident, approachable manner, named Guy Laurence.

Laurence, who had taken over as the chief executive of Rogers on December 2, 2013, five years to the day after Ted's death, had a flair for showmanship that dated back to his stints at Chrysalis Records and MGM Studios. In October 2014, he'd sported a black leather motorcycle jacket to a press conference announcing a $100 million partnership between Rogers and Vice Media. He followed with another fashion faux pas a week later, when he donned khaki shorts and a tacky striped shirt adorned with a Remembrance Day poppy to the tropical-themed launch event for the company's new roaming initiative, "Roam Like Home." (The flat-rate international roaming service was a huge hit with customers.)

At one point during the town hall, Laurence took questions from the audience. One of them, which was more of a complaint, came from a Toronto-based employee who frequently travelled out west for work. She was miffed that Rogers wouldn't issue her a laptop. While the decision likely stemmed from the company's efforts to keep a firm grip on its costs, regularly shipping her desktop computer back and forth across the country had proven to be more expensive. In an act reminiscent of talk-show host Oprah Winfrey giving away free cars to her audience, Laurence drew applause from the crowd by vowing to get the woman a laptop.

Laurence's goal in staging such a spectacle was to instill a renewed sense of corporate pride in the company's employee base, particularly in the front-line staff who interacted directly with customers on the phones and in retail stores. "You want these people to burn for your brand," one former member of his leadership team explains. "You want them to represent that pride and that brand to your customers. You've got to touch them emotionally."

Laurence's methods, while not entirely novel, were very unusual for Rogers. They seemed to resonate with some of the younger workers, many of whom cheered wildly during the town hall. But some of the senior executives—the Old Guard types—were threatened by Laurence's attempts to circumvent them by creating a direct channel to the rank and file. To them, Laurence's cringey performance exemplified why he was the wrong person for the job: at these shows, it was all about Guy.

When the Rogers board had started searching for Mohamed's replacement in 2013, there was a perception internally that the company had lost its competitive edge. The answer appeared to be Laurence, a brash 52-year-old from Manchester who had most recently served as the chief executive of Vodafone UK, a privately owned subsidiary of one of the world's largest cellphone companies. Vodafone UK was smaller than Rogers, and it wasn't publicly traded. But Edward, who was spearheading the search, felt that Laurence's experience was highly relevant. He was familiar with media, having worked on a number of packaging deals. And although Vodafone UK was primarily a wireless operation, it also had some wireline assets and an enterprise division. Laurence was deeply knowledgeable about the telecom industry, able to speak at length about everything from network architecture to marketing strategies. Edward felt that Rogers needed a hands-on, operationally focused CEO, and Laurence became his top candidate.

Laurence met with the Rogers family several times, including dining at their home in Forest Hill. During an interview at Spencer Stuart's offices, he spoke extensively about his own family dynasty— a piano business—in an effort to relate to them. "My first impression was that I liked him as a person," says Melinda.

Laurence couldn't have been more different from his predecessor. Unlike Mohamed, who was refined and well mannered, Laurence was blunt and direct. He liked to tell people that, during an interview with the board's selection committee, he had leaned across the table and proclaimed, "I want this job."

His unconventional management ideas, which sometimes bordered on the extreme, seemed like just what Rogers needed to breathe some new life into its sluggish corporate culture. In one speech, posted to the video platform YouTube, Laurence described how he transformed Vodafone's offices into workplaces of the future, built to appeal to the sensibilities of Generation Y—a cohort of workers who disdained hierarchies and thought of workplaces as communities. Offices were eliminated, as were assigned seats, replaced with empty desks that could be claimed as needed. Employees congregated in the coffee shop installed in the centre of each building.

Laurence even bragged about the lengths to which the company went to ensure that employees didn't violate the spirit of the new model by leaving items behind to symbolically claim their desks. "One hundred per cent clean desk policy means that we take anything that's left on the desk at the end of the day and we incinerate it that night—even if it's the pictures of your loved ones." The comment drew a few laughs, although it wasn't entirely clear whether he was joking.

Shortly after he was hired, Laurence spent a weekend in the Bahamas with Loretta. He did so after receiving a salient bit of advice: if he wanted to understand Rogers the company, he needed to understand the Rogers family, and in particular its matriarch. While in the Bahamas he even went fishing with Dr. Bernie Gosevitz.

Laurence spent his first three months on the job criss-crossing the country on a listening tour. He crowdsourced opinions about the state of the company, sitting down with thousands of employees and asking them questions like "What would you most like to see me do as CEO?" He even went undercover as a field technician to gain a deeper understanding of customers' pain points. His travels were chronicled via an internal blog that included the kinds of details that Canadian CEOs typically don't divulge. For instance, he wrote about buying a multimillion-dollar home in Toronto's posh Rosedale neighbourhood, and about having his Mercedes shipped from overseas.

Laurence summarized the findings from his tour in a 20,000-word report that he presented to the company's board. The conclusion he arrived at was that Rogers had lost its way. It's not unusual for a company's performance to stumble following the passing of its founder. Like many founder CEOs, Ted had been the glue that held the company together. And while Mohamed might have been the safe and logical choice to take the helm after he was gone, Laurence felt that Mohamed's conservative approach had deviated too much from the company's DNA as a bold, innovative startup. He believed that management had become bloated and overly risk-averse, and that the key to improving the company's performance was to reinvigorate its corporate culture.

Laurence outlined his vision for the company in a seven-point plan that he called "Rogers 3.0." It included improving customer service, expanding the enterprise services division, and investing in both networks and talent. He vowed to return the company to growth and put an end to its practice of scrambling to slash spending or hike prices at the end of each quarter to meet financial targets.

Laurence continued Mohamed's efforts to professionalize the company, purging the management ranks of powerful people whose values didn't align with his own. Both Edward and Melinda were persuaded to vacate their management roles. Stepping back from the day-to-day operation of the family company can be difficult for heirs, who may see it as an abdication of their duties. Charles Sirois, a prominent communications executive who sat on the Rogers board and was a strong advocate for the owner-manager model over the owner-operator model, broached the thorny topic with Melinda. Extricating family members from management roles that had outgrown their skill sets was difficult but sometimes necessary for the good of the company, he told her. The transition was challenging for Melinda, but over time she came to accept it. Edward, meanwhile, had agreed to step down during discussions with Horn prior to Laurence's arrival.

Memos went out announcing the changes in May 2014, shortly before Laurence was scheduled to present the Rogers 3.0 plan to his management team in a ballroom at the Four Seasons Hotel. The revamped management structure that he laid out divided the company into consumer, enterprise, and media divisions, while all customer service operations—including call centres, field technicians, and online sales channels—fell under the newly created "customer experience" banner. He installed Deutsche Telekom executive Dirk Woessner as the head of the consumer division, replacing former wireless and cable head Rob Bruce, and hired Cisco Canada head Nitin Kawale to lead the enterprise team. Former Google executive Deepak Khandelwal took over customer service, while one of Laurence's former Vodafone colleagues, Frank Boulben, came on board as chief strategy officer.

Laurence and his newly assembled leadership team scored a number of victories, including Roam Like Home and the acquisition of struggling wireless startup Mobilicity, which Rogers pried out of Telus's hands. But not all the initiatives that they introduced were a roaring success. A partnership that saw Vice Media create exclusive content to broadcast on Rogers networks was cancelled after just three years, as was one with Spotify that aimed to boost wireless data usage by giving customers free access to the music streaming site. Laurence had decided to import his "sharespace" concept from Vodafone, launching an ambitious renovation that would transform the telecom's dated offices into a modern, open-concept workspace. But the project was expensive and, inevitably, controversial—at least with the Old Guard, who felt alienated by the concept and still had considerable sway at the company. Although Laurence had attempted to purge them from the ranks, he sometimes met opposition from Edward, who, despite having been removed from operations, would occasionally intervene on behalf of his allies.

Laurence also found himself at the helm of the doomed Eclipse project. The telecom had spent roughly half a decade and close to half a billion dollars building its own custom TV platform. Initially, Edward and Melinda seemed supportive of the endeavour. Creating the platform in-house was in line with their father's legacy of technological innovation. But the company didn't actually have all of the technical expertise it needed, and had to outsource a lot of the work to many different vendors, which made the job significantly more complicated and expensive. Then, just as Rogers was preparing to launch the project, Swedish telecom supplier Ericsson announced that it would be discontinuing the software platform that Eclipse was built on.

Two divergent perspectives emerged within the company. Some—including Laurence, who had been hands-on with the project—wanted to move ahead with the launch. Others thought it would be wiser to cut their losses and license technology from Comcast, like Shaw was doing. The board assembled a committee comprising two of its more technologically minded directors— John MacDonald and Rob Burgess—to assess the situation. By the time the company's management team and its board convened at the Langdon Hall hotel near Cambridge for a strategy session, it was clear which way Edward was leaning. During the debate that broke out between the two sides, he grilled Laurence about working with Comcast.

Laurence stuck to his guns. He felt that Eclipse was a viable product and wanted to launch it, even if the company did wind up switching to a provider such as Comcast in the future. By that point, however, Laurence's days as chief executive were numbered, and the strategic misalignment with its controlling shareholder wasn't helping his cause. In the end, Rogers struck a licensing deal with Comcast and took a $484 million writedown on Eclipse.

When he'd first arrived at Rogers, Laurence was seen as someone who could breathe new life into the company. The problem was that he may have breathed too much new life into it, upsetting the delicate balance by ushering in too much change too quickly. Culturally, he was an outsider to the polite Canadian telecom industry and its prim ruling family. In one very un-Canadian move, he publicly called Bell a "crybaby" for griping to the federal regulator about Rogers' use of its NHL broadcasting rights.

By mid-2015, several directors, including Edward and other Rogers family members, were becoming increasingly unhappy with their hired hand. Lind, for instance, felt that Laurence was arrogant and condescending towards employees. However, some analysts believed that the company's performance had started to turn a corner. And the board had awarded Laurence a larger-than-expected bonus for two consecutive years.

Then, in August, the situation took on a new sense of urgency. Another candidate—one who had previously interviewed for the job—had unexpectedly become available.

SEVEN

JOE

While members of the Rogers family were becoming increasingly disillusioned with their company's CEO, David Peterson, the former premier of Ontario and a long-standing Rogers director, invited a friend's husband out for lunch. The friend was Melissa Martin, a tall, slender woman with long, dark hair whom he'd met during board meetings at St. Michael's Hospital, where they both served as directors. He didn't know Martin's husband well—they had met only a handful of times—but Peterson, a consummate networker, had developed a habit of taking someone out for a meal when they faced a setback. That's how he found himself sitting at the Toronto Club across from Joe Natale, the likeable and highly respected telecom executive who, not too long ago, had been fired from Telus.

A towering man with dark, bushy eyebrows and a warm smile, Natale grew up in a tight-knit family in St. Catharines, a city west of the Niagara River in a region of Ontario known for its ice wine. He was the oldest of three children—two boys and a girl—born to Italian parents who had immigrated from Europe along with his grandmother. Once in Canada, Natale's father, who had worked as a machinist in Switzerland, got a job in a restaurant while he tried to figure out what to do next. He ended up opening a hugely popular restaurant of his own, called the Roman Villa. After school, Natale would sit at a table near the kitchen and do his homework. Watching his parents running their own business imbued him with an entrepreneurial spirit and ignited his passion for cooking.

Natale showed signs of promise early on. He studied at the country's top engineering school, the University of Waterloo, and during his final year, at a summer co-op placement at Bell Canada, he impressed his colleagues by creating an electronic system for logging jobs. "He was an absolute star," a former Bell colleague recalled.

It was at Bell that Natale met Martin. They started dating sometime later, after a mutual friend played matchmaker by telling Natale where Martin was working strike duty one summer in the late 1980s.

After graduating with a degree in electrical engineering, Natale got a job at Andersen Consulting, the precursor to Accenture. His grandmother, who lived with his family and spoke only Italian until the day she died, couldn't comprehend what her grandson did for a living. "You just meet with people?" she would ask. "And they pay you for that?"

Natale was twenty-six when he and two of his Andersen colleagues decided to strike out on their own, co-founding a consulting firm called Piller Natale & Oh. One of the first people they hired was a consultant named Dave Fuller. Fuller was bright and highly educated—he had a mechanical engineering degree from Queen's University, as well as an MBA from the Schulich School of Business—and he and Natale became a formidable team. They were both strategic thinkers and had complementary skill sets: Natale was an optimist, Fuller was more skeptical; Natale was great at generating ideas, Fuller at executing them. Eventually, they were finishing each other's sentences.

Piller Natale & Oh grew to about seventy employees before being acquired by KPMG. The global accounting firm adopted Re-Build—the re-engineering methodology that Natale and his team had developed for businesses undergoing major transformations—as the new standard for its consultants worldwide. The success increased Natale's profile. In 2002, his name appeared on *Report on Business* magazine's Top Forty Under 40 list.

Sometime after Natale and his colleagues moved over to KPMG, the firm decided to split off its consulting arm through an initial public offering. The decision was hastened by the accounting scandal surrounding U.S. energy company Enron, which rocked the auditing services industry and prompted the consulting divisions of the five largest accounting firms to distance themselves from their firms' auditing practices. Natale, Fuller, and the others who had moved over as part of the takeover became managing directors at the newly formed BearingPoint.

Then, in 2003, a new opportunity arose. Darren Entwistle, the sharp, hard-driving CEO of Telus, was looking for someone to head up the Vancouver-based telecom's enterprise division serving institutional customers, such as large companies and government agencies—and a recruiter identified Natale as a candidate.

By that point, Natale was the leader of BearingPoint's global automotive practice, a role that required frequent, long flights to Asia that took him away from Martin and their three young daughters. He had risen as high up at the firm as he could without moving south of the border, where the company was headquartered. The telecom industry interested him; he felt that it presented a real opportunity to positively impact people's lives. He decided to take the job.

Telus was little more than an amalgamation of regional phone companies when an executive search committee recruited Entwistle from the senior ranks of British telecom Cable & Wireless plc to be its new leader. Fiercely ambitious and with an intellect to match, Entwistle had grown up in a middle-class, anglophone household in Montreal. He was twelve years old when his mother succumbed to cancer, leaving him not only with a hole in his life but also perpetually in a hurry. Like Ted, Entwistle was plagued by an acute sense that his days were numbered. His introduction to the telecom industry was through his father, a Bell repairman and installer.

Entwistle was only thirty-seven years old when he arrived at Telus's Robson Street office in downtown Vancouver, and he wasted no time in making his first bold move. The company that Entwistle had been hired to run was formed in 1990, when the Alberta government decided to privatize its telephone network. Telus merged with British Columbia's BC Tel nine years later, then acquired a controlling interest in QuebecTel in 2000, just before Entwistle walked through the door. The result was an awkward mishmash of copper landline networks whose very survival was threatened by the burgeoning wireless and internet boom.

Within months of his arrival, Entwistle acquired Clearnet Communications, a heavily indebted wireless upstart, for an eye-popping $6.6 billion. The deal quickly turned Telus into a national wireless carrier and put the fresh-faced Entwistle in direct competition with Ted, by then an ageing industry titan. It also brought new blood into Telus, including Clearnet CEO George Cope, who would later become the CEO of Bell.

While Cope and his team of Clearnet executives ran wireless, Entwistle needed someone to head up the enterprise group. He had big ambitions for the division, which was struggling to expand in eastern Canada and compete against Bell. Natale, who was well connected in Canada's most populous city and had plenty of experience transforming businesses, seemed like the perfect man for the job. His first interview was with Cope, who was frank about the challenges and opportunities that the role presented.

After landing the job, Natale overhauled the enterprise division by switching up its strategy. Rather than focusing solely on selling equipment, the team started pushing managed services and solutions. He also revamped the sales force, bringing in fresh blood from companies like IBM and HP that weren't in the telecom space but knew how to sell services and solutions. He hired several of his colleagues from BearingPoint as well. After about a year, he convinced Fuller to leave consulting and join him.

The turnaround was successful, and Entwistle rewarded Natale by piling new responsibilities onto his plate. Soon, Natale was in charge of overseeing not only Telus's largest corporate clients but medium-sized and smaller ones too, as Entwistle consolidated the units together under one umbrella called "business solutions." Telus's international call centre division and its fledgling health business were also brought within Natale's domain.

Entwistle was an intense, demanding boss, but he and Natale hit it off, connecting not only professionally but on a personal level as well. They bonded over their shared love of cinema and music—they were both fans of The Eagles and Bruce Springsteen—and their interest in history, particularly leaders famous for navigating through challenging times, such as Winston Churchill. Although Natale worked out of the Toronto office, he and Entwistle travelled together for work and spoke frequently on the phone. They got to know each other's families, and spent time at Entwistle's cottage on B.C.'s Sunshine Coast.

One of the keys to Natale's success was his ability to connect deeply with people on a personal level, fostering a fierce sense of loyalty among his subordinates. Although he worked long hours, many of them were not spent behind a desk but at restaurants and social functions, forging relationships. People gravitated towards Natale. He was charismatic, a gifted storyteller, and had a high emotional quotient, or EQ, a trait that proved useful in assembling teams. He understood the importance of hiring on the basis of not only competence but of character as well. "If you're in front of Joe, you're the most important person to him; you know you've got his attention," one former Telus colleague recalled. "Joe's secret sauce is that he's very human," said another. "He gets very connected."

When Monty Carter, an Alberta-based senior vice-president, travelled to southern Italy with his wife for their twenty-fifth wedding anniversary, they arrived to find a bottle of champagne and a bouquet of flowers in their room. Natale had tracked down the farm they were staying at and sent the gifts. "That endeared Joe to my wife forever," Carter later recalled.

Every division that Natale was put in charge of flourished. Over time, it became evident that Entwistle was grooming Natale to eventually replace him. In 2010, following the departure of an executive named John Watson, who frequently butted heads with Entwistle, Natale took over the consumer side of the business.

Then, in the fall of 2012, a recruiter from Spencer Stuart came knocking. Nadir Mohamed was leaving Rogers, and the Toronto-based telecom needed a new CEO.

By that point, Natale's name was on Telus's succession plan. But the recruiter was persistent. So, as a courtesy, Natale took a meeting with Edward Rogers and Alan Horn to discuss the role. He didn't tell Entwistle because he didn't want to be seen as trying to twist his boss's arm. But he also didn't have to. Everyone in the industry knew about the vacancy at Rogers, including Entwistle, who would have assumed that Natale had been approached.

It was roughly around that time that Entwistle told the board that he was ready to step down. Over the course of more than a decade, he had steered the company through a period of highly profitable growth and had amassed enough personal wealth to comfortably retire. He was ready to step back from day-to-day operations. He spoke about moving back to the U.K. and getting a job as an adjunct professor, maybe at Oxford or Cambridge, and spending more time with his twins. And he was concerned about clogging the company's progression arteries and losing Natale, an ambitious and highly regarded executive who might leave if he wasn't given an opportunity for advancement. The board of directors started planning for the transition.

But there was a hitch. Telus's board was chaired by Brian Canfield, a telecom industry veteran who, over the years, had been a prominent champion for British Columbia. Canfield, along with several other directors, was concerned that if Telus appointed a Toronto-based CEO, other senior leaders would leave western Canada to be physically closer to their boss and maintain their level of influence within the company. Over time, it would result in a hollowing-out of the company's Vancouver headquarters, they feared. They felt that being a western Canadian company was core to Telus's identity. After all, the company generated most of its revenues and profits in Alberta and B.C.

The issue came to a head during a heated board meeting in February 2014. Sitting at a rounded, dark wood table in an old-fashioned boardroom at the Robson Street headquarters, Canfield said the appointment should be conditional on Natale moving to Vancouver.

Entwistle's face visibly reddened. He told the board that Natale needed to stay in Toronto for family reasons. Entwistle feared that if the board forced the issue, then his designated successor might not take the job. Besides, the leadership transition would see Entwistle become executive chair for a period of three years, during which he would keep an eye on the company's strategy, operations, and leadership from his western perch. His presence in Vancouver would prevent a power shift from western Canada to the east, he argued.

The board agreed not to codify the move into Natale's contract. But Natale was expected to maintain a strong presence in western Canada. And, according to some, he promised to move out west eventually, when his kids went off to university and Entwistle transitioned to a non-executive chair role.

Natale's ascension to the corner office was announced in May 2014. The fact that Entwistle was ceding the CEO's chair came as a surprise to the financial community, but Natale's appointment did not. He had long been viewed as the heir apparent.

Industry analysts welcomed the news that Entwistle was sticking around. The executive chair structure was common in the U.S., and it gave the board a way to retain both Entwistle and Natale. But some corporate governance experts were critical, including York University law professor Richard Leblanc. Executive chairs were frowned upon because they possessed too much power, he told the *Globe and Mail* in an interview at the time. Best practices dictated that an independent director should serve as chair.

One former employee called it "a sleight of hand." The organizational structure had effectively stayed the same; Entwistle and Natale had simply moved chairs. "Joe still didn't have a direct line into the board. He wasn't reporting into an independent board chair; he was reporting into Darren."

In a move aimed at safeguarding the board's independence, Dick Auchinleck, a former oil and gas executive who sat on Telus's board, was appointed lead independent director. It was Auchinleck who first informed Natale that Entwistle would be staying on as executive chair. Natale was taken aback, but he didn't oppose the plan. He had worked closely with Entwistle for over a decade, and he felt that he knew how to handle him.

A role delineation agreement—a prenup of sorts—was drawn up to clarify who had the final say on various matters. Entwistle would remain in charge of external-facing areas such as investor and government relations, while internal operations such as corporate development, acquisitions, and running the monthly executive meetings fell under Natale. The two men would share responsibility for Telus's strategy. The idea was that as time went on, Natale would take on additional responsibilities and Entwistle would step back entirely.

But despite this attempt at clarifying their roles, the issues inherent in Telus's new leadership structure started to surface. Natale's management style was dramatically different from his predecessor's, and while some executives welcomed the change, others found it jarring. Entwistle liked to take charge of every situation; Natale was a consensus-seeker. Entwistle was a notorious micromanager who liked to get into the weeds; Natale was more focused on the big picture. Entwistle was perpetually bursting with energy and ideas; Natale was more thoughtful and reserved. Over time, the leadership ranks fractured into Team Darren and Team Joe.

The members of Team Darren felt that their new leader was indecisive and didn't add as much value as his predecessor had. They had become accustomed to leaving meetings with Entwistle armed with new ideas and avenues to explore, and they felt that Natale wasn't providing them with the same level of feedback. Entwistle was exacting in a way that was intoxicating to some of his subordinates, and his absence plunged them into withdrawal.

Team Joe felt differently. They favoured Natale's softer touch to Entwistle's demanding leadership style. Rather than viewing Natale as indecisive, they believed that Telus's leadership team had become so reliant on Entwistle's guidance that some senior executives struggled to make decisions on their own. They worried that Entwistle remained too involved in the company's day-to-day affairs and was effectively undermining Natale. Perhaps the obsessive Entwistle had overestimated his ability to step away from the company, they speculated.

Over time, Entwistle and several other executives started to feel that the company's performance was slipping. They were

particularly concerned about what they perceived to be skyrocket-
ing costs, as well the financial outlook for the second half of 2015.
Companies project their results several quarters ahead, and the
projections for the third and fourth quarters were worrisome,
according to multiple sources. Growth in average revenue per user,
a critical industry metric referred to as ARPU, was projected to start
slowing, and Entwistle and Auchinleck believed that a combination of revenue stimulation and cost-cutting was in order—and
that Natale was dawdling.

There were other points of friction between the two men,
according to people who worked there at the time. Entwistle felt
that his successor was constantly breaking the terms of their prenup by veering into the executive chair's territory—for instance,
by taking investor relations meetings. (A source in Natale's camp
disputed the notion that the prenup precluded him from doing
so.) And the pair butted heads over Project Falcon, a multibillion-
dollar endeavour to replace the telecom's copper network with
fibre-optic cables. Entwistle wanted to go full throttle, while Natale
favoured a more gradual approach that would protect the balance
sheet. When Natale tried to trim the project's budget, Entwistle
reinstated it.

Unlike Ted Rogers, Entwistle didn't found the telecom that he
ran, nor did he control it through dual-class shares. Telus was a
widely held public company. But he exhibited a similar level of
proprietorship. Entwistle had poured so much of himself into
Telus that at times it was hard to tell where he ended and the company began. He was a divisive figure—not everyone enjoyed working in a pressure-cooker environment, and some people found his
intensity off-putting—but his success was indisputable, and it
gave him great latitude with the board. He had transformed Telus
from a collection of utilities into a dynamic telecom and technology company, with billions in annual revenues and a share price
that outperformed its peers globally. Any degradation in the

company's financials might have felt to him like an erosion of his personal legacy.

At one point, Entwistle inadvertently discovered that Natale and his chief human resources officer, Sandy McIntosh, had set out to modernize a description of the company's values. Entwistle had consulted widely across the company when crafting the edicts, which vowed that the telecom would put its customers first, "embrace change and innovate courageously," and "grow together through spirited teamwork." He was upset when he learned that they were being modified without his input, according to several people. It was as if Natale was trying to rewrite the definition of Telus itself.

Unbeknownst to Natale or his head of HR, a senior vice-president in human resources named Donna McNicol had been tasked with compiling a report about the CEO's performance. Working alongside an unidentified national consulting firm, McNicol interviewed twenty vice-presidents, senior vice-presidents, and director-level executives from across the organization, summarizing her findings in a 27-page internal document titled "Confidential Briefing for the Lead Director."

At least some of the report's findings were derived from exit interviews with executives who departed the company during an April 2015 reorganization overseen by Natale. The nameless executives quoted in the document therefore may not have not been the most impartial of sources. They portrayed the executive shuffle as messy and chaotic, claiming that the announcement was delayed more than once on account of Natale's travel schedule, then finally sent out the day before Good Friday, leaving people scrambling over the Easter long weekend to figure out what was happening. Several people claimed that they had been left in the dark about aspects of the reorganization that impacted them or their teams. Some felt that Natale was promoting people he knew and liked, creating a sort of inner circle, rather than making personnel decisions based on performance. "The CEO rewards loyalty, not results," one person griped.

The criticisms didn't stop there. The report, which several of Natale's allies later characterized as a "hit job," also took aim at his work ethic and his allegedly lacklustre contributions on important files such as critical auctions for wireless licences, the CRTC's wireless wholesale proceeding, and Telus's failed pursuit of Mobilicity. In contrast to Entwistle, a workaholic who eschewed time off, Natale occasionally chose to unplug during what the report described as "critical times." In March 2014, during board meetings leading up to the leadership succession, Natale vacationed in Africa. He was in Costa Rica during the planning process for the 2015 reorganization, then in Europe when the reorganization was originally scheduled to be announced. "He cannot ever be reached when he is on vacation," one executive complained.

Perhaps one of the most damning allegations in the report involved an alleged incident at the Presidents Club, an annual event held as a perk for the company's top sales performers. It was held in Istanbul in 2015, and the final day of the event coincided with an election that was expected to spark violent protests. The security concerns were so great that the Telus delegation was advised not to leave the hotel grounds that day, according to one person in attendance. In an apparent attack on Natale's character, the report alleged that Natale flew home a day early, leaving more than 100 team members behind. "Although the communication to the participants claimed 'family commitments,' it was well known that he had left due to the security alert," the report claimed. But a source close to Natale rebuts the allegation, saying that he left early to attend the high school graduation of one of his daughters, who was valedictorian.

Interestingly, a significant focus of the report related to exactly the issue that had concerned Canfield prior to Natale's appointment: a supposed shift of power and decision-making from western Canada to the east. The document listed nine senior roles that were moved from either Vancouver or Edmonton to Toronto or Ottawa during Natale's tenure, including the chief financial officer and the heads of human resources, media relations, investor relations, and corporate development. It even detailed exactly how many days Natale had spent in western Canada—the equivalent of roughly 11 per cent of his time—and contrasted it against the east–west split in the company's customer base, revenues, and profits.

One leader claimed that vice-president and senior vice-president promotions were disproportionately skewed towards those who lived in Ontario: "People are shocked at the speed of how junior people were promoted in Toronto." Another complained about having a hard time getting Natale's attention: "You have to be in Toronto to be heard."

Natale was just over a year into his tenure as CEO when he walked through the doors of Telus Garden, a gleaming new office tower occupying an entire city block in downtown Vancouver. It was early August 2015, and he and several members of his team had flown into Vancouver for strategy discussions with the company's board. The so-called strat checks took place over several days at the telecom's freshly built headquarters, and included a dinner aboard the *Nova Spirit*, a sleek, 150-foot white yacht with teak decks and marble floors owned by Canadian billionaire Jim Pattison.

But while Natale was feeling positive, the board was discussing his imminent departure. Board procedures dictate that a company's CEO exit the room for a portion of the meeting, which is known as an "in camera" session. During such a session, at

1:45 Pacific Time on a Thursday afternoon, Auchinleck kicked off a discussion about terminating Natale—and reinstating Entwistle in the role.

The topic didn't come as a surprise to anyone on the board, because Auchinleck had spoken to each of them individually prior to the meeting. During these one-on-one meetings, Auchinleck, a balding man with an impressive chevron moustache, had laid out the evidence that he had gathered to support the leadership change—evidence relating to Natale's performance and his unwillingness to relocate out west. By the time the board sat down in the sleek new fifth-floor executive boardroom to discuss the issue as a group, it was more focused on the consequences of firing Natale— for instance, how much severance to pay him and the "flight risk" of other executives.

Sitting around a light brown table in the bright and airy boardroom, Auchinleck recapped the conversations he'd had with Entwistle and various employees across the company about Natale's leadership. Although he had read McNicol's report, as lead independent director Auchinleck felt he had a duty to verify its contents, so he conducted his own interviews.

He'd also spoken to Natale. In July, the two men had met to discuss several issues, including what Auchinleck felt were troubling financial projections, and the board's desire for a greater CEO presence in Vancouver. It was at that meeting that Natale told Auchinleck that, due to family reasons, he wouldn't be ready to make the move to Vancouver for several more years.

The board's discussion about Natale continued for another forty minutes after Entwistle left the room. At 4 p.m., after more than two hours, the meeting was adjourned so that several of the directors could catch their flights home. They would reconvene at noon the next day, via teleconference.

But first, the board's human resources compensation committee needed to discuss Natale's severance package. They were prepared to pay him generously to leave. In 2015, Natale would take home $11.6 million in total compensation, including a $1.3 million salary and a $6.2 million transition payment. His pension was valued at $3.2 million.

The compensation committee meeting wrapped up at around 11 a.m. About an hour later, the board reconvened to finalize the leadership change. The vote to oust Natale, who had been appointed to the job just fifteen months earlier, and put Entwistle back in the CEO's chair was unanimous.

Earlier that morning, Natale had joined Entwistle on a conference call with analysts to discuss Telus's second-quarter results. Revenue was up more than 5 per cent from a year ago, and the telecom had managed to sign up 63,000 net new wireless subscribers—14,000 more than during the same quarter the previous year. Its churn (a figure that represents the rate of customer turnover on a monthly basis) was below 1 per cent for the eighth consecutive quarter. One analyst called it an "impressive" achievement.

When Natale arrived at Entwistle's office later that day to say goodbye before heading back to Toronto, he was beckoned to the boardroom. There, he was fired by Entwistle, the man taking over his job.

McIntosh, the head of human resources, had hung back to accompany Natale on the trip home. It was a tough situation for her. She was close with Natale and had only been brought into the loop the night before by Josh Blair, a senior Telus executive who worked closely with Entwistle. Sleep-deprived and in a state of shock, she cried on the flight home.

The next morning, Natale phoned up his executive team one by one to break the news to them. He sounded stunned, as though he hadn't seen it coming.

Telus announced the news on Monday, blaming Natale's reluctance to relocate his family to Vancouver, where the telecom's headquarters were located. "Mr. Natale recently indicated that a move to Western Canada would not work for him and his family for several years and the Board determined that the Company would be best served by having its chief executive officer reside in the West," the press release read.

Nobody believed the official explanation, however. "I don't think anyone with half a brain thought that was true," said one company insider. Although east–west tensions had played into the decision, it was inaccurate to suggest that Natale had essentially forfeited the job he had so worked hard to earn by refusing to move. But Team Darren and Team Joe had conflicting views on what had really transpired.

According to those in Entwistle's camp, Telus had centred the narrative around geography in order to protect Natale's reputation. Although it was true that the board wanted its CEO to reside in Vancouver, that wasn't the only reason they had decided to part with Natale. It wasn't even the main one. Entwistle had really wanted the succession plan to work, several people said. But over time, the board had come to believe that Natale wasn't cut out for the task. The board asked Entwistle if he would return, and Entwistle, for whom Telus was something akin to an offspring, had found it impossible to say no, just as he did with his biological children.

Natale's supporters, meanwhile, believed that Entwistle had orchestrated the whole thing to get his job back. There were no real concerns about Natale's performance, or at least not for this group. Entwistle just wasn't ready to move on.

According to several industry analysts, Natale's tenure was too short to gauge whether or not there were issues with his performance. In any case, the lack of a clear consensus on the issue among the telecom's current and former executives illustrates a simple truth: not everyone agrees on what a CEO should be.

Almost immediately after Entwistle had reclaimed the top job, Telus announced that it was slashing 1,500 jobs. While some described the layoffs as painful but necessary because of Natale's inaction, others wondered whether the real purpose behind them was to justify his firing. In a press release, the company's union called the cuts "regrettable and unnecessary," noting that the telecom had just reported a $398 million adjusted quarterly profit and boosted its dividend by 10 per cent. Lee Riggs, the president of National Local 1944 of United Steelworkers, chastised Telus for reducing its headcount at a time when the company was "extremely profitable."

Amid the refined elegance of the Toronto Club, Natale pondered his next career move. David Peterson suggested that he consider teaching at a university. Being around students brimming with energy and optimism could be exhilarating, the former premier told him.

Peterson found Natale to be charming and intelligent. After lunch, he phoned Edward to suggest recruiting the former Telus CEO to the Rogers board. But Edward had another idea. He wanted Natale to take over as CEO.

The process of surreptitiously recruiting Natale to Rogers without tipping off Laurence, the company's sitting chief executive, dragged on for months. It started with a call to Natale from Edward's friend and adviser Roger Rai. As the courtship progressed, Natale was introduced to various members of the Rogers family. Melinda was particularly impressed with him. She felt that they had finally found a top-calibre executive who not only shared her family's values but also her father's belief in the need for constant innovation.

There was, however, no discussion about the contemplated leadership change at meetings of the board's human resources committee, whose mandates included overseeing succession planning, according to one source. In fact, the HR committee had just rated Laurence as exceeding his performance targets.

Firing the chief executive is arguably the board's most important responsibility, and the process normally involves assessing the CEO's performance against objectives set by the HR committee. Choosing a replacement is also usually a board-supervised process that includes a search committee, interviews, and outside consultants. But John MacDonald, one of the company's independent directors, claimed none of that took place when Edward, with the support of his family, decided that it was time for his handpicked CEO to go. "The Board was not involved in any aspect of that termination except approving the termination package, and it was not involved in the search for a new Chief Executive Officer," he later said in court documents.

Edward may have been keeping the circle small to prevent Laurence from discovering what was afoot. One board source said the leadership change had been discussed at the corporate governance committee, a group comprised entirely of independent directors. (At the time, its membership was Charles Sirois, John Clappison, and Isabelle Marcoux.) It's unclear why that particular committee, whose role is to ensure that the board is functioning properly, and not the human resources group, would have been the avenue for the discussion. Regardless, MacDonald and the others went along with Edward's plan, with all of the directors ultimately voting in favour of the change. In doing so, they may have emboldened Edward to follow the same playbook the next time that he became dissatisfied with the company's leadership.

In September 2016, Natale flew out to Vancouver to try to convince Entwistle to free him from his two-year non-compete clause early. They went for dinner at a Tuscan-inspired restaurant downtown called Giardino, where Entwistle told Natale that he'd think about his request. Ultimately, however, he decided that he couldn't accede to it. In 2015, Telus had paid Natale a significant sum of money in part because he had agreed to extend his non-compete from one year to two. Natale's $6,243,650 transition payment, which one corporate governance expert described as "anoma-lously large," meant that he couldn't work for Rogers—or any Telus rival—until July 2017.

But Edward didn't want to wait that long, and he approached Entwistle to discuss unshackling Natale from the agreement sooner. The negotiations were, according to a source close to the Telus side, "brutal." Entwistle and the Telus board were baffled as to why Rogers wouldn't just wait for Natale's non-compete to run out. Edward, meanwhile, couldn't fathom why Telus was fighting so hard to prevent an executive they had fired from working at Rogers. The deeper that Entwistle dug his heels in, the more valu-able it made Natale appear to the Rogers side.

On Thanksgiving Day weekend in October 2016, Entwistle was with his family in New York City. They were heading into a Broadway production of the highly acclaimed musical *Hamilton* when Entwistle got a call from Edward, who wanted to discuss the non-compete. Entwistle spent a portion of the play outside the theatre on his phone, before sheepishly rejoining his family during a break. The calls continued throughout the weekend, not only from Edward but from Alan Horn as well. At one point, Entwistle was in SoHo shopping with his daughter. While she tried on dresses, Edward continued to call him, wanting to know why Telus wouldn't grant his wishes. The impression that stuck with Entwistle was of someone who was used to getting his way.

Horn, meanwhile, was left with the unenviable task of firing Laurence. Despite the fact that he and Edward still hadn't con-vinced Telus to free Natale from his contract, Horn broke the news to Laurence the following Sunday at the office. Laurence disagreed with the board's decision, he told Horn, but he respected their right to make it.

His departure was announced in a press release the next day. "We have appreciated Guy's leadership over the last three years," Edward said in a statement, thanking Laurence for his "competitive spirit and many contributions." His separation payments came to more than $13.5 million, the company later disclosed.

By the end of the year, negotiations between Rogers and Telus had broken down. Telus, meanwhile, entered into arbitration with Natale, who the telecom alleged had breached the terms of his non-compete and confidentiality agreements. The issue first surfaced when Telus learned that, in the fall, Natale had made a presentation to the Bank of Montreal's board of directors about the telecom's highly successful approach to customer service, a strategy it called "customer first." According to one source, he'd been asked to give the talk by the bank's president, Bill Downe—who was a friend of Natale's—and condensed a slide deck that he'd received from Dave Fuller, which had already been shown at investor conferences. According to Telus's investigation, however, Natale had allegedly tweaked the presentation to make the strategy look even more successful than it was. The telecom was also alleging that, during the recruitment process, Natale—in an effort to impress his prospective employer—had provided Rogers with strategic advice at a time when he was subject to a non-compete. Neither allegation was ever proven in court, and one source close to Natale disputes them.

Finally, in April 2017, Edward and Entwistle reached a deal that extricated Natale from his non-compete roughly two months early. The confidential agreement, which included about $13–14 million in cash as well as non-monetary compensation—such as deals relating to broadcasting Rogers-owned sports content—was valued at nearly $30 million, according to sources.

Publicly, the leadership change was positioned as being less about the family's dissatisfaction with Laurence and more about the need to snap up Natale before someone else did. Despite having been squeezed out of Telus, Natale was a hot commodity, and there was palpable excitement that he was coming on board. "When Joe [Natale] became available, it became too irresistible," a nameless Rogers source told the *Financial Post*. "Here was a guy with real operations experience who ran one of our major competitors. The opportunity was just too good to pass."

Lind was also enthusiastic about the hire, later describing Natale as "exactly the person we need." "He has all the right instincts, and he inspires people," Lind wrote in *Right Hand Man*. He even compared Natale's approachable nature to that of the company's legendary founder, who had been known to engage with employees at all levels in the elevator or the cafeteria.

But the six months between Laurence's departure and Natale's arrival were purgatory, according to some former employees. Projects that Laurence had spearheaded stalled as the people working on them wondered whether or not to keep going.

"I personally call it the dark days," said one source, citing a lack of leadership and communication from senior management, led by Horn, who once again filled in as interim chief executive. "Guy was sort of a champion of the people and got canned with no explanation."

One day in mid-November 2016, about a month after Laurence's abrupt departure, the rows of red seats in the John Bassett Theatre on Toronto's Front Street filled up with hundreds of Rogers employees. The two days of strategic-planning sessions for the company's leadership had been in the works for some time, and on the agenda were executive speeches, breakout rooms, and a performance by a gospel choir.

In lieu of the ousted chief executive, members of the Rogers family addressed the crowd, including Melinda, Loretta, and Edward and his two sons—Edward Samuel Rogers IV, who was just days shy of his eleventh birthday, and nine-year-old Jack

Robinson Miklos Rogers. Some employees were still shell-shocked from Laurence's firing. To them, the sight of Edward's sons on stage in their navy blue Upper Canada College blazers was a stark reminder of who was really in charge.

EIGHT

CARE NATION

Not long after Natale had taken occupancy of the chief executive's office on the tenth floor of 333 Bloor, Eric Agius found himself sitting in the modern, glass-walled room with a blank sheet of paper, discussing with the new CEO how to turn around the company's languishing call centres.

In the summer of 2017, several months into Natale's tenure, Agius's boss, Dirk Woessner, had asked him to lead the transformation of the troubled division. It was an important but notoriously difficult assignment. Morale at the customer service centres that housed 7,000 employees and handled more than 30 million calls a year was low, and it showed in the numbers: complaints were rising, while net promoter scores—a widely used market research metric that measures customer loyalty—were falling.

At first, Agius, a determined and articulate executive with experience at global firms such as Nike and LG Electronics, tried to decline the task. After all, he was fourteen months into the project he had been hired to do—transforming the telecom's sales channels—and his team's efforts were finally starting to pay off. He wanted to finish what he had started.

But Agius soon realized that saying no wasn't an option. On April 19, 2017, Natale's first day on the job, the new chief executive had made it clear to the company's shareholders that improving its poor customer service was among his top priorities. Although the telecom was good at signing up subscribers, its churn was higher than that of its peers, impacting its wireless results.

Standing on stage at the Velma Rogers Graham Theatre, a 225-person venue in the basement of the Rogers campus, with Edward, Loretta, and Martha in attendance, Natale paid tribute to Ted and the "incredible company" that he built, before shifting to his own management philosophy.

Natale wasn't ready yet to lay out a detailed, strategic plan. After all, he had only been on the job for a mere eleven hours, by Horn's count. ("Alan started counting at one minute past midnight, in case you're wondering where eleven hours came from," Natale joked after Horn introduced him.) But he did provide some hints as to where he felt the telecom had gone astray.

"I have an overarching belief that everything starts and ends with culture. It's the foundation for sustainable success, especially in a fast-paced industry like ours," Natale said. He then quoted legendary management consultant Peter Drucker, who famously said that "culture eats strategy for breakfast." (Interestingly, Drucker once had this to say in a column about family enterprises: "Both the business and the family will survive and do well only if the family serves the business. Neither will do well if the business is run to serve the family.") The ideal work environment was one where employees could thrive—not only professionally, but personally as well—Natale explained. Then, he turned to the company's most pressing, perennial problem.

"Second, I believe teams only succeed if they obsess—*truly obsess*—over the customer experience. We will succeed if we look at every idea, every change, through the lens of the customer. Every great company is built on this belief."

Natale was, of course, not the first Rogers CEO to focus on the dire need to improve the telecom's relationship with its customers, who were frustrated with both the prices they were being charged and the customer service that they received. Overhauling the customer experience had been a tenet of Laurence's Rogers 3.0 plan, and he and his team had taken some steps to that end, including making bills easier to understand, introducing data management tools, and offering unlimited internet plans. Natale acknowledged these efforts in his remarks at the shareholder meeting. "I've been impressed with the inroads Rogers has made. There is definitely more work to do, but there are signs of progress."

Agius learned just how much more work there was to do when he started looking under the hood of the customer care division. His original reluctance to take on the project was validated. Morale at the call centres was low, and absenteeism was so high that more than 20 per cent of staff—the equivalent of an entire call centre—was off work on any given day. Turnover was high too, as people headed for the exits. They felt as if they were an island, disenfranchised from the rest of the organization.

After digging a little deeper, Agius determined that under-investment was to blame. Rogers had been paying its call specialists well below market rates for years, and they received poor, outdated training. The offices they worked in were shabby and uninspiring, and managers behaved more like administrators with checklists than like coaches. Agius believed it all stemmed from the fact that the telecom's leadership was too fixated on costs. Whenever the company needed to hit a particular quarterly target, management would simply cut expenses, without considering the impact on customers or employees.

Agius outlined his observations to Natale. Together they drafted a plan, which Agius scribbled down on a sheet of paper. It comprised four key objectives: change the culture within the call centres; make customer experiences frictionless; improve training and tools for call centre staff; and change how customers perceive Rogers.

In an effort to combat feelings of loneliness and isolation among front-line workers, Agius decided to rebrand the call centre operations. A masterful storyteller who had worked at Nike, the world's most valuable sportswear brand, Agius knew how powerful a name could be. He settled on one that he hoped would convey to front-line workers that their jobs mattered. Going forward, the company's call centres would be "Care Nation."

The call centres weren't the only area that the telecom had under-invested in. During Laurence's tenure, Rogers had pared back its spending on its wireless network, while Bell and Telus had continued to aggressively pump cash into theirs. Compounding the problem was the fact that Bell and Telus shared portions of their wireless networks, making the gap between Rogers and its peers even more significant. When Natale arrived, Rogers was consistently scoring below its rivals on third-party tests of download speeds and latency (an industry term for lag time). The new chief executive resolved to close the investment gap and put Rogers back on equal footing with its peers.

Natale had cut his teeth at Telus running the division that served business customers, and he quickly decided that the Rogers enterprise services unit was in need of a complete overhaul. Rogers had always lagged behind Bell and Telus in the profitable enterprise services business. Expanding the division had been one of Laurence's key priorities as CEO, and he had installed Nitin Kawale, the former head of Cisco Canada, to head up the endeavour. But efforts to meet Laurence's ambitious growth targets by introducing sophisticated new products such as cloud-based networking services and cybersecurity solutions had failed. Kawale's division had ended up relying on sales of wireless services to enterprise clients to boost its revenue. Much of the growth had come not from large corporations buying cellphone plans for their workers, but from employee purchase plans that allowed individual employees to buy their own services from Rogers at discounted rates. The strategy had created friction with the consumer division, which felt that the enterprise folks were undercutting them and signing up less profitable customers.

One of the first things Natale did was get rid of Kawale. In the weeks following his abrupt departure, the enterprise division went through several rounds of layoffs, starting at the vice-president level and flowing down to directors and junior employees. Some of the complex new products that Kawale and his team had introduced had proven difficult to sell, and the teams supporting them were let go as Natale set out to simplify the business.

Some of the sales representatives were stunned. Just five months earlier, during meetings convened in Toronto and Calgary, they had been told that the new products they were selling and supporting were the division's key growth engine. The business had just gone through a hiring spree, and they were feeling good about their jobs. Now, the same leaders who had been tasked with expanding their teams were ordered to immediately downsize them. The abruptness with which they had to pivot from onboarding new sales representatives to conducting exit interviews with those very same people gave some of them whiplash. By the end of 2017, after Natale's first eight months on the job, the company's total head-count had decreased by 700, to 24,500.

Perhaps the biggest challenge facing Natale was repairing the company's culture. In the span of five years, Rogers had been run by three different CEOs—four including Horn's second stint as interim chief executive—and the frequent leadership changes had bred uncertainty among the company's staff. At a high level, the priorities between each of the various leaders were fairly similar. But each of them had different ideas about how to achieve those goals, and with each new CEO came a fresh batch of VPs and C-suite executives. Some of the initiatives that the previous leadership had spent millions on were dropped. To some, it felt like the company was being torn down and rebuilt every few years.

The Rogers family had always taken great pride in the fact that the telecom they owned and controlled was a family business. They spoke about how the tens of thousands of people they employed were all members of their extended family. Melinda, in particular, was a firm believer that the company's dual-class share structure provided a distinct advantage: the ability to take a longer-term focus. She had some evidence to back up her perspective: the National Bank of Canada's Canadian Family Index tracked approximately forty publicly traded family-controlled companies and found that they consistently outperformed widely held companies.

But Rogers, with its revolving door of chief executives, wasn't taking a long-term focus. Rather, it was plagued by bursts of short-term thinking. Also, being a family business came with a dark side. Ted's ghost still loomed over the place many years after his death, and his friends and relatives continued to populate the company's halls. Edward had created a spy network of allies throughout the company that allowed him to continue interfering in personnel and other decisions, even after he had been ousted from his VP role. The organization was so rife with cronyism that new employees quickly learned to keep track of people's proximity to the Rogers family. Those with close ties were considered untouchable, and it was wise to avoid getting on their bad side.

That fear-based culture wasn't conducive to attracting top talent, particularly in a world where, as the role of software in telecom networks grew, telecom companies found themselves competing with deep-pocketed technology giants such as Facebook and

Google for engineering talent. The technology arm of Rogers, filled with lifers lacking in the latest technical skills, was growing stale, according to some sources.

One person who was keenly aware of the importance of staying close to the family was the company's exceptionally powerful chief financial officer, Tony Staffieri. He had survived through three successive CEOs, and it was widely believed throughout the company that he coveted the top job. Over the years, he had developed a close relationship with Edward, who shared his financial focus. When Natale's arrival was announced, there were whispers that Staffieri was upset he'd been passed over for the role. (A source close to Staffieri who has worked closely with him for years disputes this notion, saying that he has always focused on the job that the company asked him to do.)

It's normal for a chief financial officer to be focused on tightly controlling costs. But Staffieri had an outsized influence on decision-making at Rogers, according to several company insiders. He had more people reporting to him than a typical CFO, as roughly half a dozen divisions that wouldn't normally be part of finance—including the supply chain, procurement, and corporate strategy groups—were within his purview. This led some employees to view the finance department as bloated, even as Staffieri advocated for a lean organization. While the human resources division typically had three or four vice-presidents, the number of VPs in finance was in the double digits—a strong indication of the unit's power, according to some.

Several former executives blamed Staffieri for what they perceived to be chronic underinvestment. They claimed that he was behind the company's push to close a number of retail stores before Natale's arrival, hampering efforts to sign up new customers, and that he had resisted efforts to spend the money needed to modernize the telecom's sales channels. A source close to Staffieri calls the allegations "ridiculous," claiming that investments in digital sales channels increased and that there was no push to close stores "other than what was directed by Joe and his head of wireless."

When Staffieri had stepped into the CFO role, he had brought in a new financial approval process inspired by practices at the other companies he had worked at, including Bell. But some employees felt that it was overly burdensome and redundant, and that the amount of financial red tape at Rogers exceeded that at other companies. In addition to the usual process that one went through to get a budget approved, a secondary approval was required before spending the money. Executives understood that only projects expected to generate a high return on investment would be considered, and Natale often found himself mediating disputes between Staffieri and the business unit heads about spending plans. But Staffieri's allies say he was merely playing the role that Natale had asked him to play—that of the CFO.

Guy Laurence had begun the thorny task of extricating the Rogers family and some of its powerful allies from the company's upper ranks, but the brusque manner in which he had done so was likened by one former employee to open-heart surgery. If Natale were to continue his brash predecessor's work of transforming Rogers from a cozy family enterprise into a professionally run company, he would have to use a far less invasive approach. It was a challenging mandate, but one that many believed the likeable Natale was particularly well suited for. Unlike Laurence, who was seen by some as taking a bull-in-the-china-shop approach, Natale was perceived as a leader who could navigate touchy situations with grace. If anyone could transform Rogers into a high-performance culture—a meritocracy rooted in transparency, openness, diversity, and equal opportunity—it was him.

Natale believed that bringing in people who were motivated to do what was right for the customer would improve customer loyalty and, ultimately, drive better financial results. It would also, he hoped, provide stability. "One of my goals is to create a management team with strong talents and succession so the next CEO of Rogers comes from within the organization," he told the *Globe and Mail*.

Care Nation was an attempt to change the corporate culture at the grassroots level, but Natale also needed a top-down approach; he needed to bring in a new class of leaders to usher the company into the future. He started assembling the New Guard.

Near the end of 2017, Edward Rogers was finally crowned the chairman of his father's telecom empire. Some of the independent directors had concerns about whether the founder's son was suitable for the role, which had previously been held by long-time family lieutenant Alan Horn. They believed that the chair should maintain a level of detachment from day-to-day affairs and let management call the shots on things like personnel decisions—a view shared by many corporate governance experts. But eventually, Edward's ascension to the chairmanship had started to feel like an inevitability. After all, his name was on the building. After much deliberation, the board decided that Horn would step aside, ceding the position to Edward. Some directors thought that giving Edward something important to do might curb his frequent interference with management, although not everyone viewed his involvement as a negative. "He has tremendous value to add," says one of Edward's board allies, the retired investment banker Robert Gemmell.

On December 7, just seven months into Natale's tenure as CEO, Rogers issued a press release announcing the change. "The company is in great shape, there is great momentum in the business and the company is being led by an outstanding CEO in Joe Natale," read a quote from Horn. "This is the right time for the Board to make the planned transition of the Chair's role to Edward."

Although Edward had expended considerable time and money freeing Natale from his non-compete, it didn't take long for the newly appointed chairman to start souring on his hired hand. According to sources, Natale's relationship-driven approach to leadership vexed Edward and his allies, some of whom felt that the chief executive spent too much time at social functions. Some people in the company began derisively referring to Natale as "Cocktail Joe" behind his back.

Natale's strategy of recruiting superstars to his executive leadership team also clashed with Edward's desire to promote people inside the company, and the chairman tried to push back on at least one of Natale's high-profile hires: Jordan Banks. Natale had tapped Banks, a former eBay and Facebook executive, to replace broadcaster Rick Brace as president of the sports and media business. But Edward didn't think that Banks had the right skill set. He had someone else in mind for the job—a broadcasting executive and long-time Rogers executive named Colette Watson. According to Gemmell, Natale had also failed to disclose to the board that Banks was a close personal friend. "There was a hell of a fight over Jordan," one company insider said. Natale won in the end, and Banks joined the executive leadership team in the summer of 2019. But the task that lay ahead of him—modernizing the Old Media business built by the company's late founder—was daunting. It was made even harder by the $5.2 billion, twelve-year rights deal with the National Hockey League that Rogers had signed back in 2013. Although the contract boosted Rogers Media's revenues, it made it increasingly difficult for the division to be profitable, especially since the cost of the rights ramped up each year.

Natale confided in several directors that he was spending a considerable amount of time managing Edward. But Melinda reassured Natale that she thought he was doing a good job. The message was echoed by Loretta, who met regularly with Natale— a dynamic that one person likened to meetings between Canada's prime minister and the Queen. The matriarch was keenly aware of the interpersonal dynamics between her children, and of the challenges that came with the CEO role. During her monthly meetings with Natale, which typically took place over a meal and a glass of wine at her home in Toronto or in the Bahamas, she offered to help manage her offspring if Natale ran into trouble. There was "mutual affection" between Loretta and Natale, according to one person who was briefed about their meetings.

Some of the rank and file began to sense what they perceived to be a culture war within the Rogers family over how the company should be run. Melinda, who had spent years immersed in Silicon Valley's culture of innovation, wanted Rogers to be a talent magnet that focused on the future, a vision she shared with the company's new CEO. Edward, meanwhile, seemed more focused on the finances.

In early 2019, Natale and his team faced a dilemma. Globally, the wireless industry was moving away from charging customers hefty fees for exceeding their data allotments. For Rogers, overage fees represented about 5 per cent of wireless service revenue, and doing away with them would mean taking a significant financial hit. But the shift towards so-called unlimited data plans (somewhat of a misnomer, as customers would see their speeds throttled once they hit their data caps) had some advantages as well. Overage charges were a major source of customer gripes, increasing the workload on the company's call centres, and they were heavily criticized by consumer advocates for contributing to Canada's high wireless prices relative to other countries. The fees had also conditioned Canadians, fearful of facing steep charges for exceeding their data limits, to rely heavily on WiFi. Growth in consumers' data consumption had stalled just as the big telecoms prepared to spend billions deploying the latest iteration of wireless technology.

It was clear that switching to unlimited plans was the right move. Doing so would not only improve the telecom's relationship with its customers and reduce call volumes at Care Nation, but would also whet consumers' appetite for data, hopefully spurring them to purchase pricier packages offering faster speeds. The only question that remained was how quickly and aggressively to roll out the new plans.

There were some compelling arguments for migrating customers onto the new plans as fast as possible. It would hurt in the short term—there was no doubt about that—but once customers moved to unlimited they would be less likely to change carriers, and lower customer turnover would boost the wireless subscriber figures. Moving aggressively would allow Rogers to pass through the painful revenue loss more quickly and return to growth.

Rogers announced the launch of its unlimited data plans, called Rogers Infinite, on June 12, 2019. For $75 a month, customers could get ten gigabytes of high-speed mobile data. Once they hit their data caps they would see their browsing speeds reduced, rather than incurring financial penalties. Rogers wasn't the first wireless carrier in Canada to offer such a plan—Shaw's Freedom Mobile had launched its Big Gig data plan, which offered ten gigs of data for $50, back in 2017—but it was the first of the Big Three to make the switch to unlimited data, and Bell and Telus were forced to quickly follow suit. Unlike Rogers, however, which advertised the new plans heavily and trained its sales staff to push them, Bell and Telus opted for a much more gradual transition that allowed them to hold on to their lucrative overage charges a little longer.

As expected, the decision to migrate customers quickly onto the new plans caused overage revenues to plummet. When Rogers reported its third-quarter results at the end of October 2019—the first full quarter since the introduction of the Infinite plans—the telecom disclosed that more than a million customers had signed up for the new pricing model, more than three times higher than the company had expected by that point. Overage fees fell by $50 million, causing profits to fall short of analyst expectations and forcing the telecom to slash its 2019 revenue and earnings guidance. The company's stock suffered its worst trading day in six years, dropping 8.1 per cent to $61 a share.

During the company's quarterly earnings conference call, Natale and Staffieri reassured analysts that the pain would be temporary. The company had initially expected it to take six to eight quarters to transition away from its reliance on overage revenues. Now, the change would occur over just four or five quarters. By the second half of 2020, average revenue per user would be returning to positive growth, Staffieri said. And the change was already reaping some benefits. Calls to Care Nation relating to billing and overage were down by 50 per cent. Data consumption had increased by 50 per cent, while the telecom's "likelihood to recommend" score, which tracks customers' loyalty by asking them how likely they are to recommend the company's services to friends or family, was up by 30 per cent. "We believe this move was inevitable, and it was the right time before we ramp into a 5G world," Natale explained on the call.

The president of Rogers' wireless division during that time was Brent Johnston, a former colleague of Natale's from Telus who had served as the Vancouver-based telecom's senior vice-president of consumer marketing. Johnston had left Telus and was working for Apple when Natale brought him over to Rogers in 2018.

The decision to move to unlimited data was made in early 2019, roughly six months after Johnston arrived. It wasn't a decision that he made on his own—both the management team and the board had agreed with the approach. However, some felt that Johnston's team had stumbled on the execution—and that it would ultimately cost him his job.

To stop the revolving door at Care Nation, Agius's team re-engineered the training program for its call specialists. They had new hires start taking customer calls on day one, allowing those who weren't suited for the job to drop out a lot quicker. This also allowed the company to shorten the program from six weeks to four.

Agius and his team implemented other changes, as well. They made the scheduling system for front-line staff more flexible, which helped cut absenteeism in half. They launched an online suggestion site called Voice of the Frontline that allowed call centre and retail staff to communicate customer needs up the chain. They upgraded the technology in the call centres to make it easier to use, increased starting salaries, and brought in a consulting firm to teach first-level managers how to be coaches. They even brightened up the dreary Care Nation offices and equipped workers with second monitors and better chairs.

Natale's warm, empathic leadership style resonated with employees and turned him into something of a folk hero among front-line staff. He earned their trust by speaking to them openly and honestly during monthly open-mic sessions. At Telus, a laserlike focus on the customer had permeated every facet of the organization, and Natale strove to instill that same philosophy at Rogers. Every Monday morning, he would send out an email outlining how the company had let down one of its customers, and how it could improve.

Over time, the changes started to bear fruit. The "likelihood to recommend" score rose by almost 70 per cent. The proportion of customer problems resolved during the first call climbed by 50 per cent. Employee engagement improved too, not just at the call centres but across the entire organization. Jim Reid's human resources team had discovered, by surveying employees, that growth and development were the key drivers of engagement, and they introduced training programs that took advantage of those insights. In 2014, employee engagement was at 72 per cent. By 2020, it had risen to 87 per cent—a 15 percentage point increase over the span of six years.

But while morale among the rank and file was improving, hostilities between directors on the company's board were growing. Two of the telecom's independent directors—Gemmell and ex-Quebecor chief Robert Dépatie—seemed happy to let Edward call the shots. After all, as the controlling shareholder, he had the final say. But others, including the outspoken former technology executive Rob Burgess, who had crossed paths with Melinda in Palo Alto, California, believed that the independent directors had a duty to speak for all of the company's shareholders, including those who owned the non-voting Class B shares.

In late November 2019, Burgess resigned from the company's board following an incident involving an activist investor. New York–based Mason Capital Management had bought up roughly 5 per cent of Rogers' Class A voting shares and presented the company with a strategy to boost the stock price, by spinning out its cellphone towers as well as its sports and media assets. Sources say Burgess was upset by how Edward handled the issue; he felt that Edward had bypassed the board and engaged directly with Mason. Gemmell, meanwhile, portrays the situation differently. He says Mason's ideas were provided to both the board and its finance committee in "summary concept form" and were "essentially dismissed" at both levels—including by Burgess—because they were not a good use of the company's resources "or interesting in any way." (Burgess has refused to confirm or deny this on the record.) However, Edward was interested in buying the shares from Mason through the Rogers Control Trust, and he reached out to the activist investor to propose a deal. He didn't feel that he had to consult the directors because it was Rogers Telecommunications Ltd., an entity owned by the trust and not the public company, that was proposing to buy Mason out.

The following month, the Rogers Control Trust announced in a press release that it was acquiring an additional 5.7 million Class A shares—just over 5 per cent—through a "private agreement with a single vendor," bumping up its ownership stake to more than 97 per cent of the voting shares. According to one source, the board was "generally happy" that the company's management was freed up to focus on running the business, rather than having to respond to Mason's recommendations. But to Burgess, the incident was the latest example of Edward treating the publicly held company like his own private fiefdom, according to sources. It wasn't the sole reason for his departure, they said, but it was the straw that broke the camel's back. He told other directors that he was no longer comfortable with the manner in which the company was being governed and that his lawyers had advised him to step down. Burgess never publicly spelled out the reasons for his departure. But several months after his resignation, he told a class of MBA students from McMaster University's DeGroote School of Business that he had stepped down from the Rogers board because he and the chairman had conflicting views on corporate governance. "I like mine better," he said.

Despite the dysfunction in the telecom's upper ranks, there was a lot for the legions of rank-and-file workers to be excited about. Natale was an inspiring leader who seemed to genuinely care about customers and employees, and he rallied the troops by painting a compelling vision of the company's role in a 5G-enabled future. He had assembled a team of respected leaders such as Banks and Jorge Fernandes, a former Vodafone executive he successfully lured from the U.K. to become Rogers' chief technology officer. And while the telecom's rivals waited on a decision from the federal government regarding whether or not to ban China's Huawei Technologies Co. Ltd. from Canada's 5G networks over security concerns, Rogers' partnership with Swedish supplier Ericsson allowed it to race ahead and launch the service first.

The mood within the broader company was upbeat when hundreds of Rogers employees convened at the Carlu in February 2020 for the Ted Rogers Awards, an annual gala named in honour of the company's late founder. Although reports of a novel coronavirus originating from China had begun dominating headlines, COVID-19 was still deemed a fairly low risk in Canada. As a precaution, hand sanitizer stations were installed around the venue. The slick and highly scripted event, which was emceed by Rogers Media personalities, was a jubilant affair. Natale posed for photos with the winning teams. For many Rogers employees, it was the last time they would see one another in person. On March 11, the World Health Organization declared the COVID-19 outbreak a global pandemic.

NINE

"BEANS ABOUT CABLE"

On March 24, 2020, as the rapidly spreading novel coronavirus plunged the world into chaos, tributes started pouring in for JR Shaw. The founder of Shaw Communications had long ago ceded his place at the helm of his cable empire to his sons—first to the fiercely competitive and boisterous Jim, then to the softer, more spiritually minded Brad—but he remained involved in the business as the company's executive chairman, and his passing was marked by glowing statements from industry leaders. BCE Inc.'s president and chief executive, Mirko Bibic, lauded him as an "inspirational entrepreneur," while Telus's Entwistle praised JR's philanthropic work and characterized him as a "formidable competitor." Edward offered condolences to JR's widow, Carol, as well as to his three surviving kids, and described JR in a statement as a "true pioneer" whose "legacy will be felt for generations to come."

James Robert Shaw was born in 1934. He legally changed his name to JR—with no periods—many years later. His mother, Lottie, was a reserved, religious woman with plump cheeks, dark, wavy hair, and softly tapered brows framing her brown eyes. In

1922, she married Francis Shaw, a young man with a ruddy complexion and a head of copper locks who had just returned from fighting in the First World War. Lottie and Francis both grew up near Brigden, an agricultural community in southwestern Ontario, just across the border from Detroit. As children they had attended the same church, a local branch of the Reorganized Church of Jesus Christ of Latter Day Saints, a spin-off of Mormonism that eschewed polygamy.

Francis was only twenty years old when he was shipped off to France to fight in the war, and he was one of the lucky few who made it back with all of his limbs intact. After returning home, he was determined to make the most of his good fortune. His first business ventures involved securing contracts to do roadwork for various townships and using horse-driven plows to dig V-shaped trenches for a natural gas pipeline. By the time JR was two years old, his father was spending long stretches away from home on business.

Francis and Lottie had two daughters, Bertha and Dolly, a mischievous son named Les, and JR, who was the youngest and the most coddled of the four kids. The farm on which JR and his siblings grew up was a very different world from the prestigious boarding schools that Ted Rogers attended. The Shaw kids learned the value of hard work by tending to the family's cows, sheep, and hogs, as well as a hundred acres of crops. They lived in a big, square house heated by a furnace, and it was JR's job to load up the coal that lined the driveway into a wheelbarrow and haul it inside. A thick stripe of green paint visually separated the top storey of the house from the bottom portion, which was beige. Francis installed pipes that carried rainwater from the roof to a cistern in the basement that was perpetually full of drowned rats. Lottie, who despised rats, would use a ladle to scoop the rainwater into a pot and heat it on the stove to bathe herself and the kids.

As a child, JR loved lying on the carpet next to the radiator in the central part of the house, staring up at the ceiling while voices emanating from a massive console radio transported him into detective mysteries and westerns. He and his sister Dolly, who was five years his senior, often bickered over which programs to listen to.

When Francis came home on the weekends, he would sometimes push the furniture aside, get down on his hands and knees, and let the children climb all over him. He lavished them with generous Christmas presents as his business ventures flourished. While other children got oranges, nuts, or hockey pucks, JR and his siblings got bicycles. But Francis was also a strict disciplinarian with a fiery temper. Once, JR and a friend smoked a bunch of cigarette butts out of a corncob pipe at the Brigden fall fair. When JR got home and lied to his father, who asked him if he had been smoking, he was beaten from his knees all the way up to his back.

In the ninth grade, JR spotted a tall, blonde girl named Carol Bulman in the schoolyard. She was taken with JR's thick, auburn hair and his athletic build. Soon, JR was flying down the highway in his mother's two-door hardtop Oldsmobile Delta 88 to visit Carol in Sarnia, where she lived with her parents and three sisters. After baseball games—JR played third base and was a powerful batter—the couple would neck in the car at the drive-in movie theatre owned by JR's dad.

The high school sweethearts were married in 1956 and honeymooned at the Muskoka Beach Inn, a rustic, two-storey lodge with a red roof surrounded by cabins on the south shore of Lake Muskoka. That same year, JR enrolled at Michigan State University, where he studied business and economics. Carol gave birth to the couple's first child, a boy named Jim, in 1957.

After finishing his degree, JR moved his small family to Hamilton, an industrial city at the west end of Lake Ontario, to work for his father's pipeline-coating business. JR and his wife found a house perched high atop a stretch of escarpment. The elevation allowed them to receive a clear television signal from Buffalo. To unwind, JR watched sports on TV, rooting for the Boston

Red Sox, the Toronto Maple Leafs, and the Hamilton Tiger-Cats of the CFL.

The couple's second child, Heather Ann, was born on Canada Day in 1959. A third, Julie Marie, followed in 1961. By then, the family had moved into a small brick house in Toronto's west end so that JR could work with his brother Les out of the company's head office. But he spent much of his time flying back and forth to Saskatchewan, where he wooed clients in the oil and gas industry.

JR hated being away from his family, and eventually proposed moving to Edmonton to build a plant there. Carol was hesitant at first, but she could see that, for JR, the move was an opportunity to step out from the shadow cast by his father and older brother.

Once in Edmonton, JR was disappointed with his television choices. The popularity of the medium was exploding, but now that he was no longer close to the U.S. border, his rooftop antenna could only pick up three signals—and no Sunday afternoon football games. JR was working hard to establish the company's western presence and feed his growing family—Carol delivered their youngest child, Bradley Scott, in 1964—but he worried that the pipe-coating business had limited runway. Like Ted Rogers, JR saw an opportunity in cable television. The lack of over-the-air signals in Edmonton had convinced him that cable would be a booming business.

Not everyone was so certain. "Young man, cable television is nothing more than a passing fad," Joe Jeffrey, the former president of the Chamber of Commerce of Canada, once told him. Still, JR persevered, incorporating Capital Cable Television Co. Ltd. on December 9, 1966. The company was later renamed Shaw Communications Inc.

But the process of obtaining a broadcasting licence was far lengthier and more arduous than JR had anticipated, and several of his business partners lost hope and moved on. Even JR started to second-guess the plan, as his other business ventures—including

an ice cream shop, a roast-beef restaurant franchise, and a gas
reservoir near Dawson Creek, B.C.—failed to take off. It was a
difficult few years, and JR was forced to scale back costs on the
construction of the family's new home, a farm in Sherwood Park.
To soothe his anxiety, he paced around the farm with a bucket,
picking up discarded nails.

Finally, in July 1970, as he and his staff stood at the open windows of Capital Cable's office watching the noisy Klondike Days
parade march down Jasper Avenue below, JR received a phone call
with good news. The CRTC had awarded Capital a licence for half
of Edmonton.

Capital Cable signed up 10,000 customers in its first year. Then,
over the next two decades, JR worked his way across the country,
charming other families into selling him their cable systems as a
wave of consolidation surged through the sector. He started in
British Columbia's lush Okanagan Valley, known for its wineries
and fruit orchards. In 1970, shortly after securing the Edmonton
cable licence, the Shaws drove through the region in a rented
motorhome that, unfortunately, kept breaking down. But in a twist
of good fortune, a pit stop they were forced to make in Penticton
after a small electrical fire broke out led JR to a business opportunity. While he and Jim waited for the car to be serviced, they
stopped in to visit Lloyd Gartrell, a local cable operator whose
office was in a strip mall, only to discover that Gartrell had already
conditionally sold his cable system. JR told him to call if the sale
fell through, which it did. In 1971, JR bought the cable network,
which included 7,500 homes in Penticton, Kelowna, and Revelstoke,
for $2.2 million.

Even as JR's cable empire expanded, it continued to fly under
the radar of people like Ted Rogers and Maclean Hunter's Ron
Osborne. The lack of relevance bothered JR, although things finally

changed in 1992, when Shaw broke into the lucrative Ontario cable market by taking over David Graham's Cablecasting. The deal cost more than $300 million and doubled the company's size.

JR's warm and friendly nature was the key to his success. Once, in the mid-1990s, he clinched a $635 million deal in a hospital room in Miami Beach. JR was in the midst of negotiating the split-up of the Maclean Hunter properties with Ted, when an opportunity presented itself for Shaw to expand beyond its stronghold in western Canada. CUC Broadcasting Ltd., the large Scarborough-based cable system founded by the late businessman Geoffrey Conway, was for sale. In order to close the deal, JR flew out to Miami to visit the founder's widow and the company's largest shareholder, Julia Conway Royer, who was at the Mount Sinai Medical Center after giving birth to her son.

"[JR] was such a wonderfully warm person that she felt that she could entrust him with her husband's legacy," former Shaw president Peter Bissonnette told the *Globe and Mail* in an interview shortly after JR's death. The takeover of CUC turned Shaw into the country's second-largest cable operator.

Unlike Rogers, which always seemed to face an uphill regulatory battle when it came to closing mergers, Shaw's takeovers were so devoid of controversy that they typically sailed past the regulators without a hitch. Some family friends, including Bissonnette and Phil Lind, attributed that to JR's friendly approach to doing business, which extended to his relationship with regulators. "Rogers tended to be a bit more bombastic when they'd go into hearings," said Bissonnette.

But JR could be resolute as well. In 1995, he uprooted not only his family but also the cable company's headquarters, because he felt that Edmonton's mayor, Jan Reimer, was threatening the company's growth. It was a crucial moment for building out fibre-optic networks, and Shaw wanted to bring fibre lines into its technology centre in downtown Edmonton. In order to do so, the company needed to renegotiate the contract it had inked with the city back in 1970 to replace the wording "coaxial cable" with "fibre-optic cable." Reimer argued that the new lines should be public property, and that Shaw should pay to lease them.

Shaw spent four years trying to hash out a deal with the city, while its Vancouver-based rival Telus was busy building out its own fibre-optic network unimpeded. Despite how important Edmonton was to Shaw's identity, the fiercely competitive JR eventually made the difficult decision to relocate the company. In the fall of 1995, Reimer was narrowly defeated by Bill Smith, a businessman and former professional football player with the Edmonton Eskimos. But by then, Shaw had moved its headquarters into an angular tower of concrete and rose-coloured glass in downtown Calgary that it bought from Shell Oil.

Prior to the move, JR had jotted down a list of twelve reasons why Shaw's headquarters should relocate. One of them related to succession planning. In Edmonton, Shaw had been known as JR's company. In Calgary, his kids would have a chance to make the company their own.

Julie Shaw, the younger of the family's two daughters, spearheaded the extensive redesign and renovation of the newly purchased Shaw Court. Blonde with a round chin and a warm smile, Julie studied architecture and first joined the family company as a draftsman before becoming its vice-president of facilities design and management.

JR was an avid art collector, and he lined the walls of the bright and airy Shaw Court with original pieces by Canadian artists, as well as adding an art curator to the company's payroll. Regina artist Joe Fafard was commissioned to create a steel sculpture of a bison to guard the building's entrance. JR had taught his children to appreciate art as well. Julie would later recall how, at Christmas, he would wrap up four paintings and make the kids choose which one they wanted, based only on size and shape.

Initially, JR and Carol's first-born son wasn't eager to join the family business. As a teenager, Jim was rebellious and butted heads with his father. He left home at sixteen to go work on a farm in Lethbridge, Alberta, cutting off contact with his family for several months. But he knew that he needed to get an education, so he eventually asked to be enrolled at Shawnigan Lake School, a lakeside boarding school on Vancouver Island. After graduating from Shawnigan, Jim took a stab at a formal business education at the University of Calgary. But he had no patience for lectures or hours of studying, and ultimately dropped out, starting a Christmas tree business with a childhood friend instead.

Jim dabbled in tree delivery and rock hauling, and did a stint working in the family's pipe-coating factory. Eventually, in the 1980s, as the cable industry took off, JR convinced his eldest son, then in his twenties, to come on board. Jim was apprehensive about reporting to his father, but that didn't turn out to be a problem. After starting his new job, he quickly realized that the guy installing cable lines didn't report to the CEO.

From there, Jim steadily rose through the ranks. He landed his first management job in 1986, running the Victoria, B.C. cable system, before returning to Edmonton to become vice-president of operations.

The Shaw family's succession planning strategy was markedly different from the one employed by Rogers. Rather than leading the company right up until his death, JR was in his sixties when he decided to pass the torch to one of his offspring.

All of JR's kids were employed at the family enterprise by that point. Julie was working in facilities management, while Brad had a leadership role in Shaw's Star Choice satellite service. Heather, who had an MBA from the University of Western Ontario's Ivey Business School, had run several of Shaw's media properties and was slated to become the chair of a new entity called Corus. The Shaws had been buying up radio and television stations, and JR planned to spin them out into a separate unit. He had offered to appoint Heather as its CEO, but she opted for chair so that she could spend more time with her kids.

As JR's retirement loomed, Jim, who had once been so reluctant to work for his dad, was the obvious choice to take over as CEO. He had become the company's president, working closely with JR during the cable consolidation of the 1990s. On December 16, 1998, when he was sixty-four years old, JR sat down and handwrote his son a letter in neat, elegant cursive.

"Tomorrow you will become CEO, the pivotal position. You deserve it—and I pass on the mantle, very willingly, with best wishes and love. The time we have spent together, thinking and planning, is a period of such satisfaction, every dad should experience," he wrote. He advised his son to spend less time in the office and more with his family, and to turn to his siblings for support when needed. "I will always be available to assist you where possible, but you're the man."

Jim quickly became one of the most polarizing figures in the Canadian cable industry. Unlike his polite and well-mannered father, he projected the image of a boisterous, politically incorrect western Canadian cowboy. A stocky man with a bulbous nose, auburn hair, and a matching goatee, he kept a model Harley-Davidson on his desk and once showed up to a cable convention in biker gear. The walls of his childhood bedroom had been plastered with posters of a Suzuki 125.

To the chagrin of Shaw's lawyers, Jim was known to speak off the cuff at CRTC hearings, ignoring the talking points that had been painstakingly prepared for him. He saw himself as a champion for consumers, leading to frequent clashes with CRTC chairman Konrad von Finckenstein. Jim complained about Shaw being forced to carry an LGBTQ television channel that his customers didn't want, and about having to contribute to the Canadian Television Fund, which financed homegrown content and was later consolidated into the Canadian Media Fund. Jim called the fund a waste of customer money and pulled Shaw's contributions to it at one point, prompting the CRTC to hold a public hearing. When Jim learned that von Finckenstein wouldn't be in attendance, he declared he would not attend the hearing either, as he wasn't interested in negotiating with the CRTC's "B team."

Although Jim's demeanour was very different from his father's, he continued to consult JR on major business decisions. Shortly after their son took over as CEO, JR and Carol spent several months vacationing in Tuscany. Jim called JR often for advice as he negotiated with CanWest, a Winnipeg-based media conglomerate, over how to split up the broadcasting assets belonging to Western International Communications Ltd.

JR continued to receive generous compensation after he stepped down as CEO. As executive chairman, he received an annual salary of $1.2 million, and had a "founder's agreement" bonus plan that paid him 0.5 to 1 per cent of the company's profit each year. In 2019 he reduced his payout to 0.35 per cent, and still collected $6.8 million. He also knew how to enjoy his wealth. He bought a winter home in Hawaii and a secluded fishing camp called Eagle Pointe Lodge at the intersection of British Columbia and Alaska, where the waters of the North Pacific Ocean teem with salmon, halibut, and orcas. Brian Felesky, an accountant who did tax work for the Shaws, was among the small group of friends JR brought up to the lodge to discuss philosophy and commerce, over fine wine and gourmet meals prepared for them by a Calgary chef.

Felesky admired JR's flair for enjoying life, as well as his generosity. JR had been so deeply moved by his friend Donald Mazankowski's struggles with heart problems that he raised funds to advance treatment of the disease that had afflicted the Canadian politician. In order to win the Shaw family's business, Felesky was required to make a substantial donation to the Mazankowski Alberta Heart Institute.

Eventually, Jim Shaw's workaholic lifestyle, heavy drinking, and diet of cheeseburgers and steaks began to take a toll. In early 2008, he was forced to take time off after developing bleeding ulcers. Von Finckenstein was unaware of the affliction when he expressed his disappointment over Jim's absence during a regulatory hearing that April. "I thought he would have done us the courtesy of showing up personally," the chairman told Shaw's executives. "Sending you, which in his terminology I would characterize a 'B team,' I don't think adds to the process."

Jim's doctor told him that if he continued on his trajectory he would eventually "fall over dead." Fuelled by that stern warning, as well as his marriage to Meg Nicholson, a Calgary investment banker eighteen years his junior, Jim overhauled his lifestyle. The man who showed up on BNN, the business news channel, later that year was fifty pounds lighter and wearing glasses and a suit.

While he may have weighed less and dressed more appropriately for his position, Jim's antics continued to get him into trouble. The situation came to a head in 2010 when he had a meltdown during a lunch with investors at Il Giardino, a restaurant in Vancouver. He seemed to be drunk and was behaving belligerently, criticizing some of the investors. He hastily resigned less than a week later. By then, Jim's younger brother, Brad, had already been tapped to replace him. The incident accelerated the transition by two months.

Brad Shaw's leadership style was very different from his brother's. Unlike Jim, who liked to maintain an outward appearance of toughness, Brad was a spiritual man with the gentlemanly mannerisms of his father. He spoke about vulnerability and compassion as powerful leadership traits, and liked to tell a story about a

Buddhist high priest he and his wife had met in Calgary. The holy man had passed Brad a small rock that he had heated up just by chanting on it. It was so hot that it seared third-degree burns into Brad's hands.

Brad and his wife travelled frequently to Tibet, where they funded an orphanage for 250 kids run by the holy man. One year, the couple took their four children—daughters Sierra and Hannah, who was just a toddler at the time, and sons Phelan and Logan—to the orphanage, which was in a town called Zadou. It was no easy trip, but Brad and Michelle thought the journey would be eye-opening for the kids.

Growing up, Brad was an athletic teen who played AA hockey and raced his dad downhill on family ski trips. Like his older brother, he spent his summers doing manual labour for the family company, before graduating to working the phone lines at Shaw's call centres. In his early twenties, he went through a rough patch, becoming entangled with what JR and Carol characterized as a bad crowd and developing a penchant for drinking and drugs. These behaviours were intolerable to JR, and Brad wound up moving out of the house and becoming estranged from his family.

Finally, one summer night, Brad hit rock bottom. He missed his parents and his siblings and the family's two miniature schnauzers, Freckles and Fritz. But after walking the roughly twenty kilometres home, he was too anxious to face his parents. Worried that they might not take him back, he hid out in a shed on the family's property for two days, eating bits of food he had brought along in his backpack and sleeping on a stack of plywood. Eventually JR stumbled upon him by accident.

Brad was welcomed back into the family and started working his way up through the company, taking on progressively more senior roles in the cable and satellite divisions. By the time the 47-year-old took over the family business in 2010, its market cap had grown to $9.5 billion. His brother Jim had built upon their father's pioneering success by adeptly steering Shaw into internet and even home phone services, the latter of which was territory previously dominated by phone companies like Telus. But there were challenges ahead—most notably, heightened competition from Telus, which had retaliated by encroaching on Shaw's turf and launching its own television service, Optik TV. At the same time, the era of cord-cutting was underway, as consumers started cancelling their pricey cable subscriptions in favour of online streaming services such as Netflix. By 2015, Telus's internet protocol television or IPTV service had attracted more than a million subscribers. At least some of those gains came at Shaw's expense; between 2011 and 2015, Shaw lost more than half a million cable customers.

In order to revive its flattening revenue growth, Shaw needed to get into the industry's only significant growth driver: wireless. Over the years, the Shaws had flip-flopped several times regarding their wireless ambitions, and that indecision wound up costing them both opportunities and time. In the 1990s, they had bought a 10 per cent stake in Microcell, the wireless carrier that operated as Fido, for $30 million. But they sold the investment in 1998, six years before Fido was acquired by Rogers. In the 2000s, Shaw contemplated offering wireless services through a partnership with one of the Big Three telecoms, but never struck a deal.

By 2008, the telecom had resolved to build its own wireless network from scratch. That year, the company paid $189 million for wireless airwaves during a public auction. But by the time Brad took over from Jim two years later, the build had stalled. The first major decision he was faced with as chief executive was whether to pour more than a billion dollars into the project or pull the plug.

The following year, after conducting a strategic review, Brad decided to abandon the initiative. Instead of constructing a wireless network, Shaw would build a less costly network of WiFi hot spots that its internet customers could connect their smartphones and tablets to for free. The move left many on Bay Street scratching their heads. Shaw was betting that WiFi would disrupt the market for pricey cellphone plans, but it was unclear how the company would monetize its investment.

As a result of its shift in strategy, Shaw set out to sell the wireless airwaves that it had bought in the 2008 auction. They were in a band of spectrum called AWS, short for Advanced Wireless Services. Canada's Conservative government had wanted to bring down cellphone bills, and it decided that the best way to do so was to encourage new competitors to emerge by reducing one of the industry's major barriers to entry. Ottawa was responsible for issuing wireless licences, which grant companies the exclusive right to use specific frequencies on the electromagnetic spectrum. During the 2008 federal auction, the government set aside 40 per cent of those licences for new wireless competitors, allowing them to obtain access to the wireless spectrum at a fraction of the cost paid by the major carriers. Shaw was one of the companies that had benefited from the policy. The catch was that it couldn't sell the licences to one of the incumbent carriers for five years—a policy intended to prevent companies from buying discounted spectrum with the sole purpose of flipping it for a profit.

That didn't deter Rogers, which in 2013 agreed to pay $50 million for the option to acquire Shaw's spectrum licences when the five-year government-imposed moratorium lifted. But by the time the deal was finalized in 2015, Brad Shaw had once again had a change of heart. He was in Halifax when he got the call from Guy Laurence that June confirming that Rogers would buy the licences. The sale would net Shaw a profit of $158 million. But it was a poor consolation prize. Brad had decided that Shaw needed to get into the wireless business after all, and now the company had no spectrum.

There was, however, another option. Rather than build a wireless network and amass a portfolio of spectrum licences from scratch, Shaw could buy an existing carrier. Two of the three independent wireless carriers that had been born out of the 2008 auction for wireless airwaves had already been swallowed up by larger competitors. Public Mobile was bought by Telus in 2013, while Mobilicity went into creditor protection before being acquired by Rogers in 2015. But there was one scrappy carrier that, despite numerous setbacks and several ownership changes, was still standing. It was called Wind Mobile.

Wind was founded in 2008 by Anthony Lacavera, a computer engineering graduate from the University of Toronto with curly dark hair, pale blue eyes, and big entrepreneurial ambitions. Lacavera, who had founded a number of companies on the fringes of the telecommunications industry, was ready to put up $10 million of his own cash to launch Wind, but he needed a much larger war chest to secure the spectrum licences and build out a wireless network. After canvassing Bay Street for investors and coming up empty-handed, he started cold-calling his way down a list of global telecoms. He ultimately secured the funding for the licences, which wound up costing $442.5 million, from an unlikely place: an Egyptian billionaire named Naguib Sawiris. Sawiris ran the telecom arm of Orascom, a massive conglomerate founded by his father. To Lacavera, a 33-year-old from a small Ontario town called Welland, Sawiris was the embodiment of a modern-day pharaoh. The two hit it off, and Lacavera managed to talk him into the investment.

But Wind's foreign backing soon became a thorny issue. Canada's foreign ownership rules stipulated not only that 80 per cent of a telecom's voting shares had to be held by Canadians, but also that the company couldn't be controlled by foreigners. Although Lacavera and his team had structured Wind to keep Sawiris at arm's length (Lacavera had two-thirds of the vote), the CRTC, after some prodding from Telus, decided to review the matter. During public hearings, lawyers for the incumbent tele-coms argued that Wind was merely a shell for foreign interests, and that Sawiris, not Lacavera, was the one running the show.

The CRTC bought the arguments. In October 2009, the regu-lator ruled that Wind didn't meet Canadian ownership rules and therefore couldn't offer wireless services. Lacavera's firm, Globalive Communications Corp., had already spent $800 million on Wind, hired 600 staff, and secured dozens of retail stores. Unable to gen-erate revenue, the company was bleeding millions of dollars a week. But rather than give up, Lacavera turned to a provision in the Telecommunications Act that gave the federal government the power to overrule a CRTC decision. On December 11, six weeks after the CRTC ruling, Ottawa did just that. Wind was finally able to launch.

By the following July, Wind Mobile had attracted 100,000 cus-tomers. But the battle over its foreign funding wasn't over. Telus and Public Mobile, one of the two other upstarts that had emerged from the 2008 spectrum auction, challenged the federal cabi-net's ability to overturn the CRTC ruling. The battle landed in the Federal Court of Appeal, which sided with Wind, and was then appealed up to the Supreme Court.

The legal saga was a wild rollercoaster ride for Lacavera and his team. "One day we're dead, the next day we're living, the next day we're dead again," he said, years later, in an interview with the *Globe and Mail*. "I had to say to people, 'You don't need to apply for another job, we're gunna get through this.'"

When the top court declined to hear the case, it seemed like the ride was finally over. But in 2011, Sawiris decided to sell the majority of Orascom's telecom holdings, including Wind, to Russian-controlled VimpelCom Ltd.

Then, in early 2014, Vladimir Putin invaded Crimea, and the Russians at the helm of VimpelCom started dumping their hold-ings in western countries, such as Canada, that were denouncing the Russian government's actions. Lacavera's Globalive and a consortium of private equity players bought Wind and its debt for a bargain price of $300 million.

The sale meant that Lacavera no longer had control over the company; he now held just one of four votes. The others belonged to Wind's new private equity owners, a group that included West Face Capital, Tennenbaum Capital Partners, and LG Capital Investors. And those owners didn't share Lacavera's long-term ambition of owning a wireless business. When Shaw initiated talks about buying Wind, Lacavera was unable to persuade his private equity partners to hold on to the company. He was the only one who didn't vote in favour of the deal—despite the fact that it would net him a nine-figure cash profit.

In financial terms, the sale was a major victory. Just fourteen months after the consortium had bought Wind for $300 million, including debt, they turned around and sold it to Shaw for a stunning $1.6 billion. Still, Lacavera was disappointed. He felt the carrier was worth even more than that, and that his plans had been cut short. "I would have never sold the company," he later said. "I would be 90 years old on my deathbed owning that company."

For Brad Shaw, the acquisition meant he was finally in the wireless game. By the time Shaw announced the deal in late 2015, Wind had picked up close to a million subscribers in Ontario, Alberta, and British Columbia, as well as additional spectrum. It was expected to generate $485 million in revenue and $65 million in EBITDA (earnings before interest, taxes, depreciation, and amortization) in calendar 2015, Shaw disclosed in a press release.

There was, undoubtedly, a lot of work ahead. Shaw would need to upgrade Wind's network to the latest standard, known as 4G LTE, and acquire additional spectrum before Apple would allow the telecom to sell the highly sought-after iPhone to Wind's customers. But Brad could rest a little easier, knowing that the company his father had founded finally had what it needed to go head-to-head with Telus: its own wireless carrier.

Less than a year later, as Shaw prepared to launch Wind's new network, it rebranded the carrier in an attempt to shed its reputation of spotty service. Going forward, Wind would be known as Freedom Mobile.

On an extraordinarily cold day in January 2018, scores of Shaw employees gathered outside a Calgary stadium. They were undeterred by the temperature, which hovered around minus twenty-five degrees Celsius. Loretta Rogers, who had flown in from Toronto with her family and the company's CEO on a Challenger corporate jet, was undeterred as well. Edward walked with her outside while she smoked a cigarette.

The bond between the Rogers and Shaw families had been forged over decades of deal-making, playful competition, and elaborate pranks. The practical jokes started in 1997, when JR and Jim sent Ted a note, challenging him to a contest to see who could sell the most cable packages over a six-month period. The winners would dine on steak, the losers on beans. Shortly after Shaw had won, they sent Rogers cans of beans plastered with yellow-and-red labels bearing the company's logo. "We know beans about cable," it proclaimed.

Later, after giving Ted a savvy stock tip that paid off, Jim Shaw arrived at his home in Calgary's upscale Mount Royal neighbourhood to find that, in lieu of steak, Ted had sent him a live cow as thanks. The Shaws retaliated by delivering a heavy sculpture of a bull to Ted's office. With it came a card that read, "You go to Calgary to get the beef, you come to Toronto to get the bull." Another time, Ted returned from a trip to find his office filled with boxes containing 500,000 pennies, to mark Rogers hitting 500,000 subscribers.

But it wasn't practical jokes that had brought the Rogers family out to the cavernous Calgary stadium, where they took their seats among the Shaws and roughly 1,500 other people. They were there for a celebration of life. Jim Shaw, the sixty-year-old cowboy of Canada's cable industry, had died after a brief illness.

Jim had left an indelible mark on the city. As the motorcade from his funeral made its way to the stadium, it was greeted by local police officers standing at intersections in salute. Calgary's iconic 628-foot tower shone Shaw blue for days after his passing.

He'd left a mark on Edward as well. Over the years, the billionaire cable scions had bonded over their efforts to step out from their fathers' considerable shadows. Jim was like a big brother to Edward, at least in a business sense. When they spent time together, he did most of the talking.

JR lived with the grief of losing his eldest son for two years before he succumbed to illness himself. His death in early 2020 came as Shaw Communications found itself at another crossroads. The wireless industry was on the cusp of a massive investment cycle, as carriers started upgrading their networks to 5G. The newest iteration of wireless service promised to change the world by enabling bold new technologies, but overhauling the country's wireless networks to the new standards would cost billions. JR's passing meant that Brad Shaw would face the final test of his leadership without the counsel of his father, or his older brother, to guide him.

TEN

ROGERS V. COGECO

 One summer evening less than five months after his father's death, Brad Shaw met Joe Natale for dinner at Centini, a high-end Italian restaurant in downtown Calgary. Sitting in the amber-hued dining room at a table draped in white linen, Natale listened for close to an hour while Brad vented about the challenges facing his company. The cost of rolling out 5G was daunting, and it wasn't just about upgrading the network. Shaw would have to spend vast sums of money buying additional spectrum as well. Although Brad didn't say it explicitly, the message was clear enough to Natale: the Shaws were considering an exit.

The prospect of a Rogers-Shaw merger was one of the longest-running rumours in Canadian business circles. In fact, some people believed that when Ted and JR had divided Maclean Hunter's cable assets between them over dinner back in 1994, they did so with the intention of eventually joining forces. A merger between Rogers and Shaw would be historic, sealing a decades-long bond between the country's eastern and western cable families and fulfilling Ted's longstanding dream.

Overseeing such a deal would be a major achievement for Natale, who'd spent years trying to foster a relationship with Brad in case the opportunity arose. Back when he was at Telus, he and Brad were competitors. But after taking the top job at Rogers, Natale stepped into the role of suitor, trying to woo Shaw's chief executive whenever their paths crossed at industry gatherings, such as the send-off party held for Bell CEO George Cope at the Toronto Club. (Cope ceded the top job to Mirko Bibic, formerly Bell's regulatory lawyer, in January 2020.) The pair didn't discuss specifics over dinner on July 30, but Natale made his intentions known. Coming together would give both companies the scale they needed to roll out 5G quickly and compete against Bell and Telus, who benefited from a network- and spectrum-sharing deal that allowed them to pool their resources. It would put the cable companies back on equal footing with the behemoth known as "Bellus."

But while he pitched Brad on the merits of a merger over dinner, Natale had another takeover target in his crosshairs. Rogers had been approached by Altice USA Inc., a New York–based cable company, about making a joint play for Cogeco and its American cable network, Atlantic Broadband. Rogers had owned a significant chunk of the equity in Cogeco Inc. and its Cogeco Communications Inc. subsidiary for two decades, but its stake gave it no voting control over the companies—which, like Rogers, had dual-class share structures that kept the founding family firmly in charge. But that didn't deter the would-be suitors, who'd soon find themselves facing the wrath of Fortress Quebec.

Shaw wasn't the only telecom facing challenges in the summer of 2020. Although COVID cases had declined as the first wave of the pandemic abated, the crisis had created a slew of financial pressures for the industry. Store closures and a slowdown in immigration made it harder to attract new customers, while lucrative roaming charges—the fees that customers pay for using their cell-phones abroad—plummeted as travel ground to a halt. All of the Big Three telecoms reported sharply lower second-quarter profits, but the impact on Rogers was disproportionately large. Rogers had more cellphone customers than its rivals and was therefore more reliant on roaming revenues. On top of that, a significant chunk of its customer base was in Toronto, which experienced some of the longest and strictest lockdowns in the country. People were at home, worried about getting sick or losing their jobs, not shopping for cellphone plans. Meanwhile, the telecom's sports and media division was decimated as advertisers pulled back spending and sporting events were cancelled.

Compounding those structural problems was a case of incredibly unfortunate timing. Rogers had just taken a significant revenue hit from its aggressive push to move customers onto the new unlimited plans. But instead of emerging on the other side of that migration and returning quickly to growth as they had planned, the company's leadership team found themselves facing a slew of even greater headwinds. Rogers had also been in the midst of roughly half a dozen different transformational initiatives—overhauling everything from its supply chain to its credit and collections department—when the pandemic arrived. One executive likened the situation to a bomb going off outside a hospital while a patient is on the operating table.

Another pandemic-related problem at Rogers was that it heightened growing tensions between Natale and Edward. Edward initially questioned the seriousness of the crisis and pushed back on the need for public health measures, such as store closures and remote work, according to two former executives. Edward didn't comment on the allegation, although a source in his camp called it "completely false and an obvious attempt to discredit him."

At the same time, Edward and Tony Staffieri, who shared what some described as a fixation on tightly controlling costs, saw an opportunity in the crisis. According to sources, they wanted to fire the workers in the company's retail stores to slash expenses. Natale opposed the idea for a number of reasons, not least of which was the fact that it would be difficult to rehire them, one person said. However, one of Edward and Staffieri's allies said it was Natale who was looking for ways to cut costs during the pandemic, and who made the decision to furlough employees when public health measures temporarily shuttered shopping malls.

By the fall of 2020, Edward had raised concerns about Natale's leadership at meetings of the Rogers Control Trust on three occasions, starting in September of 2019. He was becoming impatient with the telecom's share price, which was stagnant and lagging behind Bell and Telus. On top of that, he was worried that Bell was picking up a larger share of subscribers in British Columbia. That concern was shared by two of the company's long-standing directors, Alan Horn and Phil Lind, as well as Rob Gemmell, who had joined the telecom's board after retiring from investment banking. Some of the board's independent directors felt that the pandemic was largely responsible for the company's lacklustre performance, and that it was unfair to pin structural problems, such as the size of Rogers' wireless division and the company's ownership of hard-hit media and sports assets, on Natale. However, according to Gemmell, Rogers was repeatedly coming in third place in a number of key performance metrics, such as service revenue growth and its share of new wireless subscribers. "That started to concern me," he says.

Internally, there was some debate over the validity of that data. Sources close to Natale say that a finance vice-president had been enlisted to cherry-pick data points that portrayed the telecom's performance in a negative light, and that Staffieri had then fed the information up to the board—an act that Natale considered to be a breach of trust. Those in Staffieri's camp, meanwhile, claimed that Natale was attempting to suppress, exclude, or amend certain metrics to show a more favourable result, and that Staffieri had refused to play along. ("When Joe took steps so the information provided by [the executive] was no longer available, I considered this a breach of his duties," says Gemmell.) But a source on Natale's side said the information, which amounted to a massive data dump with no analysis or context, was never suppressed. "It wasn't about suppressing information, it was about presenting the board with a consistent set of KPIs," the person said.

Another point of contention between Edward and Natale related to an issue that consistently arose during board strategy sessions: Rogers' ownership of a significant chunk of Cogeco. The Montreal-based cable company was founded in 1957 by Henri Audet, an engineer who quit his job at the CBC to launch a TV station in Trois-Rivières, a city in Quebec that sits at the confluence of the St. Lawrence and Saint-Maurice rivers. He financed the venture by selling his house and raising $100,000 from friends and other investors. The gambit paid off. Over the years, Cogeco picked up radio stations and cable systems, expanding into Ontario and then south of the border. In 1993, in keeping with the standard practices of dynastic families, Audet passed the reins to his son Louis. An alum of Harvard's MBA program with an undergraduate degree in engineering from Montreal's École Polytechnique, Louis served as chief executive for twenty-five years before anointing Philippe Jetté, who headed up the company's data centre division, as CEO. Louis Audet remained the chairman and controlling shareholder.

To Natale, Rogers' Cogeco stake was $2 billion of dead money that could be put to better use, particularly given the massive 5G investments on the horizon. He believed that Audet, whose role as chair gave him status in Montreal's business community, would never agree to sell the companies. Even if he did, the Audets' ownership of multiple voting shares, which carried ten to twenty times the voting power of the subordinated shares, kept the family firmly in charge of the process; Rogers, despite owning 41 per cent of the subordinated shares of Cogeco and 33 per cent of those in its Cogeco

Communications subsidiary, was powerless to force or block any potential transaction.

Natale wanted to sell the shares and reinvest the money elsewhere. Some directors supported the idea. Others, including Gemmell and Edward, were vehemently opposed. They felt that owning a very large stake in a company they wanted to buy was a smart strategic move, even if they didn't have voting control, and that Rogers didn't need the money.

The Rogers board was in the midst of one of its annual discussions about what to do with the shares when it was approached by Altice. The New York–based cable company headed up by former investment banker Dexter Goei was looking for scale, and Cogeco's Atlantic Broadband was an attractive target. Buying the ninth-largest cable operator in the U.S. would increase Altice's customer base by more than 1.1 million homes and businesses. Rogers, on account of its significant stake in Cogeco, was a natural fit for a partner; Altice could acquire the U.S. assets, while Rogers could pick up the Canadian cable network, which was of no interest to Altice.

Making an unsolicited offer for a family-controlled company was undoubtedly a long shot. But there were murmurs that the Caisse de dépôt et placement du Québec, the giant pension fund that owned 21 per cent of Atlantic Broadband, was looking for an exit. And in January of that year, Gestion Audem Inc.—the corporate entity through which the Audet family controlled 69 per cent of the votes at Cogeco and 83 per cent of the votes at Cogeco Communications—had dumped some of its stock, sparking speculation that the Audets were in need of some extra cash.

Despite the unlikeliness of success, Natale saw the play as an opportunity for a resolution to a long-standing conundrum. Rogers' network in Ontario was a doughnut, with Cogeco's assets forming the hole in the middle. If Rogers was going to eventually acquire the cable company, it didn't make sense to build out its own infrastructure in Cogeco's territory. But Rogers couldn't wait forever. The architecture of 5G networks required more integration between wireless and cable infrastructure, which meant that the telecom would need to fill the gaps in its cable network in order to fully deploy this newest iteration of wireless technology. Partnering with Altice to make a bid for Cogeco was an opportunity to test the hypothesis that owning a significant but non-controlling stake in the Cogeco companies positioned Rogers to acquire them. If there really was a way for Rogers to leverage its stake in Cogeco into a takeover, it could save Rogers a lot of time and effort building out infrastructure in cities such as Oakville and Burlington. And if the play failed, perhaps the board would agree to sell Cogeco and reinvest the $2 billion elsewhere.

Rogers and Altice tried to engage with Louis Audet, but he was in no hurry to meet with them, offering an appointment several months away. Becoming frustrated with what they perceived to be a delay tactic, the would-be suitors sent Cogeco their offer late in the afternoon on September 1. Rogers and Altice were willing to pay a combined $10.3 billion for the Cogeco companies, with Rogers shelling out $4.9 billion for the Canadian cable business. Owners of the subordinate voting shares—those that came with a single vote—would receive $106.53 per share of Cogeco and $134.22 for each share of Cogeco Communications.

It was a generous offer, amounting to more than 30 per cent above the companies' closing prices on August 31. To sweeten the deal, the Audets were offered what Altice described as a "sizeable premium" for their multiple voting shares. In total, the family would receive $800 million for their stake. But the Audets were not interested in cashing out, and rejected the overture that evening.

Undeterred, the suitors went public with their offer, each issuing its own press release before markets opened for trading the following morning. It was an aggressive Hail Mary move that appeared designed to rally Cogeco's non-voting shareholders.

Although they exerted no voting control over the company, disgruntled shareholders could put pressure on the family to sell, or even launch a class-action lawsuit. Perhaps the Caisse would seize the opportunity to recoup its investment and try to force the Audets to the table.

The Audet family holding company responded swiftly by publicly rejecting the proposal. Cogeco was not for sale, Gestion Audem stated in a press release, noting the family was unanimous in its decision. (Louis had two brothers, François and Bernard, and two sisters, Denise and Geneviève, and at least two of the five trusts that owned the family holding company appeared to be controlled by his siblings.) Cogeco's independent directors rejected the offer later that day, after meeting to discuss the proposal and speaking to Louis. The family's position was not a negotiating tactic, he told them.

It didn't take long for Fortress Quebec to come rushing to the Audets' aid. During an interview broadcast on Quebec City Cogeco station FM 93 the day that Rogers and Altice went public with their offer, Quebec premier François Legault vowed not to allow the Montreal-based cable company to fall into non-Quebec hands. "There's no way [we'll let] this Quebec company move its headquarters to Ontario," he said, adding that it was "out of the question" for the province to lose a head office as important as Cogeco's.

Others jumped into the fray as well, including Pierre Fitzgibbon, Quebec's Minister of Economy and Innovation. In a symbolic gesture, Fitzgibbon tabled a motion in the National Assembly in recognition of Cogeco's important role in the province's media and telecommunications industries, which drew the support of opposition parties. Mayors in several cities where Cogeco offered internet and cable services also spoke out in support of the company, as did the Caisse. The pension fund was a fixture of Quebec Inc., with a dual mandate of supporting the province's economic prosperity and earning returns, and it had gone to war with Rogers before, when it backed Quebecor's bid for Vidéotron. Despite rumours that the pension giant had spoken with investment bankers about dumping its 21 per cent stake in Atlantic Broadband, executive vice-president Ani Castonguay said in an interview that the fund was aligned with the Audets' acquisition-based growth strategy for the business. (The Caisse, also known as CDPQ, invested US$315 million to help Atlantic Broadband pay for the takeover of a rival cable company in 2017; the takeover offer from Rogers and Altice valued its stake at more than double that: US$750 million.)

Rogers promised to keep Cogeco's headquarters and its management team in the province if the takeover succeeded. In a press release, the company highlighted the telecom's "deep roots" in Quebec, noting that mobile carrier Fido remained headquartered in Montreal sixteen years after Rogers had acquired it, and touted Rogers' support of local communities, such as its sponsorship of Montreal's Pride Parade. For added legitimacy, it included a statement from Robert Dépatie, a prominent Quebecker on the Rogers board, touting the deal's economic benefits for the province.

Dépatie had been appointed to the Rogers board in April 2017, at the same time as Gemmell. Both men were ardent supporters of Edward, and seemed to view it as a birthright for the founder's son to rule the company as he saw fit. That perspective clashed with the views of the company's other independent directors, some of whom felt that their chief role was to serve as a check and balance to the controlling shareholder's power. Gemmell saw it differently. He believed that the independent directors were to be independent of management, not of the controlling shareholder.

Dépatie's appointment to the Rogers board came roughly two years after a five-month stint as the president of Groupe St-Hubert, Quebec's pre-eminent purveyor of rotisserie chicken. Prior to that, the shaggy-haired, bespectacled resident of Rosemère, an affluent suburb of Montreal, had spent thirteen years at Quebecor, including as the head of its telecom subsidiary, Vidéotron. He cited health reasons when he stepped down in mid-2014, after having ascended to the role of president and CEO of Quebecor Inc. and Quebecor Media Inc.

Quebec Inc.'s opposition to the takeover created an awkward situation for Dépatie and fellow Quebec director Isabelle Marcoux, a prominent businesswoman who chaired the board of Transcontinental Inc., the printing, packaging, and media conglomerate founded by her father. Marcoux, who had joined the Rogers board in 2008 and headed up its human resources committee, was no stranger to the dynamics of family-run enterprises. Like Edward, she had worked her way up through her father's company, and she was familiar with the heightened expectations that went along with being the offspring of a successful entrepreneur. "People scrutinize your moves. They test your leadership, they test your decision-making abilities, they test your judgment," she once said in an interview.

Marcoux argued against continuing the Cogeco pursuit in the wake of the Audets' rejection. She felt that it was a waste of time, and risked damaging the telecom's brand in Quebec, where it had 2 million customers. Besides, her own family also used a dual-class share structure to maintain its grip over its corporate empire, as did the Rogers family, and neither of them would have wanted to be on the receiving end of such tactics.

Despite Marcoux's objections, Rogers and Altice pressed on. According to a source in Natale's camp, Edward wasn't ready to throw in the towel and pressed the chief executive to publicly attack the Audets. "He's saying, 'We need to be more aggressive, you need to go on the record saying that what they're doing is wrong,'" said the source, who was briefed about the discussions. A source close to Edward presented a different version of events, arguing that it was Natale who wanted to pressure the Audets through a public relations campaign.

Tensions between the two telecoms reached a boiling point on September 15. Speaking at the Bank of Montreal's annual media and telecom conference, held that year in a virtual-only format, Cogeco's chief financial officer accused Rogers of trying to eliminate a potential wireless competitor from the market. "As you know, we are attempting to get into the wireless space," said Patrice Ouimet. Cogeco had been lobbying the telecom regulator to mandate wireless network sharing, which would allow the cable company to get into the cellphone business by leasing capacity from the large carriers. Shutting Cogeco out of the wireless business is "probably part of the equation" for Rogers, Ouimet contended.

That day, Natale and Goei fired off a letter to Audet, accusing him of flouting corporate governance rules. Cogeco's directors hadn't taken any of the steps they should have taken after receiving a takeover offer, the suitors alleged. Cogeco's two boards hadn't established independent committees to review the offer, nor had they referred the unsolicited offer to the existing strategic opportunities committee. "In simple terms, the boards and their independent directors failed to fulfill their most basic duties in representing the shareholders they are duty-bound to represent and protect. We do not understand how you as a board member of Cogeco Inc. and Cogeco Communications Inc., with the responsibility to act in the interests of all of the stakeholders, could have behaved in this unacceptable manner," Natale and Goei wrote. The letter concluded with a request for a meeting with James Cherry, Cogeco's lead independent director.

Cherry wrote back the next day that he wouldn't be meeting with the two chief executives. The board was confident that it had followed the correct process and given the matter proper consideration. "The support of the Audet family is necessary to complete a transaction. We assume that you know this because you each run a family-controlled company." Rogers and Altice had gone public with their offer, despite the fact that Louis Audet had already informed them that his family's shares were not for sale—a fact that the suitors had omitted from their press release, Cherry wrote. According to him, it amounted to a bad-faith tactic aimed at sowing confusion in the market: "We can only surmise that this was done with a view to misleading investors and increasing the stock price in an attempt to put pressure on the family to sell." Cogeco would not engage further in what it deemed a "futile exercise" aimed at diverting management's attention away from its business operations and creating friction among its stakeholders, he concluded. Instead, the company would focus on executing its growth strategy: investing in its broadband and media businesses and forging ahead with its plan to launch a wireless carrier.

Still, Rogers and Altice continued their pursuit, which Goei publicly characterized as a "marathon, not a sprint." But Natale, who was becoming increasingly concerned about the impact of the whole fiasco on his company's image, had seemingly changed tactics from aggression to something between damage control and a charm offensive. In late September, Natale vowed to invest $3 billion in Quebec should the takeover succeed—money that would be spent upgrading wireless networks to 5G, bringing high-speed internet to underserved rural areas, and even creating a 300-employee tech innovation hub. Cogeco quickly countered that Rogers didn't need to acquire the Quebec cable company in order to make investments in the province. In an interview with the *Globe and Mail*, Cogeco's chief executive Philippe Jetté pushed back on the argument Rogers was advancing that the regional cable company was too small to compete in a capital-intensive industry dominated by rivals with significantly deeper pockets. Cogeco, which had entered the U.S. in 2012 when it snapped up Atlantic Broadband for US$1.36 billion, could easily do another billion-dollar acquisition south of the border, where the broadband market was "highly fragmented" and contained many small and mid-sized cable operators, Jetté said.

Industry analysts had expected that Rogers and Altice might sweeten their bid, and in mid-October, as the stalemate dragged into its second month, they did just that, boosting their offer by $800 million—to $11.1 billion. That amounted to $150 per share of Cogeco Communications, the more widely held stock, up from $134.22, while shareholders of Cogeco Inc. would get $123 per share, instead of the $106.53 contemplated in the previous offer. It represented a 51 per cent premium over the company's share price before the first offer was made in September. At the same time, to generate some urgency, Rogers and Altice proposed a deadline. If they didn't see a path forward by November 18, they'd withdraw the offer.

The Audets wasted no time in rejecting the new proposal, which would have paid them close to a billion dollars for their stake in the companies. "Since this is apparently not registering with Rogers and Altice, we repeat today that this is not a negotiating strategy, but a definitive refusal," Louis Audet wrote in an email to the *Globe*. The message was clear: Cogeco was not for sale, no matter the price.

Still, the Cogeco boards began reviewing the latest offer. This review might have seemed like little more than a performative exercise, given that the Audets had already rejected the overture. But some analysts began to wonder whether Cogeco's independent directors might press the Audets to start talking with the bidders, given the new, significantly higher offer.

At least one shareholder was becoming openly agitated by Louis Audet's obstinacy. Accelerate Financial Technologies, a Calgary-based hedge fund, owned shares in both Cogeco companies, and its founder and chief executive, Julian Klymochko, felt that the company's dual-class share structure was unfairly depriving public shareholders of an enormous payday.

Klymochko wasn't alone in his belief that multiple-voting shares constitute poor corporate governance. Although such structures had proliferated in recent years, particularly in the technology sector, where founders sought to scale their companies without giving up control, investors overwhelmingly preferred the more democratic one-share, one-vote structure. Critics such as Klymochko believed that the discrepancy between control and economic ownership reduced accountability to the company's public shareholders. According to Klymochko, that discrepancy was particularly large in Cogeco's case, where the Audets called the shots despite owning a relatively small economic interest—just 3.3 per cent—of the companies' total equity. Their grip over the companies was leading to what Klymochko described as "massive economic destruction and evaporation of shareholder wealth." Frustrated, he took his grievance public in an interview with the *Globe and Mail*.

Klymochko's comments were exactly the kind of support that Rogers and Altice were hoping to receive from public shareholders. But before the sentiment could gain momentum, the boards of Cogeco Inc. and its subsidiary announced that, after consulting with lawyers, the independent directors had decided to reject the revised offer. They felt that the company still had runway for growth.

On October 21, three days after Rogers and Altice put forward their revised bid, Cogeco finalized a deal that had been in the works for over a year. It was acquiring DERYtelecom, Quebec's third-largest cable company, for $405 million. Jetté pointed to the takeover as proof that Cogeco had the capacity to grow into a larger regional player. But Vince Valentini, an analyst at TD Securities, was unconvinced. "This relatively small acquisition at a premium valuation is not the type of shareholder-friendly initiative that we would expect Cogeco to put forward as an alternate course of action to accepting a $150 [a share] takeover offer," he wrote in a research note. He suggested the company consider spinning out its Atlantic Broadband division through a public offering.

By the end of October, Goei conceded that the odds of the takeover succeeding were slim. "I think it's fair to say that there's a low chance of us being able to . . . move forward on this project," he told investors during the company's quarterly earnings call. Formally, he noted, Rogers and Altice had until November 18 to "see if anything shakes loose." But nothing did shake loose, and as the bid expired on November 18 Natale expressed his disappointment that the Audets and the Cogeco boards had refused to engage with what he called a "terrific offer."

"It just wasn't meant to be," he said resignedly during a virtual conference hosted by RBC Capital Markets.

The rejection was shrugged off by most within the organization. Rogers was simply doing what was in the best interests of its shareholders, says Gemmell. "I happen to think what we did was in the interests of Cogeco shareholders too, but there was a controlling shareholder who happened to disagree. . . . We did what we needed to do. And, in his mind, he did what he needed to do."

While Rogers had faced criticism from Quebec for getting aggressive with the Audets, who were considered royalty, one executive who was involved in the internal discussions argued that the company didn't behave in an inappropriate or disrespectful manner. "Certainly, we tried to raise the heat on saying no, with a very public proposal around a very generous offer. And it didn't go, and that's okay. There's no harm done."

That sentiment didn't seem to be shared by Louis Audet, however—at least not at the time. He and Edward spoke on the phone a handful of times during the process. During one particularly heated exchange, Louis lashed out at Edward. "Your father would be ashamed of you," he said.

ELEVEN

HELL OR HIGH WATER

Brad Shaw wanted to know just how much capital his company would need to truly compete on both the wireless and cable fronts. So in November 2020, he and Trevor English, Shaw's chief financial officer, tasked their investment bankers at TD Securities with mapping out the company's potential moves in an industry that increasingly demanded scale. Shaw had a long-standing relationship with the bank, having asked it to prepare this sort of analysis before.

To call telecom a capital-intensive business would be an understatement. Shaw had poured billions into Freedom Mobile since acquiring the carrier in 2016, including upgrading its wireless network to the latest technology and buying more spectrum licences to improve the quality of its service. In total, including the $1.6 billion acquisition price, Shaw's foray into wireless had cost the company roughly $5 billion. They financed the venture by selling two of their significant businesses: the media division, which they sold to Corus, and their U.S. data centre subsidiary, ViaWest. The investment was still net negative to the tune of $3.3 billion.

While Shaw was diverting its finite resources into the wireless business, it was being outspent on the wireline side by a rival three and a half times its size. Telus had embarked on Project Falcon, an aggressive, decade-long spending spree to upgrade its copper wires to fibre-optic cables. For every dollar that Shaw invested in its wireline network, Telus spent two, allowing it to capture a growing slice of the internet and television markets in western Canada. While Shaw lost nearly 8,000 retail internet customers in 2020, Telus picked up 157,000. Those losses and gains were reflected in their share prices, as well; Telus's had roughly doubled over the past decade, while Shaw's remained stagnant. Shareholders were unhappy with Shaw, which hadn't hiked its dividend since it began investing in wireless. During the summer, the company had launched a new wireless brand called Shaw Mobile, which offered a remarkably good deal: $0 talk-and-text plans available as part of a bundle with Shaw's internet service. The aim was to stem the bleeding of its broadband customers to Telus. But although Shaw Mobile managed to attract some subscribers, the majority of them weren't generating any revenue.

That fall, when the company's leadership team presented their three-year plan to the board, the conversation was a difficult one. It wasn't like Shaw was in financial distress or headed for creditor protection. Far from it. The telecom was still reporting solid revenue and growing profits. But that profit growth was increasingly coming from cost-cutting. And with the investments that it would need to make in both its wireless and cable networks, there was no dividend growth on the horizon.

Brad and English met with the bankers the week before Christmas to discuss the outcome of TD's review. Shaw was billions short of what it would need to compete against Telus. The Shaw family's legacy was rooted in being builders and visionaries, and it was humbling for Brad to realize that they were underinvesting. A variety of options were discussed, including maintaining the status quo and continuing to execute the company's strategic plan. But Brad was concerned that the telecom would be unable to innovate. Another option on the table was to sell the company, either to a private equity firm or to what's known as a strategic buyer—in this instance, another telecom operator.

Brad and his father had discussed the possibility of a sale more than once before JR's passing, but the time had never seemed to be right. After all, Shaw had only just gotten into the wireless game. Things looked different at the end of late 2020, however, as the company stared down the barrel of another wireless investment supercycle. The telecom had no more non-core businesses to sell—at least, nothing substantial. If it was going to forge ahead into 5G it would have to take on more debt, on top of the roughly $5 billion already outstanding on its balance sheet. The road ahead was winding and unclear, but one thing seemed certain to Brad: it would only get tougher for Shaw to compete in what was already a tough industry. A sensitive, emotional person, Brad deeply felt both the ups and downs of running the cable empire his father had built. After more than a decade at the helm, perhaps it was time for a change.

In the first week of 2021, Brad Shaw received an unsolicited offer from another telecom executive: Mirko Bibic, the chief executive of BCE Inc. and its subsidiary, Bell Canada. Bibic had heard rumours through bankers and industry sources that Brad was contemplating a sale, and that Rogers was already engaged.

Refined and articulate with a square jaw and neatly cropped salt-and-pepper waves, Bibic was born in Montreal and grew up in a city called Longueuil on the other side of the St. Lawrence River. His father, who had immigrated from Serbia, was a carpenter; his French mother worked as an administrative assistant. Bibic began his career as a lawyer, working his way up to a role as managing partner of Stikeman Elliott LLP's Ottawa office. In 2004, he followed his mentor, a lawyer named Lawson Hunter, to BCE, where he was promoted to chief legal and regulatory officer, then chief operating officer. He was roughly a year into his role as CEO when he flew out to Calgary to pitch Brad Shaw on the merits of merging with Bell. It would be a heavy lift from a regulatory perspective, he told him, but Bell could get it done. After all, the company had managed through that process in 2017 when it won the blessing of federal regulators for its $3.9 billion takeover of Manitoba Telecom Services Inc. within a relatively short time frame.

When Shaw's board met a week later, on January 13, Brad told them about his meeting with Bibic. Afterwards, he invited Natale back to Calgary to continue the conversation they had started at Centini the previous summer. Rogers was still interested in acquiring Shaw, Natale told him. This was good news for Shaw, which now had two prospective buyers and could play them off each other to fetch a higher price.

The TD Securities bankers presented their findings to the Shaw family trust in early February. After weighing the options, the Shaws decided that selling the company was their best bet. But they didn't want a financial buyer, who amounted to little more than just a chequebook; they wanted scale that would allow the company that JR had built to keep competing, even if it was no longer under the Shaw name. The overtures that they had received from Bell and Rogers were attractive. Both companies had strong balance sheets, made strategic sense, and could move quickly and quietly, ahead of the upcoming 5G spectrum auction. And they were both well positioned to navigate the lengthy, treacherous process of obtaining approvals from three different federal regulators. Brad reached out to Bibic and Natale and asked them each to submit preliminary offers.

As the process got underway, additional advisers were brought under the tent. Shaw retained Davies Ward Phillips & Vineberg as its legal counsel, while Rogers brought in bankers from Barclays and Bank of America Securities. The Shaw family trust sought its own legal advice, as did a special committee of the telecom's independent directors. The Rogers family, meanwhile, tapped its long-standing relationship with Torys. In total, roughly a dozen different law firms and investment banks were asked to provide input. But even as the circle of advisers expanded, negotiations around the largest potential takeover in Canadian telecom history somehow managed to stay out of the public eye. Bankers code-named the transaction Project Scotch, referring to Shaw as "scotch" in documents and Rogers as "rum," to mask the companies' identities.

Natale and Bibic presented their offers to Brad on February 17. Rogers was offering $35 per share, while Bell came in slightly higher, at $37. The Shaw family had decided not to seek a premium for their voting Class A shares, even though they were more valuable. (Despite the company's dual-class structure, Brad claimed that JR had always treated all shareholders as equal partners.) Although Rogers and Bell were both offering the same price to both classes of Shaw's shareholders, the proposal from Rogers still treated the two groups of shareholders differently. While the Shaw family would be paid with a mix of cash and Rogers stock, which allowed the Shaws to minimize their tax bill, the Class B shareholders would be paid only in cash. Rogers didn't want to dilute its existing shareholders by issuing too much new equity. In contrast, Bell was offering the same cash-and-stock mix to both classes of shareholders. The difference was significant, because the number of shares that the Shaw family would receive under the Rogers proposal was fixed, regardless of what happened to the telecom's stock. If Rogers' share price was higher by the time the deal closed, that would make the Shaw family's stake more valuable than that of other shareholders. If, on the other hand, Rogers shares slipped, it would hurt the Shaws.

Brad, English, and Shaw's chief legal and regulatory officer, Peter Johnson, spent several days discussing the offers with their legal and financial advisers. They decided they needed more clarity on how Rogers and Bell each planned to approach the complex regulatory process. The sale of Shaw's broadcasting assets would require the approval of the Canadian Radio-television and Telecommunications Commission, while Innovation, Science and Economic Development Canada—a department under the jurisdiction of the federal industry minister, responsible for regulating the use of airwaves on the electromagnetic spectrum—would have to sign off on the transfer of Shaw's wireless licences. A third agency—the Competition Bureau—would review whether the deal was likely to substantially reduce competition.

Bibic had been through more than one contentious takeover, including Astral Media in 2012, which was initially blocked by the broadcasting regulator. When Bell bought Manitoba Telecom Services in 2017, Bibic found that proactively identifying competitive issues and lining up divestiture partners generated goodwill with regulators, making them more open to sharing the terms under which they would approve the deal. (Bell wound up divesting a portion of Manitoba Telecom's wireless subscribers to Telus and rural internet provider Xplornet Communications.) Bibic was certain—and prescient, as it would turn out—that the federal government, which for years had sought to encourage the growth of new wireless competitors, would not allow Rogers to swallow up Freedom Mobile. He and his chief legal and regulatory officer, Robert Malcolmson, believed the wisest course of action would be to approach the regulators at the outset, even before announcing the deal, with a plan to sell the carrier. In competition law parlance, this approach is known as "fix it first." They even came up with potential buyers for Freedom that they thought could pass muster with the regulators.

Although Brad initially expressed interest in Bibic's proposal, Shaw's advisers weren't sold on the strategy. During a tense virtual meeting on February 19, Davies lawyers grilled Malcolmson about why Bell was proposing the fix-it-first approach. They were insistent that Bell agree instead to a "hell or high water clause" that would saddle it with all of the deal's regulatory risk. The clause stipulated that the buyer would agree to almost any condition required to satisfy regulators—even if that meant selling off parts of its own business. In short, it would do whatever it took to get the deal done, come hell or high water.

But Bibic wasn't prepared to take on that level of risk, despite urging from Brad, who reached out to both him and Natale the following day with feedback on their offers. Natale, whose lawyers had also met with Davies, had agreed to the hell or high water clause, Brad told Bibic. If Bell wanted to buy Shaw, it would need to agree to it, too.

By Monday, both suitors had sweetened their bids. Bell had bumped its price to $39.25 and increased the size of the retention package for key Shaw employees. Rogers now came in slightly higher, at $40.50 per share, but the company had also added a demand. It wanted an ironclad guarantee—known as an irrevocable voting support agreement—that the Shaw family would vote in favour of the deal no matter what, even if someone came in with a higher bid after it was announced. The Shaws, meanwhile, preferred what is known as a soft voting support agreement, which would give them some wiggle room.

Shaw spent the next few days reviewing the offers. By the time the board convened on February 28, Bell had raised its bid to match the $40.50 that Rogers was offering. But the company continued to argue against the hell or high water clause. Bell was also offering a smaller reverse break fee than what Rogers was willing to pay Shaw if it walked away from the deal. And while Shaw wanted to move quickly ahead of that summer's auction for 5G wireless airwaves, to avoid spending large sums of money on licences, Bell was advocating for the carrier to take part in the auction. That way, if the deal fell through, Shaw would still have the airwaves needed for 5G.

A group of senior executives, including Brad and English, walked Shaw's directors through a detailed comparison of the two offers. Both proposals were attractive to the family, Brad told them. Each made strategic sense, offered good value to shareholders, and included commitments to maintain a head office in Calgary and continue the family's investments in the community and in charitable programs. But the board was unwilling to move forward with Bell's offer unless the company agreed to the hell or high water clause. But Bibic's stance was firm. Two days later, when Brad relayed the board's feedback to him, Bell withdrew from the process.

With their rival out of the way, Natale and his team got started on the due diligence process. A confidentiality agreement was signed and a virtual data room was set up. But the telecom giant was still demanding an irrevocable commitment from the Shaws to vote in favour of the deal. After a series of discussions between its board and various financial and legal advisers, Shaw agreed to the condition—in exchange for a significant increase to the reverse break fee. If Rogers walked away, it would be on the hook for $1.2 billion.

The historic union of the country's east and west cable networks was announced before markets opened for trading on Monday, March 15, 2021. The proposed deal, if it secured the blessing of federal regulators, would see Rogers pay $20 billion and assume roughly $6 billion of Shaw's debt. The synergies were expected to exceed $1 billion annually within two years of closing, Rogers announced in a press release that touted the takeover's economic benefits: 3,000 new jobs in western Canada, a quicker 5G rollout, and the creation of a $1 billion fund to connect rural, remote, and

Indigenous communities to high-speed internet. Shaw would get two seats on the Rogers board—one for Brad, the other for another individual to be nominated by the family.

It didn't take long for analysts and other industry observers to identify the hitch in the companies' plan. Reducing cellphone bills had been identified as a priority for the Liberal government, and regional carriers like Freedom Mobile were seen as playing an important role in affordability. Although there was virtually no overlap between Rogers' and Shaw's cable networks, allowing Rogers to gobble up Canada's fourth-largest wireless carrier would lead to greater consolidation in the wireless sector, which was already dominated by an oligopoly of three powerful players. Together, Rogers, Bell, and Telus would have roughly 95 per cent of the country's wireless subscribers, up from 88 per cent, according to an analysis by Kaan Yigit of Solutions Research Group, a Toronto-based consumer research consultancy. To appease the regulators, Rogers would have to part with Freedom, industry analysts predicted.

While Rogers was negotiating the largest takeover in its storied, sixty-year history, the tensions on its board were reaching a flashpoint. The company's lead director was a man named John Clappison, a chartered accountant and former managing partner from PricewaterhouseCoopers. Clappison had joined the board back when Ted was still around, after Garfield Emerson pushed the founder to recruit a director with deep financial expertise to strengthen the audit committee. He took over as lead director from Charles Sirois in 2018. At companies such as Rogers, where the board chair is also the controlling shareholder, one of the independent directors is appointed to act as a sort of captain for the group. The role often involves serving as a liaison between the company's CEO and its chair, making it an easy job when things are going well and a very difficult one when they aren't. And in early

2021, things were not going well in the highest ranks of Rogers Communications.

Clappison had the unenviable task of meeting separately with Edward and Natale with the goal of forging a more constructive relationship between them. Edward felt that Natale was a mile-wide-and-inch-deep type of leader who lacked the solutions to the company's most pressing problems. He was particularly concerned that service levels—the percentage of customer calls answered within twenty seconds—had fallen by about 20 per cent. But according to a source in Natale's camp, the drop had occurred during the pandemic, as customers looked to upgrade their internet speeds and other telecom services as workplaces, schools and virtually every other facet of their lives shifted online. In fact, Natale felt that the company had fared exceptionally well throughout that chaotic period. And while Edward was complaining to various members of the family trust about the chief executive's performance, Natale was complaining to Clappison that he was spending a considerable amount of his time trying to constrain Edward, who Natale claimed was interfering with his ability to run the company. According to sources in Natale's camp, Clappison tried to persuade Edward to step back and operate within the confines of his non-executive chair role. But Edward, despite having been persuaded to abandon his ambition of serving as chief executive of his father's company, seemed intent on remaining involved in decision-making to a greater degree than Natale would have liked.

The growing divisions on the company's board were reflected in director evaluations. The common governance practice involves directors assessing each other, as well as the chair, via anonymous questionnaires. In 2019, the year after Edward became chair, he received a number of negative comments, according to sources. For instance, one director suggested that Edward join other boards in order to learn how a chair should operate. The feedback "was pretty brutal," one person said, while another described Edward's reviews as "terrible." But certainly not everyone had a negative view of Edward's performance. Some directors were effusive in their praise, calling him an "excellent chair" and an "effective leader" whose years of industry experience were of great help to the board.

There were also disputes about how to fill vacancies on the board. Directors are generally thought to lose their independence from management after a period of time, and David Peterson had been there for three decades and was looking to step down. There were discussions at the board about the need to bring in fresh blood—there were too many family members and too many Old Guard types still hanging around. The independent directors had lined up several experienced candidates, according to sources. But Edward, who was the chairman of the board's nominating committee, had his own candidates in mind—described uncharitably by one of his opponents as "sycophants."

In January 2021, Clappison's relationship with Edward hit a breaking point, and he left the board. There are conflicting explanations for his departure. In one version of events, Edward told him it was time to go, citing a declining level of support for him on director surveys. In 2020, Clappison's scores were drastically lower—by as much as 33 per cent—than in the previous year, according to a source in Edward's camp. His favourability score on one question pertaining to his overall leadership dropped to 57 per cent that year, down from 80 per cent in 2019, the person said. But according to Clappison, he left of his own accord. "No one indicated to me that, as a result of my performance review from the board members, I should resign, or not stand for reelection the following April. Nobody said that. I resigned based upon my concerns about constant interference and override of governance within the company," he says.

Clappison's worsening scores merely reflected the growing divisions on the company's board, with Edward's allies responsible for the decline in the lead director's support, one person said.

Clappison told John MacDonald that Edward constantly tried to override board-approved policies and interfered with the decisions and mandates of the human resources and corporate governance committees, MacDonald later stated in court documents. He also interfered with Natale's decisions to hire or fire company executives. In short, he tried to operate as an executive chairman, even though that wasn't his title, MacDonald alleged.

Clappison's departure left the lead director role vacant. Edward wanted Robert Gemmell to take on the position, but the lead director was supposed to be appointed by the independent directors, not by the chair. Peterson spoke to each of the directors individually. The consensus was that John MacDonald should step into the role.

A seasoned telecom executive, MacDonald had worked at Bell Canada, first as its chief technology officer and later as its president and chief operating officer. He'd also served as the president and coo of AT&T Canada, which was rebranded as Allstream and subsequently acquired by MTS. He ran the enterprise division of MTS Allstream for five years before joining the Rogers board in 2012.

At first, MacDonald didn't want the lead director role, but eventually he agreed. Peterson, meanwhile, was talked into sticking around for another year because there weren't enough independent directors.

Edward's dissatisfaction with the company's performance, meanwhile, continued to grow. He and some of his allies felt that the wireless business was not attracting as many subscribers as it should have been relative to Bell and Telus, particularly in the west. "There's a competitive spirit here. We like to win," one Old Guard executive said. And the wireless division wasn't winning. In each of 2018, 2019, and 2020, Rogers added fewer net new wireless subscribers than its two main rivals.

Natale apparently shared some of Edward's concerns, because in early 2021, he fired the company's wireless president, Brent Johnston. Company insiders described Johnston as a bright and personable executive who was doing many of the right things. The problem, according to some, was a lack of priorities. Some believed that Johnston's team had too many projects on the go, and that some of those projects—such as the repair business, accessory financing business, and mobile retail store—weren't sufficiently profitable. Others believed that Johnston had become the scapegoat for the shift to unlimited data plans. The industry-wide move away from overage revenue had been unavoidable. But although some executives agreed that the switch should have been made as quickly as possible, others felt that Johnston had been, in the words of one company insider, "a little too bloody minded about it." At times, this person said, Johnston had failed to convince certain board members of the merits of his approach.

To fill the role, Natale brought over his long-time ally and close personal friend Dave Fuller. But the highly regarded telecom executive was joining the company at a time when at least one person suspected that the CEO's own days were numbered.

As head of the human resources committee, Isabelle Marcoux sometimes found herself at odds with Edward over the telecom's compensation policies. Although several sources downplay this conflict—with one person calling such differences of opinion "a sign of a healthy board"—to several directors it seemed like Marcoux was becoming frustrated with Edward. "She routinely called into question the lack of rigor around key areas of governance and Edward's preference for unilateral decision making," one person said. Part of the telecom's long-term compensation strategy for senior executives was to award them with performance-restricted stock units, or PRSUs, which would turn into equity—or "vest"— when the company hit specific targets. According to one source, Edward wanted to remove the performance criteria, going against the best practices espoused by proxy advisers. Marcoux insisted that the vesting of the grants be tied to EBITDA, the person said. Sources in Edward's camp denied this account, with one calling it "total fiction," while another stated that the board "was aligned and voted for the company's various compensation decisions over the years."

In June 2021, Marcoux vacated her seat on the Rogers board. She had been there for thirteen years and felt that it was time to bring in a fresh pair of eyes. Before she left, she made a prediction. It had become apparent to Marcoux that the company's chief executive and its controlling shareholder had conflicting philosophies on how the telecom should be run—relating, for instance, to its organizational structure. Marcoux told at least one director that she believed Edward would soon fire Natale.

TWELVE

A SPECIAL WAY TO
END THE NIGHT!

Anthony Lacavera had unfinished business. When he launched Wind in 2008, his goal was to bring Canadians globally competitive wireless prices. For a time, he had enjoyed a measure of success. The network was patchy, full of dead zones and prone to dropped calls, but the company still managed to attract subscribers. It also appeared that Wind's competitive prices were having a ripple effect throughout the broader industry. From 2008 to 2014, wireless prices declined by more than 25 per cent, according to federal government data, although by 2015 they had started to climb back up. After years of startup challenges and legal battles with the incumbent telecoms, Lacavera thought he was finally on track to execute the plan that he and Sawiris had crafted when the company was sold from underneath him. The proposed deal between Rogers and Shaw presented an opportunity to finish what he had started.

Canadians had long griped about excessively high cellphone bills relative to other countries, a fact that was borne out by several studies. While the telecoms quibbled with the data and argued that wiring up the country's vast and sparsely populated geography was costly, there was also the fact that a three-player oligopoly controlled 90 per cent of the market. And telecom was far from the only Canadian industry where this was the case. Canadians also paid some of the highest air fares and financial service fees in the world, owing to the fact that two large airlines controlled 80 per cent of the air travel market, while five big banks held 85 per cent of the financial services market. (In contrast, in the United States, the five biggest banks made up just over a third of the market.) But the contempt that many Canadians felt for their telecom providers seemed to eclipse their anger towards other industries. This may have been because the price gouging was more obvious—most Canadians had experienced reverse sticker shock when purchasing SIM cards abroad—or because of poor customer service. Whatever the reason, the situation had taken on such significance that, during the 2019 election, the Liberal Party campaigned on a promise to slash wireless prices by 25 per cent. It wasn't surprising, therefore, that Canadian consumers reacted negatively to the prospect of further wireless-industry consolidation, which flew in the face of years of policy-making by two successive federal governments that had advocated for a fourth national wireless carrier.

During federal spectrum auctions, blocks of airwaves had been set aside for less established players, allowing them to purchase the licences for considerably less money than what Rogers, Bell, and Telus had to pay in the open auction. The Big Three telecoms despised these set-asides, referring to them as "government subsidies" and arguing that they drove up wireless prices by artificially constraining the supply of spectrum licences for the larger carriers. Still, the policy appeared to have had some success in encouraging the growth of smaller, regional players, although the effectiveness of the government's efforts was hampered by what the smaller companies characterized as anti-competitive actions by a telecom oligopoly determined to protect their entrenched positions. According to the regional carriers, the Big Three telecoms were refusing them timely access to cell towers and charging excessive rates for allowing competitors' customers to roam on their networks.

Still, by 2020, there were some promising signs that the federal government's efforts were starting to bear fruit. An analysis by the Competition Bureau found that wireless prices were 35 to 40 per cent lower in markets where regional competitors—carriers like Shaw's Freedom Mobile, Quebecor's Vidéotron, and Eastlink in Atlantic Canada—had captured more than 5.5 per cent of the market. The takeover threatened to undo that progress.

Freedom was the last of the three wireless startups born out of the 2008 auction that hadn't been snapped up by one of the Big Three telecoms. Although it operated in only three provinces—Ontario, Alberta, and British Columbia—it was the closest thing that Canada had to a fourth national wireless carrier. It was also the country's fourth-largest wireless provider, having amassed roughly 1.7 million customers. Allowing it to be swallowed up by Rogers would be the final nail in the coffin of the government's four-carrier policy.

On a bright day in early April, as he walked through Toronto's Yorkville neighbourhood, Lacavera called Edward to congratulate him on the Shaw deal. If Freedom was for sale, he'd love to buy it back, he said. It seemed obvious to Lacavera that the country's largest, most dominant wireless provider would not be permitted to acquire the scrappy carrier that had been credited with helping to drive down wireless prices. But the voice on the other end of the call didn't seem to agree. There was nothing to discuss, Edward told him. Freedom wasn't for sale.

Two weeks after the takeover had been announced, Joe Natale and Brad Shaw were summoned to appear virtually in front of the House of Commons industry and technology committee. The committee, which was made up of members of Parliament

from the Liberal, Conservative, and New Democratic parties, and
the Bloc Québécois, had convened four days of virtual hearings
into the proposed takeover. It was a star-studded affair; in addition
to top executives from both Rogers and Shaw, the guest list
included Matthew Boswell, the head of the Competition Bureau,
and Pierre Karl Péladeau, the charismatic billionaire at the helm
of Quebecor Inc.

Like Lacavera, Péladeau had sensed an opportunity when he
first heard about the proposed merger, and he too had phoned
Edward to express his interest in Freedom Mobile. He received
essentially the same answer. Rogers didn't have to sell anything,
Edward told him. They thought that they could hold on to Freedom. That view was shared by Robert Gemmell, who was hopeful
that Rogers would be able to persuade regulators to let them buy
the carrier.

Péladeau disagreed, and he used his appearance in front of
the industry committee to urge Ottawa not to abandon its long-
standing ambition to foster a fourth national wireless carrier.
"History shows that when you have four operators, you'll be able
to enjoy more competition and that will be shown in the prices
and different offers that are available for consumers," Péladeau
said. He pointed to wireless prices in Quebec, where Vidéotron had
captured 22 per cent of the market, characterizing them as 40 per
cent below those offered in other parts of the country. "Less players, less competition." He pitched Quebecor as the natural buyer
of Canada's fourth-largest wireless carrier, arguing that his company had the expertise, the experience, and the financial resources
needed to be successful.

Natale, who looked laid-back in a dark blazer and white dress
shirt with no tie, seemed to leave the door open to a divestiture.
"We're open and flexible as to how to best solve any questions the
Competition Bureau may have on the wireless front," he told the
committee. But it would take some time—"the better part of nine

to twelve months"—to reach a conclusion. "It's premature at this point to do or say something, when we haven't really started that process in earnest."

Natale was pressed about his claim that the takeover would actually increase competition in the telecom sector. "I guess I'm not seeing how eliminating a competitor is going to be advantageous in the long run for competition," said Brian Masse, a New Democrat with an interest in telecom policy. "That's a big issue for me."

Liberal MP Nathaniel Erskine-Smith noted that Shaw's own executives had previously touted the importance of having independent regional players to compete against Bell, Rogers, and Telus. "If we take your past statements at face value, shouldn't we expect a negative impact on affordability of telecommunication services in this country if this deal goes through?" he asked pointedly.

Natale waxed poetic about 5G, defended the country's cellphone prices as "right in the middle of the pack," and touted the deal's benefits for consumers in western Canada, where the merged Rogers-Shaw entity could go head-to-head with the dominant telecom, Telus. Combining forces would give Rogers and Shaw access to national infrastructure, Natale said, allowing them to speed up their rollout of 5G wireless services, a technology that promised to power everything from remote surgeries to autonomous cars.

Brad Shaw, who also appeared before the committee, argued that the takeover had already had a positive effect on competition. Just days after the deal had been announced, Telus had gone to the capital markets for $1.3 billion to accelerate the expansion of its high-speed internet network and its deployment of 5G.

By early April, Telus had also joined forces with BCE in pressuring the federal government to prevent Shaw from participating in an upcoming auction for wireless airwaves critical for 5G. Bell, Telus, and several other smaller telecoms argued in letters to Ottawa that the integrity of the auction, slated for the summer, would be compromised if Shaw was permitted to bid independently from

Rogers, with whom it had entered into a merger agreement. The lobbying turned out to be unnecessary. On April 7, when the federal ministry responsible for regulating the scarce and valuable public resource published a list of applicants for the June 15 auction of 3,500-megahertz spectrum, Shaw's name was absent from the list. That meant that if the takeover fell through, Shaw would be left in a precarious position, without the spectrum it needed to deliver the latest iteration of wireless technology. In short, Shaw was all-in.

As the country grappled with a surging third wave of COVID-19 infections in the spring of 2021, Rogers found itself in the midst of a particularly ill-timed crisis. Just over a month after announcing its historic and highly contentious deal to acquire Shaw, a software upgrade from its Swedish equipment supplier Ericsson caused customers' cellphones to disconnect from the Rogers network, knocking out wireless service nationwide for nearly twenty-two hours. Customers were unable to make calls, send text messages, or use wireless data on their phones, just as the pandemic had left them more reliant than ever on connectivity. Some Canadians who had just become eligible for the COVID vaccine ran into difficulties booking their appointments.

The global health crisis had created both challenges and opportunities for the industry. Network traffic surged as the country went into lockdown, with schools and many workplaces moving online. Canadians were suddenly consuming more data than ever before, relying on their phones and internet connections for everything from commerce to entertainment to staying in touch with loved ones while they isolated in their homes. That placed an unprecedented level of demand on the country's telecom networks—which, thankfully, had proven to be remarkably resilient, aside from a hiccup in the pandemic's early days. In March 2020, shortly after the federal government announced emergency funding for Canadians who had lost their jobs due to the crisis, a flood of calls congested the networks, causing busy signals and dropped calls. Telecom engineers worked around the clock to resolve the issue, laying additional fibre-optic cables, installing new equipment at their central offices, and restructuring legacy telephone networks. Work that would have taken weeks was completed in a matter of days, even while the telecoms grappled with the same logistical challenges as most other companies, including a rapid shift to remote work.

Their Herculean efforts paid off. Throughout the crisis, society developed a greater appreciation for how critical connectivity had become, and the Canadian telecom industry's strong performance relative to those of other countries gave it greater sway with regulators. The sector's fraught relationship with the federal government appeared to have finally turned a corner. In the summer of 2020, the first year of the pandemic, industry minister Navdeep Bains sided with the incumbent telecoms in an appeal relating to mandated wholesale rates, noting that if the rates that the big telecoms were permitted to charge smaller competitors for network access were set too low, they could stifle future investments in infrastructure.

However, the heightened level of demand for telecom services also meant that the sector faced heightened scrutiny. Outages, which had always been problematic, became catastrophic, and the public backlash to the day-long Rogers outage in April 2021 was swift.

When Rogers reported its first-quarter results a few days later, Natale apologized to the telecom's customers and vowed to win back their trust. "We're not just going to get to the bottom of this but work very hard to make sure it doesn't happen again," he promised. In the wake of the service disruption, the telecom implemented a number of measures to prevent the issue from recurring. While most of them were tailored to the specific circumstances of that particular outage, others were broader. But none of them, it would later turn out, were able to completely eliminate the possibility of an outage. And when the next one occurred, its scope would be even larger.

The photograph that plunged Suzanne Rogers into the centre of a roiling controversy was one that she had posted on her own Instagram account in early May 2021. The woman who has been referred to as "Canada's fashion fairy godmother" was thirty-six when she and Edward tied the knot, and their lengthy courtship gave her ample time to think about what marrying the cable scion might allow her to accomplish. "I wanted to have my own identity; I wanted to be more than wife of, or daughter-in-law of," she later told the *Toronto Star*. She threw herself into philanthropic work, reading to children at the Sick Kids Hospital library and chairing a $10 million campaign for the Covenant House youth charity. Her love of fashion led her to launch a series of fundraising galas called Suzanne Rogers Presents, which raised more than $3.7 million for children's charities and featured prominent designers such as Zac Posen, former Spice Girl Victoria Beckham, and Oscar de la Renta. After attending runway shows put on by the graduating classes at the city's most prominent fashion school, then known as Ryerson University (later renamed Toronto Metropolitan University), Suzanne saw an opportunity to nurture talent. In 2016, the Edward and Suzanne Rogers Foundation donated $1 million to the university to launch a fellowship program called the Suzanne Rogers Fashion Institute, which aimed to support emerging Canadian designers. A second gift followed in November 2020, extending the program for another five years.

These endeavours turned Suzanne into a prominent figure in Canada's fashion industry. Her Instagram page, which had amassed a sizable following, depicted a woman with bright pink lips, icy blue eyes, and Dolly Parton-esque blonde hair, wearing pastel colours and floral patterns as she posed with fashion icons, family members, and fellow socialites in exotic locales. Her big hair and extravagant get-ups courted attention, so much so that *Toronto Life* once likened her to a "bejewelled pageant queen at a minimalist Calvin Klein show." But the photo that attracted the most attention of all did so for the wrong reason. On the left of the shot was a smiling Suzanne in a boho-chic ruffled white crop top and skirt, her hair in a half up-do. On the far right was Edward— khaki pants, collared shirt, black blazer, no tie—next to their two sons, Edward Samuel IV and Jack Robinson Miklos, who, their mother gushed in another post, were "happy to dress up" in preppy spring blazers. It would have been just another relatively innocuous snapshot of life for the Rogers, were it not for the man in the centre of the photo. Dressed in one of his comically oversized suits and outdated ties, and flashing the camera an awkward thumbs up, was none other than the former U.S. president, Donald Trump. "A special way to end the night!" Suzanne had captioned the shot.

It wasn't the first time that Edward's family had shared Trump-related content on the social media platform. In February 2017, just weeks after Trump was sworn in as president, Edward had posted a selfie in a signature Trump "Make America Great Again" hat. However, May 2021 was a particularly fraught time to be publicly associated with the former U.S. president. Four months earlier, a mob of Trump's supporters had stormed the Capitol in a violent insurrection, spurred on by the president himself and his false claims that the election had been stolen from him. He had also become a symbol of white supremacy at a time when race riots in the wake of the death of George Floyd—a Black man killed by a white police officer—had sparked international discourse about racial inequality.

Not to mention, Ontario was in the midst of an extended stay-at-home order intended to curb the spread of the novel coronavirus.

And although Canada's policies on non-essential travel were merely recommendations, the public outcry about wealthy jetsetters flouting public health guidelines had grown into a chorus.

It was against this backdrop that Edward, Suzanne, and their two sons dined at the Mar-a-Lago Club, Trump's lavish members-only resort in Palm Beach, Florida. They had been invited there to celebrate the first birthday of their godson Rocco with his mother, Toronto socialite Jenna Bitove Naumovich, the granddaughter of food industry titan John Bitove Sr. It wasn't just the fact that the chairman of Rogers and his wife had travelled to Mar-a-Lago while the province that housed their company's headquarters was under lockdown, or that they had posed for a photo with the former president/persona non grata Donald Trump that was so shocking. It was also that, rather than being caught in the act by the paparazzi or a gossip hound, Suzanne had outed the family herself through a series of remarkably tone-deaf social media posts. "Dinner last night at @themaralago club," she wrote proudly overtop one video that she shared to her Instagram stories on Saturday morning. It began with a shot of a plaque denoting Trump's 1985 purchase of the mansion, which was formerly the estate of American businesswoman and cereal heiress Marjorie Merriweather Post, before panning to an arched doorway of ornamental iron and carved stone. "With my godson and @jennabitovenaumovich" she captioned a photo of herself and Naumovich seated at a table in a gold-hued dining room, a small child in Suzanne's lap.

The backlash from Canada's fashion community was swift. Designer Michael Zoffranieri, who had benefited from Suzanne's philanthropy, was one of the first to call her out. "We do not stand for white supremacy," he wrote in an Instagram post, noting that while his statement could impact his livelihood, he couldn't stay silent. Two members of the advisory group to the Suzanne Rogers Fashion Institute resigned, including Lisa Tant, the former editor of *Flare* magazine, and Hudson's Bay vice-president Tyler Franch.

Sports journalist Andrew Stoeten, who writes about the Rogers-owned Toronto Blue Jays baseball team, took aim at the team's chairman, calling him a "billionaire failson" in a post entitled "Jesus Christ, Edward Rogers."

"It truly takes a staggering amount of ignorance, and a similarly immense lack of empathy, to not understand or care how dispiriting and infuriating a thing like this was going to be for people," Stoeten wrote.

The university's fashion school invited Suzanne to consider Trump's harmful impact on members of the fashion community who are "low income, Black, brown, Asian, disabled, Indigenous, trans, queer and/or part of other systemically marginalized communities." But shortly after the statement was posted to the fashion school's Instagram account, it was deleted and replaced with a different message. The previous post was not endorsed by the university and didn't reflect the institution's views, the new message read. "We do not believe social media is the appropriate platform to judge the actions of others."

This was not particularly surprising. After all, the Rogers family was one of the university's most generous supporters, having donated more than $34 million to the school over the years. The Rogers name was plastered all over the university's campus, including its business school, the Ted Rogers School of Management, and the building that housed its media, communications, and journalism program, the Rogers Communications Centre.

But the retraction created an even larger controversy, as faculty, students, and alumni criticized the university for silencing its fashion school. "This is what happens to the academic mission of free inquiry when you financially starve public postsecondary institutions to the extent that they depend on the philanthropy of wealthy individuals," English professor Colleen Derkatch wrote on Twitter.

Meanwhile, some irate customers began phoning the telecom to cancel their services, according to sources. They were shocked and angry that the family would publicly associate themselves with Trump, given his track record. In the end, the call centre staff managed to convince some of the customers to stick around by going through the company's usual customer retention process, according to two of the sources, who pegged the number of calls at roughly 200. It was a drop in the bucket for a telecom with more than 11 million customers, but the experience was an unpleasant one for the employees, who were caught off guard and were unsure how to respond to the irate callers. However, one of Edward's supporters challenged this account, calling it "lies being perpetrated by disgruntled former leaders."

Suzanne issued a statement the following day, proclaiming her belief in "equality, diversity, inclusiveness and respect for all." She did not have any kind of relationship with Trump, she wrote, "good or otherwise." In fact, she had never met him before that night, she said. Her family had interacted with him for "mere seconds" as they were leaving after dinner, and no political statement had been intended by the photograph. She had posted it "without considering the false assumptions" that would be made about her personal beliefs. "I regret that my actions caused anyone to question my values or commitment to the communities and causes my family and I hold so dear."

The photograph stirred up unrest among the company's ranks, as well. After George Floyd's death, Natale's leadership team had worked to build a more inclusive culture within the organization. They held listening sessions with employees and revamped their inclusion and diversity strategy, putting in place measurable targets to hit by 2025. The sports and media division launched a campaign providing $10 million in free advertising and creative services to business owners from equity-seeking groups. To some Rogers employees, seeing a photo of the company's chairman posing with Trump—a man whose legacy was at odds with those values—flew in the face of those efforts.

At first, Edward—who, according to sources, told people that he had fallen ill with COVID after his visit to Mar-a-Lago—said nothing publicly about the photo. Sources in Natale's camp say the chief executive pressed the chairman to issue a company-wide statement, further straining their fraught relationship, but Edward initially didn't see the need for one. However, Edward's supporters dispute this account, calling it "fiction" and "completely inaccurate," and stating that Edward did not, in fact, have COVID following his trip. The incident also seemed to deepen the rift between Edward and Melinda—who, according to one family friend, was deeply upset and spent time speaking with employees about diversity and inclusion in an attempt to reverse the perception that the family was pro-Trump. She spoke to her brother as well, offering to help him with the fallout even though she felt that the photo was a mistake, according to one source.

Finally, after about a week, Edward was spurred into action when questions about the photo arose at a company town hall. In a carefully crafted email to the company's employees—one which, according to a source, was written by Melinda and then edited by Edward—he apologized for his family's "total lack of judgement" in posting the photo. "We recognize Trump is a polarizing figure and to many does not align at all with our values," the statement read. "We are so disappointed that this mistake caused any of you to question our commitment to inclusion and I unequivocally stand with you against the intolerance, systemic racism and inequality too many people experience daily."

THIRTEEN

THE "BUTT DIAL"

David Peterson pushed his bike along a gravel road, his son-in-law's cellphone pressed against his ear. Every year, the former Ontario premier rode fifty kilometres through the rolling hills of Caledon, a municipality northwest of Toronto, to raise money for the Headwaters hospital in nearby Orangeville. But that year—a warm Saturday morning in September 2021—his efforts were thwarted by a confluence of unexpected events. Roughly two kilometres north of Terra Cotta, a tiny hamlet on the banks of the Credit River, he experienced a problem with a gear on his grey Cannondale cyclocross bike. Then, just as the bike broke down, he received a call—one so urgent that it managed to find him despite the fact he didn't have his phone.

Peterson had left the device at home, hoping for some peace of mind. But his disconnection from the outside world wound up being short-lived. Natale was desperately trying to reach him. It was an absolute emergency, he said when he got a hold of Peterson's wife, Shelley, who had stayed home on account of a bad knee. Shelley then called their son-in-law, who was with Peterson on the bike ride and passed him the phone.

While his daughter, son-in-law, and two grandchildren continued the bike ride, the white-haired Peterson, who played the role of elder statesman on the Rogers board, headed towards a nearby restaurant called the Terra Cotta Inn, where he planned to rendezvous with Shelley. While he walked, pushing his malfunctioning bike, he listened for close to an hour while Natale recounted what had transpired the previous evening. The events that he described were so bizarre and absurd that they almost strained credulity.

The night before, Natale's wife had been in the kitchen making chicken stir fry when he walked through the arched doorway of their red-brick home in Toronto's Rosedale neighbourhood. It was the end of a busy week of investor meetings, and Natale was keen to catch up with Staffieri to discuss an issue involving credit ratings agencies in relation to the Shaw deal. He opened a bottle of wine, poured himself a glass, and dialled. What followed would later become the subject of intense fascination, intrigue, and dispute.

One fact that wasn't in dispute was that Staffieri was meeting that evening with David Miller, the telecom's former chief legal officer. As a pandemic safety precaution, the two men, who were old friends, had opted for an outdoor setting: a park in front of the Four Seasons Hotel in Yorkville, where Staffieri and his wife owned a condo that they had bought in 2016 for $5.7 million.

What Natale relayed to Peterson and several other directors the following morning went like this, according to multiple accounts:

Natale found himself on a call with Staffieri, but Staffieri didn't seem to be aware that the call was taking place. His phone tucked inside his suit jacket pocket, he was engrossed in conversation with Miller, whose voice would have been familiar to Natale.

Natale attempted futilely to get Staffieri's attention before he caught a snippet of the conversation. Through the crackling wind and the murmur of other voices, it sounded like Staffieri and Miller were discussing the future of Rogers, the company that Natale supposedly ran. He muted himself, hit the speakerphone button, grabbed a notebook out of his briefcase, and, sitting on his living room floor, began to take notes.

To Natale's ear, it sounded like Staffieri was soliciting Miller to come back in the role of general counsel. Then things got worse.

Miller wanted to know what exactly he'd be stepping into. So Staffieri outlined a detailed plan that involved ousting Natale, taking over his job, and culling the vast majority of the senior leadership team.

Dave Fuller and Jorge Fernandes, the company's chief technology officer, were the only two members of Natale's executive team worth keeping around, according to Staffieri. The other nine should go—including Eric Agius, the executive who had led the call centre transformation project, and chief communications officer Sevaun Palvetzian. Dean Prevost, who ran the telecom's consumer division, Connected Home, was also on the chopping block. Rogers Bank was a good idea, but Lisa Durocher was the wrong person to run it. Jim Reid, the company's long-standing head of human resources, who had survived through four CEO changes, was "too soft"; a former Rogers executive named Bret Leech would be brought back to take over from him. Jordan Banks was "useless" and should be replaced as president of Rogers Sports and Media by Colette Watson, while the role of chief financial officer— the post that Staffieri still occupied—would be filled by Shaw's Trevor English once the merger was completed.

The alleged plan also involved a significant restructuring of the company, essentially undoing changes that began when Nadir Mohamed consolidated the cable and wireless divisions back in 2009. Instead of the current structure, which split the telecom into consumer and business divisions, the plan was to put it back to how it used to be. There would once more be a cable division, and Robert Dépatie, the former Quebecor head who sat on the Rogers board, would be put in charge of it. Natale would be given the option to leave amicably, the departure positioned as his idea.

After twenty-one minutes, he told the directors, Natale had heard enough and ended the call. He was gutted and in disbelief. Until that moment, he'd thought that things were going well. His relationship with Edward had become increasingly fraught, but he believed that he had Loretta and Melinda's support, and the feedback that he'd received from the board regarding his performance had been positive. In fact, they had rated him as outperforming their expectations on all of his performance reviews. He had assembled his dream team, poaching executives from other companies and even luring Fernandes from Europe. And he had achieved what none of his predecessors had by outmanoeuvring Bell and striking a deal to acquire Shaw. The plan, as recounted—which couldn't have been cooked up without Edward's support—threw all of that into doubt.

Natale plotted his next steps with his closest confidante, his wife. She had allegedly overheard the whole thing and was equally stunned. By then, the stir fry she had been making was completely forgotten. It sat in the kitchen while they strategized, getting cold.

Initial reports provided to the *Globe and Mail*, which first reported the existence of an inadvertent phone call, suggested that Staffieri had accidentally dialled Natale during his discussion with Miller. The implication was almost poetic: the chief executive of Canada's largest wireless carrier had learned of a covert plot to unseat him through a butt dial. The version of the narrative that later emerged, including in affidavits sworn by both John MacDonald and Loretta Rogers, was that it was actually Natale who had initiated the call, making the incident technically more akin to a butt answer. (Or, as one person aware of the call described it, a "reverse butt dial.") To many, the debate over whether or not the call technically met the definition of a butt dial (or was simply a "butt dial in spirit," as one *Toronto Star* story described it) was rather trivial and pedantic. The result was the same: the plan to oust Natale and the majority of his senior team was beginning to unravel because of the conversation that he had overheard.

However, some people insisted that Natale had not learned of the plan through a phone call at all. When Staffieri later checked his phone log, he saw that there had been an incoming call from Natale. But his conversation with Miller was nothing like what Natale claimed to have overheard, according to one source. Staffieri didn't know exactly how Natale had figured it out, but he suspected that he had pieced the plan together later in some other way, for instance by going through Staffieri's emails, this person said. (After Natale had learned of the plan to replace him with Staffieri, he had tasked Reid and Lisa Damiani with conducting an investigation into the CFO, which included having the telecom's corporate security compile copies of Staffieri's communications, including his emails, text messages, Outlook calendar, phone logs, and Microsoft Teams history, the company later alleged in court documents.) Besides, Staffieri had actually spoken with Natale about the credit rating agencies that evening, and his boss had said nothing about overhearing a conversation. But a source in Natale's camp denied that the two men spoke on the phone that evening.

No one ever requested a correction or a retraction of the *Globe*'s story. Instead, roughly a year and a half after the incident, Staffieri denied the entire existence of the "butt dial" in an interview with the *Toronto Star*. "There was no call to Joe," Staffieri told Richard Warnica. "There was no call by accident to Joe."

Staffieri appeared to be carefully parsing his words. After all, according to several accounts, the call was, in fact, to Tony, and not to Joe. But Warnica's story went beyond what Staffieri appeared to have said, stating that he had denied the existence of any overheard phone call whatsoever. "The entire story—about Natale listening in on the details of the coup—was made up, he said," Warnica wrote. Warnica then went on to explain that sources close to Edward believed the tale had been fabricated to cover up the fact that Natale had been leaked "confidential board discussions." The story didn't specify who had allegedly done the leaking, although some believed that the sources were pointing a finger at Melinda.

"I don't think that butt dial actually took place," says Robert Gemmell. "Tony says it never happened." He questioned the credibility of Natale's narrative—"I mean, who has a pen and paper out if they get a butt dial?"—and why the chief executive hadn't declared to Staffieri that he was on the line.

Despite how muddy the situation had become, one thing was clear: someone was wrong about the butt dial. In one version, Natale, in a desperate fight to save his job, had concocted an elaborate tale, apparently with the help of a board ally such as Melinda, and either managed to convincingly sell it to the other directors or was in cahoots with them all along. In the other, Staffieri was attempting to save face following a slew of embarrassing headlines.

Staffieri's allies pointed to the fact that the story from Natale's camp had changed over time, from a butt dial to a butt answer. But there were problems with the version of events that had emerged from Staffieri's camp, as well. For one thing, the inadvertent phone call was described in both Loretta and MacDonald's sworn affidavits. Besides, for Melinda to have leaked the plan to Natale, she would have had to know about it. And at that point, there had been no formal discussions about replacing Natale or making any of the changes that Staffieri had spoken of during official board meetings. By his own admission, Edward had only told Melinda about his desire to replace the CEO two days earlier. It seemed unlikely that he had provided his sister, who he didn't trust, with the level of detail that Natale had become privy to. In fact, when Edward revealed the plan to MacDonald, the company's lead independent director, on the same day that he spoke to his sister, he allegedly concealed one specific part of the scheme. According to MacDonald, it seemed that Edward didn't want anyone to know about Dépatie's involvement.

Edward first began socializing the idea of ousting Natale during late summer and early fall. He had been unhappy with the chief executive's performance for some time, and by that point had decided that it wasn't going to improve, he later stated in court documents. The Shaw takeover was the biggest deal that the company had ever done, and Edward didn't think that Natale was the right person to handle the process, from lining up funding to securing regulatory approvals to planning and executing the complex process of integrating the two companies. But rather than bring the matter to the full board, Edward engaged in a series of confidential discussions with a handful of close confidants—long-time lieutenants Lind and Horn, as well as his two most devout supporters on the board, Rob Gemmell and Robert Dépatie. It was around that time that he also spoke with Staffieri about taking over the top job. Edward was impressed with Staffieri's performance as CFO, and he knew that Staffieri aspired to do more in his career. But although Natale and his allies would later position the situation as a covert coup, according to Gemmell the discussions were preliminary and conceptual. "There literally was no plan. I would have known if there was a plan to change management."

Although Edward positioned the change as being in the company's best interests, sources close to the company would later speculate that it was driven by something else. He seemed to become dissatisfied with every CEO after several years. Perhaps it was because they couldn't live up to his father, or because he felt that he could run the company better himself, even though he had long ago abandoned his ambitions to do so. Others suspected that he had become overly fixated with the company's financial performance because he craved larger dividend payments to invest in his privately held real estate company, Constantine Enterprises. Staffieri, given that he was the company's CFO, shared that focus on the bottom line, and appeared amenable to doing Edward's bidding.

On September 11, Alan Horn paid a visit to the family matriarch and her youngest daughter, Martha. The two women were virtually inseparable, having spent much of the pandemic hunkered down together in the Bahamas or up in Muskoka. Loretta typically relied on people like Horn and Edward to keep her apprised of what was happening at the company. Until that day, she had been under the impression that Natale was performing well—despite the fact that Edward later said that he had raised concerns about the chief executive at four separate meetings of the Rogers Control Trust, starting in September 2019. After speaking to Horn, Loretta realized that Edward had a different view on Natale. Although at the time she trusted the information that she was given by her late husband's trusted confidant, she would later say that her trust had been misplaced.

Edward didn't tell Melinda about his plans until the morning of September 15. He was worried that she would take the information straight to Natale. She had done so in the past, relaying confidential discussions about Natale's performance that had taken place at the family trust to the CEO, Edward later alleged in court documents. Still, Melinda was the vice chair of the Rogers Control Trust and the deputy chair of the telecom's board. Edward had no choice but to bring her up to speed.

Melinda disagreed that there were problems with Natale's performance, but Edward was resolute. Later that day, he logged onto a regularly scheduled video call with MacDonald, the lead independent director, to discuss company matters. The call wound up being "anything but ordinary," MacDonald would later recall.

It was then that MacDonald first learned that Edward planned to oust Natale. The company's performance was not where it should be relative to Bell and Telus, Edward told him. He believed it was time for Natale to go. But rather than hire from outside the organization again, Edward wanted to promote from within. He wanted to put Staffieri in the role, and he wanted the change to be made quickly, before Rogers started integrating with Shaw. Natale would be given a choice: retire and leave amicably, or be fired.

But the shakeup that Edward was planning went beyond the corner office. He intended to reorganize the whole executive leadership team, and told MacDonald that he was already in talks with a senior cable executive from the U.S. about joining the company. In truth, the person he intended to put in charge of the cable division was Dépatie. Edward eventually admitted to MacDonald that he had misled him about the U.S. cable executive to conceal Dépatie's involvement, MacDonald said in an affidavit later filed in court, although a supporter of Edward's later stated that what was said in MacDonald's affidavit about this was untrue.

MacDonald was stunned, not only by the timing—after all, the company was in the midst of trying to consummate one of the most significant deals in its history—but also by the choice for Natale's replacement. MacDonald had always viewed Staffieri as a highly capable executive, but he wasn't sure that a CFO without operating experience was the ideal candidate to lead Rogers in Natale's absence. Regardless, he felt the matter should be left up to a selection committee. MacDonald asked Edward who else he had shared his plan with, and was told that only Horn and Edward's family were aware of it.

Edward depicted the September 15 video call differently in his own court filing. According to Edward's version, he told MacDonald that he planned to implement a formal process to review Natale's performance and to consider who might potentially replace him. Although he had a "strong preference" for Staffieri, he was open to the views of other directors, and hoped to reach a verdict by November.

But MacDonald said there had been no mention of a formal review. "I clearly would have recalled such a statement," he stated, adding that he would have been supportive of a review, "to the extent that it was run in accordance with RCI's formal governance processes."

The call left MacDonald feeling disturbed. To him, Edward's approach to assessing the CEO's performance and choosing his replacement demonstrated a blatant disregard for the board's most important duties. There had been no discussions at the board or, as far as MacDonald knew, at any of its committees about replacing Natale. In fact, the board was of the view that Natale had exceeded the goals that they had set for him, which included turning around the company's lagging wireless network, improving customer service, and assembling a new management team. Melinda was particularly happy that Natale had brought them the Shaw deal. Although the timing of the transaction had been driven by the Shaw family's desire to exit the business, Bibic could have snatched the deal out of Natale's hands.

MacDonald told Edward that he needed time to think, and encouraged him to bring the matter to the full board. More than two years before his death, in a memorandum to the board dated June 26, 2006, Ted had outlined the steps that he wished to be followed whenever the chief executive's chair was vacant. A special committee was to be established to identify and screen potential candidates. The board was to make the final call, after factoring in the committee's advice.

MacDonald then called Peterson, who advised him to set up another meeting with Edward. Thinking they had time, Peterson suggested scheduling it for the following Monday. That way, MacDonald could spend the weekend preparing a presentation that laid out why it wasn't the right time to replace the CEO. Peterson also suggested that MacDonald bring along a written document outlining the steps for making such a change.

But MacDonald never got the chance. As he and Peterson learned that weekend, Edward's plot appeared to be further along than either of them had imagined. To them, it seemed that not only was there a detailed plan to revamp the company's upper ranks, but the recruitment process was already underway.

Shelley Peterson grabbed her husband's cellphone, hopped into her Lincoln, and drove from the couple's farm in Caledon to the Terra Cotta Inn. There, sitting in his wife's car in the restaurant parking lot while he waited for the rest of his family to finish the bike ride, Peterson made a series of phone calls as he tried to get a handle on the looming crisis. Among those he spoke to were MacDonald, Melinda, Loretta, and Martha. Everyone seemed stunned, some of them wondering if they had an insurrection on their hands.

MacDonald also made a flurry of calls that day. He first spoke with Natale, who had reached out and asked if they could talk. MacDonald began the call by bringing up the concerns that Natale had recently raised about Staffieri to the board's human resources committee. The CFO had spent some of the pandemic in Florida and, according to company sources, had largely withdrawn from Natale's executive team. "He was kind of AWOL," one person said. And although Staffieri's name remained on the company's emergency CEO plan—meaning that he was poised to take over should Natale suddenly vacate the role—Natale had begun laying the groundwork to replace him.

That was precisely what Natale wanted to talk to him about, he told MacDonald. Then he laid out what he had learned the night before.

For the second time in a matter of days, MacDonald was floored. After hanging up with Natale, he began reaching out to the company's independent directors, with whom Natale had requested

a meeting, to bring them up to speed. In total, there were six independent directors on the Rogers board, including MacDonald,
Peterson, Dépatie, and Gemmell. The group also included Ellis
Jacob, the president and CEO of cinema chain Cineplex Entertainment, and Bonnie Brooks, the former head of the iconic Canadian
retailer Hudson's Bay. Only five of them dialled into the call with
Natale; Dépatie did not, although MacDonald said in court documents that he did invite the ex-Quebecor head to participate.

Natale was animated as he told the independent directors
about the inadvertent call he claimed to have had with Staffieri.
He no longer trusted his CFO and wanted to fire him, he said.
Gemmell thought it was inappropriate for Natale to table the issue
with the independent directors, and suggested that he take it up
with Edward instead.

MacDonald filled Edward in on what had transpired. According
to MacDonald, Edward admitted to him during this call that he
was aware of "most of the details" of the plan that Natale claimed
to have overheard. He also confirmed that Staffieri and Miller
had met the previous evening. To MacDonald, it appeared that,
contrary to what Edward had told him a few days earlier, the plan
had been shared with several people and was already in motion.
MacDonald urged Edward to convene a board meeting before the
situation spun out of control, but his request went unheeded.

Edward and Natale spoke on the phone later that evening.
Edward told Natale that he saw no basis for firing Staffieri. They
agreed to meet the next day at the telecom's corporate headquarters. At Melinda and Natale's behest, MacDonald decided to
attend the Sunday morning meeting. He felt it would be good to
have another set of eyes and ears there.

MacDonald showed up at Edward's tenth-floor office shortly before
the meeting was scheduled to begin. Edward seemed surprised

to see him, but he welcomed his presence. At 10 a.m., Edward, MacDonald, and Natale convened in the CEO's office. For several minutes, Natale described the conversation he had overheard, and outlined his reasons for wanting to fire Staffieri. He felt deeply betrayed by Staffieri, who had been openly plotting to usurp him, and could no longer work with the CFO. He presented Edward with an ultimatum: either he or Staffieri would have to go.

Edward responded that Natale shouldn't blame Staffieri. The whole thing wasn't his idea—it was Edward's. He apologized for how things had unfolded, but he'd lost confidence in Natale as CEO.

Natale was taken aback. He asked Edward if he was being fired. Edward repeated that he had lost confidence in him, but said he preferred that Natale leave of his own accord. He was willing to negotiate with him on an exit package that would pay him more than the normal severance that he was owed, as well as a consulting agreement that would allow him to remain involved in closing the Shaw deal.

Natale told Edward that he needed some time to process the news. As he left the meeting, one thing was clear. Regardless of how his departure was framed, he understood that he was being fired. All that was left was to hammer out the terms of his exit.

The first time that the board met to discuss Natale's imminent departure was at 9 a.m. the following Wednesday, three days after he had effectively been fired by the company's chair. MacDonald, in his capacity as lead director, had formally requested that Edward call the meeting. The directors gathered in a modern, airy boardroom studded with skylights that was named after Nadir Mohamed and occupied the seventeenth floor of the green-domed tower at 1 Mount Pleasant Road, a building that employees referred to as OMP. Present were eleven of the company's directors, with Loretta, Martha, Lind, and Ellis Jacob attending virtually. Absent were

Natale, whose employment at Rogers was the topic of the discussion, and Dépatie. The reason for Dépatie's absence would later become the subject of great controversy.

Several of the independent directors were outraged when Dépatie's plan to join the management team came to light. The most vocal of them was Bonnie Brooks, who, along with MacDonald and Dépatie, formed the human resources committee, the group that oversaw the company's compensation policies. When Isabelle Marcoux had stepped down from the board, Dépatie had taken over her role as the chair of the group. According to sources, Brooks argued that Dépatie had effectively created, with Edward's input, the reward system that he would be a beneficiary of when he joined the management team. There was talk of an ethics inquiry, although not all of the directors were convinced that one was needed. After all, it wasn't money in Dépatie's pocket; as an executive, he would still have to hit certain performance targets.

According to MacDonald, Edward told the board at the September 22 meeting that Dépatie had resigned the previous day because he was conflicted by virtue of Edward's plan to put him in charge of cable. This was corroborated by at least one other person present, as well as a draft of the meeting minutes that was later filed by Edward's lawyers in court. "The chair reported to the rest of the board members that Mr. Dépatie had resigned from the board of [Rogers Communications] effective the day before," the document read. However, it went on to note that Dépatie had not followed the "formal requirements" for tendering a resignation, and therefore remained on the board.

But Edward and Gemmell took the position that Dépatie had never stepped down at all. "At no time . . . did Edward or anyone else report that Robert Dépatie had resigned from the board. That never happened," says Gemmell, who was present at the meeting. Rather, it was "clearly understood" that Dépatie would resign as part of the leadership transition. "I am confident in saying that no board member in attendance at the September 22 meeting was under any other impression. To suggest so is, in my opinion, disingenuous."

The minutes from the board meeting were later changed to reflect this. According to the final version, Edward had said that Dépatie would resign "upon signing an employment agreement" for a role as the president and chief operating officer of cable. Natale would later argue in a court filing that the company had committed an "egregious violation of ethics" by modifying the document to support its false version of events.

Edward kicked off the board meeting by flipping through a series of gloomy slides that sought to demonstrate just how poorly Rogers was performing relative to its peers. The first graph charted the company's share price performance relative to Bell, Telus, and Shaw since Natale had joined in April 2017. Another showed Rogers in second and third place across a series of sixteen performance metrics—including revenue and earnings growth, monthly turnover of wireless customers, and complaints to the telecom ombudsman. One set of charts illustrated the level of investor confidence in the leadership teams of the major Canadian telecoms, based on data attributed to Brendan Wood International. Natale and his team were ranked third of the Big Three telecoms. But when it came to chief financial officers, Rogers took the top spot.

The slide deck spelled out only two paths forward. The first scenario involved a leadership transition with Natale's support; the second, without it. There was even a tentative date set for a retirement party at the Toronto Club, where the Rogers family would host the company's board and management team for a celebration of Natale's "tenure and accomplishments."

At least at first, things seemed to be going according to Edward's plan. Loretta read out the statement that Edward, with Martha's input, had written for her the night before. She urged the board to come together and support Natale's retirement, Staffieri's promotion, and the choice of Dépatie to lead cable. "Joe is a good man. We all like him. He has been here four and a half years and he has had his chance." While she was hopeful that Edward and MacDonald could "come to terms" with Natale, the company needed to move forward. "Tony will be a strong CEO at Rogers and I look forward to working with him in his new role. He is all about results and execution and that is what we need as we have a tough five years ahead of us with integrating Shaw and achieving the objectives of that deal."

Not everyone was persuaded. Four of the five independent directors—MacDonald, Peterson, Brooks, and Jacob—were furious with Edward. (Gemmell was not part of this contingent.) They were all prepared to resign in protest over what they saw as a major breach of corporate governance rules. A corporate board's most critical job is to oversee the hiring and firing of the CEO, and according to the block of independent directors, Edward had stripped them of that duty by essentially firing Natale and choosing his replacement without convening a board meeting. However, corporate directors also have what's known as a fiduciary duty to act in the best interests of the corporation. And the director group was worried that a mass exodus from the board in the wake of Natale's departure would draw too much attention to Rogers just as it was trying to acquire Shaw. They felt that the best thing to do was to stick around and try to ensure that nothing like this ever happened again.

During the meeting, the four directors were blunt about what Edward had done. They openly challenged his narrative about Natale's performance, noting that a number of external factors—including the pandemic, the transition to unlimited data plans, and the uncertainty surrounding the Shaw takeover—were weighing on the stock price and financial results. They cautioned about the potential perils of firing the CEO in the middle of the Shaw deal. And they lambasted Edward for circumventing the board.

Brooks and Peterson were particularly vocal in their objections. That caught the attention of Loretta, who had always respected

Peterson. She started to wonder if she had been wrong to support her son.

Edward conceded that the process had been unfortunate. He suggested hiring external consultants to conduct a corporate governance review, although some of the independent directors had doubts about how committed he was to the idea.

By the end of the meeting, nothing had been resolved. The board agreed to reconvene later that week.

In the meantime, Alan Horn met with Natale to work out the details of his severance. Over the course of several meetings, they hammered out an agreement and shook hands. "It was a very rich deal," one person said.

Under normal circumstances, Natale would have walked away with $13.7 million of severance. The terms that he and Horn agreed on would see Natale receive a lump-sum payment of $6.8 million, consisting of 24-months' base salary, allowance, and target bonus, the company later disclosed in court documents. His 2019, 2020, and 2021 performance-related restricted stock units, or PRSUs, would vest on an accelerated schedule and would be valued at the five-day average closing price prior to the announcement of his retirement, making them worth approximately $12 million. Natale would also stay on as a contractor until the conclusion of the Shaw deal, receiving his usual $1.3 million annual base salary, as well as a $4 million cash bonus if and when the takeover closed. Finally, he would then enter into a two-year consulting agreement, for which he would receive $20 million.

The board met to vote on the offer two days later. Gathered in a wood-panelled boardroom on the third floor, the directors took their seats around a large, trapezoid-shaped table, where Edward summarized the terms of Natale's resignation, which was to take effect on October 1.

By that point, the pressure that had been steadily building over the past week had erupted into open hostility. Brooks, whose role on the board's human resources committee made her privy to executives' performance evaluations, was blunt. Staffieri was just not capable of running the organization, she argued.

But when it came time to approve Natale's severance package, she, MacDonald, and Jacob still voted in favour of it. They continued to feel that the company would be better off with Natale in charge, but Edward had already fired him, and they didn't have the votes to reverse that. They saw themselves as approving a generous exit package to ensure that Natale was treated properly on the way out—not as endorsing his termination, which is how Edward's camp would later position the vote.

The only director who voted against the resolution was Peterson. He was livid. In an emotional speech, he chastised the board for using shareholder money to cover the mistakes of what he characterized as an autocratic chairman. For years, Edward had displayed a pattern of complete disregard for any compliance and governance obligations, Peterson argued. The chairman's latest move—to single-handedly fire Natale without board approval—was deplorable. In fact, it was the most distasteful process he had ever experienced in his life. After thirty years on the Rogers board, he was stepping down.

Melinda pleaded with Peterson to reconsider. Stay until the next board meeting on Sunday, she entreated him. Cooler heads will prevail. He reluctantly agreed.

Despite the intense criticism, Edward's plan was nearing the finish line. All that was left was to finalize Staffieri's contract. But the seeds of doubt that Peterson's objections had planted in the minds of two of the plan's supporters were beginning to take root. And by the time Edward logged on to the virtual meeting two days later, things had taken an unexpected turn.

FOURTEEN

DILL PICKLE MARTINI

Shortly before 10 a.m. on Saturday, September 25, 2021, Martha Rogers appeared beneath the arched doorway of a two-storey, French-inspired mansion on Forest Hill Road. The house, which was guarded by a heavy metal gate, sat across the street from Upper Canada College, just steps away from where the Rogers kids had grown up. It belonged to her sister Melinda.

Martha and Melinda weren't exactly seeing eye to eye at the time. The COVID pandemic had kept them physically apart, and, according to Melinda, left them with doubts and uncertainties about what was going on at the telecom company that bore their family's name. A situation involving pandemic precautions had also created tension within the family, according to sources. At one point, Melinda had received a letter from the advisory committee to the Rogers Control Trust—a group that included her sister Martha—prohibiting her from visiting her cottage for the season. Melinda, Martha, and Loretta all had cottages on the family compound on Tobin Island, property that was owned by the family trust. (Edward and Suzanne's cottage was on a different part of the island and not owned by the trust.) Melinda had contracted COVID earlier that year, and Loretta and her doctor were apparently concerned that she could still infect others. Melinda was hurt by the reaction, but she respected the concerns and had all family members and staff regularly tested for COVID by the Cleveland Clinic, one person said.

There was another reason why Martha's sudden appearance on Melinda's doorstep was surprising. The youngest of Ted and Loretta's children had never taken much of an interest in the family business. While all three of Martha's older siblings had, at some point in their lives, worked for Rogers Communications, Martha had not. Having allowed her registration as a naturopathic doctor to lapse, she spent her time keeping her mother company, particularly after Ted's death, and serving on the boards of various nonprofit organizations. She chaired the Rogers Foundation, which her parents had created as a vehicle through which to donate to health-, education-, and environment-related causes. Like her mother, she was passionate about protecting wildlife and nature. Once, as the two women stood by a marina near their cottages and watched a turtle dig a nest in the sand, they were so struck by the decline they had witnessed in Muskoka's turtle population that they launched a program aimed at protecting the species.

Despite Martha's lack of corporate experience, her father had given her a seat on the Rogers board. She chaired the environmental, social, and governance committee, but that was the extent to which she involved herself in the company's affairs. All of that was about to change, however. Martha was about to play a crucial role in the escalating power struggle that would soon engulf the telecom's board.

By that point, Martha was becoming increasingly concerned that the independent directors seemed to have a different set of facts regarding Natale's performance than the ones that she and her mother had been presented with. The morning after David

Peterson's impassioned speech, she embarked on a fact-finding mission. She called Peterson and peppered him with questions. Over the course of more than an hour, he laid out his perspective on the situation.

Then, she showed up at Melinda's house. She wanted to know if what Peterson had told her was true. Together, Melinda and Martha phoned up the contingent of independent directors. The conversation was, according to one source, "the breaking of the dam." The directors spoke about years of what they perceived to be bad behaviour, describing Edward with words like *arrogant* and *bully*. The more that Martha heard, the more convinced she became that firing Natale had been the wrong move. She was insistent that they find a way to bring him back.

Loretta was also beginning to have a change of heart. She spoke first to Martha, who relayed to her the independent directors' concerns. Then she discussed the situation with MacDonald and Brooks. That conversation afforded her a "more complete and unbiased" picture of Natale's performance, leading her to conclude that she had been misled by her son and her late husband's long-time lieutenant, she later said in court documents. Her decision to switch sides in a fractious battle between her adult children would have been difficult for any parent. But by that point, Loretta had also decided that her son's actions needed to be undone.

That afternoon, Melinda's driver deposited her at Peterson's Caledon farmhouse, roughly an hour outside the city. They settled into a pair of armchairs in the den, a welcoming room with pine wainscoting on the walls and a fireplace filled with crackling flames. There, they devised a plan to reinstate Natale and address the corporate governance shortcomings that had resulted in his termination.

They knew that to convince Natale to return, Staffieri would need to go. They also wanted to ensure that Natale was free to run the company without interference from Edward. The solution, they decided, was a compromise, one that would allow Edward to remain the chair by putting ring-fencing around him. William Braithwaite, a Stikeman Elliott lawyer, helped them draft the resolution.

That day, Natale informed a handful of his leadership team— Dave Fuller, Jim Reid, and Jordan Banks—of his imminent departure. He planned to tell the rest of the team on Sunday. But the situation wasn't sitting well with him, despite the generous severance package that he had secured. Thinking back to the conversation that he had overheard, Natale knew that the bulk of the senior leaders he had brought on board would soon be trailing him out the door. So when Peterson and Melinda called from Peterson's den to ask Natale if he'd consider sticking around, he told them that he was open to the idea, but needed to consult with his wife and his lawyer first.

The pieces of Peterson and Melinda's plan were falling into place. They had an ousted CEO interested in reclaiming his job, and enough board votes to push the change through. They toasted their progress with the house specialty cocktail: a dill pickle martini.

Edward and his allies, meanwhile, were completely oblivious to the scheme that was quietly unfolding among a subset of the company's board. According to Edward's account, neither MacDonald nor Brooks said a word about it when they met with him the next day to finalize Staffieri's compensation. As far as Edward could tell, Natale seemed pleased with the arrangements. A press release was drafted, praising Staffieri's "incredible work ethic" and his "track record for results." But the announcement appointing "one of the company's and telecom industry's most highly regarded leaders" as its new chief executive wouldn't cross the wire on September 27 as planned. Because when the board convened virtually on Sunday afternoon and Edward began outlining Staffieri's compensation package, he was interrupted by MacDonald. He and several of the directors had a better plan, MacDonald said. Then he passed the floor to Edward's baby sister.

Martha's voice was clear and forceful as she read out a new resolution that would rescind the board's approval of Natale's resignation, sweeten his employment contract, and fire Staffieri, replacing him on an interim basis with a finance executive named Paulina Molnar. The motion also proposed reinstating Clappison as a director, conducting a corporate governance review, and establishing an executive oversight committee that would allow Melinda, MacDonald, and Clappison to supervise Edward's interactions with Natale and his management team.

Edward and his remaining supporters on the board—a group that had, by that point, dwindled to just Horn, Lind, and Gemmell—were completely blindsided. Horn was especially outraged. A cool-headed man who often played the peacekeeper role, he was rarely riled up, which made his anger that much more salient. After all the complaining that the contingent of independent directors had done about bad corporate governance, here they were springing this resolution on everybody else without warning. It was hypocrisy, he said.

Edward and Lind were furious as well, as was Gemmell. While the dissident directors saw themselves as opposing the unilateral actions of an authoritarian chairman, Gemmell later characterized their actions as a "display of duplicity."

"This is not how you conduct yourself if you're a serious group of people," Gemmell says, seemingly invoking Logan Roy, the fictional patriarch from HBO's hit television series *Succession*, who in one episode, told his adult children, "I love you, but you are not serious people."

In the end, the meeting—held via Microsoft's Teams platform—adjourned without a vote. The plan was to give everyone time to think it over and reconvene in three days.

The next day, Edward, Melinda, and Horn crammed into a friend's float plane at the Buttonville airport, just north of the city, and flew forty-five minutes to visit Loretta and Martha at the family compound in Muskoka, in the hopes of resolving the impasse. They sat around the dining room table in Loretta's homey cottage, which looked virtually the same as it had when Ted built it in the 1950s, down to the furniture. Over the course of the discussion, which lasted no more than two hours, the family tried to hash out a compromise. Despite the breakdown in the relationship between Natale and Staffieri, Edward suggested they both stay on through the closing of the Shaw deal. The fact that it would have been difficult for Natale to work with Staffieri—the man who had tried to usurp his job—didn't seem to trouble Edward. The executives who ran his company were merely the hired help, and he expected the butler and the maid to get along.

It appeared to Edward that Melinda was open to the idea. As the impromptu family gathering ended—cut short by text messages from their pilot friend Steve, who was getting antsy about getting back to Toronto before it got dark and became unsafe to land on water—Melinda told Edward she'd get back to him. There might be a path forward, she said.

That night, Edward called MacDonald to fill him in. MacDonald asked if he should tell the other independent directors about the compromise that Edward had proposed. That was up to him, Edward replied. But he was still waiting for Melinda's response and thought it would be better if the family could get on the same page first.

Working with Staffieri was a non-starter for Natale, however. He felt deeply betrayed by Staffieri's actions, and believed that keeping him on the executive leadership team would create a toxic work environment. Edward may have put Staffieri up to the scheme, but Staffieri had agreed to go along with it. "Tony was Judas," said one of Natale's allies. "He stuck a knife in Joe."

In the end, Melinda never responded directly to Edward's proposal. Instead, a one-sentence email from MacDonald landed in Edward's inbox at 1:44 p.m. the following day. Copied on it were Melinda, Martha, and Loretta, as well as Peterson, Brooks, and Jacob. "Edward, we have reviewed the proposal you suggested to me yesterday and have rejected it," it read.

Like all large, publicly traded companies, Rogers had an executive leadership team, a CEO, and a board of directors that was headed up by a chair. But what most members of the public—and even many savvy industry observers—didn't fully grasp prior to the fall of 2021 was that ten individuals had an outsized level of influence over the $30 billion telecom and media giant. These ten people were the advisers to the Rogers Control Trust, the corporate entity through which the Rogers family held the company's voting Class A shares. And while Edward may have lost control of the Rogers board, he still had another lever to pull. On September 28, the same day that MacDonald informed him that his proposal had been rejected, Edward called a meeting of the Rogers Control Trust advisory committee. It was to take place at 11:30 the next morning.

There was a significant amount of overlap between the advisory committee and the Rogers board. Six individuals—Edward, Loretta, Melinda, Martha, Lind, and Horn—occupied seats on both. The remaining four spots on the advisory committee were occupied by Lisa Rogers, Ted's childhood best friend Thomas "Toby" Hull, Loretta's nephew David Robinson, and the sitting mayor of Toronto, John Tory. As chair of the trust, Edward had the ability to vote the proxies that came with the Class A shares, allowing him to replace directors. But he had a duty to consult the committee, who could restrain him or replace him with a two-thirds vote.

Roughly an hour before they were scheduled to meet, a man by the name of Bob Reeves, who handled the investments made by the family holding company, advised the committee via email that the meeting was being pushed until later in the day. In fact, it was being rescheduled to 4:15 p.m., the same time that the Rogers board was scheduled to meet. The board meeting, meanwhile, would be pushed back by two days, until October 1, Edward told MacDonald. He justified the postponement by telling MacDonald that he needed time to get advice on how firing Staffieri would impact the Shaw deal.

But that wasn't the sole reason for the delay. According to MacDonald, Edward told him that day that he wasn't prepared to lose control of the company. He was planning to call a shareholder meeting and replace the independent directors who had moved against him. He needed to get some advice on how that would impact the Shaw deal, too.

The problem was that, even as board chair, Edward didn't have the power to simply reschedule the meeting as he pleased. He needed consent from the majority of the board, and he didn't have it. Shortly after 2 p.m., MacDonald informed him that the majority of the directors were opposed to the adjournment, and therefore the board meeting would proceed as planned.

That afternoon, in what was almost certainly a first for the telecom company, duelling meetings took place. The Rogers board met without its chair, while the trust's advisory committee met without Loretta, Martha, and Melinda.

Those who attended the advisory committee meeting backed Edward, who believed that Natale and his management team were entrenching themselves in the company and had manipulated the board into doing their bidding. "The members of the Advisory Committee expressed strong support for me as Control Trust Chair," Edward later wrote in an affidavit. Several of them expressed the view that the independent directors had acted inappropriately, and that Melinda was using the situation to challenge the structure of the Rogers Control Trust and Edward's role as chair. Lisa was particularly vocal, according to a source. She was known for being resolute, and when she didn't agree with her brother, she would typically be the first to speak up. "She is not pro-Edward," the person said. But in this particular instance, Lisa took her brother's side. She felt that she was honouring the wishes of their father, who had wanted his son to play a significant role in the company.

Meanwhile, in the third-floor boardroom of 333 Bloor Street East, Melinda, acting in her capacity as deputy chair, called the other meeting to order. Horn and Lind were both absent, having chosen to accompany Edward to the family trust meeting. But they sent a mercenary: Richard Willoughby, a corporate lawyer from Torys who served as an adviser to the committee. Willoughby tried to persuade the directors to adjourn the meeting until October 1. He told them they had a legal responsibility—a fiduciary duty—to consider the position of the company's controlling shareholder, Edward. Not surprisingly, Willoughby's speech fell on deaf ears. He was asked to leave, and the meeting continued.

Loretta spoke about the importance of good governance to Ted. He would have wanted to avoid disruption to the company's employees, investors, and lenders. She said that she remained confident in Natale, who had received an "outperform" rating on his most recent evaluation.

The board discussed a variety of matters, including the implications of firing the chief financial officer in the midst of a takeover that required the telecom to borrow billions of dollars. They knew there was a risk that the advisory committee would strike back by removing some or even all of the directors who had supported Martha's motion. But in the end, the resolution was passed, with only Gemmell voting against it.

Jim Reid, the chief human resources officer, delivered the news to Staffieri. He'd been kept apprised of the situation, so the termination didn't come as a surprise. Given the company's dual-class structure, Staffieri was confident that he would end up with the top job. But he worried about the tumult that lay ahead for the company and his team, as well as the headlines that his family would read.

The press release announcing Staffieri's departure crossed the wire shortly before 8 p.m., sending shockwaves through Toronto's business community. The company provided no explanation for its decision to part ways with its chief financial officer during its proposed takeover of Shaw, but tried to reassure investors that the deal was going ahead as planned.

Edward wasn't shown the press release, or consulted on its contents, before it went out. He spoke to each member of the advisory committee, aside from his mom and two of his sisters, in the aftermath of Staffieri's firing. According to Edward, all of them were upset that the board had ignored his wishes.

The retaliatory strike that the independent directors had been bracing for came four days later, on October 3, via a letter from Willoughby. It was addressed to the directors who had gone against Edward, a group that had grown to five members with the reinstatement of Clappison. Willoughby claimed to be writing on behalf of the advisory committee to the Rogers Control Trust, which had been a client of Torys for many years. But Loretta, Melinda, and Martha found this assertion alarming. After all, they also sat on the committee, and yet they hadn't authorized such a letter. It outlined the breakdown in the relationship between Edward and the five independent directors, and reminded them about the structure of the family trust. The way that it was set up allowed a single individual—the chair—to exercise the family's control over its telecom empire. That gave Edward, with the advisory committee's support, "the power to deal with this untenable situation by unilaterally reconstituting the board." Willoughby said he hoped that wouldn't be necessary. He suggested a meeting between the directors, the advisory committee, and Edward, to see whether a "mutually agreeable path forward" could be found. "If, however, you believe that there is no prospect of agreeing on such a path, then the advisory committee requests that you resign from the board," he concluded.

Braithwaite, the Stikeman lawyer, responded on the directors' behalf. None of them had any intention of resigning, he wrote. They had acted the way that they had in response to a scheme that Edward had designed, without the board's input, which they believed would be "extremely harmful" to the company. "These directors have in this entire process been motivated by one thing, which is to act in the best interest of [Rogers Communications], which includes all stakeholders and not any one particular shareholder."

But by the time Braithwaite sent the letter on October 5, Edward had already taken the first step towards enacting his plan. The day before, a Torys lawyer had written to Lisa Damiani, the telecom's chief legal and regulatory officer, requesting a list of the names and addresses of the company's shareholders. The request was initially met with silence.

In early October, Melinda invited a communications adviser named Wojtek Dabrowski to her home. A former journalist, Dabrowski had worked for the CEOs of two of the country's largest financial institutions before starting his own firm, Provident Communications, in 2016. By the time he found himself sitting on a cream-coloured sofa in Melinda's living room, whispers were spreading through Bay Street about the reason behind Staffieri's exit. It seemed like only a matter of time before the story blew up, and Melinda and her long-time adviser, Gareth Seltzer, wanted to be ready.

Before the meeting, Seltzer had done some due diligence on Dabrowski, who he had been introduced to by Melinda's lawyer Walied Soliman, the chair of Norton Rose Fulbright Canada. (Provident and Norton Rose had worked together previously on cybersecurity cases.) Sitting in a room filled with photographs of her four children, who ranged in age from five to fourteen, Melinda spoke with Dabrowski for over an hour. Seltzer and Melinda's husband Eric Hixon listened, as did the family's two yellow English labs, Pluto and Astro, named in honour of Hixon's love of astronomy.

Melinda struck Dabrowski as a thoughtful, principled person. Her priority, she told him, was to protect her family and its greatest asset, Rogers Communications. "Within minutes of starting to talk about this, she went to the governance issues," he later recalled.

Melinda wasn't the only one thinking about how to respond to what was about to become a very public battle between warring factions of the Rogers family and the company's board. Around the same time, Edward had retained the services of Navigator, a high-stakes crisis management firm that had trademarked the slogan "When You Can't Afford to Lose." The firm's primary point person on the Rogers file was a dark-haired, bushy-eyebrowed Queen's University graduate named Jonathan Lowenstein.

Navigator, in turn, introduced Edward to Jonathan Lisus, a partner at a boutique law firm called Lax O'Sullivan Lisus Gottlieb. A fearless litigator with narrow eyes and a receding hairline that accentuated his oblong face, Lisus had been named Canada's Trial Lawyer of the Year by Benchmark Litigation in 2020. But at least part of the rationale for retaining him was an act of gamesmanship; Lisus had just represented Soliman, Melinda's lawyer, in a defamation case against a self-described news commentator who had accused Soliman, a Muslim, of supporting terrorism.

Rogers Communications, meanwhile, worked with Scott Davidson, a personable, bespectacled managing director at a New York–based public relations firm called Teneo that had been brought on board during the Cogeco fiasco and had stuck around to advise Rogers on its takeover of Shaw.

As the parties lawyered up and retained communications advisers, at least one journalist was piecing together what had transpired. Then, on October 8, the Friday night that marked the start of the Thanksgiving long weekend, the thing that for weeks had seemed inevitable finally happened. The *Globe and Mail* published a story online that revealed that Staffieri's unceremonious exit from Rogers had been preceded by a power struggle between Edward and several other members of the telecom's board, including his sister Melinda.

In the week after the story broke, Loretta, Melinda, and Martha embarked upon a war against Torys. The firm was founded in the 1940s by John S.D. Tory, the grandfather of the Toronto mayor, then passed down to his twin sons, John A. Tory and James M. Tory. Ted Rogers had briefly articled at the firm early in his career, then turned to it for legal advice on his estate arrangements, including the creation of the family trusts. It had acted for the advisory committee since its inception over a decade earlier. Now, Melinda, Martha, and Loretta wanted to replace it.

Their unhappiness with the firm stemmed from the fact that it had sent two letters claiming to be on the advisory committee's behalf, without consulting three of its members. The first was the October 3 letter that had threatened to fire the independent directors; the second, the request for the shareholder list.

Willoughby tried to rectify the problem. On October 12, he wrote to the committee, advising them that Torys would no longer act for those members who had secured their own lawyers. That included both Edward and Melinda. "We will continue as counsel to the balance of the [advisory committee] members, assuming you wish us to continue," he noted.

But this arrangement was unacceptable to Loretta. "The Advisory Committee needs impartial and independent counsel, which our long-time friends at Torys have not demonstrated," she replied via email. She urged her children to work together to find a firm that they could all agree on.

Melinda wasn't satisfied with the arrangement either. She planned to speak with her siblings about finding a new law firm to represent the trust, she told Willoughby. They also planned to discuss proposals that lawyers had assembled in the hopes of bridging the widening gulf between family members. "In the interim, I would ask Torys to respect Loretta's instructions and immediately stand down in a dignified manner," she added. She ended the letter—one in which she had threatened to fire the law firm that had advised her family for two generations—with "warmest personal regards."

Martha took things even further, accusing Willoughby of being conflicted, "tone deaf" to the family's situation, and disrespectful to the matriarch. "You've lost the moral capability to advise our family through this difficult period."

But Willoughby wasn't backing down. He had meant no disrespect to Loretta, he wrote, but he intended to continue representing the subset of six advisory committee members—John Tory, Phil Lind, Alan Horn, Toby Hull, David Robinson, and Lisa Rogers—who had not hired their own lawyers.

The exchange continued, with Martha accusing Willoughby of engaging in conduct that was "quite unbecoming of the law firm our father spoke so highly of for so many years." She fired off a list of questions, asking, for instance, when Torys had stopped representing her and who was currently paying the firm's invoices. "Kindly let me know your answers on these four questions by end of business today," she concluded, "at which time, I will be conferring with other family members for your forced removal."

FIFTEEN

SCHRÖDINGER'S BOARD

A young lawyer by the name of William Stransky marched through the front doors of a 35-storey skyscraper in downtown Vancouver on October 19 with clear instructions from his boss: "William, please do not return, but wait in the main lobby if they do not let you up."

After two weeks of unsuccessful attempts to obtain the shareholder list from Rogers, Edward and his lawyers had had enough. Stransky, an associate at Vancouver-based law firm McEwan Partners, which Edward had retained, was dispatched to Fasken's offices to inspect the document.

Edward didn't receive an answer to his original request—which he had sent to Lisa Damiani on October 4—for more than a week. When he finally did get an answer on October 12, it came from Kareen Zimmer, a partner at Fasken. The firm, which had been retained by Rogers, raised what Edward's side referred to as "various technical objections," asking for clarification as to how the lists would be used, as well as for proof that the trustees had signed off on the request. The firm's client was also demanding a larger payment. The law required a person requesting a shareholder list to pay a "reasonable fee," Zimmer noted, and Rogers had determined that the $1,000 that Edward had remitted wasn't reasonable. It wanted five times that much.

Jonathan Lisus replied that the amount they had already paid was in line with market rates. But in order to avoid any further delay, he agreed to courier over a cheque for the additional $4,000. By October 18, Edward's side was growing impatient, and Ken McEwan, a partner at the firm that employed Stransky, informed Fasken that he would be sending the associate to their offices the next day.

Fasken replied the following morning that sending Stransky wouldn't be necessary; they would provide the shareholder list in an electronic form by the end of the week. But McEwan didn't want to wait that long. By the time Zimmer responded that she would circulate the firm's COVID precautions for visitors, Stransky was already en route. "Mr. Stransky is wearing a mask and is double vaccinated," McEwan wrote in an email. "He also has his record of vaccination. There is no reason for delay."

If Fasken was indeed delaying—an allegation that the firm repeatedly denied in the increasingly hostile back-and-forth that ensued—it was because its client knew exactly what Edward was planning to do with the lists. He needed them so that he could notify the company's shareholders of his intention to reconstitute the telecom's board.

Stransky returned bearing bad news. The lists were kept in a designated office outside of British Columbia, he had been told. McEwan argued that this made Fasken non-compliant with the province's securities laws, and dispatched Stransky back to 550 Burrard Street. That, in turn, angered Fasken lawyer Tracey Cohen, who derided McEwan's conduct and the tenor of his emails as "unnecessarily aggressive and adversarial." While McEwan quarrelled with his counterparts at Fasken, Stransky waited for nearly four hours in the firm's lobby, unbeknownst to the Fasken lawyers, who assumed that he had left.

That evening, the dissident directors, the family trust advisers, and a phalanx of lawyers crammed into the telecom's third-floor boardroom hoping to resolve the ongoing dispute. The five directors took their places along a table across the front of the room, facing the trust advisers, who were seated in a U-shape. Lisa, who attended the meeting virtually from Victoria, B.C., appeared on a screen mounted on the wall behind the directors, while lawyers and support staff were seated in chairs that had been arranged along the room's back wall.

For the dissident directors, the "without prejudice" session, chaired by Toronto mayor John Tory, was an opportunity to explain their actions to the trust. John MacDonald and Bonnie Brooks read prepared remarks that highlighted their experience as corporate directors—Brooks noted that she was a recipient of the Order of Canada—and how it had shaped their understanding of good governance. What had happened at Rogers—the manner in which Edward had, according to the dissidents, single-handedly terminated Natale—was not good governance, they said. Brooks went even further, telling the trust that Staffieri was not the right person to lead the company. They spoke, too, about what they perceived to be a pattern of behaviour by the company's chair—one characterized by a flagrant disregard for process. It was an intense meeting. "David Peterson was in a lather," one person who was in attendance later recalled. "He was red-faced and angry." Another attendee described the gathering as a "dump on Edward" session. Loretta read a statement that criticized not only her son but also her late husband's most trusted lieutenants, Horn and Lind. But Edward took solace in the fact that his mother hadn't written the words herself. When she was later asked by her daughter Lisa who had crafted the statement, Loretta responded, "Counsel," according to one source.

Edward, meanwhile, remained composed as he sat next to his wife, who was dressed in pink and visibly distraught. Suzanne had never been directly involved in the company, but she liked to be visible around Rogers, sometimes accompanying Edward to the telecom's annual general meetings. Before Rogers sold off its magazine publishing business in 2019, she was known to occasionally call up employees in the division to request coverage of her charity fashion galas.

An agenda that was circulated before the meeting indicated that Larry Tanenbaum, the chair of Maple Leaf Sports & Entertainment, would be in attendance. Tanenbaum, who co-owned MLSE with Rogers and Bell through a three-way partnership, was very close with Loretta, having lived across the street from her and Ted for thirty years. But it was no secret that he and Edward didn't get along. Sources said they butted heads during meetings of the MLSE board, on which they both sat along with Melinda, Staffieri, Bibic, and several others. Still, some of the people who attended the without-prejudice session were surprised that Tanenbaum would wade into a messy spat between Rogers family members. Those people, it turns out, were correct, because in the end it wasn't Tanenbaum but his lawyer, Dale Lastman of Goodmans, who showed up to address the meeting on Tanenbaum's behalf.

Lastman's various roles in the conflict epitomize the cozy, insular nature of Canada's corporate world. In addition to being a director of MLSE, he had also represented Natale in negotiating the terms of his later-rescinded resignation, and his firm had advised Rogers on its acquisition of Shaw. Now, the son of former Toronto mayor Mel Lastman was to make a presentation on behalf of one of the owners of the city's most valuable sports teams to warring factions of a prominent business family at a session mediated by the city's sitting mayor.

Lastman's remarks, which focused on Edward's conduct on the MLSE board, wound up being less forceful than the anti-Edward camp had hoped. The dissident directors waited outside the room while Lastman spoke about how aggressive a negotiator Edward had been on Rogers' behalf at the MLSE board, and how his unwillingness to play ball had irked Tanenbaum. He referred to the tough stance that Edward had taken during negotiations that summer with Toronto Raptors head Masai Ujiri. Edward attempted to ask questions but was silenced by his lawyer, Lisus.

The presentation was an attempt by the anti-Edward camp to demonstrate a pattern of behaviour. But some observers were left scratching their heads, wondering what it had to do with the situation at Rogers. By the time the meeting was over, Edward was convinced that his opponents' plan had backfired. Based on the comments and the body language of the other trustees, he believed that the meeting had reaffirmed for his allies that the independent directors were disingenuous, combative, and uninformed—and that they needed to go.

In attempting to mediate the family dispute, John Tory was fulfilling a promise that he had made to his dear friend Ted before he passed away. While his motivations may have been honourable, his decision to chair the three-hour-long meeting soon attracted public scrutiny. This was a familiar theme for Tory, whose ties to the Rogers family had been an ongoing source of conflict since he was first elected mayor in 2014.

Tory had stayed in close contact with Ted and Loretta after he left Rogers in 2003. In 2010, following a five-year run as the leader of the Ontario Progressive Conservative Party, he joined the Rogers board. But unlike his father, John A. Tory, who had served as a director for decades, John H. Tory stepped down after just

four years to focus on his new job as city mayor. He decided, however, to hold on to his various roles as a trustee, adviser, and director at several Rogers family trusts, citing a "moral obligation" to
the family. Fortunately for Tory, fulfilling that obligation also happened to pay a non-trivial amount of money. According to the
Toronto Star, Tory earned $100,000 for serving on the advisory
committee to the Rogers Control Trust—roughly half of his 2020
mayoral salary, which came to $198,834.

The corporate structure through which the Rogers family
wielded its power over the telecom and media conglomerate that
bears their name was convoluted. The family owned 97.5 per cent
of the company's voting shares and 10 per cent of the non-voting
ones, but those shares weren't all held in one place. Instead, they
were spread across a dizzying array of corporate entities, a structure established primarily for tax planning purposes. At the top of
that structure was the Rogers Control Trust and the ten-person
advisory committee that steered it. Tory served as a bridge between
generations, sitting down with each of the four Rogers kids when
they turned twenty-one and explaining this structure to them.

Municipal laws require city council members to declare a conflict if they or a family member have a financial interest in a matter
being voted on. Tory did so more frequently than other councillors,
and more than half the time it related to Rogers. He also owned
Rogers shares, although the size of his position in the company was
not publicly disclosed. In 2014, the last year that he served on the
Rogers board, his holdings were worth close to $5.5 million, accord-
ing to securities filings. After that, he was no longer classified as a
company insider, which meant that he didn't have to disclose his
holdings. But public scrutiny of his ties to the telecom giant continued to dog him. Some questioned whether it was appropriate
for the mayor to mediate a Rogers family feud.

At a media scrum the day after the meeting, Oliver Moore,

the *Globe*'s urban affairs reporter, asked Tory whether it was a good use of time for the mayor to chair a meeting that could determine the future of Canada's largest wireless carrier. Tory, who was known for working long hours, curiously took the question as an attack on his work ethic, responding that he had worked from six in the morning until six at night before heading to the meeting at 333 Bloor. "I don't think there are too many people that call into question my devotion to my job," he told Moore. "If I had a hobby, if I had some other kind of activity that I did, frankly, if I'd wanted to spend time with my family, I don't think after a twelve-hour day anybody would deny me that opportunity."

All the while, the battle over the shareholder list raged on. When the board met the morning of October 20 to sign off the telecom's third-quarter earnings, MacDonald said the company's management had been instructed not to release the list until the directors had an opportunity to discuss governance issues later that day. Based on conversations he'd had with his sister Martha and others, Edward interpreted this to mean that they were planning to remove him as chair.

In the meantime, emails continued to fly back and forth between the high-powered lawyers embroiled in the clash over the shareholder list. By that point, Melinda's lawyer, Walied Soliman, had also entered the fray, arguing that certain members of the advisory committee—namely, Melinda, Martha, and Loretta—had not approved Edward's request for the list. Torys countered that Edward didn't require the committee's approval to request the list. "Folks, respectfully, this is getting silly," Lisus wrote shortly before 2 p.m. "These are publicly available records."

Sometime after the lunch break that afternoon, MacDonald told those in the meeting that management had been instructed to release the list. It was provided to Edward's camp shortly afterwards. However, the board had run out of time to address the governance matters they had been planning to discuss. It appeared that Edward's removal as the chair of Rogers Communications would have to wait until they reconvened the next day.

That night, shortly before midnight, Bonnie Brooks fired off an email to Tory on behalf of the independent directors. She told him that she was concerned that the key issues had not come across forcefully enough at the previous night's meeting and wanted to underscore them.

Edward's interference with the company's management over the past seven years had become impossible to control, she wrote. "The chair wants to run the company, believes that he runs the company, and no CEO or management team can operate effectively under these conditions." Replacing Natale with Staffieri would give Edward so much power, she argued, that it would de facto turn him into an executive chair.

The leadership changes that Edward was contemplating could also have dire consequences for the Shaw deal, she cautioned. The ratings agencies might downgrade the company if they learned of the turmoil engulfing its board and management team. Natale had been the primary point of contact for the lenders financing the deal—and, over the years, he had forged relationships with the heads of the CRTC and Innovation, Science and Economic Development Canada, two of the federal regulators reviewing the takeover. "His being at the table is critical," Brooks argued. "Both government agency leaders involved do not know Tony [Staffieri], have never met him." Besides, she added, Brad Shaw had requested no further changes to the board or management team—an assertion that Shaw would later deny.

The independent directors felt that they had run out of options. Edward's decision to eschew governance protocols had put the company in grave danger, according to Brooks. The directors had no illusions about where things were likely headed; they knew that Edward was plotting to replace them. But in the meantime, they were prepared to remove him as the chair of the Rogers board, she concluded.

Shortly after the email was sent, its contents were leaked to the *Globe and Mail*, prompting the first public statement from Shaw since the conflict began. The Shaws had kept their heads down, intent on staying out of the fray of what they viewed as a family matter. But after the contents of Brooks's letter to Tory went public, Brad issued a written statement to the *Globe*, noting that his company remained committed to the takeover. "Any recent reports or descriptions regarding comments made by me or Shaw Communications with respect to the composition of the Rogers Board of Directors or its management team are false," he stated. "This is a Rogers Family and Board matter and out of respect for the Rogers Family it is not appropriate for Shaw Communications to comment on recent developments."

Dave Fuller's efforts to turn around Rogers' wireless business were starting to bear fruit. In many respects, his strategy was a continuation of Brent Johnston's, although he had made some tweaks. Under Fuller's leadership, the wireless team zeroed in on two key priorities. The first was to improve the customer experience as a way of reducing churn. Rogers had always been great at winning new customers, less so at keeping them. Retaining more subscribers would boost its total net additions. The second was to continue shifting away from mass-marketing and towards micro-marketing campaigns that focused on specific segments of the market and that would be more difficult for competitors to match.

On the morning of October 21, with the board in turmoil, Rogers reported that it had added 175,000 net new wireless postpaid subscribers during its third quarter—"our best result in 13 years," the company boasted in a press release. (Postpaid subscribers are those who are billed at the end of the month for the services they used, versus prepaid customers, who pay upfront for wireless services.) Its churn, meanwhile, fell to 0.95 per cent, its "best third-quarter churn result ever."

But the positive news was quickly overshadowed by what would almost certainly go down as one of the most dramatic days in the telecom's history. That morning, at eight o'clock, the advisory committee members convened at the offices of Torys, located on the thirty-third floor of a sleek, black tower in the heart of Toronto's financial district.

Edward felt that the situation with the dissident directors had become untenable. They were ignoring his wishes and, in his view, trying to entrench themselves on the board, much like how Natale and his team were trying to entrench themselves in the company. Rogers needed independent directors who behaved professionally and worked cooperatively with the controlling shareholder, he told the other members of the advisory committee. Unless the committee voted to restrain his powers, he would be replacing the five dissidents with a slate of his own hand-picked candidates. The manner in which he planned to enact the change had never been used at Rogers before. Rather than call a shareholder meeting, Edward was planning to reconstitute the board through a written resolution, a strategy that Lisus had concocted.

The meeting was disbanded to focus on trying to negotiate a settlement. Loretta, Melinda, Martha, and Soliman were put up in one room at the law firm, while Edward, Lind, Horn, and Lisus occupied another one. John Tory again tried unsuccessfully to mediate between the two factions, shuttling various proposals back and forth and occasionally stepping out to deal with city business.

The proposals put forward on behalf of the three Rogers women contained many of the same elements that were present in the resolution that the board had passed on September 29. They wanted Natale to remain as CEO, and for measures to be put in place that prevented Edward from interfering with how he ran the company. Melinda, Martha, and Loretta also wanted Edward to pause his plan to reconstitute the board. But according to one source, the proposals also contemplated changes to the control trust will. Melinda, Martha, and Loretta were proposing that an independent third party oversee the trust for a specified period of time. They saw this as a way of strengthening governance. But according to Edward's side, the three women were using the crisis as leverage to change Ted's will, away from having just one set of hands on the wheel. This was untenable for Edward's camp, who were seeking a compromise that would reinstall Staffieri and have him work alongside Natale through the closing of the Shaw deal.

At times, some of the lawyers thought that a settlement might be within reach, although Lisus advised Edward not to take the deals that were on the table. He didn't believe that keeping Natale and his leadership team, who were fundamentally at odds with the controlling shareholder, was a good idea, nor did he wish to return for another day of negotiations, as the other side was suggesting. Lisus argued that the situation needed to be dealt with quickly— there was simply too much chaos, and too much at stake. Negative headlines were drawing attention to the company, the Competition Bureau had commenced its review, and the Shaw family wasn't happy about the feud.

To trigger the nuclear option, Edward's lawyers had to send instructions to Computershare, the transfer agent, by 4:30 p.m. Before they could do that, they needed to know whether Edward had the advisory committee's support. As the negotiations dragged on, Edward's lawyers became increasingly impatient with the other side, who seemed to be trying to run out the clock. If they didn't pull the trigger that day, Edward's legal team would have to redo the complex logistical process that had taken them roughly a week to set up.

Finally, the two sides reconvened in the main boardroom to take a vote. But as the minutes ticked by, they found themselves grappling with technical issues trying to connect Lisa Rogers and Toby Hull to the meeting remotely via Teams.

Loretta delivered a heartfelt speech to the advisory committee, urging them to consider her late husband's wishes. She spoke about the early days of Rogers, recalling how one year she and Ted drove around during an ice storm delivering coffees to the workers who were de-icing the towers. She believed that Ted had made it clear that the trust's chair had a duty to consult "earnestly and widely" with other family members, and to go through the "public gauntlet" of a shareholder meeting before removing or appointing directors. There were clear protocols in place—including the board's nominating committee, which existed solely to identify and review potential candidates—to ensure that such changes weren't made at the whim of a single individual. As Loretta saw it, Edward had disregarded those checks and balances when he set the wheels in motion to replace the five independent directors who had done exactly what the non-voting shareholders would have expected them to do.

But by that point, both sides were firmly entrenched in their positions. For the motion to pass, two-thirds of the advisory committee—or seven people—would have to vote in favour of constraining Edward's ability to exercise control over the company. Only four of them did—the three Rogers women, as well as Tory, who wanted more time to try to reach a settlement.

The retaliation was swift. Immediately after the trust meeting concluded, the board reconvened without Edward, Horn, or Lind present. Loretta personally put forward the motion to oust her son as chair, replacing him with John MacDonald. It was a difficult decision, but Loretta felt that her son needed to be stopped. The final straw had come when she learned—not from Edward but through a media report—that Edward was planning to replace the majority of the board's independent directors through a written resolution, without even consulting his mother or two sisters about the replacements.

MacDonald agreed to step into the role because he believed that having an independent director as chair was in the company's best interests, signalling a commitment to good governance. To him, the notion that he and the other directors were attempting to entrench themselves on the board was preposterous. Although Rogers directors were paid $110,000 annually for their roles, MacDonald later wrote in court documents that the dissident directors had nothing to gain from remaining in their positions or from engaging in a highly public battle with Edward. In fact, from a personal perspective, it was tempting to resign, MacDonald said. They didn't because they took their responsibilities as independent directors at a significant public company seriously. Still, the board meeting proved stressful for MacDonald, who was sitting so tensely in his chair that he cut off a nerve to his foot and had to visit the hospital.

Loretta, Martha, Melinda, and Tory looked exhausted as they filed out of Torys after more than nine hours of discussions. Martha emerged first, guiding her mother towards a black SUV limousine that had been parked outside the building all afternoon. Melinda followed several minutes later. "As my late father would say, the best is yet to come at Rogers," she told the *Globe*'s Andrew Willis, who was stationed outside. "This was a long, tough day."

However, the day was not over yet. Before they left the building, Edward's legal team had instructed Computershare to mail a written resolution to the company's registered Class A shareholders, triggering a chain of events that would land Rogers Communications in a bizarre and unprecedented stalemate.

According to Edward, the board of Rogers Communications was reconstituted the morning of October 22, when the family trust, through its trustee, the Bank of Nova Scotia Trust Company, executed a written shareholders' resolution. That resolution removed MacDonald, Peterson, Brooks, Jacob, and Clappison from the board, replacing them with real estate mogul Michael Cooper, famed dealmaker and former Brookfield Asset Management head Jack Cockwell, ex-Rogers executive Jan Innes, media executive Ivan Fecan, and forestry magnate John "Jake" Kerr. Interestingly, almost all of the new directors were publicly linked to Phil Lind; four of them were mentioned in his book, some several times. For instance, Lind had worked closely with Innes for years, and described Kerr, who he met on his first day at UBC, as a long-time friend. They attended events together, from the Kelowna Regatta to the exclusive Bohemian Grove summer retreat in Monte Rio, California. "Jake is a tremendous guy who's travelled similar paths as my own, socially and in business," Lind wrote.

Normally, public companies replace directors at their annual meetings—or, if they wish to act sooner, at special shareholder meetings convened with advance notice. This gives shareholders the opportunity to consider the candidates and, if they have the power to do so, vote on them. But corporate law in British Columbia, where Rogers was incorporated, was unique in allowing for such changes to be made through a written resolution, as long as it was signed by shareholders who held at least 66.67 per cent of the company's voting shares. As the chair of the Rogers Control Trust, Edward controlled 97.5 per cent of the votes.

The company issued a press release expressing concern that Edward would try to make such a fundamental change to its governance structure in this unprecedented manner. As far as the telecom's leadership knew, no Canadian company had ever used this mechanism to overhaul its board before. That didn't appear to faze Edward and his allies. That evening, he, Lind, and Horn called for a meeting of the new board to take place that Sunday at 4 p.m. in the main boardroom. Its purpose was to reinstate Edward as chair and appoint directors to the board's various committees.

However, after conferring with lawyers, the company deemed Edward's resolution invalid. "Accordingly, the board of directors of Rogers, including its independent directors, remains unchanged," MacDonald said in a statement.

That view was shared by Melinda, who argued that her brother had miscalculated his legal position. There was no precedent that allowed him to simply fire five independent directors and replace them with whoever he pleased on a whim, she told the media. Such changes could only be made at a shareholder meeting, with proper notice and disclosure to the company's shareholders, including those who held the non-voting Class B shares.

Declaring the resolution invalid appeared to be little more than a delay tactic. After all, no one was questioning Edward's ability to make the changes that he was seeking at a shareholder meeting. But that process would take many months, according to Melinda's lawyer, Walied Soliman. "Any assertion that the independent directors of Rogers could be removed by a written resolution is simply false at law," Soliman stated. "The board of RCI remains constituted exactly the same as it was yesterday."

After a series of strange and dramatic twists, the telecom and media giant found itself in an odd predicament. The company had two boards, and no one could say for certain which was the real one. A source close to the company termed the situation "Schrödinger's board," in reference to the famous quantum physics thought experiment known as Schrödinger's cat. "Rogers Chairman Fires Board for Firing Him for Firing CEO" read the headline on a story by prominent American financial columnist Matt Levine that captured the absurdity of the situation.

The management team, meanwhile, was becoming concerned that the governance chaos was disrupting operations. During a meeting that Friday, multiple members of the eleven-person leadership team said they were prepared to leave if Edward got his way, according to two people present. That prompted a response from

Edward, who, despite earlier plans to purge much of the management ranks, now said he was open to working with the company's leadership—provided that they were committed to the business and to closing the Shaw deal. "If Mr. Natale is no longer committed to our company, its employees, and our shareholders, he should resign and we will turn the page," Edward said. He also took issue with the company's switching law firms from Fasken to Goodmans, who had advised Natale in a personal capacity regarding his resignation arrangements. But Goodmans denied the existence of any conflict, noting that those negotiations were completed.

It had come to the point where both sides were in open warfare, exchanging increasingly harsh words in duelling statements to the press. But the harshest words of all came not via the newspapers' front pages, but through the Twitter account belonging to Martha Rogers.

Martha couldn't sleep that night. She had the telecom's 24,000 employees on her mind. So she did what any insomnia-stricken second-generation billionaire embroiled in a bitter corporate governance battle with her older brother would do. She logged onto Twitter and, beginning at 3:19 a.m., released a torrent of criticism aimed squarely at Edward and his "old boys club Trump cabal." She didn't care if Navigator, hordes of lawyers, or Trump supporters came after her. "We'll spend every penny defending the company, employees & Ted's wishes, nothing you can do will deter us," she wrote. "Bring. It. On." The only way to stop her was by "ceasing, desisting & stepping down." She had receipts from the past twenty-plus years, she said cryptically, as she vowed to reveal the truth about her brother's "Trump scandal"—even if it meant blowing up her own life in the process. She was driven by what she saw as the sole reason her father had put her on the board in the first place: to serve as a check and balance and ensure that "nothing this insane" ever happened. "This is for you Dad," she said.

Joe Natale and the three Rogers women boycotted the Sunday meeting. They felt that attending what Martha had deemed a "pretend 'board meeting'" and a "waste of time" would have only legitimized it. But that didn't stop Martha from voicing her opinions about her brother's "play date" with his "Old Guard puppet masters" Lind and Horn. Her father had trusted them to do the right thing, but money, power, and control had gone to their heads, she tweeted. "Like in a bad movie, Ed and his old guard literally meet in dark boardrooms. All men. All white. All old. They think they are masters of the universe instead of thinking about the impact their instability is causing tens of thousands of people." Ted would be "so disappointed" to see how his former lieutenants were destroying his company.

Edward found the tweets childish and embarrassing, both for the company and for his sister. That afternoon, he regained his title when his board of hand-picked loyalists appointed him chair. This was, according to Martha, about as valid as if her brother had appointed himself the King of England. Robert Gemmell, meanwhile, was given the role of lead director.

But the *other* board was still insistent that nothing had changed. MacDonald, Peterson, Brooks, Jacob, and Clappison remained duly elected directors, they said in a statement supported by the Rogers women. "No other group of individuals has any authority to purport to act as the Board of Directors of Rogers Communications Inc.," it read. Loretta, meanwhile, urged her son to back down.

Edward had repeatedly stated that he was acting in the company's best interests. Gemmell agreed. He believed that the board needed to be independent of management in order for the company to be run effectively. But Edward's mother called the path that her son was on "misguided," accusing him of putting his own interests before those of the company's employees, customers, and shareholders. "He should stop immediately, as his behaviour simply serves to underscore his seemingly wanton disregard for good governance," she said in a statement provided to the press. But while Loretta's words were biting, Edward didn't believe that she really meant them. He was convinced that his mother was unwell, and that she wasn't the one responsible for the actions that were being taken or the statements that were being written. In Edward's view, it was Natale who was driving the whole thing. However, sources close to Loretta challenged the notion that she was a passive observer in the family dispute, as well as any suggestion that she was experiencing cognitive decline. They described the matriarch as mentally sharp and "intimately involved" in the conflict, instructing advisors on how to proceed. According to one source, Edward had borrowed money from his mother for both personal and business reasons, which caused problems between them. However, a source in Edward's camp disputed this account, calling it "fiction." Still, despite the tensions that were spilling out into public view, Edward and his mother continued to speak to one another during the feud, engaging in what one source described as "lovely conversations."

Meanwhile, the legal stalemate continued. The company's law firm, Goodmans, put Edward's board on notice that anyone relying on the consent resolution to conduct Rogers business would be held responsible for any damage to the company or its shareholders. "The unseemly threat at the end of your letter is noted," Jonathan Lisus retorted. "Have you communicated the same message to the former directors of RCI who were removed on Friday and have chosen to publicly obstruct the business and affairs of the company? For convenience, we have copied their counsel."

On the evening of October 24, after the first meeting of his new board, Edward announced that he would be taking the matter to court. He would petition the Supreme Court of British Columbia to sanction his move to replace the five dissident directors without holding a meeting.

Ken McEwan, one of Edward's lawyers, urged the telecom to back an expedited hearing in a letter to the company's lawyers.

The uncertainty was hurting Rogers' share price, triggering down-grades from analysts, and prompting multiple inquiries from the Ontario Securities Commission. "Obviously it would not be in the best interests of Rogers Communications to have the regulator consider it necessary to intervene," he added, without specifying what the securities watchdog was inquiring about.

The B.C. court filing resulted in a trove of documents being released, as Edward and his opponents laid out, in painstaking detail, conflicting versions of the events that had transpired in the preceding weeks. Edward defended his actions by taking aim at Natale's performance, noting that while the CEO had gotten "some positive reviews," the company was lagging its peers, missing its budgets, and watching its stock price stagnate. The firing was not, he claimed in a sworn affidavit, an action that he had taken unilaterally; rather, he had raised his long-standing concerns about Natale at four separate meetings of the Rogers Control Trust, and all but one of the directors—Peterson—had voted in favour of Natale's retirement before the majority of the directors inexplicably reversed their positions in the span of forty-eight hours. "My mother Loretta and sister Martha in particular expressed the firm view that Mr. Natale had had more than four years to prove himself and that it was time for a change," he wrote. Martha countered on Twitter that "Ed's always been a fan of specious claims. Like Trump won the 2020 election."

John MacDonald submitted his own affidavit, in which he stated plainly, "I do not agree with many of the statements in the [Edward] Rogers affidavit, many of which are simply factually inaccurate." Loretta, meanwhile, accused her son of misleading her about Natale's performance and acting against his father's expressed wishes, which were contained within a memorandum that had also been filed in court. But Edward believed that his actions were in line with what Ted would have wanted. "Before his death, my father frequently told me he believed in the importance of consultation and discussion, but emphasized the need to have one final decision maker," he wrote. The filings illustrate the problem with trying to run a company in accordance with the wishes of a dead man—namely, that surviving family members can have wildly differing interpretations of those wishes. Both sides in the legal battle tried to bolster their position by quoting from the memorandum as if it were the Bible.

Other documents among the mountains of evidence filed in court included minutes of board meetings, a selection of Martha's most inflammatory tweets, and private family documents such as Ted's will that were made public for the first time. One of the exhibits submitted by Edward's side—his September 22 presentation to the board about the company's lagging performance—created an awkward situation for Dave Fuller. On a slide entitled "Next steps," Edward revealed that after appointing Staffieri as CEO and Dépatie as head of cable, he intended to promote Fuller—Natale's most trusted, long-standing ally—to president and chief operating officer of wireless. This, of course, made it appear as if Fuller was a willing participant in Edward's scheme. To set the record straight, Fuller submitted his own affidavit, in which he threw his support behind Natale. Firstly, Fuller noted, the presentation that Edward had publicly disclosed contained twenty competitively sensitive data points that, in Fuller's view, should have been redacted. Secondly, neither Edward nor any of his associates had spoken to him about the president and COO of wireless role. If they had, he would have declined it. Natale was the only reason he had joined Rogers and he had no interest in working for any other CEO. "I have worked with Joe Natale for over 20 years. I consider him to be a leader of outstanding capability, integrity, and quality. There is no doubt in my mind that he is the best possible CEO for RCI both prior to, and after, the Shaw acquisition. Anyone who suggests otherwise does not understand his capabilities or our business."

Meanwhile, the chaos enveloping the company was expanding. Someone had leaked an explosive story to the *Toronto Star*, alleging that, over the summer, Edward had attempted to sabotage plans to keep Masai Ujiri at the helm of the Toronto Raptors franchise—which, during the sports executive's tenure, had won the NBA championship. (Edward had celebrated that 2019 victory by purchasing NBA championship rings for the company's directors.) Bell and Larry Tanenbaum, MLSE's other owners, were ready to lock down Ujiri, who had boosted the franchise's value by $500 million and was being pursued by other sports franchises. But, according to three sources who spoke to the *Star*, Edward didn't think that Ujiri was worth the $15 million salary that Bell and Tanenbaum were willing to pay him, and believed that the team could be managed without Ujiri, by general manager Bobby Webster. Edward denied the story, telling the paper that negotiations can "test both sides" and that he had the "utmost respect" for Ujiri. Regardless, the story immediately drew the ire of Raptors fans; the championship win had turned Ujiri into one of the most beloved men in the city.

The Ujiri incident wasn't the first time that Edward had made headlines for fumbling a sports negotiation. His 2014 attempt to replace Blue Jays president Paul Beeston with Chicago White Sox executive vice-president Kenny Williams was characterized by the *Globe*'s sports columnist Cathal Kelly as "more slapstick than cunning." Edward phoned White Sox owner Jerry Reinsdorf to ask for his blessing to hire Williams, apparently without realizing that Reinsdorf and Beeston were best friends. "Attempting to nickel and dime Raptors boss Masai Ujiri was even less smooth," wrote Kelly.

On October 29, three days before Edward and his family's telecom empire were set to square off in a Vancouver courtroom, Vidéotron sued Rogers for $850.3 million, alleging that Rogers was attempting to deliberately sabotage their long-standing network sharing pact. Meanwhile, Bell and Telus, who were already lobbying the telecom regulator to block the transfer of Shaw's broadcasting assets, were plotting ways to leverage the chaos and throw another wrench into the takeover.

Martha continued her onslaught of personal attacks against Edward and his allies. In a series of tweets bearing hashtags such as #EdRogersSaga and #OldGuardDown, she accused her brother of committing "elder abuse" by preying on their mother, and of throwing "perpetual tantrums" whenever he didn't get his way. She also criticized Tory's claim that he was mediating the dispute in his spare time ("Actually no, that's not the truth, John. We were there 9-10 hours, outside of you leaving for 45 mins to do a press conference.") and took aim at Edward's crisis firm, Navigator, who she accused of trolling her online. (A Navigator spokesperson calls Martha's allegation "baseless," saying that the firm "never undertook personal or online attacks of any kind.")

The conflict was clearly weighing on Martha, and on October 28, she once again found herself unable to sleep. "Seize the day," she tweeted shortly after 5 a.m., adding, "Navigator, I hope I'm not tweeting too early for you boys. I'd hate to miss out on today's onslaught." Then, over the course of several tweets, she revealed that she had been victimized for the past three years by an alleged stalker, who had been lobbing death threats her way whenever the company was featured in the news. "Yup, Ed's Trump scandal brought him out again," she wrote, adding that she spoke to Horn about it "numerous times after as the deafening online hate conflated the rest of us to Ed." Over time she began to isolate herself, she added. "Alan encouraged this for 'my safety.'"

While some Twitter users expressed support for Martha, including telecom consultant Eamon Hoey, who praised her for being a "strong voice for governance," others called her tweets embarrassing, or suggested that they were having the opposite effect of the one she had intended. While Martha saw herself as standing up for employees and non-voting shareholders, some people accused her of hurting the company and its investors by airing her family's dirty laundry. One day in early November, she simply tweeted a list of years, with no context or explanation: "2007, 2009 & 2019." A few days later she asked rhetorically, "Who wants to talk about Ed & Suzanne's Trump play date?" Later still she asked her brother whether he was "ready to come out from Navigator's skirt," adding, "You've spent a lifetime behind mom's."

But the most biting words were contained in a tweet linking to a *Financial Post* article by journalist Robert Brehl. Fifteen years earlier, as a seventy-fifth birthday present for their dad, the four Rogers kids had hired Brehl to help Ted write his memoir. Brehl's article in the *Post*, which was headlined "How Ted Rogers planned for family conflict and set up rules to resolve it," described what he had learned through conversations with the company's founder about the structure of the Rogers Control Trust. Martha retweeted the story with a one-liner: "Ted knew what his son was."

SIXTEEN

ROGERS V. ROGERS

Courtroom 67 is housed within a large concrete and glass structure situated in the centre of downtown Vancouver. The high-tech and high-security courtroom was built in 2012, at a cost of nearly $3 million, to house one of the four high-profile gang-related criminal trials clogging the city's justice system that year. On November 1, 2021, the red-carpeted room, with its small spectator area divided, for safety reasons, from the main courtroom with Plexiglas, was the venue for a very different kind of case—the showdown between Edward Rogers and the management team of the telecom bearing his family name.

More than a dozen lawyers passed through the metal detectors and filed into the courtroom for the hearing of Edward Rogers v. Rogers Communications Inc., or Rogers v. Rogers for short. Inside, under the harsh glare of fluorescent lighting, a screen displayed a live feed of the nearby overflow room, where reporters sat in chairs spaced several feet apart as a pandemic precaution. Others across the country dialled in via phone to follow the unprecedented case. As far as anyone was aware, no shareholder of a major public company had ever attempted to use a written resolution to recon-stitute the majority of its board.

The high-stakes governance battle had renewed long-standing calls for stricter regulations governing dual-class share structures. It was widely known that holders of non-voting shares at compa-nies such as Rogers had no say over changes to the board. But the dramatic internecine battle at Rogers, which had dominated the front pages of newspapers for weeks, had made that fact much more salient. The Canadian Coalition for Good Governance (CCGG), an organization representing major institutional investors, argued that stock exchanges should attach conditions to dual-class share com-panies, such as sunset provisions that would either dissolve the structure after a period of time or allow shareholders to periodically vote on whether or not to maintain it. "You may have bought into Rogers under Ted Rogers. But the reality is that situations change and there should be an opportunity for shareholders to reassess what they bought into—and they didn't sign up for the offspring run-ning the company, most likely," Catherine McCall, CCGG's executive director, said during an event about corporate governance at Rogers.

Others, such as the Shareholder Association for Research and Education, a shareholder rights advocacy group known by the acro-nym SHARE, went even further, arguing that the construct should be eliminated entirely, with existing dual-class structures phased out over a period of time. "I'm sympathetic to the idea that some-one has built up a company, been that innovative owner, and that for a certain period you probably do need to protect that control, in the early stages of a company," says Kevin Thomas, the non-profit's CEO. The problem is that, over time, "the insiders start to take advan-tage of special perks and indulgences and feel that they're owed something beyond the reward for their initial innovation."

Those on the other side of the debate, including David Beatty, academic director at the David and Sharon Johnston Centre for

Corporate Governance Innovation, caution that banning dual-class shares would push technology companies, who tend to favour the structure, away from listing on Canadian exchanges. Family-controlled companies outperform widely held ones because of their longer-term focus, argues Beatty.

Regardless, the case in front of B.C. Supreme Court Justice Shelley Fitzpatrick was not an examination of the merits of dual-class shares, according to Ken McEwan. A balding man with grey-ing facial hair and icy blue eyes, McEwan was accompanied by two other lawyers from his firm, Emily Kirkpatrick and William Stransky—for whom the long hours spent camped out in the Fasken lobby had seemingly paid off—as well as Jonathan Lisus and several of his colleagues.

According to McEwan, the case hinged on a "simple and narrow" legal question: Can the person who controls 97.5 per cent of the company's voting shares use the "consent resolution" powers under the B.C. Business Corporations Act to replace directors on the board of Rogers? He posited that they could. "We are here as a shareholder exercising clear shareholder rights," he told the court.

The B.C. Business Corporations Act, which came into force in 2004, contained a number of changes intended to ease the administrative burden on provincially incorporated businesses and give them more flexibility. One of the ways in which the province's corporate laws differed from those in the rest of the country was in allowing for directors to be replaced through a written resolution. "I'm sure the Toronto types are discovering how unique we are," quipped Justice Fitzpatrick.

The telecom, represented by David Conklin and a Vancouver-based litigator named Stephen Schachter, argued that the kind of changes Edward was attempting to make required him to call a shareholder meeting. The idea was that doing so would offer more time for public discourse about Edward's plans, giving minority shareholders the opportunity to vote for or against those plans by buying or selling shares. To make their case, lawyers cited the company's publicly disclosed governance practices, its articles of incorporation, and the memorandum of Ted's wishes. "When you're changing five independent directors, effectively changing control at the board level, it is, we would submit, a fundamental change to the company," said Conklin, the bespectacled, brown-haired Goodmans lawyer. "It's a change that shareholders and stakeholders have a direct interest in, and a right to be fully informed about. It is not a private company."

The company's position hinged largely on four words contained within Rogers' articles of incorporation, which state that "the shareholders may by ordinary resolution remove any director from office and the vacancy created by such removal may be filled at the same meeting." Schachter argued that "at the same meeting" meant, quite simply, that there had to be an actual meeting. The company's lawyers also noted that in his memorandum of wishes, Ted had anticipated precisely the type of situation that had transpired. Should the company's board ever find itself at odds with the best interests of the Rogers family, as represented by the control trust chair, Ted expected that the chair would go through the "public gauntlet" of a shareholder meeting to appoint new directors.

Finally, they relied on an independent opinion from Garfield Emerson, the former Rogers chairman who specialized in corporate governance. Emerson wrote that reconstituting the board through a written resolution flew in the face of best practices for the governance of publicly traded companies. Edward's actions had deprived the company's shareholders—including the holders of non-voting Class B shares and the small minority of Class A shareholders who weren't Rogers family members—of their right to ask questions and voice their concerns about the proposed changes. Nor was it only shareholders to whom the company was accountable. Other stakeholders—including employees, customers, and creditors, as well as federal regulators and stock exchanges—were also impacted by the lack of transparency and accountability from the company's controlling shareholder, Emerson argued.

Edward's lawyers posited that Emerson's report should be ignored, in part because he had left the board after a falling-out with the company's founder. This, they claimed, raised questions about his independence. The exact circumstances surrounding Emerson's departure from the board were in dispute. In *High Wire Act*, Caroline Van Hasselt reports that Ted asked Emerson to step down as chairman over an incident involving a corporate governance failing relating to the audit committee that the founder wanted to sweep under the rug. But in his memoir, *Relentless*, Ted called it "simplistic" to suggest that Emerson's departure was related to a single incident. In any case, McEwan argued that corporate governance was "irrelevant and beside the point."

If the judge sided with Edward, it would give him unfettered powers to reconstitute the board in this manner whenever he pleased, the company's lawyers argued. He could change his mind in six months and once again replace the independent directors and the management team. "He cannot thumb his nose at due process," Schachter said. "This is a public company. It's subject to public processes, and a walk through the Act, as my friend has done, to say he can do whatever he wants, on whatever terms he wishes, should be rejected."

Whatever the decision was going to be, Justice Fitzpatrick believed that it needed to be made quickly. "I recognize the urgency of the situation," she told the parties. The internal power struggle had attracted extensive media attention and hurt the company's share price. It had also created uncertainty for Rogers at a time when stability and proper governance were particularly critical for the company.

That day, BCE, along with two advocacy groups, sent letters to the CRTC, urging the regulator to delay its hearing into the Shaw takeover, which was scheduled to take place in Ottawa later that month. The telecom watchdog was reviewing whether Rogers should be allowed to acquire Shaw's broadcasting distribution business, including satellite TV service Shaw Direct and cable networks in British Columbia, Alberta, Saskatchewan, Manitoba, and northern Ontario. The two groups—an Ottawa-based consumer advocacy called the Public Interest Advocacy Centre, and a non-profit called the National Pensioners Federation that advocated for elderly Canadians—argued that the confusion over who was really in charge of Rogers made it impossible to properly conduct that hearing.

"The CRTC cannot be certain that the officers on the Rogers panel that will be answering its questions at the hearing, or the board of directors that is instructing them, will actually be the persons in charge of executing the proposed transaction," the advocates wrote. There was, therefore, no guarantee that any assurances the executives made would be respected by the telecom's future leadership. Even if the case were resolved quickly, the judge's decision could be appealed, stretching out the uncertainty over which of the duelling boards had the authority to oversee the company's affairs for potentially several months.

Bell expressed support for the request in a separate letter, calling the situation unprecedented. "To our knowledge, the commission has never before been asked to approve a change of control transaction in circumstances where the legal control of the acquirer is itself uncertain." That alone should be enough reason to delay the hearing, the telecom argued. Telus echoed that sentiment in its own letter, which it sent to the regulator the following day.

Rogers and Shaw were dismissive of these requests, with the latter labelling them as disingenuous and driven by the rival telecoms' own competitive interests. There was no dispute between members of the Rogers family about the importance of the Shaw deal, Rogers stated in its response to the CRTC, promising that all commitments it made to the regulator would be honoured regardless of who wound up in charge. "Rogers' and Shaw's commitment to this transaction has never wavered," the filing read. The hearing, the cable companies insisted, should proceed as planned.

It was against this backdrop—as Rogers' competitors tried to throw a wrench into the pending regulatory hearing for a deal that both factions of the warring family agreed was critical to the telecom's future—that Justice Fitzpatrick decided to move swiftly. She would issue a ruling at 2 p.m. on Friday, she told the parties, before adjourning the hearing.

Lisus was feeling confident when the hearing reconvened in courtroom 67 four days later. In fact, in the preceding days, he had told Walied Soliman that he was certain that his side was going to win. Soliman, who had attended the November 1 hearing as a spectator, didn't agree, although there would have been good reason for him to trust Lisus's judgement. After all, Lisus had just helped Soliman win a victory in an unrelated legal matter—his defamation suit against the online commentator who had accused him of supporting extremist terrorist Islamic organizations. On October 21, while Lisus and Soliman were on opposite sides of the fractious family and boardroom battle at Rogers, an Ontario Superior Court judge had ruled in Soliman's favour in the libel suit, awarding him $500,000 in damages. The two men, who were camped out at Torys with their respective clients that day, briefly stepped outside for a quick hug, then went back to fighting.

Lisus and Soliman had tried to negotiate a deal ahead of Justice Fitzpatrick's Friday ruling. Melinda had proposed a compromise that she believed would bring peace to the company for at least five years, while keeping Edward in his role of chair of the trust, ensuring an orderly board transition at Rogers Communications, instituting a governance review, and giving trustees the ability to annually review director appointments. Melinda's side felt it was a good offer for both sides, and it won the blessing of both John Tory and Alan Horn, one person said. But according to a source on Edward's side, the proposal went against both Ted's will and good governance practices and had "absolutely no support." The offer died when both Edward and Horn failed to show up to an advisory committee meeting convened just hours before the judge's ruling. It would be up to the B.C. court to settle the issue of the telecom's duelling boards.

Justice Fitzpatrick had reviewed, and then subsequently disregarded, much of the voluminous evidence that had been filed, particularly those documents that, in her view, related more to "family squabbles" than the legal issue at hand. These squabbles, she wrote in her detailed reasons, were "an interesting backdrop to this dispute that would be more in keeping with a Shakespearean drama." They had lended a voyeuristic element to the dispute, giving Canadians a window into the lives of an extraordinarily wealthy family. But they had no bearing in determining the narrow legal issue that was in front of her, she noted. "At best, they are a distraction."

Nor was she concerned with Natale's performance or Edward's alleged meddling with the company's management. The debate between the two sides over corporate governance was interesting, "but, in my view, it is not one that I need wade into." Ted's memorandum of wishes was interesting as well, but irrelevant because it had been drafted after the company had adopted its articles of incorporation in May 2004. The singular legal issue that Justice Fitzpatrick was concerned with was whether the so-called consent resolution was "valid and effective in accordance with the Act."

She had determined that it was. "RCI argues strenuously that Edward is 'thumbing his nose' at the proper process and that he improperly seeks to exert rights 'with the stroke of a pen.'" But as Justice Fitzpatrick saw it, "Edward has closely followed the strictures of the articles, as informed by the act where appropriate. This can only be described as respecting the process, not disregarding it." Accordingly, she was granting the order that Edward was seeking, as well as legal costs. Rogers Communications would have to correct its register of directors, striking out the names of the five dissidents and replacing them with Edward's new appointees.

The ruling revealed an uncomfortable truth: that at the end of the day, one person—Edward Rogers—held ultimate control over the telecom and media giant. And as long as Edward had the support of the majority of the advisory committee, there was virtually nothing that the company's board, or his mother or sisters, could do to stop him.

There was, however, still another matter to discuss. Schachter wanted Justice Fitzpatrick to stay the decision for a few days, arguing that if it were to take effect immediately, it might preclude his clients from seeking an appeal. "Given the order that you have made, and given that it results in a reconstitution of the board, unless and until the appeal is allowed, there's a serious risk that the appeal would be rendered moot by actions of the new directors."

But Justice Fitzpatrick wasn't so sure. "I'm not really understanding how it would be," she responded.

The management of a public company is accountable to its board. And the problem for Schachter's clients was that as soon as the judge's ruling took effect, the telecom's reconstituted board could simply instruct management to abandon the appeal. Worse, they could immediately fire Natale and his management team, as Edward and his allies had been planning to do. "To ensure that does not happen, it's necessary for us to have a stay of your order, to at least get us into the Court of Appeal," Schachter implored.

But McEwan assured the court that no such steps would be taken. He urged the judge to deny the request for a stay. The confusion regarding the composition of the telecom's board had become untenable, he argued.

"The balance of convenience does favour certainty here," Justice Fitzpatrick noted as she rejected the request. "The order will be effective today."

Melinda, Martha, and Loretta swiftly denounced the ruling, calling it a "black eye for good governance and shareholder rights" that set a "dangerous new precedent" by allowing a company's independent directors to be removed from the board "with the stroke of a pen."

"The company now faces a very real prospect of management upheaval and a prolonged period of uncertainty, at perhaps the worst possible time," they said in a statement provided to the press.

Edward also issued a statement that night, one that left many observers puzzled. After waging a successful war to oust the five directors who had tried to stop him from firing Natale, Edward appeared to have suddenly changed his mind about the chief executive. "Mr. Natale remains CEO and a director of Rogers Communications and has the board's support. Our focus must be on the business, a return to stability, and closing our transformational merger with Shaw Communications."

He went on to say that his family's disagreements were not unlike those experienced by every other family. "I am hopeful we will resolve those differences privately. . . . I know every member of our family wants the brightest future for Rogers Communications."

For a moment it looked like maybe—just maybe—everybody was going to get along.

SEVENTEEN

PINKY SWEAR

On the Sunday evening after the court ruling, Natale and his lawyer, Dale Lastman, rode an elevator up to the twenty-seventh floor of the boxy beige tower at the corner of King and York. After walking through a set of glass doors, they took their seats at a rectangular oak table in a small boardroom housed within the law offices of Lax O'Sullivan Lisus Gottlieb. Sitting across from them were Edward, Alan Horn, and Jonathan Lisus.

Edward had tried to meet with Natale the day before, to see whether there was a path forward that would allow the telecom's senior leadership team to remain in place until the Shaw deal closed. But the chief executive of the company that Edward was now firmly back in control of was eluding him. Natale, who was trying to figure out his next steps, was taking hours to respond to Edward's texts, and when his replies did finally arrive, they were curt. He wasn't available to meet until Sunday evening, he'd told Edward, while he and his senior leadership team met with their lawyers. Lisus had suggested contacting Lisa Damiani, the telecom's chief legal and regulatory officer, but she was also being coy.

Brad Shaw, meanwhile, was keen to put the conflict in the rear-view mirror, particularly in light of how Bell and Telus had tried to leverage the chaos into a regulatory delay. Around 7 p.m. on Saturday, he had fired off an email marked "Urgent" to Edward and Natale. Contained within it was a confidential letter addressed to the CEO and the chairman of the company to which he had entrusted his family's legacy.

Brad urged Natale not to appeal Justice Fitzpatrick's decision. Shaw had reviewed the court decision and believed it to be sound. "Now is the time to move forward, not perpetuate uncertainty," he wrote.

His second request was for continuity in the management team, an ask that was not dissimilar from the one that he had previously denied making. There was a considerable amount of work remaining to consummate the takeover and integrate the two companies. Brad was encouraged by Edward's statement that Natale and his leadership team had the board's support, and he hoped that it would allow Natale and his team to remain at the company and focus on the takeover. "Let's get this deal done so we can deliver on its promise of transformational change in our industry, for the benefit of all Canadians," he concluded, a statement so grandiose that it read more like a political campaign than a correspondence between corporate leaders.

For Joe Natale to remain at the company's helm, he needed certain guarantees from Edward. When they finally met in the boardroom at Lisus's law firm on Sunday, Natale came armed with a document. It laid out a list of five conditions under which he would stay on as CEO. The first, which was titled "commitment," detailed a series of promises by Natale and his leadership team to steady the organization after weeks of upheaval, and focus on completing the acquisition of Shaw—including securing the required regulatory approvals and planning for the integration. They promised to conduct detailed orientation sessions to help onboard the new directors, as well. "The CEO and executive leadership team will focus their attention, and the attention of the organization, on the future, not the past," one bullet point read.

While the first item was innocuous and seemed to be in everybody's best interests, the second was bound to stir up controversy. Considering the breakdown in his relationship with Edward, Natale was seeking a number of commitments aimed at protecting his authority as CEO, including a stipulation that Edward would function as a non-executive chair. Hiring and firing decisions would be made by management, and a two-person committee would be put in place to mediate disagreements between Edward and Natale. The board was not to engage directly with Rogers employees, save for members of the executive leadership team, without Natale's approval. The governance review that the previous board had agreed to undertake was to continue in a timely manner, and Robert Dépatie was not to join the management team. Staffieri, meanwhile, would have no role at the company—not as a director, an employee, or even a consultant.

The third principle, titled "choice," stipulated that Natale was willing to stay in the role at least until the Shaw deal closed, or June 15, 2022—whichever came first. If he were fired before June 15, any member of his executive leadership team would be given the option of leaving the company with their full severance, as if they were terminated without cause. The fourth dealt with the management team's compensation. In addition to honouring existing agreements, Natale thought it would be wise if Edward considered, at his own discretion, sweetening their compensation packages. Lastly, point five referred to a press release that would be drafted to demonstrate to the world that the board and the management team were on the same page.

Edward's side had expected Natale to accept the olive branch that had been extended to him when Edward issued a statement expressing support for Natale as CEO. They felt that Natale was in no position to be making demands about how the company should be run after the judge had handed Edward a clear victory. Lisus told Natale to reflect on the situation, and both sides left the meeting without reaching a resolution.

Earlier that day, Lisus had written to the Goodmans lawyers, Lastman and Conklin. Natale and his management team had been advised that there was a decent chance of Justice Fitzpatrick's ruling being overturned on appeal, according to a source briefed about those discussions. But with a new board in place—one that wasn't in favour of an appeal—they found themselves in a tricky spot. "It cannot be disputed that the best interests of RCI lie in heeding Shaw's strong concern that pursuing an appeal is disruptive to the consummation of the transaction," Lisus wrote. He asked the lawyers to confirm by 5 p.m. that the appeal would be dropped. If they didn't, Edward would ask Fasken to review the judge's reasons and provide the board with an independent opinion on the viability of an appeal, he cautioned. That evening, the telecom issued a one-line statement: "Rogers Communications Inc. announced today that it will not seek an appeal of last week's British Columbia Supreme Court ruling."

Natale had a message for the executives gathered in a conference room at Hotel X, a luxurious hotel on the Lake Ontario waterfront. The company had gone ahead with its annual vice-presidents-and-up offsite event, scheduled for two days in early November, despite the uncertainty hanging over Natale and his leadership team following the court ruling. Natale kicked off the session by throwing a picture of Mark Twain up on screen. It was accompanied by the famous quote "The reports of my death are greatly exaggerated."

The image was intended to be an icebreaker, and it drew a laugh from the crowd. Not surprisingly, the Staffieri allies in attendance were unimpressed. To them, the stunt came off as arrogant and premature.

For the first several hours of the event, an external consultant spoke to the attendees about managing stress. The session had been arranged months earlier in the context of dealing with the mental challenges of the pandemic, although by the time the off-site was underway, there was an entirely new crisis for the company's leadership to stress about. While many in the audience found the session to be helpful, one of Natale's opponents described it as a "waste of time" that should have been focused on the Shaw takeover instead.

The two-day affair probably served the opposite purpose of what was intended: it widened the growing division between the company's two factions—Natale's New Guard, and the dwindling Old Guard of Edward loyalists and Staffieri recruits—rather than helping to find common ground between them. Natale was a leader who fostered loyalty among his team, and throughout the two days he received an outpouring of support from many of his executives. During that evening's dinner, some of his allies went up to microphones placed around the room to express their respect and admiration for the chief executive. The Old Guard found this display distasteful and unnecessary. The following day, when the attendees were divided into teams, Dan Golberg, the brash, outspoken senior vice-president of strategy and corporate development who Natale had brought over from Telus, barrelled into a room full of reserved, buttoned-down finance executives, many of whom were loyal to Staffieri, loudly proclaiming, "Joe's the man!" according to one person present.

While tensions were playing out within the company, Martha Rogers walked out of Jong Young Flower Market with an assortment of brightly coloured orchids and headed towards Mount Pleasant Cemetery. For years, Martha had been writing her dad messages by arranging flowers in the grass in front of the tombstone that marked his final resting place. She used orchids because of how long they lasted, and typically chose blues and purples, Ted's favoured hues. Jasmine, the woman who ran the flower shop at Avenue Road and Davenport, had come to know her over the years as the girl who always bought orchids for the cemetery.

Occasionally, Martha posted photos of her arrangements to Instagram. Other times she simply sent them to her mom, her cousin Carolyn, and her aunt Ann "Rooney" Graham Calderisi before she passed away in 2016. On that day in early November 2021, however, with the leadership of her family's telecom empire still in limbo, Martha decided to disseminate her message more broadly, via Twitter. The photo that she uploaded depicted an assortment of yellow, purple, blue, and pale pink blooms arranged in front of a monument inscribed with the Rogers family crest. They spelled out, "We will fight for you!"

A week after their initial meeting on November 7, Natale, Edward, Horn, and their respective lawyers gathered again, this time at Goodmans' offices on the thirty-fourth floor of the Bay Adelaide Centre. Edward had spoken with Natale twice in the intervening week—once on November 9, then again that Friday, November 12. He had urged Natale to pick up the olive branch and to stay on as CEO through the close of Shaw. But he told him he couldn't support the principles document. Rogers would need an exceptionally experienced finance team to raise the capital needed to fund the $20 billion takeover, Edward said. He believed that Staffieri, with his long history at Rogers and the respect he commanded at the financial institutions, was the right man for the job. Bury the hatchet and work with Staffieri to get the deal done, he implored.

But Natale made it clear to the chairman that he didn't support Staffieri's return. He told Edward that he would reflect on the situation and get back to him.

Now, at Goodmans, Natale popped open his silver Mac laptop and began reading from the screen. He was willing to stick around, but he could never work with Staffieri again, he said. If that wasn't acceptable to Edward and the board then he would resign. When Natale was finished, Edward, Horn, and Lisus scurried off to huddle in a separate room. Lisus was insistent that there was no way that keeping Natale in the role would work. When they returned, they told him that they would accept his resignation. They agreed to work together on the terms of Natale's exit package and the wording of the press release announcing his departure.

The parties shook hands and parted ways. Lisus remarked to Edward and Horn that he was pleased with how the meeting had gone. To him, it seemed a done deal and that this was the logical conclusion. Horn, though, cautioned Lisus not to get ahead of himself. Natale had previously shaken his hand, too, after negotiating the terms of his departure, only to later renege on his word. It would turn out to be an astute warning.

The next day, Lisus wrote to Dale Lastman, emphasizing the need to move "with alacrity" in finalizing Natale's exit and the communications surrounding it. Lastman agreed and said he would wait to hear from Fasken, which would be helping with the arrangements. But when Faskens reached out, Goodmans was unresponsive. Late that afternoon, the firm advised that Natale was unavailable because his father-in-law was unwell.

Then, on Tuesday morning, Lisus received an email from the Goodmans lawyer David Conklin. At first, he thought it was a joke. "Mr. Natale asked that we advise you he has concluded it is in the company's best interests that he remain as the Chief Executive Officer," it read. "To be absolutely clear, Mr. Natale has no intention of resigning. He is focused on running the business and completing the Shaw transaction."

The board was scheduled to meet that day, and Natale wanted to attend and speak to the directors. He felt that they should hear his plans for the company. That afternoon, he sent the board a memorandum, telling the directors that he looked forward to working with them.

Natale's sudden reversal stunned Edward's camp. Although the chief executive's departure had not yet been finalized, they had thought it was a done deal. Ahead of the board meeting, Edward assembled a report summarizing the previous week's events. He sent it to each of the directors along with Natale's document of principles—which, by Edward's account, conflicted with basic governance principles and with the board's ability to perform its duty of overseeing management. Edward believed that Staffieri's return would put the company in the best possible position to conclude the acquisition of Shaw. He instructed the board to discuss the situation. "This discussion should include whether Joe continues in his role as CEO in light of the events over the past 10 days," he concluded.

When Natale addressed the board that day, Rob Gemmell told him he found the principles document astonishing. Gemmell's view was shared by several directors, who felt that Natale was demanding that the board cede a number of its responsibilities to management. For instance, one bullet point stipulated that the board could only increase, and not decrease, managers' scores on their performance evaluations, and therefore their bonuses. Some directors viewed the request as an attempt to usurp the human resources committee of its powers. Another sticking point was Natale's suggestion that board members, including established business leaders like Jack Cockwell, be prevented from speaking to Rogers employees without management approval. The notion of creating a committee to mediate disputes between Edward and Natale also ruffled some feathers. The chair and the CEO of a public company had to be able to work together, one director said.

After Natale left the meeting, several directors expressed outrage about the situation. "It's almost like he wanted to be declared czar," one of them said. Melinda addressed the board, speaking of her desire to work constructively with the new directors, although she, Martha, and Loretta continued to lobby for Natale to remain at the company's helm. When it came time to vote on his termination, the three women abstained. Everyone else voted in favour of giving Natale the boot.

When the meeting adjourned, Edward personally called Natale to break the news to him. After a fractious and sometimes personal battle that had lasted two months and unseated the majority of the company's independent directors, Natale was out and Staffieri was back in, as interim CEO with an almost-guaranteed shot at the top job.

Martha, meanwhile, took to Twitter to remind the world that, less than two weeks earlier, her brother had publicly expressed support for Natale as CEO. "Guess he didn't pinky swear," she quipped.

Sometime after Joe Natale's departure, Brian Cox, an award-winning Scottish actor, sank into an armchair, peered into a camera and pressed record. White-haired and in his seventies, Cox was an accomplished Shakespearean actor who had gained prominence in the 1990s for his portrayal of King Lear, before crossing over into film and TV.

In late 2021, while a turbulent fight rocked the boardroom of Canada's largest wireless carrier, Cox was entangled in a strikingly similar scenario playing out on television screens. *Succession*, the HBO series about three siblings fighting for control of their ageing father's media empire, was airing its third season and Cox was playing the lead role: Logan Roy, the ruthless patriarch with a penchant for profanity.

For months, news outlets and *Succession* fans had been comparing the Rogers family conflict to the acclaimed television drama. "Real life *Succession* battle plagues Canada's top wireless firm," read a headline on the BBC website. "*Succession*-style feud gripping

Canada settled as court sides with Edward Rogers," blared *The Guardian*. Even Martha weighed in on the matter, although she wasn't fond of the comparison. "Succession? Please. It feels more like GoT [*Game of Thrones*]," she tweeted, "and I hope to God I'm Arya."

Although the show's creator, Jesse Armstrong, had stated that the Roys were a fictional family, many viewers couldn't help but see the similarities between them and real-life business families, such as those of conservative media baron Rupert Murdoch or the late media tycoon Sumner Redstone. For Canadians, the most obvious parallel was to the Rogers family.

Some of that likely had to do with timing. The first episode of the show's hotly anticipated third season aired on October 17, while Edward's lawyers were fighting to obtain the shareholder list. The two storylines were essentially playing out simultaneously; while viewers tuned in to the escalating tensions between members of the ruling family of the fictional media and entertainment conglomerate Waystar Royco, the Rogers family clash was intensifying as well. The parallels likely contributed to the prominence that the Rogers story received in the press—it had garnered an outsized level of attention for a business story, dominating the front page of newspapers such as the *Globe and Mail* for weeks—as well as in Canadian society more broadly.

The borders between the two storylines started to blur in late November, when the *Globe and Mail*, which had broken the Rogers story and led much of the subsequent coverage, unexpectedly received a shout-out on the show. ("Maybe I buy you a diamond the size of the Ritz-Carlton and a few illustrious newspapers," Kendall Roy, the heir apparent to the Roy family dynasty, muses to his girlfriend about how he might spend the spoils if his father buys him out of the company. "The *Globe and Mail*, the *L.A. Times*.")

Then, in early January 2022, a nineteen-second video clip surfaced that brought the walls between reality and fiction crashing down altogether. It was a message recorded by Cox through the video platform Cameo, where fans can buy personalized greetings from celebrities. The fans ordering the video messages, typically as a gift for a family member or friend, can provide detailed instructions to the celebrities recording them.

In the video, Cox, who charged more than $800 a pop for a Cameo video, was dressed in a collared black shirt and seated in front of a window with wooden shutters.

"Edward," he began, "This is from Suzanne. Congratulations on your real-life *Succession* at Rogers Communications."

He paused for a beat. "And also," he continued, raising his thick, prominent eyebrows as Logan Roy's characteristic smirk crept across his face, "having Joe Natale to fuck the fuck off."

Then he flashed the camera a quick thumbs up.

"Well done, Edward," he concluded, scrunching his face into his signature scowl. "Congratulations."

EIGHTEEN

PROJECT MARS

Tony Staffieri spent his six weeks of unemployment reading, burning off his pandemic weight gain on the treadmill, and catching up with old friends. He also fielded several calls about potential job opportunities. It was the longest that he had gone without a job since graduating from business school. But Staffieri was still committed to Rogers, and periodically, various board members, including Edward, Alan Horn, and others, called him to check in and ask whether he was still interested in the job.

In mid-November, when a slimmed-down Staffieri marched back through the doors of 333 Bloor after being crowned interim CEO, there was no time to waste. First he'd need to secure the financing and the three regulatory approvals needed to close the Shaw takeover. Then he'd have to integrate the companies and pay down the deal's roughly $20 billion debt load.

On his sixth day at the job, Staffieri accompanied a delegation of more than two dozen representatives of Rogers and Shaw to Gatineau, Quebec for a public hearing in front of the country's telecom regulator. But rather than taking a seat in the front row, the newly minted CEO, who'd been away for more than a month while the preparations for the hearing were underway, blended into the sea of suits as he sat quietly in the second-last of five rows, Phil Lind to his left.

Even after the two-board situation at Rogers had been resolved, Telus had pushed for the five-day hearing to be postponed. There was still "considerable uncertainty" surrounding the company's leadership because of Edward's earlier plan to reshape the telecom's upper ranks, the Vancouver-based telecom argued in a letter to the Canadian Radio-television and Telecommunications Commission. The regulator reviewed the matter to satisfy itself that the Rogers executives who planned to appear had the authority to do so. In the end, it decided that the hearing would go ahead as planned.

If there had indeed been any doubt as to whether the executives appearing in front of the commission were doing so with the blessing of the controlling shareholder, it was soon quashed. Because, when the hearing kicked off, it was Edward Rogers and Brad Shaw, the progeny of the cable companies' founders, who were seated side by side in the front row, directly facing the three commissioners. After a round of introductions by Ted Woodhead, the telecom's senior vice-president of regulatory affairs, Edward took the floor and delivered a speech that invoked their fathers' legacies as visionaries who started with next to nothing and took big risks. The companies that they founded always upheld their commitments to regulators, and this deal was no different, Edward said. "Our board, our management team, and I are totally committed to this deal. We will stand behind each and every commitment made by our team today."

Bell and Telus were urging the commission to reject Rogers' takeover of Shaw's broadcasting distribution business. They argued that allowing Rogers to acquire Shaw's licences to deliver television channels through cable, satellite, or the internet would give the combined entity too much control over the availability of programming. But Edward contended that Canadian broadcasters needed to grow to survive the threat posed by global streaming giants. Canada was "no longer an island," he said. "Today's telecommunications networks require scale to compete on the world stage."

The only hint of the chaos that the company had just emerged from came when one of the commission's lawyers asked whether Rogers would be paying Natale to consult on the deal as part of his severance agreement. (The commission's practice was to include consulting fees in the calculation of a deal's value, she explained.)

"I'm not aware of that," responded Woodhead. A brief silence followed before Edward chimed in.

"I can just add, uh, that the, uh, termination arrangements with Mr. Natale are still being worked—are still being worked through," he stammered.

On a rainy day in late November 2021, Melinda Rogers-Hixon settled into a beige couch in the den that, for the past several months, had served as her war room. Her outfit—a stylish burgundy blazer with a black turtleneck, dark blue jeans, and knee-high black boots—had attracted a light dusting of dog hair from her two labs. Gareth Seltzer, the energetic, bespectacled adviser who had also spent the better part of several months in that room, was nearby, as was Melinda's communications adviser, Wojtek Dabrowski. A mug printed with a photograph of all four of Melinda's kids sat on the glass table in front of her; in the corner of the room was a barren Christmas tree, freshly unfurled and waiting to be decorated.

The beige-and-gold-hued room, overflowing with family photos, was an apt setting for Melinda's first media interview about the conflict that had riven her family. She was thoughtful and deliberate as she spoke of her desire to rebuild her relationship with her brother. In addition to her roles at Rogers, Melinda had a day job advising other multi-generational family businesses as a partner of a global firm called Generation Transition Advisors. The conflict, while painful, had presented an opportunity to bolster her brand as an adviser by centring her discussions around themes such as governance and corporate citizenship. "I think she feels very satisfied that she's bringing a lot of eyes to the issue, even if it's a little embarrassing, even if she feels more people are looking at her when she picks the kids up from school," Seltzer told the *Globe*.

Melinda mused about a debating technique that she and Edward had honed around the dinner table as kids. Ted would make them switch sides halfway through and argue the opposite position. The purpose of the exercise, he explained, was to teach them how to challenge their own assumptions and understand the other person's perspective. She wondered whether employing the technique might have prevented the highly public meltdown that had recently embroiled the family and its company in turmoil.

Melinda and Edward were on speaking terms, and had even taken a walk together through Forest Hill, the neighbourhood they'd grown up in and lived in still. But the siblings were having difficulty seeing eye to eye. To Edward, it felt like, although Melinda had initially been receptive to the idea of a discussion, she wasn't in the right frame of mind to engage. Melinda told the *Globe and Mail* that emotions were still raw, and that it would take time to repair their bond. As she saw it, they didn't have much of a choice. "It's not even up to us whether we want to fix it or not," she said. The fate of their company depended on it. "We have to find a way to work together in a constructive manner, where all voices are heard."

Regardless, she remained steadfast in her opposition to the leadership change enacted by her brother and his allies on the board, and in her support for Natale. "I think he was the best CEO we've had—100 per cent—since my father passed," she said. He had impressed her with his people skills—his ability to build strong teams and to motivate people—and with the manner in which he had steered the company through the early days of the pandemic.

He also had outmanoeuvred Bell to win the Shaw deal, which was, to Melinda, "no small feat."

Most of all, Melinda explained, she had wanted to maintain stability at a crucial moment in the company's history, as it worked to consummate the deal of their father's dreams. With every new CEO—and there had been four such changes in the thirteen years since Ted's passing, plus two interim CEO stints by Alan Horn— there came a new senior leadership team and a new strategy. "When you're a revolving door, it's extremely hard to be competitive and make your mark and actually follow a direction and execute it." To Melinda, the biggest advantage of being a family-run company was the ability to take a longer-term focus, and she didn't believe that the company was doing that. After all, her brother had just cited a short-term metric—share price performance—as his primary justification for ousting the management team.

Melinda, Martha, and Loretta also maintained that Torys was conflicted by taking sides in the family squabble. Early in the new year, lawyers for the three Rogers women filed an application with the Ontario Superior Court of Justice seeking to block the firm from representing a subset of the advisory committee members. They argued that doing so without Melinda, Martha, and Loretta's consent was a conflict of interest, and that it violated the Law Society of Ontario's rules of professional conduct. "Torys cannot act or give advice against the applicants, who are now former clients, in advising other advisory committee members," the lawyers wrote. (Melinda et al. had apparently bolstered their legal team, which still included Norton Rose, by adding high-profile criminal lawyer Frank Addario.) They also claimed that they were being denied access to legal files, including minutes from the September 29 trust meeting that they had skipped in favour of the concurrent board meeting. (Torys' position was that the meeting had not been duly constituted because the trustee was absent, according to court documents.) They were asking the court to order the firm to hand over its files, and to step down as counsel to any members of the advisory committee.

Not long after it was filed, the application was withdrawn. According to a source, Lisus convinced Melinda, Martha, and Loretta to move the dispute to private arbitration. This was partly due to the standstill agreement that the two sides had entered into in the hopes of avoiding another public spectacle that could derail the Shaw deal. Under the agreement, which was to remain in place at least until the merger closed, both sides had agreed to temporarily shelve their various disputes. They had also agreed not to disparage one another in the press. Edward's side believed that Melinda had breached her duties as a director by speaking about management performance and other board matters during interviews with the *Globe and Mail* and Bloomberg News. The standstill meant that she would refrain from criticizing the company's management in the media, and that Edward and the board would refrain from taking any action against her for the alleged transgression.

Prior to the warring factions falling silent, the public was given one more glimpse inside the fraught state of affairs within one of Canada's wealthiest and most prominent business families. In early January, shortly after the holidays and before the lawsuit against Torys had been filed, the *Globe and Mail* obtained a copy of the Cameo clip that Brian Cox had recorded for Edward. Jonathan Lowenstein, Edward's spokesperson, told the newspaper that the video had been sent to Edward as a "practical joke." He didn't deny that Suzanne was behind the prank, although some speculated that she'd been framed. Regardless of who was behind the gift, it was clear that Edward had gotten a kick out of it; he and Suzanne had allegedly sent it around to friends, family members, and colleagues.

Natale was, unsurprisingly, not amused. Many of his friends, family, and business contacts saw the video, which was shared widely on social media and covered by major media outlets. Natale considered it an attack on his reputation.

Martha, meanwhile, fired up her Twitter account, where she posted a link to the *Globe*'s story alongside a photo of a glass adorned with silver starfish. "Huh. I got mom a vase for Christmas," she wrote.

In the immediate aftermath of Natale's departure, Edward and Staffieri had told a BofA Securities analyst that they weren't planning to make any other changes to the management team. The idea was to "maximize stability heading into the Shaw merger," the analyst, David Barden, wrote in a research note. That sentiment was echoed by Robert Gemmell, who praised the telecom's strong leadership team in an interview with the *Globe and Mail* on November 18.

But just two weeks later, the company announced the first of a slew of changes to its upper ranks. They unfolded almost exactly as Staffieri had laid out during his allegedly overheard conversation with David Miller back in September. Robert Dépatie joined the management team in early December, taking on a newly created position that effectively put him in charge of cable, giving him oversight of the Connected Home business, which offered internet, television, and smart-home monitoring services; Rogers for Business, which served large, small, and medium-sized enterprises; and the customer service division.

Barden also wrote that, although Staffieri was initially given the CEO job on an interim basis while a search was carried out, Edward's support—and his control of the board—made Staffieri a shoo-in for the position. The observation was an astute one, although not much of a stretch. In January, Staffieri was appointed to the CEO role permanently—at least, as permanently as any Rogers CEO, several company insiders joked.

Soon after, Staffieri began purging the New Guard that Natale had assembled and replacing them with executives with long-standing ties to Rogers. He brought back or promoted Old Guard types who he believed could hit the ground running and execute on his plan to regain a leadership position in the thirteen key performance metrics where he felt that Rogers was lagging.

Unsurprisingly, the first high-profile departure was Natale's most trusted ally, Dave Fuller. He was replaced by company veteran Phil Hartling, lured out of early retirement to become president of the wireless division. Close behind Fuller were Dan Golberg and chief communications officer Sevaun Palvetzian.

As planned, chief human resources officer Jim Reid was replaced by Bret Leech, while Colette Watson, the shrewd cost-cutter who had left for a role as president of the Cable Public Affairs Channel, came back to claim Jordan Banks's title of president of Rogers Sports & Media. Also out were Eric Agius, the chief customer officer who had spearheaded the Care Nation project (the position was eliminated), and Dean Prevost, who was booted from the executive leadership team but stayed on with the company as president of integration. Glenn Brandt, a 31-year company veteran, stepped into Staffieri's previous role of chief financial officer. The executive leadership team saw a new position added as well—Mahes Wickramasinghe, a chartered accountant and ex-Rogers employee, rejoined the telecom as chief administrative officer. David Miller did not return to Rogers in the role of chief legal officer as some had anticipated, although according to sources he did some consulting work for the company. Instead, Lisa Damiani's former chief legal and regulatory officer role was split into two positions. Ted Woodhead, who was playing a key role in the company's effort to secure regulatory approval for the Shaw deal, was promoted to chief regulatory officer and head of government affairs. The chief legal officer title went to Marisa Wyse, a lawyer who spent seven years at Goodmans before joining Rogers. By the time the overhaul was complete, only three members of Natale's original, eleven-person executive leadership team remained: Staffieri, chief technology officer Jorge Fernandes, and Lisa Durocher, who headed up financial and emerging services, including Rogers Bank. The Old Guard was back in charge of Rogers Communications, making everything old new again.

The departures were not confined to the executive leadership team. In the months following Staffieri's return, attrition "skyrocketed," according to one former executive, who noted that the departures were justified due to the imminent merger with Shaw. Some employees were let go. Others left because they disagreed with the company's new direction, which several of them described as a single-minded focus on controlling costs. They said that, in contrast to Natale's Rogers, which had cared about their professional growth, they felt Staffieri's Rogers treated them like interchangeable numbers on a spreadsheet, free to be manipulated as needed to hit quarterly financial targets. By the end of 2021, the company's headcount had shrunk by roughly a thousand. It declined by another thousand employees the following year—such that, by the end of 2022, the total number of staff clocked in at around 22,000, making Rogers roughly 8 per cent leaner than it had been at the close of 2020. The decreased numbers did not trouble Staffieri, however. "We have the people we want," he told the *Globe and Mail* in an interview.

The sale of Shaw's Freedom Mobile was code-named Project Mars. No one involved seemed to have a good explanation as to how the moniker had been chosen. In all likelihood, it was simply the next item on some investment banker's list of prospective code names, one person speculated. Despite Rogers' reluctance to part with the carrier, the federal government had made it clear in November 2021 that it wouldn't allow Rogers to acquire Shaw's entire portfolio of wireless spectrum licences. The company spent the next several months exploring alternatives that would see it acquire some, but not all, of the Freedom Mobile spectrum, while ignoring repeated overtures from Pierre Karl Péladeau and Anthony Lacavera. Then, in January, shortly after his permanent appointment to CEO, Staffieri asked industry minister François-Philippe Champagne if the government was still committed to having four wireless carriers. Rogers was willing to part with Freedom if that's what Ottawa wanted, Staffieri told the minister, who he referred to as "mister minister," a title that at least one government official found excessively formal.

Champagne didn't give Staffieri an answer during their January meeting. However, on March 3, 2022, his office issued a public statement that made it clear to the telecom that it would have to divest Canada's fourth-largest wireless carrier. Champagne shared Canadians' "serious concerns" about further consolidation in the telecom sector, and was committed to ensuring cellphone affordability. "The wholesale transfer of Shaw's wireless licences to Rogers is fundamentally incompatible with our government's policies for spectrum and mobile service competition, and I will simply not permit it."

There was no shortage of interested suitors for Freedom. The loudest of them was Lacavera. The carrier's founder had put together a group of investors—including pension funds, private equity, and family offices—to help Globalive buy back its former business. The group included Twin Point Capital, a U.S. principal investment firm founded by Lawrence Guffey and Jonathan Friesel, and the Baupost Group, a Boston-based investment manager. (Guffey was familiar with both Freedom and Lacavera; he had been part of the consortium that owned Wind before it was sold to Shaw.) But Lacavera's repeated text messages to Edward had largely gone ignored. By December 2021, frustrated by the stonewalling, Lacavera made his intentions public via an interview with the *Globe and Mail*. "Freedom Mobile may be up for sale again, and founder Anthony Lacavera wants to buy it," the headline read. But the icy reception from Rogers continued. In February 2022, Globalive tried reaching out to Barclays, the investment bank that Rogers had retained. They were told that there was nothing to discuss.

Globalive wasn't the only suitor who was turned away. Other prospective bidders, including Quebecor's Vidéotron subsidiary and internet wholesaler Distributel, had also expressed interest in Freedom and been rebuffed. They were all told roughly the same thing. There was no sale process underway; not now, maybe not ever, because Rogers believed it would be able to hold on to Freedom. But after Champagne's announcement in early March, word began to spread through financial circles that there was, in fact, a sale process underway. Rogers had set up a data room, and several interested parties, primarily private equity types, had been permitted to take a look. Vidéotron, Globalive, and Distributel were not invited to the party.

Quebecor's top brass were not particularly surprised that Rogers wouldn't engage with them. To say that there was bad blood between the two cable companies would be an understatement; there was roughly $850 million worth of it. In the lawsuit that Vidéotron had filed in the Quebec Superior Court in the midst of Rogers' boardroom meltdown in late October 2021, the company alleged that Rogers had made an increasing number of demands on Vidéotron in a deliberate attempt to sabotage their network sharing pact in Quebec and the Ottawa area.

Rogers and Vidéotron had struck the twenty-year network sharing pact back in 2013. The premise behind it was that, by pooling their resources, each company could improve coverage for its own customers while minimizing its costs. But things started to go sideways after Nadir Mohamed left the company in 2014, Vidéotron alleged. When Jorge Fernandes took over as chief technology officer in 2018, he reviewed the deal and called it the worst partnership agreement that he had ever seen, stating that anyone who negotiated it and still worked at Rogers should be fired, according to court documents.

There was another strike against Vidéotron. The company had plotted a national expansion before, buying up discounted spectrum in the 2008 auction only to later scrap its plans and sell the airwaves at a profit. This angered the Big Three telecoms, who felt that it amounted to awarding a federal government subsidy to a cable company controlled by a billionaire separatist. What was stopping Péladeau from acquiring Freedom Mobile and then flipping the spectrum for an easy profit, some wondered.

In public speeches and media interviews, Péladeau insisted that this time would be different. The regulatory environment was much more conducive to a fourth carrier than it had been years earlier, when Vidéotron had cancelled its national expansion. Péladeau believed that Vidéotron was the natural buyer for Freedom, and he and his team lobbied their contacts in the federal government hoping that officials at Innovation, Science and Economic Development Canada would pressure Rogers into letting his company into the data room.

Lacavera was pursuing a similar approach. In addition to his attempts at lobbying the government, he continued to press Rogers to allow him into the process. After more than half a dozen unsuccessful attempts to contact Edward and his advisers, he reached out to Barclays a second time. He told them that he knew there was a process underway, and that they were accepting bids that Friday. With two days to go before the deadline, the bankers told Lacavera that he could submit an offer, and they would present it to Rogers. But they failed to provide Globalive with all of the information and materials that a bidder would normally receive, Lacavera later claimed in a letter to Ottawa. Fortunately for Globalive, they knew the asset well. After all, they had built it. Relying heavily on their previous knowledge from when they had owned Wind, Lacavera and his team submitted a blind $3.75 billion offer.

The offer failed to get any traction, however. Lacavera claimed that Rogers refused to enter into discussions with Globalive unless the company signed a confidentiality agreement. This was standard business practice, but the document itself was not, according to Lacavera and at least two other prospective bidders. Staffieri would later describe it to a House of Commons committee as a standard commercial non-disclosure agreement, or NDA. But Lacavera took issue with several provisions, including one that prohibited Globalive from communicating with regulators in relation to its bid. Globalive made several changes to the document, signed it, and sent it back. But Rogers rejected the modified NDA and, relying on the absence of a confidentiality agreement, refused to engage with Globalive's bid.

Vidéotron and Distributel also made unsolicited offers, but Rogers wasn't willing to entertain those either. According to a letter that Vidéotron sent to the Competition Bureau in early April, Staffieri told Péladeau that Rogers wasn't interested in an offer from Vidéotron at that time. Vidéotron and Distributel also refused to sign the Rogers NDA. As a telecom operator, Vidéotron had spent years forging relationships within the government, and Péladeau and his team believed that those relationships gave them an edge. The company was unwilling to sign anything that forbade it from using its back channels to regulators.

Both Péladeau and Lacavera suspected that Rogers was attempting to sell Freedom to a "friendly" buyer—someone who either didn't have the means or the appetite to compete aggressively, or who, as a friend of the family, would serve as a convenient place for Rogers to park Freedom and its valuable wireless licences for some time, with the hope of eventually buying it back.

The first buyer that was presented to regulators was Stonepeak Infrastructure Partners, a New York–headquartered global private equity firm that owned a small rural internet provider called Xplornet Communications Inc. based in Woodstock, New

Brunswick. However, industry observers were skeptical that this option would pass muster with the government. For one thing, private equity is typically shorter-term capital, and Ottawa wanted a sustainable fourth carrier. In addition, Xplornet had served as the remedy partner for Bell when it acquired MTS. To appease both the industry minister and the Competition Bureau, Bell had agreed to transfer 24,700 wireless customers, forty megahertz of wireless spectrum licences, and six retail stores to Xplornet, creating a new wireless player called Xplore Mobile. But that divestiture had failed to create a robust competitor. By the time Xplore Mobile shuttered in the summer of 2022, it had fewer than 7,000 customers. Stonepeak did not own Xplore Mobile; the division had been spun out when the firm acquired Xplornet in 2020. Still, some experts believed that the carrier's failure had tarnished the credibility of Xplornet's owner as a prospective buyer.

Rogers also tried putting forward a consortium that included the $10 billion LiUNA Pension Fund of Central and Eastern Canada, infrastructure investor Fengate Asset Management, B.C. First Nations, and the Aquilinis, the billionaire family who owned the Vancouver Canucks hockey team. That option might have been even more controversial, on account of Rogers' longstanding ties to the Aquilini family. The relationship dated back to 2009, when Phil Lind had negotiated naming rights for the Canucks' arena with Francesco Aquilini, the team's chairman, turning GM Place into Rogers Arena. In his memoir, Lind described Aquilini as "a great friend." On top of that, one of the vice-presidents at Fengate was none other than Anthony Staffieri, the Rogers CEO's son. But the biggest knock against the consortium's bid from the federal government's perspective was the group's distinct lack of experience operating a telecom business.

Lacavera, meanwhile, wasn't the sort to give up easily. When he was six years old, he had tried to scale the fence in his family's backyard with a ladder. After his mother ordered him to stop out of concern that he could fall, he endeavoured to dig a trench underneath the fence instead. At one point he even attempted to take the whole thing apart. If Rogers and Shaw wouldn't let him into the sale process for Freedom, perhaps he could dismantle that process altogether.

By spring, Lacavera was engaged in a full-blown campaign against Project Mars. He published an open letter on social media, urging Ottawa to ensure that Freedom went to a "truly independent" buyer—one without historical ties or "cozy personal relationships" to the Big Three telecoms. In a separate letter, which he sent to Champagne, competition commissioner Matthew Boswell, and the Prime Minister's Office, he accused Rogers of running a "closed and secretive sales process" from which he and other viable competitors had been intentionally excluded. He argued that the aim of the operation, which he characterized as a "non-competitive sham," was to shepherd Freedom into the hands of a weak and ineffective owner.

Rogers and Shaw secured the first of three regulatory approvals in late March, when the CRTC blessed the transfer of Shaw's broadcasting services to Rogers with some conditions attached, among them that Rogers contribute $27.2 million to several funds supporting Canadian content and local news. The telecom also lined up financing for the deal, tapping credit markets for roughly $19 billion ahead of an expected rise in interest rates.

But Rogers still needed to secure approvals from François-Philippe Champagne and the Competition Bureau, and, in the company's view, neither was being particularly helpful. By early 2021, the bureau was becoming impatient with Rogers, arguing in correspondence that the company had missed disclosure deadlines and provided incomplete answers to the watchdog's queries. Rogers disputed those claims, countering with an itemized list of alleged inaccuracies and omissions in one of the Bureau's letters. At the same time, Rogers was pressing Champagne's office to tell them who they considered to be an acceptable buyer for Freedom, but the government officials wouldn't name names. Instead, they provided the company with a four-point framework. The buyer should be competitive, well capitalized, an owner and operator of telecom infrastructure, and in it for the long haul—not a short-term private equity investor, for instance. To Rogers, it seemed that only one suitor ticked all four boxes: Vidéotron.

Finally, after months of rejecting Vidéotron's advances, Edward and Staffieri flew to Montreal to visit the Quebec cable executives. The regulatory process had dragged on for too long, they told Péladeau. Rogers had come to the realization that a deal with Vidéotron had the best chance of being approved, and they were ready to negotiate.

Vidéotron was still interested in Freedom. Rogers, however, had waited until the eleventh hour to invite the company into the process, and now Péladeau felt that he had all the leverage. Rogers needed Vidéotron badly, and he knew it. So did the rest of the world, for that matter. Because in early May, hours after the *Globe and Mail* broke the news that Vidéotron had finally been admitted into the data room, Rogers and Shaw put out a press release that went off like a grenade in financial circles. The Competition Bureau had notified them of its plans to oppose their merger at the Competition Tribunal, Canada's merger court.

The Competition Bureau argued in its application that Rogers' takeover of Shaw would lead to higher cellphone bills. None of the potential buyers that Rogers had put forward were deemed sufficient to maintain wireless competition by the watchdog, which was asking the tribunal to block the takeover.

It was against this backdrop that Rogers tried to hammer out a deal with Quebecor. The negotiations were challenging, according to sources. The Quebec-based telecom had a lot of requests, and many of them were complex and technical in nature, such as allowing Vidéotron to access various Rogers infrastructure at favourable terms.

While the negotiations were underway, Lacavera was finalizing a network and spectrum sharing deal with Telus that he hoped would bolster Globalive's bid. The twenty-year agreement was conditional on Globalive acquiring Freedom, which, by then, seemed like a long shot to everyone, including Lacavera. Still, he announced the deal in mid-May, describing it as a "substantial strengthening" of Globalive's offer that would enable Freedom to expand nationally in exchange for giving Telus access to its spectrum. "I am hopeful that Rogers will now see us as the preferred buyer," he said.

Rogers didn't, however, and continued down the path it had embarked on with Quebecor. In early June, Lacavera tried bypassing Rogers and taking his $3.75 billion offer directly to Shaw. Not surprisingly, the overture was met with silence. Under the terms of its Arrangement Agreement with Rogers, Shaw was not permitted to engage in any such discussions, even if it had wanted to.

Finally, on June 17, Rogers and Shaw announced that they had reached a deal to sell Freedom Mobile to Quebecor's Vidéotron for $2.85 billion. The price was lower than the earlier, unsolicited bid that Quebecor had made, and the Quebec telecom had extracted other benefits as well, through a series of agreements that would see Rogers provide it with transport and roaming services, among other things.

To many industry observers, the divestiture of Freedom to Quebecor was a win for Ottawa. The government had forced Rogers to sell the carrier to an existing telecom operator, one with a stated desire to expand beyond its home province and bring down prices. Lacavera was unconvinced. To him, the deal was further proof that the sale process was an uncompetitive sham. Rogers had accepted an offer that was $900 million lower than Globalive's, and Lacavera believed that the only justification for doing so was that Rogers expected to glean some other benefit—namely, a weaker competitor. To him, Quebecor represented the status quo, and the only way to truly bring down wireless prices was to create a pure-play wireless carrier like the U.S.'s T-Mobile, one whose ability to compete wouldn't be hampered by a need to protect a legacy cable business from retaliatory attacks by the Big Three telecoms.

Lacavera continued to wage a battle against the merger, emailing statements to journalists, posting videos to social media, and even launching an online petition called NoMerger.ca. The question was, why bother? After all, Freedom Mobile was no longer on the market. Even in the unlikely situation that the deal with Quebecor somehow fell through, Lacavera had made himself such an enemy of Rogers that the company would certainly never agree to sell it to him. This apparently didn't bother Lacavera, who seemed to be getting a kick out of criticizing the cable companies and bringing heightened attention to the issue of wireless affordability. As the founder of Wind, he had endured relentless attacks from the Big Three telecoms, who in 2013 had banded together and taken out full-page ads against the proposed sale of Wind to U.S. telecom Verizon. (The sale ultimately fell through for other reasons.) On some level, his campaign against the deal was payback.

But Lacavera wasn't the only one whose position hadn't wavered. A week after the sale was announced, Vidéotron sent the Competition Bureau a detailed proposal laying out the merits of its plan. It took the bureau's staff just three days to reject it. The agency didn't even meet with the telecom's representatives beforehand. Although a meeting between them did take place a few days later, the Vidéotron executives felt that Boswell's mind was already made up.

NINETEEN

CANADA'S MOST RELIABLE NETWORK

Friday, July 8, 2022 started out just like any other day for Arnaud Verdier. The twenty-year-old aviation student was awoken by his alarm at 6 a.m. as sunlight streamed in through the small window of his third-floor rental in Saint-Hubert, Quebec. He slathered on some deodorant, let out his roommate's white and orange cat, and grabbed a protein bar as he dashed out the door to drive the twelve minutes to the aviation firm he was interning at.

The first sign that something was amiss came at around 6:30 a.m., when Verdier sat down at his desk and pulled out his iPhone 13 Pro to check his email. It wouldn't load. Next, he tried to text a friend, but the message failed to deliver. All of his apps seemed to be offline as well.

At first, Verdier suspected a billing issue. Maybe something was wrong with the credit card he had on file, he thought. But it didn't take long for him to realize that several of his co-workers, who also had Rogers phones, had no service either.

During his morning break, Verdier found the cafeteria in chaos. Although credit cards still worked, the Interac debit system, which relied on the Rogers network, was down. Some patrons were scrawling down their names and contact details on a sheet of paper. Verdier scarfed down his breakfast sandwich and coffee and started the ten-minute trek back to his car to fetch his credit card.

By then, the engineers assembled at Rogers' network operations centre in Brampton were in crisis mode. Several hours earlier, at 2:27 a.m., they had started rolling out the sixth phase of a seven-phase process to upgrade the company's network core. The pre-dawn upgrade was not unusual; telecoms typically perform network maintenance in the dead of night, when traffic is the lowest.

Rogers used one common core to support both its wireless and its broadband services, which meant that all traffic—internet, voice, data, and TV—flowed through it. The core was essentially the network's brain, receiving, processing, transmitting, and connecting all of that traffic.

The engineering and implementation phases of the project had begun months earlier, back in February, after a planning process that included budget and project approvals, risk assessment, and testing. The first five phases had gone smoothly. But at 4:43 a.m., a piece of code was introduced that deleted a routing filter. Routers guide and direct packets of data through a network, and filters are what prevents those routers from becoming overwhelmed, by limiting the number of possible routes presented to them.

Rogers used equipment from multiple manufacturers in its network core. This was a common industry practice, as vendors had different strengths in terms of the various types of equipment that they produced. That practice, however, turned out to be fatal for the Rogers network that day. Differences in how routers from two of the telecom's suppliers operated were at the centre of the unprecedented network outage that left more than 12 million Rogers customers without internet, wireless, or home phone service—and created a whole new set of problems at quite possibly the most inopportune moment in the company's history.

The configuration change that was introduced in the early hours of July 8 allowed all possible routes to the internet to pass through the routers. That caused some of the telecom's networking equipment to become flooded, exceeding their memory and processing capabilities. From there, the situation unravelled too quickly for the engineers to contain. By 4:45, two minutes after the coding change had been introduced, the core began to fail.

At first, the network team had no clue why the core had gone down. Because of the outage, many of them were unable to connect to the company's IT and network systems and had to travel to centralized locations to physically access the equipment. Complicating matters further, they had lost access to the virtual private network that connected to the nodes in the network core, preventing them from being able to diagnose the problem.

Staffieri, who was at his home on Lake Simcoe that morning, was also in the dark. Shortly before 7 a.m., after he'd finished lifting weights and running on the treadmill, he turned on his phone and discovered that the internet wasn't working. His news apps were still stuck on the previous day's headlines. Then he flipped on the radio, which informed him that the multibillion-dollar telecom company that he ran was experiencing an outage.

Back in 2015, as part of an emergency-planning working group, Bell, Rogers, and Telus had agreed to provide each other with SIM cards so that they could communicate in the event that one of their networks went down. But when Staffieri popped his emergency Bell SIM card into his phone, he still couldn't get a signal. By this point, rather than waiting to see whether the SIM would complete the activation process, he got into his car and started driving. The company's emergency continuity plan instructed staff to head to the locations that they normally worked out of. For Staffieri, that was 333 Bloor. But he decided instead to go to the heart of the problem—the telecom's network operations centre, or NOC, in Brampton. On the way there he stopped at a Starbucks and used the Wi-Fi to call Jorge Fernandes. The telecom's chief technology officer was vacationing in his native Portugal that week, and the time-zone difference had given him an early start.

Fernandes was notified of the outage shortly before 5 a.m. Toronto time. About an hour later he reached out to his counterparts at Bell and Telus to inform them of the situation. Fearing that his company might have been hit by hackers, he cautioned his rivals to be on the lookout for cyberattacks.

Both Bell and Telus offered to help, but Rogers quickly realized it wouldn't be able to transfer its customers onto their networks. For one thing, the telecom would have needed access to its centralized user database and other elements of its network that had been knocked offline by the outage. Besides, no rival network could handle the sudden surge of traffic associated with more than 10 million additional wireless subscribers. Even attempting to make such a transfer risked compromising the other networks and deepening the nationwide communications crisis.

As the extent of the Rogers outage became clear, employees who had received backup SIM cards started swapping out the Rogers SIM cards in their phones, allowing them to join the recovery effort. Staff began to converge at the rally points set out in the continuity plan. At the network operations centre in Brampton, where Staffieri spent the day, engineers had managed to re-establish access to the network and set about trying to diagnose the problem. Staffieri was given an alternate phone and got in touch with Edward through a Wi-Fi-based chat app.

Meanwhile, millions of Rogers customers were waking up to discover that their cellphones, modems, televisions, and home phone lines had gone dark. Even those abroad trying to roam on their cellphones had lost connectivity, as foreign telecoms weren't able to verify their identities by pinging the Rogers core.

The outage plunged the country into chaos. Interac, a Rogers customer, lost connectivity, impacting debit card transactions as well as its popular e-Transfer service that enabled Canadians to transfer billions of dollars each year. Those businesses that relied on Rogers to power their payment systems were also unable to process credit card transactions, forcing them to either switch to cash or close for the day. Long lines formed at ATMs. Small businesses, already stretched after many months of pandemic-related closures, suffered another hit to their revenues. Travel plans were disrupted as those with Rogers phones were left without navigation apps. Even the federal telecom regulator was impacted. "Please note that our phone lines are affected by the Rogers network outage," the CRTC said on Twitter. Worst of all, some Rogers customers were unable to reach 911, leaving them cut off from emergency services in potentially life-threatening situations.

Early on Friday morning, social media was abuzz with chatter about the service disruption, while thousands of reports poured into outage-tracking websites such as Downdetector. But the telecom's own social media accounts were oddly quiet, making no mention of the widespread outage that was paralyzing businesses, consumers, and essential services from coast to coast. It wasn't until shortly before 9 a.m.—roughly four hours after the network had gone down—that the company finally acknowledged the situation on its customer service account on Twitter. "We know how important it is for our customers to stay connected," the company tweeted from its RogersHelps account. "We are aware of issues currently affecting our networks and our teams are fully engaged to resolve the issue as soon as possible. We will continue to keep you updated as we have more information to share."

That morning, Langham, a small town thirty-five kilometres northwest of Saskatoon, went into lockdown. The Saskatchewan division of the RCMP, the national police force, had responded to a fatal shooting, and they believed that the suspected gunman—a six-foot-three, brown-eyed man named Justin Heimbecker—was still at large. At 7:40 a.m. local time, a dangerous-person alert flashed across some phone screens in Langham and the surrounding cities of Saskatoon, Prince Albert, and North Battleford, urging people to shelter in place and lock their windows and doors.

After issuing the alert, Pelmorex, the company that manages the emergency alerting system, contacted Rogers to ask if they had received it. The company had indeed received the alert, but the telecom had no idea whether it had successfully disseminated the message to its customers. It soon determined that it hadn't, and it informed Pelmorex.

Three more alerts were issued in Saskatchewan that day as a string of four tornadoes tore across the province, one of them killing a horse and ripping the roof off a farm outside of Blaine Lake, north of Saskatoon. But none of those warnings were distributed through the Rogers network.

The outage had far-reaching impacts across the country. A Montreal bail hearing for Peter Nygard, a Canadian fashion mogul accused of sexually assaulting teenage girls at his sprawling residence in Lyford Cay, had to be put off until the following week because it was impossible for Nygard, who was being detained in a Toronto jail, to appear via video conference. In Toronto, the tour-opening concert by Canadian singer-songwriter The Weeknd was postponed, in part because the outage had made it impossible to open the doors of the Rogers Centre, where some 40,000 fans were expected to converge.

While havoc swept across the nation, Shawn Dionisio, the telecom's retail strategy lead, sent an email to all Rogers stores. "We currently have the following sign in the windows," he wrote, attaching an image of a poster positioning Rogers as "Canada's most reliable 5G network."

"Can you please have your stores remove this poster and store it safely," Dionisio continued. "We will communicate when the posters can be returned to the window. We are currently attempting to turn off all digital signage that refers to the claim."

In Hamilton, Gregg Eby was out running errands with his sister Linda that morning when she started to feel ill. Eby could tell that the situation was serious, but he couldn't get through to 911. After sitting Linda down in a parking lot, Eby, in his seventies, was forced to leave her alone while he ran towards the street in search of someone with a non-Rogers phone.

Several times throughout the day, Rogers had considered shutting down the portion of its network that connected phones to the network core via radio signals. Canada's telecom infrastructure was configured such that if a customer trying to call 911 was unable to connect to their carrier's radio access network, or RAN, their phone would automatically jump to the strongest signal available. However, because the Rogers RAN was still operational, its customers' phones remained connected to it. Shutting it down would have allowed them to make emergency calls through other carriers' networks. (Emergency calls could also be made by removing Rogers SIM cards from phones, although most customers didn't know this.)

But the company felt that shutting down the RAN wasn't the best solution. With the core offline, it would have to be turned off manually. That meant visiting 6,000 towers across the country. Plus, it would take time to bring the radio access network back online. The whole process could extend the outage by another day, or even longer. The best way to restore emergency services was to focus on getting the core back up and running, the telecom decided.

The decision was not a factor in Linda Eby's death. Doctors at the hospital told her family that the aneurysm she had suffered likely would have been fatal even if her brother had been able to reach 911 immediately. But the incident left her relatives—and many others across the country—with questions about the resiliency of Canada's emergency communications networks.

The drive from Saint-Hubert to his parents' place in Blainville typically took Arnaud Verdier about an hour. But without Google Maps guiding him around the rush-hour traffic, he found himself at a standstill in Montreal, the engine of his grey 2012 Honda Civic making a worrisome clacking sound. He suspected a faulty spark plug.

Normally, it wouldn't have been a big deal. He could always call for roadside assistance. But that Friday, as he tried to navigate gridlock without the aid of cellular service, Verdier realized that he would be a sitting duck if his car broke down. The thought made him nervous as the sixty-minute drive stretched into ninety minutes, guzzling up more gas than usual.

Verdier had been a Bell customer until just two years earlier, when he'd walked into a Rogers store and inquired about switching carriers. A customer service representative had told him that the Rogers network was the most reliable one. It was one of the reasons he'd decided to make the change.

While Verdier drove home, Rogers technicians were still working to restore services. At 5:40 p.m., as the outage stretched into its thirteenth hour, the company acknowledged its impact in a tweet. "We have every technical resource and partner fully deployed to solve the problem," it wrote on the RogersHelps account. "As soon as we know the specific time the networks will be fully operational, we will share that with you." The company promised to provide customers with credits.

The telecom still had not disclosed the cause of the outage, and that was beginning to make some people suspicious. Social media was rife with speculation that the telecom had fallen victim to a ransomware attack. Why else would they be keeping such a tight lid on the situation? Even a public statement from the Communications Security Establishment, which said there was no indication of a malicious attack, did little to quell the rumours.

It wasn't until late that evening that wireless services started to recover. After physically disconnecting the malfunctioning routers, engineers redirected the traffic and checked to see whether the network was stable. Determining that it was, they started slowly bringing services back online. The process had to be done carefully and methodically to avoid overloading the network and triggering another outage.

That night, the company posted an apology from Staffieri on its website. "Today we let you down. We can and will do better," it read. The network team had made meaningful progress and wireless service was returning for most customers, Staffieri said. He vowed to get to the bottom of what had happened and promised that a root cause analysis would be done. Changes would be made. "I take full responsibility for ensuring we at Rogers earn back your full trust." But the company still did not have an ETA on when its networks would be fully restored. Nor did it have an answer for its millions of customers as to why the outage had occured.

The following morning, the company announced that services were back online for the vast majority of its customers, although intermittent issues continued to persist throughout the weekend. In his second open letter, posted online Saturday evening, Staffieri said the company had finally identified the cause of the network failure. The maintenance upgrade had caused some routers to malfunction. "Our leading technical experts and global vendors are continuing to dig deep into the root cause and identify steps to increase redundancy in our networks and systems," he said, promising to take "every step necessary" to improve the resilience of his company's networks.

Over the following days, Rogers first announced it would be offering customers a two-day credit for the outage, then bumped it up to a five-day credit, costing an estimated $150 million. But the credits felt like measly compensation to disgruntled Rogers customers. Over the weekend, Arnaud Verdier spoke with Joey Zukran, a class-action lawyer at Montreal law firm LPC Avocat Inc. Zukran told him that he felt there was a case, but they needed to move quickly; the first application filed was the one most likely to be certified.

On Monday, Zukran's firm filed an application in the Superior Court of Quebec, seeking authorization to launch a class-action against Rogers. The proposed class included all customers of Rogers and its discount brands, Fido and Chatr, as well as all Quebec residents who were impacted by the outage, including those who were unable to make Interac transactions. The telecom's claims about having the most reliable network amounted to false advertising, the proposed suit alleged. It sought $200 per class member in damages, a significant financial hit to Rogers. Verdier was the lead plaintiff.

On the last night of a week-long visit to Japan, François-Philippe Champagne was having a drink with two of his staffers in the dimly lit lounge of a Tokyo hotel, decompressing before the long flight back to Ottawa. It had been a gruelling trip, with stops in Tokyo, Nagoya, and Osaka, and the energetic 52-year-old industry minister had pushed through jet lag and a packed schedule of meetings with automotive and manufacturing executives. Despite the fatigue that was starting to set in, Champagne was upbeat. He had achieved his objective of pitching Canada as a green supplier to businesses looking to clean up their supply chains.

As business travellers milled about the lounge, Champagne and his small entourage discussed the day's events. Earlier, during a roundtable with members of Japan's Business Federation, they had learned that former Japanese prime minister Shinzo Abe, who had been a strong ally to Canada, had been shot. They were still processing his death when the phone belonging to one of Champagne's staffers buzzed, delivering more shocking news: the Rogers network was down.

Champagne had spent his teenage years living with his business-man father in Shawinigan, a city on the shores of the St. Maurice River in Quebec. After finishing law school he moved overseas to establish an international legal career. He eventually returned to Canada and entered politics, winning a seat as an MP in his home-town riding in the 2015 federal election. Many suspected that he harboured ambitions of becoming prime minister, following in the footsteps of Jean Chrétien, who had also grown up in Shawinigan and who Champagne considered "somewhat of a mentor."

The friendly and ambitious cabinet minister was quickly entrusted with a variety of important posts, including the trade, infrastructure, and foreign affairs portfolios. In early 2021, as part of a cabinet shuffle, he took over as Minister of Innovation, Science, and Industry from Navdeep Bains, who announced he was leaving politics to spend more time with his family.

Champagne stepped into the role just a few months before Rogers and Shaw announced their plan to merge. He suddenly found himself responsible for a crucial review of the Canadian tele-com industry's largest-ever proposed merger. Unlike the Competition Bureau, which had to prove to a tribunal of judges that the deal would substantially lessen competition, Champagne had the ability to veto the transfer of Shaw's wireless licences—and his decision had just become more complicated.

It was late evening in Tokyo when Champagne and his team learned about the network outage. Initially, it was unclear how serious or widespread it was. Champagne went to bed, instructing his staffers to keep an eye on the situation. By the time he got up at 5 a.m., the circumstances looked dire.

Champagne was baffled that Staffieri still hadn't reached out to notify him. Surely it shouldn't be up to the minister to chase down the CEO of Rogers during a national communications crisis, he thought. Regardless, Champagne's team hunkered down in the minister's hotel room and started trying to contact Staffieri. Unfortunately, the alternate phone that he was using had a different phone number that few people knew, which made him nearly impossible to reach.

Eventually, Champagne's team got a hold of someone who was in Staffieri's proximity and could pass him the phone. Without mincing his words, the minister told the chief executive that the outage was unacceptable and needed to be resolved as quickly as possible. He asked Staffieri about the status of the network and how quickly services could be restored. By then, Rogers had a rough idea of what had caused the network to go dark and was working on a fix. On their flight home, Champagne's team started reaching out to the heads of all the major wireless carriers. The minister wanted to ensure that nothing of this magnitude ever happened again.

The following Monday, Staffieri and the CEOs of Bell, Shaw, Vidéotron, SaskTel, and Eastlink all dialled in to a conference call with Champagne. (Entwistle, who was undergoing a medical procedure that day, sent his chief operations officer, Tony Geheran, in his place.) After Staffieri provided a network update, Champagne told the telecoms that he wanted them to enter into a formal agreement to assist one another during future network outages. The mutual assistance pact that he was proposing was modelled after one that the U.S. Federal Communications Commission had implemented just days earlier, and Champagne wanted it to be in place within thirty days.

The executives expressed support for the idea. But thirty days wasn't enough time, they told the minister. In the end, they settled on sixty.

Privately, some of the executives grumbled about having to clean up Rogers' mess. While other telecoms had designed their networks in such a way that outages could be contained to specific geographic locations, creating what's known as a maximum blast radius, Rogers had not built these sorts of partitions, according to senior executives at rival telecoms. Because of that decision, the whole industry was now being cast in a bad light.

The outage thrust a reluctant Staffieri into the spotlight as he embarked on a high-profile "apology tour"—not the sort of thing that any CEO wants to do, especially one brand-new to his job. The CRTC, meanwhile, launched an investigation into the shutdown, firing off dozens of detailed questions to the company. The regulator grilled the telecom not only about the most recent outage but also about previous ones. It wanted to know what measures Rogers had put in place after the wireless outage it had experienced just fourteen months earlier, and why they hadn't prevented the more recent one from occurring.

The telecom's answers were posted online, albeit in a partially redacted form. The redactions triggered a backlash from consumer advocates, who felt that Rogers had a duty to be more transparent, particularly given the severity of the situation. Nonetheless, the responses were illuminating, suggesting that the company's delayed communications had stemmed from problems logging in to its social media accounts, which had been protected by two-factor authentication linked to Rogers devices.

Needless to say, the whole ordeal had come at a terrible time for Rogers. The outage's breadth—the way that it was able to take out everything from hospitals to payment systems—had reinforced the telecom giant's ubiquity at a time when it was asking regulators for permission to swallow up Shaw and become an even bigger company. Even prior to the outage, the deal had not been going smoothly. The takeover, which had already seen its deadline extended from mid-June until the end of July, was facing the prospect of a lengthy hearing in front of the Competition Tribunal.

Unless Rogers could reach a settlement with the Competition Bureau soon, and get the blessing of Champagne's ministry, the deal was unlikely to close before the end of the year. That meant Rogers would have to bear additional financing-related costs. The telecom had tapped debt markets back in March, raising US$7.05 billion south of the border and $4.25 billion through Canadian bond issues in order to replace the $19 billion bridge loan it had secured from a consortium of banks. But the bonds contained a clause that required them to be redeemed at 101 per cent of their value if the deal didn't close by the end of the year. The company would be forced to either pay hundreds of millions of dollars in fees to extend the bonds' redemption dates or find other sources of capital. Even more troubling was the fact that mediation talks aimed at resolving the impasse with Matthew Boswell had gone nowhere.

Meanwhile, public outcry over the deal grew into a chorus. On social media, consumers griped about wireless prices and the telecom oligopoly. Some questioned how the federal government could allow Rogers—the company that, hot off a corporate governance fiasco, had left millions of its customers without wireless or internet service for at least a whole day—to become an even larger behemoth. At the annual Calgary Stampede rodeo and festival, advocacy group OpenMedia sent out a street team to hand out flyers and rally opposition to the takeover. They were overwhelmed by the response. Grappling with the highest levels of inflation seen in years, Albertans were concerned that the takeover would kill thousands of jobs and increase wireless prices. Anger over the catastrophic outage had only poured more fuel onto the fire of discontent.

After returning from Asia, Champagne had flown to Calgary to attend the Stampede and meet with local business leaders. At a ground-breaking ceremony for the SAM Centre, a cultural centre celebrating the history of the Stampede, he was asked by Canadian Press reporter Amanda Stephenson whether the outage would have a bearing on his decision in the ongoing merger review. "This is certainly going to be on my mind, and the minds of all Canadians," he told her.

Later that month, as Rogers reported its second-quarter results, analysts zeroed in on how the service disruption would impact the telecom's bottom line. The company's results for the three-month period stretching from April to June—its second full quarter under Staffieri's leadership—were bouncing back from pandemic lows. Quarterly revenue had grown by 8 per cent from a year ago to $3.87 billion, while profits had jumped 35 per cent year-over-year to $409 million as the return of travel boosted wireless roaming revenues. However, the outage, which had occurred during the third quarter, hung over the promising results like a dark cloud.

Staffieri downplayed the situation. "Since the outage of July 8, we did see an impact on our subscriber results, but we're encouraged by the patience our customers have shown," he told analysts during the conference call.

Later, during BCE's earnings call, Mirko Bibic reassured investors that his company's network was not susceptible to a complete outage like the one experienced by Rogers. BCE's telecom subsidiary, Bell Canada, uses separate infrastructure for its wireless and broadband networks, so a problem with one of the networks would not take down the other, he told analysts. "Now it's clear that no network is perfect and no network is immune to outages, but network architecture clearly does make a difference."

By then, Rogers had announced plans to physically separate its wireless and wireline network cores. The project would be expensive—Staffieri estimated it would cost at least $250 million—but it would provide a backup in case one of the cores went down.

Jorge Fernandes announced the plan to the company's employees at an all-hands meeting a week after the outage. A well-regarded executive who had served as chief technology officer of Vodafone's U.K. division, Fernandes had been recruited by Natale, and he remained one of the last holdovers from the ousted CEO's senior leadership team.

But Fernandes wouldn't be overseeing the separation of the two network cores. Five days after the all-hands meeting, the company quietly updated the leadership team section of its website, scrubbing Fernandes's name, bio, and headshot from the page. Ron McKenzie was listed as chief technology and information officer.

McKenzie was less than a week into his tenure as CTO when he sat down next to Staffieri at a long wooden desk in room 415 of the Wellington Building in downtown Ottawa. The structure, built in the 1920s in the architectural style taught at Paris's École des Beaux-Arts, had once been the Canadian headquarters of the Metropolitan Life Insurance Company. Decades later, it was bought by the federal government and repurposed for parliamentary functions, such as the public flogging session that the House of Commons industry and technology committee had convened on July 25.

Although the House had been adjourned for the summer, the committee had called a special hearing into the Rogers outage. The telecom's top brass had been summoned to appear, along with Champagne, CRTC chair Ian Scott, and a smattering of academics and consumer advocates.

McKenzie, a silver-haired technology executive whose eye corners crinkled when he smiled, had arrived at Rogers after more than a decade at Calgary-based Shaw, including a stint as chief operating officer. Before becoming the Toronto telecom's chief technology officer, he'd served as president of Rogers for Business, the division responsible for providing connectivity to enterprises ranging from small businesses to government departments. McKenzie's bio on the Rogers website boasted about his deep technology experience, including leading the company's technical transformation at the onset of the pandemic, when commerce rapidly moved online. But some of the former executives who had worked with McKenzie suspected that he had been promoted not only for his technical skills but also because he was easy to get along with—some thought he was overly obsequious, even going so far as to suggest that he was a yes man.

Staffieri called on McKenzie several times during the hearing to provide technical explanations. Otherwise, the executive mostly sat quietly in a crisp dark blue suit accessorized with a striped pocket square, letting his boss do the talking.

Members of Parliament, as well as Champagne and Scott, criticized the telecom for its sluggish public response during the outage. Scott called the communications delay unacceptable, while Champagne lambasted Staffieri for not reaching out to him during the crisis. Several MPs questioned whether the investments that the company was promising to make in its networks should have been made sooner. Had a business decision to underinvest put the network—and people's safety—at risk?

One MP asked about diversity on the company's board. Another questioned why a company as complex as Rogers didn't have a chief risk officer on its executive leadership team. "I look forward to seeing an estimate of the cost of this outage to the Canadian economy," remarked Liberal MP Iqwinder Gaheer. Viviane Lapointe, another Liberal MP, asked why the routing issue hadn't been caught during testing. "It's difficult to have a test environment that replicates the entirety of a very complex network across the nation," Staffieri told her.

Not content with the level of pillorying thus far, Conservative MP Tracy Gray questioned whether Staffieri should lose his job. "You've had two system-wide failures within your organization, created by your organization, putting public safety at risk," she noted. "So who is losing their job? Or should it be you? Do you have the confidence of your board?"

Throughout the grilling, Staffieri remained calm and composed, almost to the point of sounding robotic. "I'm accountable to ensure this doesn't happen again. And as I've said, we have already undertaken processes and actions to make changes," he responded in a flat tone. Over the course of the hour-long beating, he stuck to his talking points. The company was sorry, and it was taking all of the necessary steps to prevent another outage.

Nathaniel Erskine-Smith, an outspoken Liberal MP who would later enter the Ontario Liberal leadership race, used the hearing as an opportunity to hammer Staffieri about the level of concentration in the sector.

"We work every day in a very competitive environment. And we work hard to bring the best value for money for our customers and for Canadians," Staffieri said in a stilted, rehearsed manner. "It's in our interest to do so. They have alternatives and they have choice."

"Wait, wait, wait—so you think Canadians have alternatives and choice in this marketplace?" Erskine-Smith retorted.

"Very much so," Staffieri replied.

"And you're saying that with a straight face?" Erskine-Smith paused briefly, as if to allow Staffieri to answer, but then quickly continued. "Okay, I'm running out of time, so here's another one you can maybe answer with a straight face. Do you think this is the end of the Rogers-Shaw deal?"

TWENTY

MONOLITHIC WIRELESS

There are many things Pierre Karl Péladeau had done in his life to have caused a stir, but his choice of shoes had not been one of them. That is, until late October 2022, when the billionaire cable scion strode into the lobby of the reflective tower in downtown Ottawa that housed the Competition Tribunal wearing a pair of black sneakers with a three-piece suit. For at least a moment, Péladeau's choice of footwear became the subject of conversation among some government staffers, rather than the business at hand. But it was not, as some might have assumed, an eccentric fashion statement. While Péladeau and his counterparts at Rogers and Shaw were trying to negotiate a compromise aimed at resolving the competition commissioner's objections to their three-way deal, the roguish, charismatic president of Quebecor Inc. was dealing with a ski injury. He had fallen on his knee and damaged his meniscus, causing his leg to swell up and forcing him to forgo the standard dress shoes.

PKP was a polarizing figure in Ottawa, in large part due to his brief stint as leader of Quebec's separatist party, the Parti Québécois. Then there was his messy personal life, including a bitter divorce and child custody battle with his ex-wife, TV personality Julie Snyder; a high-profile inheritance dispute with his youngest sister that dragged on for two decades; and a temper so legendary that it occasionally generated news coverage.

Quebecor's Vidéotron had previously contemplated a national expansion and then cancelled its plans, selling the discounted spectrum it had bought in the Toronto area during the 2008 auction for nearly double what it paid and netting an $87.8 million profit. Spectrum-flipping wasn't against the rules, although it was frowned upon as an inefficient use of the scarce and valuable publicly owned resource. In spite of that blemish on the telecom's track record, Quebecor's top brass believed they had a strong case that wireless competition would flourish if they were permitted to acquire Freedom. Péladeau and his entourage, which included his chief financial officer, Hugues Simard, were feeling hopeful as they headed into the mediation talks alongside their counterparts at Rogers and Shaw and the requisite army of lawyers. It was the cable companies' last shot at avoiding a drawn-out public hearing in front of the Competition Tribunal.

Less than two days earlier, Champagne had walked up to a podium flanked by four Canadian flags and read a statement that, although vague enough to give him wiggle room, was seen by many as tacit approval of the merger. "I want to make very clear the lens through which I will consider this proposed spectrum transfer," he stated. He expected Vidéotron to hold on to Freedom's wireless licences for at least a decade, not sell them for an easy profit. He also wanted to see wireless prices in Ontario and western Canada come down to the level Vidéotron was charging in Quebec, which he estimated to be about 20 per cent lower on average. Within hours, Péladeau had announced that he accepted the terms, calling them "in line with our business philosophy."

Some critics, including telecom researcher and Carleton Ph.D. candidate Ben Klass, noted that Freedom's pricing on some entry-level plans was already lower than Vidéotron's offerings in Quebec. Regardless, the street was jubilant. Some of the hedge fund investors poised to profit from the takeover believed that Champagne had boxed the Competition Bureau into a corner by signalling that he was essentially ready to approve the deal, with some conditions attached.

The next morning, Rogers and Shaw saw their stock prices surge on the Toronto Stock Exchange. Even a negative statement from the Competition Bureau, which said that it remained firm in its decision to challenge the proposed deal, didn't entirely dampen investors' exuberance.

Ahead of the negotiations, the telecoms had put forward a settlement proposal that aimed to address the commissioner's concerns that separating Freedom Mobile from Shaw's cable network would weaken the carrier. Rogers was proposing to give Quebecor access to some fibre-optic infrastructure—specifically, strands of glass contained within the cable sheath. The fibre strands were located within Freedom Mobile's B.C. and Alberta footprint in what's known as the "last mile," which connects cellphone towers to the backbone of the network.

Inside the tribunal's offices at 90 Sparks Street, the four parties—competition commissioner Matthew Boswell and his staff; Staffieri and his Rogers delegation; a team of Shaw executives that included Trevor English and Paul McAleese; and the Quebecor group—were all set up in separate rooms. The mediator, a white-haired retired Federal Court Justice named Michael Phelan, went back and forth between them, a process called shuttle diplomacy. It was the second attempt by the Competition Tribunal to find a middle ground between the telecoms and Boswell, who seemed intent on fighting the merger to the bitter end. The first, a virtual session mediated by Associate Chief Justice Jocelyne Gagné in July, just weeks after Rogers had struck a deal with Vidéotron, had been unsuccessful.

Although Boswell had moved to block the merger before the sale of Freedom to Vidéotron had been announced, the divestiture hadn't assuaged his concerns. In court documents filed in early September, the Competition Bureau described the divestiture as an ineffective remedy that would leave Freedom a "substantially weaker competitor."

Any optimism that the cable company executives might have had going into the second mediation session evaporated quickly. They felt that Boswell was refusing to engage with them and wouldn't divulge the terms under which the bureau would approve the deal. But the Competition Bureau's staff believed that they had been clear from the outset. In their minds, Freedom Mobile was inextricable from Shaw's cable network. And short of divulging significant cable infrastructure—the precise thing that Rogers was looking to acquire—there was nothing that Rogers and Shaw could do to win the bureau's blessing.

Staffieri asked Phelan, the mediator, if Boswell would meet with him face-to-face to try to resolve the impasse. Boswell agreed, and he and Staffieri, along with Ted Woodhead, Rogers' chief legal and regulatory officer, sat around a table in a small boardroom. But the meeting, which proved fruitless, was over in minutes.

After several hours, Phelan informed the parties that there was no compromise to be found. Their positions were simply irreconcilable. The frustrated cable executives and their lawyers filtered out of the building shortly after 1 p.m. The whole thing, they felt, had been a waste of time. While it was still technically possible to reach a settlement before the hearing began, or even while it was underway, Desjardins analyst Jérome Dubreuil pegged the odds at "close to zero per cent." The case was now, in all likelihood, headed for a month-long hearing that not only would further delay the merger but that also carried the distinct possibility of failure.

The lawyers rushed back to their gleaming office towers. They didn't have a minute to spare. The largest, most complex case in the Competition Tribunal's history was set to kick off in just eleven days, and they had a ton of work to do.

From a young age, Matthew Boswell believed that what drove the Canadian economy was much more than just the large corporations and the major urban centres in which they resided. This belief was fostered by his father, a logging supervisor who spent much of his time visiting lumber mills and factories in various towns across the country. Whenever Boswell and his three older brothers started to give off an urban, city-slicker vibe, his father would recite his "Mid-Canada speech." Don't get fooled into thinking that Ottawa, Toronto, and Montreal are all there is to Canada, he would tell them. The country's tapestry is made up of many smaller towns, and most of its residents are employed by smaller companies. "I still think about it," Boswell says years later of the speech, as he reflect on his upbringing. "I guess it's kind of in my DNA now."

After finishing his law degree at the University of Manitoba and Queen's, Boswell landed in the litigation group of a Bay Street law firm called Smith Lyons. However, once he realized that the opportunities to actually get into a courtroom and litigate were scarce for an associate, he wound up taking a job as an assistant Crown attorney. The former shoe factory that housed the courtroom that he worked out of was a world away from the shiny law offices on the sixty-first floor of Scotia Plaza, but he loved being the public's representative. It was an incredibly rewarding, albeit at times incredibly challenging, job.

After a stint at the Ontario Securities Commission, Boswell landed at the Competition Bureau, where, over the course of nearly a decade, he worked his way up to the role of Commissioner of Competition in 2019. Over time, he came to believe that Canada had fallen significantly behind the rest of the world when it came to competition law, despite having been one of the first countries to implement such a framework back in 1889, one year before the United States. He felt that the country lacked a robust enforcement framework, which hampered the bureau's ability to conduct investigations and promote competition. The agency couldn't levy the kinds of financial penalties that its global peers could, nor could it compel companies to disclose the information that the watchdog needed to conduct proper market studies. Its budget had stagnated for years, even as the economy grew.

According to Boswell, this translated into very real, very negative effects on the country's economy. Competition was, after all, a "key pillar of a capitalist society." The country's productivity growth was "weak if not anemic," the gap between Canada and its international partners was widening, and the regulatory barriers to competition were, in his view, "depressing." Multiple sectors of the Canadian economy could be described as oligopolies, characterized by coordinated behaviour between a small number of players that dominated the market. In 2008, the federal government commissioned a report that provided a succinct summary of the situation: "Canada has been identified as a country that does not place sufficient importance on competition in the conduct of its affairs." Boswell jotted the quote down on a sticky note and attached it to a folder. Even in 2022, as the end of his five-year term neared, it continued to serve as a reminder of how little the situation had changed.

In the lead-up to the hearings, media reports characterized Boswell as a man fighting a "holy battle" to modernize Canada's competition laws. In fact, some believed that Boswell had a weak case, and that his opposition to the merger amounted to little more than a kamikaze mission aimed at proving just how badly the laws needed to be changed. To Boswell, this was a ludicrous and insulting suggestion. Staff in the bureau's mergers directorate had worked around the clock for months reviewing 3 million records, including internal documents from the companies themselves, and interviewing over 100 industry participants and stakeholders for what was arguably the agency's largest-ever merger investigation. The task had become so encompassing for the bureau that, at times, the merger team had to borrow staff from other areas. After conducting that work, the bureau arrived at what Boswell characterized as an "inescapable conclusion": the deal was going to substantially reduce competition.

Still, the task ahead of Boswell and his litigation team was daunting. The Competition Bureau had taken several merger cases to the tribunal, and had won some concessions, including remedies that aimed to lessen the impact on competition. But, according to University of Ottawa law professor Jennifer Quaid, it had never convinced the tribunal to block a merger completely, as it was now asking it to do.

A palpable sense of urgency permeated the virtual hearing that kicked off on November 7, 2022. The Competition Tribunal, a quasi-judicial body established to hear cases brought by the bureau, had set aside twenty days, and there were tens of thousands of pages of filed evidence to get through. Paul Crampton, the Federal Court chief justice presiding over the hearings, was worried about how long it would take the three-member panel to weigh all the evidence and issue a ruling.

Crampton had been appointed to the Federal Court in 2009 and joined the Competition Tribunal the following year. Prior to that he had practised competition law himself, spending a decade at the Bay Street firm Davies Ward Phillips & Vineberg. (Coincidentally, the same firm was representing Shaw in the proceedings.) He was joined on the panel by two laypeople—a business professor at the University of New Brunswick named Dr. Wiktor Askanas, and Ramaz Samrout, a consultant specializing in regulatory economics.

"This is a very complex case, and it's going to be a real challenge to get a decision out in the time frame that the respondents have requested," Crampton told the parties, urging them to avoid adding to that complexity. If the merger didn't close by the end of the year, Rogers would have to pay its bond holders $262 million. That was on top of $557 million it had already paid to extend its financing—money that, according to lawyers for the cable companies, could have otherwise been invested in networks. Shaw, meanwhile, was in limbo, bleeding talent as it waited to consummate the takeover.

The Competition Bureau opened its case with a surprise appearance from a Hollywood star and former Freedom Mobile spokesperson, Canadian actor Will Arnett. To demonstrate the carrier's role in the wireless sector, the watchdog played a 2019 television ad featuring Arnett, best known for his role in the television series *Arrested Development*. It began with an ominous nighttime shot of an office tower for a fictional telecom company called Monolithic Wireless. Inside, three executives—a parody of Bell, Telus, and Rogers—sat around a table in a dimly lit boardroom, laughing maniacally about their plans to hike data charges—"Because they always pay!" That's when Arnett swivelled around in his chair, cutting them short as he launched into a sales pitch for what was, at the time, a highly competitive offer: ten gigabytes of data for $50.

"That was the kind of disruptive, competitive player that Shaw has been in the marketplace," explained John Tyhurst, a battle-hardened competition lawyer who had honed his litigation skills prosecuting criminal price-fixing and bid-rigging cases for the Department of Justice. White-haired and sharply dressed in a dark blue blazer and tortoiseshell glasses, Tyhurst had been lured out of semi-retirement to assist the bureau with what would have been, for someone like him, the case of a lifetime.

The perception that Freedom Mobile was a scrappy, disruptive competitor—a maverick—was central to the Competition Bureau's case. Although wireless was a small component of Shaw's overall business, responsible for just a fraction of its revenues, it played an outsized role in the hearings. There was, after all, no overlap between Rogers' and Shaw's cable networks. The only real competition between them was in the wireless sector, where they fought over customers in Ontario, Alberta, and British Columbia.

The bureau's position was that, prior to the merger announcement, Shaw had been a competitive force in the wireless market, using offers such as the Big Gig plan that Arnett was peddling to snatch customers away from the Big Three telecoms. When it launched its Shaw Mobile service in 2020, a disproportionate share of Rogers customers had switched over, according to porting data that tracked customer movement between carriers. Even as it negotiated a deal to sell itself to Rogers, Shaw was on the cusp of rolling out 5G; window posters announcing the new service were already in retailers' hands.

According to the bureau, all of that had changed within months of the merger announcement. The 5G rollout was halted, and Shaw sat out the summer auction for airwaves in the 3,500-megahertz range, a critical band for 5G on account of its ability to carry large volumes of data over long distances. The telecom went about hiking prices, slashing promotions, and curtailing its investments, particularly on the wireless side. In essence, Shaw had stopped competing before the deal had even closed, the bureau argued.

Boswell stood firm on his opposition in spite of the proposed divestiture of Freedom, because the bureau's investigation had convinced him that severing Freedom from Shaw's cable network would weaken it. He was particularly concerned about western Canada, where Vidéotron didn't own any infrastructure at all and had no track record of successfully competing. Although it could lease capacity from other telecoms, the bureau argued that such an arrangement would leave Freedom Mobile with razor-thin margins, hampering the carrier's ability to compete by lowering prices. Additionally, Rogers was poised to acquire a number of assets that, according to the bureau, supported Freedom, including a network of Wi-Fi hotspots, 450,000 Shaw Mobile subscribers, and the Shaw brand.

To prop up Freedom, Rogers had entered a series of commercial agreements granting Vidéotron access to various infrastructure at what the telecoms characterized as highly favourable rates. However, the commissioner saw those agreements as problematic, too. Tyhurst argued that the "complex web" of thirteen deals would make Vidéotron overly dependent on Rogers as its supplier, leaving the regional cable company vulnerable to anti-competitive actions by its much larger rival. These concerns weren't merely hypothetical, he said; Vidéotron was already alleging in its network sharing lawsuit that Rogers had deliberately sabotaged their pact in Ottawa and Quebec. He was also concerned that the agreements would create an incentive for Vidéotron to coordinate with Rogers, rather than competing against it. In essence, the bureau believed that instead of three suits sitting around the boardroom table at Monolothic Wireless conspiring to protect their margins, there would be four.

Representing the cable companies was a cadre of the country's toughest commercial litigators. Rogers had enlisted Jonathan Lisus's firm, while Shaw was represented by a contingent from Davies headed up by Kent Thomson, who had a massive courtroom presence and a friendly manner that belied his ferocity. Vidéotron, which was intervening in the case, was represented by John Rook, a gruff, white-haired partner at Bennett Jones.

The telecoms' position was, in a nutshell, that the deal was good for consumers, and that Boswell had been convinced otherwise by aggressive lobbying from Bell and Telus, who were threatened by the prospect of increased competition. The telecoms' lawyers argued that combining the country's two largest cable networks would put Rogers and Shaw on more equal footing with their

telephone company rivals, particularly in western Canada, where
Telus had gained the upper hand. If the merger went through,
Telus would finally have something it hadn't had for a long time—
a real competitor. "Rogers will be able to hammer away at Telus
in a way that Shaw currently cannot and hasn't been able to for
years," Thomson told the tribunal.

They also argued that Freedom would become an even stron-
ger competitor in Vidéotron's hands. Acquiring Freedom's 1.7 million wireless customers would double Vidéotron's customer base,
creating a near-national carrier with a substantial war chest of
spectrum licences and a "springboard" of favourable network
access agreements. The commissioner's claim that Freedom would
be unable to compete without Shaw's cable network was "untethered from reality," Lisus argued. Freedom didn't own any of the
fibre-optic infrastructure it used for backhaul, the portion of a cellular network that connects the towers to the core. Instead it relied
on leased fibre, a commodity readily available on the open market.

After Lisus finished delivering his opening arguments,
Crampton briefly interrupted the session to address an unusual
development. He was being "bombarded," he told the public hearing, by a massive volume of emails whose subject lines were all
slightly different variations on a theme: "Say No To Rogers-Shaw,"
"Bad idea Rogers-Shaw," "I am against Rogers-Shaw."

"Whoever is organizing these needs to stop," Crampton said
sternly, noting that he wouldn't be opening the messages. "They're
being deleted. I just wanted to say that this is very, very improper."

The Competition Tribunal was accustomed to operating largely
out of the public eye. The institution was created in 1986, when
Parliament revamped the country's competition laws. Its role was
to adjudicate cases brought forward by the bureau, an independent
law enforcement agency tasked with policing not only mergers but

also anti-competitive behaviours such as price-fixing and abuse
of dominance. Most people didn't even know that Canada had a
merger court, much less how it operated. Although it served an
important role in the country's economy, the majority of the cases
it heard didn't generate a tremendous amount of public attention.
For instance, just before the Rogers-Shaw hearings got underway,
the tribunal had issued a decision relating to the acquisition of a
grain elevator near Virden, Manitoba. Some tribunal hearings were
so sparsely attended that when they moved to in-camera sessions,
there was no one to kick out of the hearing room.

The immense public interest generated by the proposed merger
between Rogers and Shaw was almost entirely due to the deal's
implications for users of one of society's most critical and widely
used services. Consumers were fed up with paying cellphone bills
that, according to some (heavily disputed) studies, were among
the highest in the world, and many were concerned that the deal
would only increase them further. The nearly 8,000 people who
had written in to the Competition Bureau after the merger was
announced to voice their opposition to the deal forcefully punctuated this sentiment. The number of submissions was more than
four times higher than the merger that had generated the second-
highest level of response: BCE's takeover of Manitoba Telecom
Services in 2017. The acquisition of propane retailer Canwest
Propane by Superior Plus LP, in contrast, had generated just thirty-
eight comments. It didn't hurt that a pandemic-driven shift to virtual hearings had made it possible to observe the proceedings from
anywhere, including the home office or the couch. The net result
was that the Competition Tribunal found itself thrust into the
spotlight in a manner that it likely had never been before, and some
of the hundreds of viewers who logged in to the hearings were
surprised to discover a system that was far more opaque than they
had imagined.

It was common for significant portions of Competition Tribunal hearings to take place during in-camera, or confidential, sessions, to protect competitively sensitive business information.
But to many observers, the amount of content that had been labelled
commercially sensitive in the Rogers-Shaw case was shockingly
high. Some days, less than two hours of witness testimony took
place in public sessions. The rest of the day, attendees found themselves staring at blank screens in the breakout rooms they had been
seconded to. Documents were heavily redacted. Witness statements
were posted online only after the witness had finished testifying,
making cross-examination difficult to follow. Even the schedule
of witnesses was treated as a state secret. The result was a process
that was discombobulating even for those deep in the weeds on
the file. Many chalked this up to the fact that the tribunal was not
accustomed to such a high level of public scrutiny. Some mused
that, due to the time crunch it was facing, the tribunal might have
been more inclined to remove things from the public record than
spend precious time challenging requests for confidentiality.

Crampton was made aware of the public discontent via an article in the *Globe and Mail*. "Rogers-Shaw hearings not so public
despite tribunal's pledge to hold open process," read the headline
in the paper's weekend edition after the first week of hearings. The
following Monday, Crampton opened the hearings by responding
to the concerns. He vowed to be more diligent in ensuring that the
public was able to follow the process, and that sessions were only
held in-camera when absolutely necessary. One of his first moves
towards greater transparency was determining that an internal
Telus document that had been labelled confidential didn't warrant
the designation. The document—an internal presentation to the
telecom's board—confirmed what many had suspected: that behind
the scenes, Telus had been working overtime to derail the merger.
The company had dubbed this initiative Project Fox. It included

providing talking points to NDP leader Jagmeet Singh, who repeatedly grilled Prime Minister Justin Trudeau about the merger during Question Period; using the Rogers outage as an opportunity to warn the Competition Bureau about the risk of eliminating network redundancies; and deploying executives to Ottawa to—in Telus's own words—"kill, shape, and slow the deal." One bullet point indicated the company was lobbying Champagne about what it framed as the dangers of allowing Vidéotron to acquire Freedom.

Another Project Fox document, which was also made public, appeared to be the product of a brainstorming session, with various ideas grouped by the level of risk and effort associated with each one. It was unclear from the document whether Telus had acted on any of the ideas, which ranged from erecting billboards in Shaw's territory, to mobilizing unions over the prospect of job cuts, to enlisting "friendly academics" and former public servants to write op-eds in the media. The telecom apparently even contemplated working with "meme factories" such as Canada Proud, a right-wing group committed to ousting Prime Minister Justin Trudeau that has been accused of spreading misinformation.

According to the cable company lawyers, the existence of Project Fox called into question the motives and credibility of several expert witnesses from Bell and Telus. The commissioner was relying heavily on their testimony to support his claim that Freedom would be unable to succeed without the benefit of Shaw's cable network. Meanwhile, Telus had been hatching elaborate schemes to stop, or at least delay, the deal.

Over the course of seventeen days, the tribunal heard evidence from roughly forty witnesses, including industry consultants, economic experts, and telecom executives. Despite Crampton's efforts to make the process more transparent, a significant portion of the hearings still took place during confidential sessions. Those parts that were public were punctuated by tense moments of cross-examination and squabbles between lawyers who couldn't seem to

agree on even the most basic facts. Everything from the gravity of
the Rogers outage to the effectiveness of the wholesale regime
(Vidéotron would be relying on it to resell internet services as part
of its bundling strategy in western Canada) was debated. At times,
the two sides were so openly hostile towards one another that a
Financial Post columnist described the hearings as "worthy of
Netflix" and as "a Hollywood parody of a trial." But for the most
part, they were focused on the minutiae of anti-trust economics,
with expert witnesses sparring over issues such as how to correctly
model the merger's likely impact on prices. (This, it turned out,
was not at all a straightforward matter, as it required making quite
a few assumptions.) Often, the data that they were arguing about
was redacted from public view.

One unconventional aspect of the bureau's case, which was
puzzling to some of the cable company lawyers, was its argument
that the takeover would create a massive transfer of wealth from
consumers to a small handful of Canada's richest families. To support that argument, the watchdog had retained the services of a
poverty researcher and Dalhousie University professor named
Lars Osberg. Dr. Osberg characterized the Rogers and Shaw families as being within the top 1 per cent of the top 1 per cent, even
before the deal closed. Just a 5 per cent return on their telecom
shares would generate $450 million in annual income for the
Rogers family and $100 million for the Shaws, his analysis found.

In one particularly heated exchange, an intense Competition
Bureau lawyer named Alexander Gay grilled Brad Shaw about the
roughly $2.3 billion his family stood to receive in cash and Rogers
shares if the deal went ahead. Brad had testified that the Shaws
had decided to sell the business they had run for half a century
because it was the right thing to do for the company's shareholders, customers, and employees.

But Gay wasn't buying the altruistic explanation. "You may
very well have some overriding interest for shareholders, but

certainly you stand to gain, and you stand to gain *big*," he said. "So I find it hard to believe that you stand here today and suggest that somehow it's all about the constituents and not yourself." Two of Shaw's top executives—Trevor English and Paul McAleese—were also questioned about the large payouts they stood to receive if the deal closed, a strategy that appeared designed to call into question the earnestness of their testimony.

Brad replied that the merger was a last resort for his family, which had ruled out every alternative. "At the end of the day it's not about the dollars. It's about the business and how we support it."

Throughout their testimony, Shaw's executives characterized Freedom Mobile as an unsuccessful investment, one that had cost the company a lot of money without generating any free cash flow. The bureau was overstating its significance in the market, their lawyers argued. Gay pushed back, claiming that the company was using a skewed definition of free cash flow that it chose not to include in any of its financial reporting. In 2020, the overall company had generated $750 million of free cash flow, which it returned to its shareholders through dividends and buybacks, he noted. "Seems to me, these aren't the actions necessarily of a company that's in financial distress."

But English wasn't suggesting that the company was in distress, the chief financial and corporate development officer explained. Rather, he was speaking about the long-term strategic challenges that it was facing. Shaw's portrayal of its wireless business as a costly and unprofitable endeavour ended up prompting a question from Justice Crampton: if the Shaws couldn't make it work, why would Péladeau's chances be any better?

John Rook, Vidéotron's lawyer, argued that the deal his client had struck with Rogers and Shaw left the regional telecom in an advantaged position. Vidéotron would be acquiring Freedom for a "very attractive price" that was significantly below the $4.5 billion that Shaw had poured into it, he said, and it had secured access to Rogers' infrastructure at favourable terms. Additionally, Vidéotron had snapped up discounted 5G spectrum licences during the most recent federal auction in all three of the provinces where Freedom operated. Vidéotron was a proven competitor with a track record of gaining market share—in Quebec it had captured roughly 22 per cent of the wireless market—by offering lower prices. Adding Freedom's 1.7 million customers to its own would double Vidéotron's size, creating a near-national competitor with a larger portfolio of wireless licences and a credible path to 5G.

The bureau was not convinced. Its lawyers depicted Vidéotron as vulnerable and dependent. Quebecor was a smaller company than Shaw, Gay noted, and less well capitalized. Its credit rating was not just lower; it was non-investment grade. It might stave off bankruptcy and remain viable after acquiring Freedom, said Derek Leschinsky, one of the bureau's lawyers. But it would most likely putter along at the bottom of the market, with a view to one day selling itself to one of the larger telecoms. It would certainly not replace Shaw as a competitive force, Leschinsky argued. "That's not the competition that Canada deserves."

In late November, as the hearings drew to a close, the focus shifted to a bit of wording contained within section 96 of Canada's Competition Act. Known colloquially as the "efficiencies defence," the provision allowed a merger, even an anti-competitive one, to proceed if the potential cost savings, or efficiencies, for the merging parties outweighed the harms borne by consumers. Call it a trump card that could be played when the bureau tried to stop a takeover. Canada was the only G7 country to have such a rule, which was crafted in 1986, when consolidation was far less prevalent and free trade with the U.S. did not yet exist. At the time, the concern was that, because Canada was such a small market, domestic companies didn't stand a chance at achieving the scale they needed to compete abroad.

Naturally, Boswell believed that the provision should be eliminated. He was of the view that it was permitting mergers that were harmful to the Canadian economy, and that private benefits to merging companies shouldn't be financed by the costs incurred by Canadians.

For Rogers and Shaw, the efficiencies defence was a last resort. If they had to rely on it, that would be because the tribunal had determined that their merger was likely to reduce competition. This would put Champagne in a tough spot, as approving the spectrum licence transfer would mean greenlighting an anti-competitive deal and going against the Liberal government's promise to bring down wireless prices. Plus, the government had already committed to modernizing the Competition Act, and section 96 was almost certainly going to be part of that review. Allowing a telecom megamerger to skate through on efficiencies alone would be a bad look.

Rogers and Shaw predicted that they wouldn't have to rely on section 96. On the opening day of the hearing, Lisus proclaimed that the deal was so pro-competitive the tribunal wouldn't even have to weigh the cost savings. Still, the parties presented their evidence with regard to efficiencies, in case it came to that. And although expert witnesses from both sides bickered over the math, there was little doubt in financial circles that the efficiencies generated by the merger would be enormous. (The precise numbers, however, were not made public.)

By the time the hearings concluded in mid-December, the year-end deadline loomed large in Crampton's mind. While Rogers lamented the possibility of having to pay a quarter of a billion dollars to its bondholders to extend its financing for another year, Tyhurst implored the tribunal not to rush its decision. The case was complex, and there were fewer than ten days remaining before

Christmas. Normally, the tribunal took months, sometimes over a year, to issue a decision.

The closing arguments during the last two days of hearings coincided with the World Cup semifinals in Qatar. Hours after France had defeated Morocco by two goals, securing a spot against Argentina in the finals, Justice Crampton concluded the month-long anti-trust case with a soccer analogy. He likened the tribunal's pretrial process to the World Cup's qualifying tournaments, and the arduous, weeks-long evidentiary phase to the group stage of the sporting event. But unlike the World Cup, whose outcome would be settled within days, Crampton didn't know how long it would take for the tribunal to reach its decision.

"You've given us lots to think about," he said, "and given us a lot of documentation to go over and then discuss with each other." The tribunal was "very sensitive" to the companies' commercial deadlines, he added, but he stopped short of committing to any particular timeline. "We're going to bend over backwards to do what we can in recognition of those realities, but we're going to take the amount of time that it takes to produce a solid, robust decision that is well grounded in the evidence," he explained. "And so, not sure how long that's going to take."

TWENTY-ONE

PINOCCHIO AND GEPPETTO

One day in the summer of 2022, a document landed in the Toronto integrity commissioner's inbox. It was from Adam Chaleff, a bearded, 37-year-old civic activist with a keen interest in the inner workings of the municipal government.

Chaleff ticked all the boxes required to earn the "progressive urbanist" label in his Twitter bio. He worked as a communications adviser for a labour union called the Society of United Professionals, and at one point had served on the board of the Toronto Public Library. His life as an activist began in grade five when he opposed the closure of his alternative elementary school. By high school he was a familiar face at City Hall.

Chaleff had made a name for himself in 2012 by lodging a high-profile complaint against then-mayor Rob Ford. The wheels that Chaleff set in motion resulted in Ford being ousted from office for breaching conflict-of-interest rules, although the mayor obtained a stay that allowed him to hold on to the job until a higher court overturned the decision.

At the peak of the pandemic, the City of Toronto had launched an initiative that aligned with Chaleff's views of what a progressive city should be. Lake Shore Boulevard, a major artery running along the Lake Ontario waterfront, was closed to vehicles on the weekends to create recreational space for cyclists and pedestrians. Chaleff took advantage of the opportunity, strapping his toddler into a seat affixed to the back of his bike for twenty- to thirty-kilometre rides. When a debate broke out in City Council over the stretch of road that he had been riding, Chaleff watched closely.

The conflict began with a letter from Toronto Blue Jays president Mark Shapiro, imploring Mayor John Tory to vote against continuing the Lake Shore closures at an upcoming City Council meeting. "As a sports organization, we support folks getting outside and being active," Shapiro wrote in the June 6 letter. But the closures were a nightmare for fans trying to get to baseball games at the Rogers Centre, Shapiro complained. Couldn't the city close down some other, less vital street? "Toronto has many options and routes to use, whereas our fans do not."

When Shapiro received backlash online over his letter, Tory jumped in to defend him. The mayor then went on to vote in favour of an amended ActiveTO plan—one that didn't include Lake Shore.

Chaleff had never been a supporter of Tory's. He felt that the mayor was so tightly enmeshed in the city's elite business and social circles that he was essentially a walking conflict of interest. That was especially so when it came to Rogers, in Chaleff's view. Tory not only influenced the company's direction via his role on the trust; he was also a shareholder.

The mayor had declared conflicts and recused himself from votes on account of his involvement with the Rogers family trusts on dozens of occasions, and Chaleff believed he should have done so with ActiveTO as well. After all, both the Blue Jays and the

Rogers Centre were owned by Rogers. That meant the mayor had an indirect interest in their financial success, Chaleff felt. He asked Jonathan Batty, the city's integrity commissioner, to look into whether Tory had contravened the Municipal Conflict of Interest Act by supporting Shapiro.

Five days later, Batty responded to Chaleff's request. There were indeed sufficient grounds to warrant an investigation, he told him in a letter. If Tory was found to have breached the act, the potential penalties ranged from minor—a reprimand—to severe: removal from office.

There was, however, a complication. Tory planned to seek a third term as mayor in the fall. As per the city's laws, the investigation would need to be wrapped up before the deadline for candidates registering to run in the election, meaning that Batty had just three weeks to complete his probe.

By mid-August, the clock had run out. Although Batty had started collecting documents and interviewing witnesses the moment he received Chaleff's application, he wasn't in a position to issue a finding by the August 19 deadline. Torontonians would go to the polls without knowing whether or not Tory had violated the city's conflict-of-interest laws. Chaleff vowed to request that Batty resume the inquiry following the election.

Tory, for his part, denied any wrongdoing. He had simply cast a vote on a broad public issue—one which impacted *all* road users in the city—one of the mayor's spokespeople said in emails to reporters. "When the mayor does have any conflicts, he studiously declares them," Lawvin Hadisi wrote. "He did not have one in this case."

Notwithstanding the allegations of coziness between Toronto's mayor and the city's pre-eminent telecommunications company, one member of the Rogers family openly opposed Tory's re-election.

"It's tough to tell anymore if John Tory's Twitter is legit or a parody account," Martha Rogers tweeted in the weeks leading up to the election. She criticized the mayor for running on a platform of protecting parks and making housing more affordable after failing to address those issues during his previous two terms. "Maybe he thinks third time's a charm?" she asked rhetorically, before cutting to the chase: "Instead of the same tired promises from the same Old Guards, elect Gil Penalosa." Months earlier, Martha had hugged Tory outside of St. James Cathedral after Loretta's funeral. Now she was very publicly endorsing his rival for mayor.

Tory was re-elected mayor on October 24, beating Penalosa, who was the runner up, by a significant margin. The satirical news website The Beaverton took a shot at him in a story announcing his election win: "Rogers exec keeps side hustle," read the headline.

Tory was handed another victory a few months later. During the second-last week of December, as the Competition Tribunal mulled the Rogers-Shaw merger, Batty finally completed his conflict-of-interest investigation. He concluded that Tory did indeed have an indirect financial interest in the Blue Jays due to his involvement with the Rogers family trusts. It was duly noted that he also hadn't done himself any favours by coming to Shapiro's personal defence, causing people to question whether the mayor was conflicted. But Batty's investigation found that, contrary to Shapiro's letter (which, it turned out, had actually been ghostwritten by a city councillor named Mark Grimes), the closures had no impact on attendance at Blue Jays games. As a result, Tory's financial interest in the matter was "too remote" to have influenced his vote. "The outcome could have been different if my office obtained information or evidence that demonstrated the Blue Jays' business operations had been materially affected by ActiveTO as Mr. Shapiro's ghostwritten letter had initially suggested," Batty cautioned.

Tory was happy to put the incident behind him. Chaleff, meanwhile, was disappointed. He commended the commissioner for conducting a thorough investigation but disagreed with the report's conclusion. He continued to believe that the sitting mayor shouldn't hold an influential role in one of the country's most significant companies. Chaleff would ultimately end up getting his wish, but for a completely unrelated reason.

It took the tribunal just over two weeks to weigh the mountains of evidence in what one lawyer characterized as unquestionably the largest and most complex merger case in the institution's history. Late on the evening of December 29, in the week of dead space between Christmas and New Year's Eve, it published a brief summary of its decision, with full reasons to follow within forty-eight hours.

The three-member panel had determined that the deal was unlikely to significantly increase cellphone bills. Vidéotron was an experienced and disruptive competitor with a proven track record of competing through aggressive pricing. Its entry into Ontario, Alberta, and B.C. would ensure that competition remained robust, the tribunal predicted. It was dismissing Boswell's application to block the takeover.

The decision represented a major victory for a deal that, by then, had dragged on for nearly two years. Finally, the end seemed to be in sight. But any hopes of the deal closing before the end of the year—and Rogers avoiding a $262 million payout to bondholders—were dashed by the following afternoon. In a surprise move, the Competition Bureau served the cable companies with a notice of appeal before it had even had the chance to read the tribunal's detailed reasoning. The cable companies responded with disappointment, portraying Boswell as the villain depriving consumers of the deal's benefits. Their frustrations with Boswell spilled out into court documents. The commissioner had been intransigent and unreasonable, never budging from his all-or-nothing demand for a full block of the merger, they argued. "That decision should now have consequences," the telecoms said in a document in which they sought to be reimbursed for a quarter of their nearly $20 million legal bill.

Critics, meanwhile, glommed on to the speed with which Crampton, Samrout, and Askanas had arrived at their decision. One Ottawa-based consumer advocacy group, the Public Interest Advocacy Centre, characterized it as an "unseemly rush to judgment." That position was shared by the Competition Bureau, which argued in its notice of appeal that the tribunal had made legal errors in its rush to get a ruling out before the year's end. "The rapidity of the decision is unprecedented in tribunal history," the agency wrote in documents filed with the Federal Court of Appeal, noting that prior to the Rogers-Shaw case, the quickest decision the tribunal had ever issued in a merger challenge had taken almost three months.

Boswell's side seemed concerned that Rogers and Shaw might attempt to consummate their marriage before the appeal could be heard. As a preventative measure, the Competition Bureau asked the court for a stay and an injunction. Without one, Rogers could "cross the Rubicon" and close the takeover, the agency cautioned in court documents.

Rogers countered that the bureau's request was premature. In a letter to the court, Lisus noted that François-Philippe Champagne would want to read the tribunal's reasoning before he signed off— and it hadn't even been posted yet. "Put simply, there is no way that a closing can occur today or over the weekend, or well into next week."

The minister's office tried to quash the notion that he might greenlight the takeover ahead of an appeal. The morning of December 31, the last day for Rogers to avoid a quarter-billion-dollar financial hit, Champagne tweeted that he would wait for clarity on the legal process before rendering his decision. By that point, Rogers and Shaw had already extended their deadline until January 31, signalling to investors that their merger was not going to close before the end of the year.

Still, Champagne's assurances weren't enough for Boswell, who continued to push for an expedited hearing into his request for an injunction. In letters to the court, a Competition Bureau lawyer named Jonathan Hood noted that Rogers and Shaw were refusing to give an undertaking that they wouldn't close the deal until the court had decided whether to grant the injunction. "Once the respondents receive approval from the Minister they can start closing their transactions within minutes, causing irreparable harm," he cautioned.

By 9 p.m. on New Year's Eve, the tribunal's self-imposed 48-hour deadline had come and gone with no sign of its detailed reasons. There were murmurs that the delay stemmed from issues with the process of getting the document translated into French. But while everyone waited for the document that might shed some light on the competition commissioner's chances of winning an appeal, Justice David Stratas was carefully reading the letters flying back and forth from both sides. On January 1, he decided to act. The Federal Court of Appeal issued an emergency stay. It would remain in place until the Competition Bureau's application for a stay and an injunction could be heard.

The 88-page document outlining the tribunal's reasoning for permitting the takeover was finally published just before midnight on January 1, 2023, more than twenty-four hours later than planned. It offered a scathing critique of the commissioner's witnesses, especially the Bell and Telus executives, whose testimony "strained credulity" in light of their intense opposition to the deal.

Despite the considerable amount of time spent dwelling on efficiencies during the hearing, the tribunal hadn't bothered to weigh the cost savings that would likely result from the merger. It didn't have to, because it had concluded that the deal was unlikely to substantially lessen or prevent competition. On the contrary, the tribunal believed that the deal positioned Vidéotron to compete even more aggressively than Shaw would have been able to in the absence of the merger. The reasons for that included the fact that acquiring Freedom would double the size of Vidéotron's wireless business, creating a carrier with higher revenue and a larger port-folio of wireless spectrum licences. Additionally, the $2.85 billion that Vidéotron had agreed to pay for Freedom was substantially less than the $4.5 billion that Shaw had invested in the carrier since 2016, giving Vidéotron a "much more advantageous cost-base from which to compete."

The cable companies felt the decision was so strongly in their favour that Shaw publicly suggested that Boswell withdraw his appeal. In a statement late that evening, the telecom noted that the Competition Bureau had acted before having access to the full reasons. "It is now clear that the Tribunal rejected the evidence of the most important witnesses of the Commissioner, as well as all of his key complaints and theories. In the circumstances, Shaw urges the Commissioner to reconsider his decision to pursue an appeal."

Far from backing off, Boswell doubled down. His original notice of appeal had cited two alleged errors of law. He soon added two more. The crux of his case stemmed from Rogers and Shaw having struck their deal with Vidéotron only after the Competition Bureau had already filed its application to block the merger. As a result, the bureau believed that the tribunal should have followed a two-step process—first, assessing how the original deal would affect competition, and only then considering whether the pro-posed sale of Freedom alleviated those issues. Doing so would have placed the burden on the cable companies to prove that the dives-titure remedied any potential harm to competition. Instead, the tribunal had evaluated the version of the deal that included the Freedom sale, stating that it would be a waste of time and resources to consider a deal that could never happen.

The problem with that approach, according to the bureau, was that it set a precedent with profound implications for competition policy. By accounting for a side deal that had been struck *after* the bureau had moved to block the takeover, the tribunal was reducing the incentive for settling contested mergers before going to court. Instead, it was encouraging merging companies to go around the commissioner and straight to the tribunal, weakening the agency's ability to fight anti-competitive deals, according to Boswell.

The tribunal said it would have reached the same conclusion even if it had analyzed the deal in the manner that the bureau was suggesting, but it failed to spell out why. That was its second legal mistake, according to the commissioner. The third alleged error related to the way that the panel had applied the legal test for mergers. It had failed to consider the magnitude of the price increases or the duration and scope of the deal's impact, the bureau argued. Lastly, the commissioner claimed that the tribunal needed the bureau's consent to rely on what the agency termed "behavioural commitments," such as Péladeau's promise to reduce prices.

"This appeal is as important as it gets for merger law," Hood asserted at a hastily convened hearing on January 3. The implications for the enforcement of future mergers in Canada were profound, he argued. Shaw's lawyer Kent Thomson, meanwhile, suggested that the case dealt only with minor, confined legal issues.

Overseeing the hearing was Justice David Stratas, a jovial, no-nonsense judge who had no patience for what he perceived as an attempt by the commissioner to stall for time. He pushed back on Hood's request for a January 30 deadline for the bureau to file its legal brief, telling him, "You have already done an extensive briefing before the Competition Tribunal. I'm having difficulty understanding why it would take twenty-seven days to reinvent the wheel."

The schedule that Hood was proposing would push the hearing into February, past the deal's January 31 deadline, which would be disastrous for the telecoms, their lawyers contended. There was a significant risk that the deal would not move forward—either in its current form, or at all, Lisus cautioned in a letter to the court.

Hood was not convinced. Rogers and Shaw had already extended their deadline several times and, no doubt, could do so again, he pointed out. Besides, the financing that Rogers had secured would remain in place until the end of 2023. But just as Lisus launched into a diatribe about his opponents' cavalier approach to the deal's deadline, Stratas interrupted him.

"We don't need to cast aspersions on other counsel," he said. "I'm a substance guy." The appeal, he decided, would be heard on January 24. That meant if Rogers and Shaw won, there would still be enough time for them to secure the final approval from Champagne and close their deal by the end of the month.

Alexander Gay approached the wooden lectern in the centre of the small, packed courtroom separated by clear plastic dividers. Dressed in a black gown with white barrister tabs, he cleared his throat before introducing himself to the three Federal Court of Appeal judges hearing the case. The venue for the latest round in Matthew Boswell's legal battle against Canada's largest telecom merger was housed within 90 Sparks Street, the same reflective building in downtown Ottawa where, several months earlier, a mediator had tried in vain to find a compromise between the two diametrically opposed sides. Now, Boswell's lawyers were asking the Federal Court of Appeal to send the decision back to the Competition Tribunal for redetermination by a different panel.

Justice Stratas, the appellate court judge who had overseen the scheduling of the appeal, was joined on the panel by Montreal natives Richard Boivin and George Locke. After reviewing and analyzing volumes of documents, legal cases, and precedents, the judges were ready to hear oral arguments from both sides. Because they already knew what those arguments would be, the real purpose of the hearing was to afford the parties an opportunity to answer the judges' questions, Justice Stratas explained. "We wish to test their arguments and give them one last chance to deal with the issues that we think matter. . . . We may well interject quite a bit."

Less than five minutes into Gay's opening remarks, Justice Stratas did just that, challenging the notion that the alleged legal errors made any difference at all to the outcome of the Competition Tribunal's review. "According to the tribunal, this was not a particularly close case," Stratas said. In fact, he noted, the tribunal had identified several pro-competitive aspects of the deal. "I don't want to trivialize this at all, but just to make my question clear, the score might be five to two." Even if the alleged legal errors were corrected, it might only shift the score to five to three, he suggested.

This line of questioning appeared to agitate Gay, whose answer morphed into a rant. It was impossible to speculate on the outcome without first conducting the proper analysis, he argued. "You've got to go through steps one and two, before you can get to that conclusion. That was never done."

The court heard from Gay's colleague, Jonathan Hood, before adjourning for lunch around noon. The second half of the hearing was to be allotted to the three cable companies. But by the time Stratas, Boivin, and Locke returned to their seats, they were ready to deliver their decision.

Stratas opened by commending the bureau's lawyers for performing admirably in what he described as a difficult case. However, the judges had determined that Boswell's arguments were without merit. Asking the Competition Tribunal to examine the merger alone, without the divestiture, would be "a foray into fiction and fantasy," Justice Stratas said in what amounted to a scathing critique of the bureau's legal strategy. Even if the tribunal had erred on what the judges felt were "narrow legal points," they were not convinced that the result would have been any different. Sending the case back to the tribunal would therefore be pointless, they concluded.

Most of the lawyers in attendance had never experienced such a swift dismissal of an appeal before. Thomson, a veteran litigator, had—oddly enough, in a case involving Freedom predecessor Wind Mobile.

Lawyers for both sides shook hands like athletes at the end of a game before filtering out of the room. Boswell was disappointed by the outcome but stood by his decision to challenge the take-over. "We brought a strong, responsible case to the Tribunal after conducting a thorough examination of the facts," he said in a statement issued later that evening. While he continued to disagree with the tribunal's findings, the bureau accepted the appellate court's decision. It would not be seeking leave to appeal to Canada's Supreme Court.

Paul McAleese had decided to make Anthony Lacavera his punching bag. Sitting behind a long wooden table alongside his counterparts at Rogers and Vidéotron, Shaw's president laid into the former telecom executive whose agitating in Ottawa had prompted the House of Commons industry and technology committee to call a second public hearing into the proposed takeover.

The committee had already recommended against the deal, in a report tabled nearly a year earlier, in March 2022. But that was before Rogers and Shaw had agreed to sell Freedom Mobile to Vidéotron. Then, in January 2023, they called another meeting, this time to examine the process through which Rogers and Shaw had settled on Vidéotron as the buyer. It took place the day after the Federal Court of Appeal dismissed the Competition Bureau's case.

To many, the hearing felt largely performative. There was, after all, little doubt that the deal would ultimately get approved. "It sort of feels like a post mortem," remarked Vass Bednar, executive director of the master of public policy program at McMaster University, although she noted that she was "super glad" to be discussing such an important competition issue.

It's safe to assume that the six Rogers, Shaw, and Vidéotron executives—a group made up entirely of white, suited men—were not as glad as Bednar to be appearing before the committee. Neither was Bloc Québécois MP Sébastien Lemire, who used some of his limited allotted time to express his discomfort with the whole spectacle, on the grounds that the hearing had allegedly been convened at Telus's behest.

Telus's opposition to the deal was proof of its competitive benefits, McAleese told the committee. Part of Telus's Project Fox initiative, which aimed to "kill, slow, and shape" the merger, involved conspiring to replace Vidéotron with Globalive as the purchaser of Freedom Mobile, he argued. "What we learned is that Globalive is a very clear surrogate for Telus," McAleese said, referring to the Project Fox document that described Telus's tentative network- and spectrum-sharing deal with Globalive as an attempt to "boost" Globalive's bid for Freedom. "Globalive's chairman, Mr. Lacavera, who is very clearly comfortable playing Pinocchio to Darren Entwistle's Geppetto, is an odd choice for an operating partner," McAleese said in his opening remarks. He took aim at Lacavera's track record as a wireless operator, which he characterized as dubious. "I know that because I have a unique first-hand perspective," he continued. "I operated what was Wind Mobile after Mr. Lacavera exited the building, and I have a deep understanding of the effort required to fix the many challenges that we inherited."

Lacavera, who had appeared in front of the committee earlier in the day, bristled at the notion that he was Entwistle's puppet. "I'm coming up on fifty years old, and I've never worked for anyone yet," he noted. "I'm not about to start working for anyone. So there's no scenario where Globalive is in bed with Telus or working for Telus."

After hearing from telecom executives, academics, consumer advocates, and government officials, the session neared its end, and Tony Staffieri once again found himself facing a barrage of questions from Nathaniel Erskine-Smith. The Liberal MP wanted to know why Rogers had accepted an offer that was $900 million lower than Globalive's. Moreover, he asked Staffieri why the choice of who its competitor would be should belong to Rogers in the first place. "Why should you, Rogers, the most dominant player in a heavily concentrated sector that matters so much to Canadians— why should you get to decide who the fourth player is?"

Erskine-Smith asked the question several different ways, each time eliciting essentially the same response. Rogers had gone through an iterative process with the federal government and chosen the buyer most likely to meet the minister's criteria—one with a strong balance sheet, operating experience, and a credible path to 5G.

"Not my question," Erskine-Smith said, interrupting Staffieri as he repeated the answer again. "Why should you decide?"

"We went through the process to ensure the outcome was the most viable fourth player—" Staffieri began.

"I know these are lines you have memorized, but those are not answers to my question," Erskine-Smith said, cutting him off again. He lobbed a few questions at Shaw, then concluded by telling the panel that he wasn't convinced by the promises being made by a group of "very wealthy individuals" that the deal was pro-competitive. "This is something they've said time and time and time again, and Canadians just don't trust it anymore because these wealthy individuals are wealthy at the expense of our pocketbooks, for an essential service," he said. "Anyway," he finished, "thanks very much for the scripted answers."

As the two-year anniversary of the takeover's announcement neared, rumours about the transaction's imminent approval began to swirl. They were trafficked primarily by the arbitrage traders at hedge funds that stood to reap huge profits if and when the deal finally closed.

But Champagne appeared to be in no rush to complete his review of the spectrum licence transfer. The deal blew past one self-imposed deadline after another. Each time, the three companies—because it was now a tripartite agreement between Rogers, Shaw, and Vidéotron—agreed to extend the so-called outside date, which, naturally, attracted criticism considering the parties' threats in court that the deal was at risk of falling apart if it did not close by January 31.

As far as Champagne was concerned, these deadlines were meaningless and artificial. Therefore, he would issue his decision in "due course," he said repeatedly during press conferences and scrums. "I'm the regulator. I don't have any deadline," he told reporters on February 17, as the companies announced yet another extension, this time until the end of March.

Considering the concerns that critics such as Erskine-Smith had raised regarding the enforceability of Péladeau's commitments to reduce cellphone bills, Champagne wanted something iron-clad, including signed written undertakings that imposed penalties on Vidéotron and Rogers if they broke their promises. In Rogers' case, the promise he wanted to enforce was the telecom's pledge to spend $1 billion rolling out high-speed internet to rural, remote, and Indigenous communities. As the weeks dragged on, the telecoms worked with the federal government to hammer out the precise wording of those undertakings, as well as to address other commercial issues, such as reducing the rates charged when Freedom Mobile customers roamed on the Rogers network.

The minister was also facing political pressure not to rush his approval. In the wake of the hearings by the industry and technology committee, several Conservative members of Parliament had published an open letter urging Champagne to wait for the outcome of a new review by the telecom regulator. The CRTC had already approved the transfer of Shaw's broadcasting assets to Rogers but was now probing whether the agreements that Rogers had struck with Vidéotron, which underpinned the Montreal-based telecom's ability to offer wireless and internet bundles in western Canada, were so favourable towards Vidéotron that they gave the telecom an unreasonable advantage over its competitors. (The Telecommunications Act prohibits carriers from awarding themselves or others an unreasonable advantage, or "undue preference," through rates or the provision of services.)

The review was prompted by a complaint from TekSavvy Solutions Inc., one of the country's largest internet wholesalers, and it quickly attracted the support of other companies, including Globalive. By that point, Lacavera's firm had resolved to get back into the wireless industry, despite having been blocked from acquiring their former business, and they were concerned that the agreements between Rogers and Vidéotron would negatively impact their re-entry. In February, federal NDP leader Jagmeet Singh wrote to Champagne, urging him to block the deal over concerns that it would lead to higher cellphone bills and job losses, despite Staffieri having said that while some overlapping positions would be eliminated, overall the deal would result in a "net investment" in new jobs.

Meanwhile, some industry observers were beginning to question whether the economics of the deal still made sense, as regulatory delays had driven up financing costs and given rivals BCE and

Telus more time to aggressively build out their fibre-optic networks in preparation. Plus, Rogers was now expected to face heightened competition from a growing wireless rival.

In his public comments, Staffieri treaded a fine line between trying to convince regulators that Vidéotron would be a disruptive competitor and reassuring his company's investors that the increased competition wouldn't be too disruptive to Rogers. Competing was the telecom's "strong suit," he told the *Globe and Mail* in February, after the telecom reported higher fourth-quarter revenue and profit. "We've thrived in building our business based on competition. That's how we grew up—it's in our DNA—and we're comfortable with continuing to compete in a four-player wireless market."

At the end of his first full year at the company's helm, Staffieri was feeling proud of what he and his team had accomplished. Rogers was now first in ten out of thirteen key metrics, including year-over-year growth in its service revenue and EBITDA, both generally and in its wireless and media businesses. (Its cable division did not fare quite as well.) It had also taken the top spot in terms of how many net new cellphone customers it had added.

The improvements were at least partly owing to tailwinds from the abating pandemic, industry analysts noted. After all, the company that had been the hardest-hit by the crisis also had the most to gain when the world returned to a semblance of normalcy. Additionally, some of the changes that had been implemented by Natale's team—for instance, the work done by Fuller's team on the wireless side—had only started to yield improvements after Natale left the building. The telecom's stock price—Edward's primary justification for removing Natale—briefly rallied, hitting a high of nearly $76 in mid-April 2022. But by mid-June it had slipped below $60, roughly the same level it had been when Edward moved against the previous chief executive.

Still, Staffieri deserved credit for how he had steered the ship, several analysts said. "I think Tony's done a fine job," one of them remarked. But the true test of Staffieri's leadership was still to come, he added. Integrating Shaw would be a complex task, one requiring solid execution.

Edward's two-year battle to fulfill his father's vision of uniting the country's east and west cable systems came to a close on the last day of March 2023 in rather anti-climactic fashion. Roughly twenty of the company's senior leaders, including Edward and Staffieri, filed into a boardroom named after Ted on the tenth floor of the company's headquarters. There, over McDonald's breakfast sandwiches and coffee, they watched Champagne's 8:30 a.m. news conference.

Prior to the announcement, the minister had not explicitly told the telecoms what his decision would be. By that point, however, the fact that he planned to approve the spectrum transfer was a foregone conclusion. It had even been reported in the media the night before. To the public, the only question that remained was just how strict, and how enforceable, the conditions that accompanied the approval would be.

Rogers and Vidéotron had signed written undertakings agreeing to twenty-one conditions relating to the affordability and accessibility of wireless services. For instance, Vidéotron had promised that, over a period of ten years, it would offer cellphone plans that cost 20 per cent less than those offered by the major wireless carrier on a benchmark date in February 2023. Starting in year three, it would pay the government $25 million for each year that it failed to meet that promise, up to a maximum of $200 million. The company had also pledged to spend more than $150 million upgrading Freedom's network, and to enable 90 per cent of its customers to access 5G within two years, among other things.

Rogers, meanwhile, had codified and expanded upon the promises it had made when it first announced the takeover, including that it would spend $1 billion over five years bringing high-speed internet and 5G to underserved areas. The company also promised to maintain a Calgary headquarters for at least a decade and to create 3,000 new jobs in western Canada—a commitment that didn't preclude it from eliminating other positions, particularly in eastern Canada, in order to realize the synergies associated with the merger. For every year in which it failed to meet its commitments, it would fork over $100 million to the government, up to $1 billion.

Skeptics questioned whether the penalties were high enough to hold the companies accountable. Laura Tribe, the executive director of non-profit OpenMedia, believed that the companies might simply end up paying the fines if it made business sense to do so. Lacavera, meanwhile, predicted a "massacre of layoffs" on the horizon. Following his unsuccessful attempt to acquire Freedom, he had shifted gears to trying to re-enter the wireless sector by attempting to acquire airwaves from Xplore Mobile, the defunct carrier that had been born out of Bell's takeover of MTS. Lacavera maintained that the only way to meaningfully bring down prices was by creating a truly independent wireless carrier whose ability to compete wasn't constrained by its need to protect its legacy cable or phone business. To him, the conditions that Champagne had announced were "window dressing on the burning house."

But Champagne assured the public that the commitments he had extracted from Rogers and Vidéotron were not only unprecedented but also enforceable. "I'm a lawyer, and it's a contract," he told reporters, adding that he would watch "like a hawk" to ensure that the companies upheld their promises. He was confident that the spectrum transfer that he was approving would create a strong fourth wireless carrier that could go "toe to toe" with the three wireless giants.

Over at 333 Bloor, relief washed over Staffieri. For two years, uncertainty had hung over the company, impacting everything from its employees' morale and job security to its contracts with suppliers.

For its CEO, it had felt like wading through murky, muddy waters and having to pause every step of the way. Finally, with the last of the regulatory approvals secured, the telecom's future came into sharper focus. The Ted Rogers boardroom erupted into applause.

EPILOGUE

The sound of Martha's heavy breathing filled the cavernous cathedral at the corner of King and Church streets. It was a bright June day in 2022, and Ted and Loretta's youngest daughter was struggling to compose herself. Dressed in wedge heels and a sleeveless, knee-length black dress, a pair of sunglasses perched atop her auburn hair, Martha's voice cracked as she began reading a eulogy into the microphone, sunlight glimmering through the colourful stained-glass windows behind her. More than a decade earlier, she and her three siblings had said goodbye to their father in the same church. Now, it was time to say goodbye to their mother.

The Rogers family remained deeply divided more than six months after the company's board replaced Joe Natale with Tony Staffieri, capping a fractious boardroom battle. According to some family friends, Loretta had never forgiven her son for his behaviour in the dispute. He had not only gone against her, but had also, in her view, contravened the most sacred of edicts—his father's wishes. Edward, though, didn't believe that he and his mother had any outstanding issues.

At a reception hosted at Bishop Strachan the evening prior to the funeral, Melinda and Martha had stood inside the chapel, greeting the procession of mourners that snaked from the casket past two sets of doors and onto the stone walkway outside. Edward and his posse, which included his wife Suzanne, his sister Lisa, Staffieri, and the telecom's new chief financial officer, Glenn Brandt, stuck to the courtyard.

Despite their apparent reluctance to be in one another's presence, the warring factions were brought together under the vaulted roof of the Cathedral Church of St. James for the funeral. The executive leadership team—the victors—were in attendance, as were several of the recently defeated, including Jordan Banks, who sat near the front of the church with former chief communications officer Sevaun Palvetzian, a polished-looking woman with dark, bouncy curls. They were joined by Natale, whose unceremonious ouster from the company had been softened by a $14.1 million severance payment.

In honour of Loretta, who had loved to paint corals, turquoise waters, and bright tropical fish, mourners were encouraged to forgo the usual all-black funeral attire in favour of livelier hues. Most of them acceded to this request, including Palvetzian, who had donned a green dress, and two of the dissident directors—Clappison and Peterson—who were designated as casket bearers. Peterson wore his signature red tie, while Clappison paired a green shirt and lime green tie with a dark blue suit. Suzanne, who was arguably the most fashion-conscious person in attendance, either didn't get the memo or simply chose to disregard it; she opted for funeral black.

One person who was notably absent was Alan Horn. Throughout the family conflict, he had been quietly battling melanoma. He'd confided in Gemmell, who had battled throat cancer fifteen years earlier and admired the courage with which Horn faced his diagnosis. "It was a difficult time, but his focus and his commitment never wavered," says Gemmell. The cancer spread, and by the time Loretta's funeral came around, Horn was too sick to attend.

Martha spoke about her mother's love of nature, her fierce independence, and her generosity. Loretta was an early feminist who quietly wrote cheques to help women pay for their education. Her intelligence was often underestimated, and she played a crucial role in the family. While Ted may have been its face, Loretta was its backbone. She picked her battles carefully and had an impressive ability to let things roll off her back. "It's no secret that she meant everything to me," Martha said. "One of the things I learned from her was that kindness and weakness are not the same thing."

After Martha had finished speaking, an older, blonde woman in a flowing yellow dress was escorted to the podium by two young boys. Judith McMurray, who had been Loretta's best friend, recalled a mischievous woman who was happiest painting in her small Muskoka art studio or on her yacht in the Bahamas. But Loretta was also sharp—so sharp, in fact, that she could have run RCI herself, according to McMurray. She just didn't want to.

Melinda, in a navy blue dress adorned with bright flowers, praised her mother's business savviness ("she helped guide decision-making every single day") and her warmth. "She lived in perpetual summer," Melinda said poetically. "The sun and water were not just her passion, but the essence of her spirit."

Lisa went up last to read a poem called "Loving Memories."

Throughout the tribute, there were only a handful of subtle indications of the rift that had split the family apart. One came from a clergyman who commented that Loretta was a person, not a headline.

Perhaps the loudest statement of all came in the form of what was left unsaid—or rather, who. Although he had delivered a eulogy at his father's funeral, Edward didn't speak at his mother's ceremony. Melinda had organized the event, and he didn't want to cause a stir.

Loretta's death left nine members on the advisory committee to the Rogers Control Trust. The group shrank further in January 2023, roughly seven months later, when Horn passed away. Lind followed another seven months later, on August 20, 2023—incidentally, the day of his eightieth birthday.

With the Old Guard and both of their parents gone, the Rogers children were left to fend for themselves as they contemplated the company's future. Ted's will had set out a process for eventually replacing his four kids on the advisory committee with their own offspring. The issue had become top of mind for Melinda during the recent conflict. She was concerned that the structure of the trust pitted family members against one another, and that her own children could one day end up in a similar battle with their cousins. Preparing the kids for their roles as stewards of the family empire was of utmost importance, she believed, even though her eldest, Zachary, was more interested in becoming an entrepreneur. Edward and Suzanne's eldest child, Chloé, didn't seem interested in working at Rogers either, although she did pay tribute to her family heritage in her own way. After studying fashion history and theory at Central Saint Martins, a campus of the University of the Arts London in England, she had launched a luxury lingerie brand, Scarlett Gasque, which took its name from her maternal great-grandmother, Scarlett, and her paternal great-grandmother, Maysie Gasque.

However, there was nothing in the document stipulating that Loretta, Horn, and Lind's seats were to be filled—only that new appointments required the approval of two-thirds of the existing members. And so, in the months following their deaths, the trust simply continued along with fewer members. Eventually, the advisory committee did add at least one new member—a longtime Rogers executive named Thomas Turner. Rogers did not publicly disclose Turner's appointment, although two sources confirmed it

to the *Globe and Mail*. According to one of them, Turner, who was
the president of Rogers Business, had been appointed by Edward,
who was solidifying his grip over his empire by bolstering his support at the advisory committee.

John Tory, meanwhile, was no longer conflicted by virtue of
his dual roles as both the city's mayor and an adviser to its largest
telecom company. In February 2023, several months after winning
a third term, Toronto's 68-year-old mayor resigned after the
Toronto Star revealed that during the pandemic he'd been engaged
in a months-long affair with a 31-year-old female staffer.

Shortly after obtaining the final regulatory approval for its
takeover of Shaw, Rogers parted ways with its chief regulatory officer, Ted Woodhead. Concurrently, the company stoked controversy by hiring former industry minister Navdeep Bains to the
newly created role of chief corporate affairs officer. The announcement prompted the House of Commons ethics committee to invite
the lobbying commissioner to appear before them and explain
why the move didn't contravene federal lobbying rules. Woodhead,
who was part of the contingent of Telus executives who had followed Natale to Rogers, sued his former employer for wrongful
dismissal, breach of contract, and unjust enrichment, claiming
that Rogers had denied him his Shaw bonus despite how integral
he'd been to the deal's eventual success. Another executive, a
senior human resources vice-president named Moheni Singh
who was let go as part of the post-takeover restructuring, sued as
well, alleging that she had been promised certain compensation
in exchange for postponing her retirement, then dismissed shortly
before she became entitled to receive it. The company denied
Singh's claims, saying it had "honoured its contractual obligations" to her. In its response to Woodhead's suit, Rogers alleged
he'd been let go due to poor performance that had resulted in others becoming "more involved than they should have had to have
been" in the Shaw deal.

But the highest profile employment suit was filed by none other than Joe Natale. In August 2023, three days before Lind's death, Natale sued his former employer for more than $24 million, including an unpaid $4 million Shaw bonus, claiming wrongful dismissal and breach of contract. On top of that, he was seeking "punitive, aggravated, and moral damages," alleging that Edward and his wife Suzanne had behaved in a "malicious, high-handed, and oppressive" manner by hiring *Succession* actor Brian Cox to film a disparaging viral video about him and then disseminating it to their friends.

Rogers countered that it was retroactively making Natale's termination "with cause" after an independent investigation found that he'd engaged in "serious misconduct" by awarding himself "excessive compensation" without proper board approval. The investigation, which was led by law firm Bennett Jones LLP, lasted months and involved interviews with multiple former employees, including Natale himself. The former CEO's alleged misconduct was outlined in the company's statement of defence and counterclaim, which was filed in court several weeks after Natale's lawsuit. Rogers argued that Natale had pressured several of his subordinates into amending his employment terms without proper board approval—for instance, so that he would receive the same severance payments regardless of whether he was terminated on a with-cause or without-cause basis—and that these changes were "premised on an unlawful quid pro quo: his subordinates approved these improvident arrangements at the same time that Natale unilaterally offered and approved generous amendments to their own employment agreements." (Natale disputed the notion that he had benefitted from these amendments to his subordinates' employment contracts, claiming that it was Melinda, Bonnie Brooks, and David Peterson who had suggested the changes to ensure that the senior leadership team stuck around and continued to perform.)

The company also alleged that Natale had delayed providing the shareholder list to the board for sixteen days so that he could finalize the changes to his employment agreement, and that he had fired the company's corporate counsel, Fasken, because they had advised him that the reconstituted board was valid.

In court documents, the company characterized Natale as a "self-interested executive who resisted board oversight and refused to accept the authority of the Control Trust Chair," claiming that he had used company resources to orchestrate an aggressive media campaign against Edward and threatened to orchestrate an exodus of the company's senior leadership. His actions, they argued, demonstrated a "wanton, high-handed, and outrageous disregard for the interests of Rogers Communications and its shareholders." They were seeking, among other things, the repayment of at least $15.4 million in severance that Natale had received for being terminated without cause. As for the *Succession* video, they said only that "there is no basis for punitive, aggravated, or moral damages as sought in the statement of claim." One of the key issues was whether or not Dépatie was still on the board at the time that Natale's sweetened compensation terms were finalized. The company's position was that he was—and that as chair of the human resources committee, his signoff would have been required.

Dépatie, for his part, didn't plan to stick around until the matter was resolved. In September 2023, less than two years after he'd joined the management team, the company announced that the 64-year-old executive would be retiring at the end of the year. "As many of you know, Robert stepped down from our Board in 2021 to join our executive leadership team and to help bring Rogers and Shaw together," Staffieri said in a note to employees. "Given the merger is now closed and integration is progressing ahead of schedule, Robert believes now is a good time to transition into retirement."

Matthew Boswell continued to stand by the Competition Bureau's decision to challenge the merger, even after the tribunal ordered the agency to pay Rogers millions of dollars of costs. In a written document outlining its reasons, the Competition Tribunal criticized the commissioner for taking what it characterized as an "unnecessarily contentious approach at numerous points during the litigation," describing him as "intransigent" due to his refusal to shift focus from the original deal to the one that included divesting Freedom.

The merger court ordered the Bureau to pay $9.3 million to Rogers and $2.8 million to what was formerly Shaw for costs relating to the expert witnesses who produced reports and testified at the hearing. The federal agency was to fork over another $414,720 to Rogers and $416,187 to Shaw for legal fees. Although it amounted to a small fraction of the legal fees incurred by the merging telecoms, the tribunal said it appeared to be the largest legal fee award in its history.

The Competition Bureau expressed disappointment with the tribunal's characterizations of Boswell's conduct. "The commissioner acted in the public interest to protect competition throughout the entire proceeding and we fundamentally disagree with any suggestion to the contrary," a spokesperson for the agency said in a statement.

The *Globe*'s business columnist Andrew Willis called the wording in the costs order a "legal smackdown," arguing that the bureau had squandered taxpayer dollars. But University of Ottawa law professor Jennifer Quaid noted that it's normal for the losing party to pay a portion of the winning party's costs. To Quaid, it was "worrying" that the decision was being "portrayed as an indictment of the vigorous enforcement and outspoken advocacy that has characterized Boswell's tenure," she wrote on The Conversation Canada. The order, she added, came at a critical moment—amid an ongoing modernization of the country's competition laws.

Questions about corporate governance continued to hang over Rogers long after the board dispute had been resolved. Ahead of the company's annual shareholder meeting in the spring of 2023, proxy advisers Glass Lewis & Co. and Institutional Shareholder Services recommended withholding votes from roughly half a dozen of the telecom's directors, including Edward, over governance issues. Glass Lewis cited a number of reasons, including a lack of gender diversity (only three of the thirteen director candidates listed in the shareholder proxy circular were women) as well as "concerning pay practices." In the company's two most recent fiscal years, Glass Lewis identified what it termed a "potentially severe disconnect" between pay and performance. Staffieri had received $31.5 million in total compensation during his first year as CEO—a staggering figure—in large part due to a $9.9 million change in actuarial assumptions relating to the value of his pension. That put him above Telus's Entwistle, who had held the title of highest-paid Canadian telecom CEO for several years.

Although Staffieri's massive compensation package was likely to be a one-off, Glass Lewis took issue with other aspects of the company's compensation practices, calling it "puzzling" that executives received above-target cash bonuses despite having suffered a severe network outage that led to heightened regulatory and public scrutiny and exposed Rogers to the possibility of more than one class-action lawsuit. (The one filed by Joey Zukran of LPC Avocat with Arnaud Verdier as the lead plaintiff was still working its way through the system.) Glass Lewis recommended withholding votes from David Robinson, Jack Cockwell, Ivan Fecan, and Jan Innes, who all sat on the compensation committee. Seven other directors, including the Rogers women and Toronto Metropolitan University president Mohamed Lachemi, who had joined the board the previous year, got a pass. (Although both Cockwell and Jake Kerr—another one of the five directors who had joined the board via written resolution—were standing for re-election, both would quietly leave the board a few months later, less than two years into their terms.)

Meanwhile, Robert Gemmell, the telecom's lead director, had gotten caught up in an entirely separate corporate governance controversy, in his role as the chair of Agnico Eagle Mines Ltd. That spring, ISS and Glass Lewis recommended that Agnico's shareholders withhold their votes from Gemmell over the mining company's decision to pay one-time bonuses to reward top executives for completing a merger with Kirkland Lake Gold Ltd. Gemmell, seeing that the early votes coming in were mixed and that he was unlikely to be given a strong mandate as chair, wound up withdrawing his name ahead of the meeting.

At Rogers, Glass Lewis had also identified a skills gap among the company's directors. The depth of experience in IT and network infrastructure on the board was, in the firm's estimation, "relatively shallow." But rather than recruit a technologist, Edward continued to stack the board with allies, adding his sister Lisa, who had backed him at the trust, former Shaw CFO Trevor English, and Brad Shaw. Brad's appointment to the Rogers board came as no surprise—it had been baked into the takeover from the start—but it meant that the former Shaw CEO would receive a $110,000 retainer—on top of $400 million for his Shaw shares; a $20 million, two-year consulting contract; and a severance payment that was at one point estimated to be $18.73 million.

For all the hard work and recommendations in Glass Lewis's 23-page report, it had precisely zero impact. The firm might have saved itself the trouble entirely. There was, after all, no longer any ambiguity about who was in control of Rogers Communications. At the shareholder meeting, which was held at the Velma Rogers Theatre in the basement of 333 Bloor, with his wife and three sisters in attendance, Edward called on Gemmell to make the director nominations. The motion, which was seconded by David Robinson, passed with more than 99 per cent of the votes.

ACKNOWLEDGEMENTS

This book would not have been possible without the many sources who guided my reporting and helped me unravel and reconstruct the strange and dramatic events that occurred in the fall of 2021, as well as the circumstances leading up to them. I am deeply grateful to them for taking the time to share their insights with me—sometimes at great personal risk and against the advice of their spouses or lawyers—because they felt, as I did, that this story needed to be told. Most of these individuals spoke on the condition that their identities remain confidential, so I am unable to thank them here by name.

Thanks to my agent, Martha Webb of CookeMcDermid, for suggesting this book and for finding it a fantastic home. I'm extremely grateful that it landed in the capable hands of Doug Pepper at McClelland & Stewart/Penguin Random House Canada, whose confidence in me kept me going and whose sense of humour and acerbic wit made the process enjoyable. Gemma Wain provided thoughtful edits. Thanks to Kristin Cochrane, the CEO of Penguin Random House Canada; Stephanie Sinclair, the publisher of McClelland & Stewart; and Kimberlee Kemp, the senior managing editor of McClelland & Stewart for believing in this project.

I first started covering this story in the fall of 2021 for the *Globe and Mail* in my role as the paper's telecom reporter. Throughout that coverage, which continues to this day, I have been privileged to work with Mark Heinzl, who has served not only as a shrewd and thoughtful editor but also as an invaluable sounding board and a fierce advocate for my work. He also read an early draft of this book, which has greatly benefited from his astute observations. Dennis Choquette, the deputy editor of the *Globe*'s Report on Business, is a master strategist who helped me overcome more than one reporting obstacle. Sinclair Stewart offered sage advice, and he and the rest of the *Globe*'s masthead—including Gary Salewicz, David Walmsley, and Angela Pacienza—as well as *Globe* publisher Phillip Crawley, provided support and gave me time off to write this book.

I'm fortunate to work with incredibly talented colleagues, many of whom contributed to the *Globe's* reporting on this saga. Andrew Willis, Susan Krashinsky Robertson, and Jason Kirby deserve special mention, although many others chipped in as well. Irene Galea filled in for me while I was on book leave and contributed her architectural history expertise to this book. Brent Jang, a reporter in the *Globe*'s B.C. bureau, diligently lined up early to grab one of the only available spots in the Vancouver courtroom where the hearing took place, while Mike Hager and Wendy Stueck took on the unglamorous but crucial task of fetching documents from the courthouse. James Bradshaw passed along a critical piece of intel. David Milstead weighed in on executive compensation matters and enlisted the help of his mother in shipping an eight and a half pound book across the country for me. Stephanie Chambers pulled documents to help me locate sources and other leads.

This book also benefited from the guidance and advice of many colleagues who I am blessed to consider among my mentors and friends. I am eternally grateful to Rita Trichur for her unwavering support and friendship over the years, and to fellow author and *Globe* reporter Josh O'Kane for countless pep talks and for helping me navigate the publishing process; without his encouragement I might not have embarked on this journey. Thanks to Joe Castaldo for his indispensable storytelling advice; to Sean Silcoff for regularly checking in on me; and to Greg McArthur for taking me under his wing as a mentor. A special shoutout goes to Robert

Cribb for teaching the investigative journalism course at Toronto Metropolitan University (formerly Ryerson) that instilled in me the desire to dig deeper. Thanks to my good friend Brent Rose for taking my author photo and to the eagle-eyed Nicholas Maronese for the proofread, the executions, and the Oxford comma jokes.

This book is not only about business but also about family—the people who shape us—so I would be remiss not to mention mine. Thank you to my parents, Jacek and Małgosia, who taught me the joy of reading at a young age. I might not have become the sort of person who writes a book were it not for your unconditional love and support. Thanks as well to my chosen family—my ride-or-dies—for cheering me on, and for tolerating my extended absences. Now that this book is out you'll be seeing a lot more of me. Lastly, a heartfelt thanks goes out to my partner Roland Csach, who kept me fed, caffeinated, and grounded throughout this process, and who came up with the title for this book. I love you more than words can express.

A NOTE ON SOURCES

This book draws on hundreds of conversations with more than 120 people, including current and former executives and directors of Rogers Communications Inc., family friends, lawyers, investment bankers, government officials, executives from other telecoms, investors, and financial analysts. The vast majority of these individuals spoke only on the condition that I agree not to use their names because they feared reprisal, and in some cases they were contractually bound not to discuss certain matters. Some people took significant personal risks to provide information that they felt the readers of this book should have; I am extremely grateful for their assistance.

My reporting has also been informed by nine books, countless news articles, and thousands of pages of documents. While most of these documents are available to the public, either through the courts, industry regulators, or the Competition Tribunal, others—including email exchanges and confidential board reports—were provided to me during the course of my reporting. The B.C. court case resulted in a trove of previously confidential files becoming public, including minutes and presentations from board meetings, Ted's will and memorandum of wishes, and email exchanges between family members and attorneys. Although Ted Rogers is no longer alive, his perspective on many things, including business decisions, succession, and his family, is contained in a book called *Relentless: The True Story of the Man Behind Rogers Communications*, co-written with Robert Brehl. Other books to which I am particularly indebted are Caroline Van Hasselt's *High Wire Act: Ted Rogers and the Empire That Debt Built* and Gordon Pitts's *Kings of Convergence: The Fight for Control of Canada's Media.* Phil Lind's perspective on Ted and other matters is gleaned from his memoir, *Right Hand Man: How Phil Lind Guided the Genius of Ted Rogers, Canada's Foremost Entrepreneur,* which Brehl also co-wrote, while Jim Reid's book, *Leading to Greatness: 5 Principles to Transform Your Leadership and Build Great Teams,* provided valuable insights into some of the work undertaken by Natale's leadership team. The Shaw family history is drawn largely from a massive tome called *Above and Beyond: The JR Shaw Family History in Life and Business,* which was commissioned by JR and Carol Shaw and written by Kirstie McLellan Day.

Information that I have obtained via on-the-record interviews, conducted either for this book or for the *Globe and Mail,* is attributed as such in the text and/or the endnotes. Quotes that are in the present tense are from on-the-record interviews specifically for this book. No member of the Rogers family provided me with such an interview, although I did speak to Melinda for the *Globe* in November 2021. As I have written earlier, my reporting has since revealed that Edward's side felt that Melinda had breached her duties as a director by discussing certain matters during that interview and a subsequent one with Bloomberg News. Following those interviews, both sides entered into a standstill agreement, effective at least until the Shaw deal closed, that precluded them from disparaging one another in the press. Melinda and Martha did provide written responses to a number of questions about their upbringing, while declining to comment on the conflict that is at the heart of this story.

No Rogers CEO, current or former, spoke to me on the record specifically for this book, although I have had the opportunity to interview both Joe Natale and Tony Staffieri for the *Globe* and to speak "on background" with many people who have worked with them. The only representative of Rogers Communications who

provided an on-the-record interview for this project is the company's lead director, Robert Gemmell.

On July 19, 2023, as I was finishing this book, I sent Rogers a
list of detailed questions seeking comments from Edward and
Staffieri on various matters. Neither of them opted to comment,
although I did receive answers to some of my questions from Rob
Gemmell; I have incorporated them throughout the book.

Several people helped shape my perspective on corporate governance and competition policy, including Matthew Boswell, the
Commissioner of Competition, who generously gave me an hour
of his time. I also spoke to a number of experts, academics, and
researchers, including W. Glenn Rowe, professor of general management and strategy at the University of Western Ontario's Ivey
Business School; Dimitry Anastakis, a professor at the University
of Toronto's Rotman School of Management; Kevin Thomas, the
chief executive officer of Canadian shareholder advocacy group
SHARE; and Keldon Bester, a fellow at the Centre for International
Governance Innovation (CIGI), an international think-tank.
Andrew Rogerson of the Rogerson Law Group helped me better
understand the intricacies of trust and estate law.

As this is a work of narrative non-fiction, I have done my best
not to put words into people's mouths or thoughts into their heads.
Dialogue comes primarily from regulatory proceedings that I personally observed, although I have occasionally reconstructed bits
of conversation based on people's recollections or quoted from
other books. Some of that dialogue has been condensed for brevity.

In cases where I have described what a person was thinking or
feeling, it is because they shared those thoughts either with me or
with someone else I have spoken to, or documented them somewhere such as in an affidavit or a book. It should not be assumed
that the people whose actions, feelings, and thoughts are being
described were themselves the sources of that information.

While several of the scenes contained within this book were ones that I witnessed myself, the majority were reconstructed based on the recollections of people who were present. Because human memory is fallible, where possible I have attempted to verify such information with multiple sources as well as photographs, documents, and online research. All of the external sources that I have relied on are documented in the endnotes. Any information that is not attributed comes from confidential sources or my own observations, based on my extensive reporting on this file.

Untangling fact from fiction can be a thorny task, made more difficult by the armies of communications advisers employed by companies and wealthy individuals to manage their reputations. While researching this book, I was frequently confronted with starkly different conflicting accounts from the two camps. In some instances, even the most basic of facts—such as whether or not a director had resigned or a particular phone call took place—remain in dispute as of this writing. The fall of 2021 was an emotional time for many of those involved, and emotions can have a profound effect on memory, which at least partially explains why people can remember the same event in very different ways. In instances where people's recollections of events vary, I have either highlighted the discrepancy or used my personal judgement—informed by the extensive research that I've conducted over the course of two years—to determine the most plausible version. Some people will undoubtedly disagree with my conclusions and characterizations.

Many of the people I contacted about this story declined to speak with me or simply ignored my attempts to reach them. Some of them were concerned about jeopardizing the Shaw deal, which was still under review while I did the bulk of the reporting for this book. Others expressed concerns about legal reprisals or about taking sides in a messy family dispute. Despite these obstacles, I managed to convince quite a few of the people who were directly involved in this story to share their perspectives with me. These conversations, despite being mostly on background, allowed me to gain a deeper understanding of what was really at the heart of this saga. My overarching goal throughout this process has been to share those insights with you.

NOTES

Prologue

1   **The house was built:** Mark Meredith, "Mrs R.J. Christie Mansion," House Histree, last updated October 31, 2020, https://househistree.com /houses/mrs-r-j-christie-mansion.

1   **The present:** Ted Rogers and Robert Brehl, *Relentless: The True Story of the Man Behind Rogers Communications* (Toronto: HarperCollins Publishers, 2008), pp. 85–6.

2   **Loretta was born:** Many of the details of Loretta's childhood come from a eulogy delivered by her daughter, Melinda Rogers-Hixon, at Loretta's funeral, which was held at the Cathedral Church of St. James on June 21, 2022 and which I personally attended. It is hereafter referred to as Loretta's eulogy.

2   **The master bedroom:** Descriptions of Loretta's bedroom, friendships, life, personality, and illness, as well as details from her deathbed, come from on-the-record interviews that I conducted for her obituary in the *Globe and Mail.* The ten people I spoke to for that story were Judith McMurray, Inta Kierans, Dr. Bernie Gosevitz, Dr. Heather Ross, Robert and Birgit Freybe Bateman, John Tory, David Peterson, Larry Tanenbaum, and Melinda Rogers-Hixon.

2   **whale sharks:** Judith McMurray, "At ages 79, 82 and 83, we still find it fun to swim with whale sharks," *Globe and Mail,* May 17, 2022, https:// www.theglobeandmail.com/life/first-person/article-at-ages-79-82-and-83 -we-still-find-it-fun-to-swim-with-whale-sharks/.

3   **navy-hulled, 154-foot *Loretta Anne* yacht:** Peter, "The Loretta Anne Yacht: A Marvel of Luxury and Power," SuperYachtFan, accessed November 13, 2022, https://www.superyachtfan.com/yacht/loretta-anne/.

3   **One person was conspicuously absent:** Confidential sources.

5   **In court documents, Loretta claimed:** Affidavit of Loretta Anne Rogers, *Rogers v. Rogers Communications Inc.*, File No.: S219325, October 29, 2021 (hereafter referred to as Loretta's affidavit).

5   **it was Loretta who moved:** Confidential source speaking to the *Globe and Mail* for a story published on October 21, 2021.

5   **It wasn't the first time:** Confidential sources.

5   **pattern of behaviour:** Affidavit of John A. MacDonald, *Rogers v. Rogers Communications Inc.*, File No.: S219325, October 29, 2021 (hereafter referred to as MacDonald's affidavit).

5   **According to several people close to Loretta:** Confidential sources.

5   **Edward, however, did not feel:** Confidential source.

6   **Loretta was hurt:** Confidential source.

One A heavy burden

7 The small community: "A History of International Style," Lyford Cay Club, accessed July 1, 2022, https://www.lyfordcay.com/web/pages/a-history-of-international-style.

7 450 homes: Nancy A. Ruhling, "Lyford Cay in the Bahamas Offers a Clubby—And Unflashy—Vibe," Mansion Global, December 28, 2019, https://www.mansionglobal.com/articles/lyford-cay-in-the-bahamas-offers-a-clubby-and-unflashy-vibe-210562.

7 high-net-worth residents: Whitney Robinson, "The Private World of Lyford Cay," *Town & Country*, March 29, 2016, https://www.townandcountrymag.com/leisure/travel-guide/g2137/lyford-cay-bahamas/.

8 was staying in the Bahamas: Rogers and Brehl, *Relentless*, p. 46.

8 afflicted with health problems: Ibid., pp. 19–47.

9 panicking because he had: Ibid., pp. 44–5.

9 talking politics: Ibid., pp. 46–9.

10 Despite her family's wealth: Loretta's eulogy.

10 an intimidating woman: Caroline Van Hasselt, *High Wire Act: Ted Rogers and the Empire that Debt Built* (Mississauga: John Wiley & Sons Canada, 2007), pp. 64–5.

11 "She could be stubborn": Interview with Judith McMurray for Loretta's obituary in the *Globe and Mail*, hereafter referred to as Loretta's obituary, published June 27, 2022.

11 "We danced, and danced": Rogers and Brehl, *Relentless*, p. 47.

11 Ted and Loretta spent: Ibid., pp. 49–57.

12 talk his way into: Van Hasselt, *High Wire Act*, pp. 41–2.

12 In 1959, standing between: Rogers and Brehl, *Relentless*, pp. 57–84.

14 The station's owners: Van Hasselt, *High Wire Act*, p. 60.

14 "She was my rock": Rogers and Brehl, *Relentless*, p. 80–4.

15 "Without victory": Ibid., p. 75.

15 After a series: Van Hasselt, *High Wire Act*, pp. 60–7.

15 in February 1967: Rogers and Brehl, *Relentless*, pp. 94–8.

16 $225,000 down payment: Ibid., p. 95.

16 trouble conceiving: Ibid., pp. 86–8.

16 political storm clouds: Ibid., pp. 100–104.

17 Loretta was a rock: Interview with David Peterson for Loretta's obituary.

17 A notorious troublemaker: Phil Lind and Robert Brehl, *Right Hand Man: How Phil Lind Guided the Genius of Ted Rogers, Canada's Foremost Entrepreneur* (Toronto: Barlow Book Publishing, 2018), pp. 11–74.

18 On July 14, 1971: Rogers and Brehl, *Relentless*, pp. 106–8.

18 including his young son: Confidential source.

18 "I've got to build": Van Hasselt, *High Wire Act*, p. 74.

19 barred from the premises: Rogers and Brehl, *Relentless*, p. 26.

19 Loretta sat him down: Ibid., p. 129.

19 Loretta may have hoped: Confidential source.

19 "Need new mountains": Rogers and Brehl, *Relentless*, pp. 130–71.

21 From Ted's perspective: Ibid., pp. 170–1, 186

21 Meanwhile, bankers were: Ibid., pp. 146–151.

21 The junk bonds also: Van Hasselt, *High Wire Act*, pp. 285–9.

22   On a Sunday afternoon: Rogers and Brehl, *Relentless*, pp. 152–3.

22   It was clear: Lind and Brehl, *Right Hand Man*, pp. 151–4.

22   doctors had found an aneurysm: Rogers and Brehl, *Relentless*, pp. 153–86.

23   vicious screaming match: Ibid., p. 187.

23   "the worst business disaster of my life": Ibid., p. 189.

Two   Fast Eddie

25   Built in 1889: Don Wall, "Major Toronto Club restoration a painstaking team effort," *Daily Commercial News*, November 4, 2022, https://canada .constructconnect.com/dcn/news/projects/2022/11/major-toronto-club -restoration-a-painstaking-team-effort.

25   understated elegance: "About the Club," Toronto Club, accessed July 15, 2023, https://www.torontoclub.ca/Visitors.

25   Buckingham Palace: Gordon Pitts, *Kings of Convergence: The Fight for Control of Canada's Media* (Canada: Doubleday Canada, 2002), pp. 35–9.

25   Ted was feeling: Rogers and Brehl, *Relentless*, pp. 206–7.

25   While recovering: Ibid., pp. 186–210.

26   The offer came as: Pitts, *Kings of Convergence*, pp. 35–7.

27   Muskoka, an idyllic region: Agatha Farmer, "Did you know Muskoka has 1,600 lakes? 5 engaging facts about the region," MuskokaRegion.com, August 20, 2019, https://www.muskokaregion.com/life/did-you-know -muskoka-has-1-600-lakes-5-engaging-facts-about-the-region/article _729cc309-de43-54d9-a3db-e9a4d0c539ba.html.

27   Timeless and homey: Confidential source.

27   Loretta, then nineteen: Rogers and Brehl, *Relentless*, p. 49.

27   For Melinda: Melinda's recollections of summers in Muskoka and her upbringing in general come from her written answers to dozens of questions that I sent to her, hereafter referred to as Melinda's written answers.

28   In 1977, Ted and Loretta bought: Rogers and Brehl, *Relentless*, p. 122.

28   Collegiate Gothic: Janice Bradbeer, "150 years ago, a Toronto reverend wanted to educate his four daughters so he founded Bishop Strachan all-girls' school," *Toronto Star*, October 12, 2017, https://www.thestar.com /yourtoronto/once-upon-a-city-archives/2017/10/12/150-years-ago-a -toronto-reverend-wanted-to-educate-his-four-daughters-so-he-founded -bishop-strachan-all-girls-school.html.

29   wrangling donations: Interview with Larry Tanenbaum for Loretta's obituary.

29   Edward was eight: Van Hasselt, *High Wire Act*, p. 120.

29   As a teenager, Edward: Ibid., p. 444.

29   childlike spirit: Melinda's written answers.

29   disappeared into his binders: Interview with John Tory for Loretta's obituary.

30   Some family friends: Confidential sources; Van Hasselt, *High Wire Act*, p. 444.

30   Ted later regretted: Rogers and Brehl, *Relentless*, p. 88.

30   Loretta loved her children: Melinda's written answers.

30   Lisa was told early in life: Rogers and Brehl, *Relentless*, p. 87.

31   "Lisa was older": Melinda's written answers.

31   a rebellious phase: Rogers and Brehl, *Relentless*, p. 159.

31   **In 1855, six students:** Douglas Richard Carlson, *History of the Sigma Chi Fraternity 1955 to 1980* (Sigma Chi Fraternity, 1990), pp. 1–57.

32   **Ted was able to secure a dinner meeting:** Rogers and Brehl, *Relentless*, p. 37.

32   **Edward took on the role of treasurer:** Catherine McLean and Grant Robertson, "Out of the shadow," *Globe and Mail*, May 24, 2008, https://www.theglobeandmail.com/report-on-business/out-of-the-shadow/article17986670/.

33   **Like her brother:** Melinda's written answers.

33   **on-and-off courtship:** Confidential sources.

33   **They were eighteen:** Confidential source.

33   **She was born in Elliot Lake:** Leanne Delap, "How Suzanne Rogers became Canada's fashion fairy godmother," *Toronto Star*, December 24, 2020, https://www.thestar.com/life/fashion_style/2020/12/24/how-suzanne-rogers-became-canadas-fashion-fairy-godmother.html.

34   **"every lousy job they could":** Rogers and Brehl, *Relentless*, p. 213.

34   **One long-time cable executive:** McLean and Robertson, "Out of the shadow."

34   **"negative option billing":** Rogers and Brehl, *Relentless*, pp. 119–20, 212.

35   **throwing rocks:** Lind and Brehl, *Right Hand Man*, p. 277.

35   **Rogers gained a reputation:** Rogers and Brehl, *Relentless*, pp. 211–12.

35   **endless barrage of memos:** Van Hasselt, *High Wire Act*, p. 438.

35   **People who flocked:** Pitts, *Kings of Convergence*, pp. 25–6.

35   **perpetually dissatisfied:** Lind and Brehl, *Right Hand Man*, pp. 244–6.

36   **Not everyone took:** Melinda's written answers.

36   **When Ted flew off:** Van Hasselt, *High Wire Act*, p. 66.

36   **"At home, he was just dad":** Melinda's written answers.

36   **Among the most high-profile:** Rogers and Brehl, *Relentless*, p. 215.

37   **Tall and lanky:** Van Hasselt, *High Wire Act*, p. 359.

37   **mirroring both his work ethic:** Confidential sources.

37   **Horn became integral:** "Rogers Communications Announces the Passing of Alan Horn," Rogers Communications Canada Inc. press release, January 16, 2023, https://www.globenewswire.com/en/news-release/2023/01/17/2589529/0/en/Rogers-Communications-Announces-the-Passing-of-Alan-Horn.html.

37   **The late 1990s were difficult:** Rogers and Brehl, *Relentless*, pp. 219–24.

37   **entering the internet business:** Van Hasselt, *High Wire Act*, pp. 346–7.

37   **lost millions:** Rogers and Brehl, *Relentless*, p. 234.

38   **investors soured:** Van Hasselt, *High Wire Act*, p. 361.

38   **hitting $4.80 per share:** Rogers and Brehl, *Relentless*, pp. 219–20.

38   **But Edward and Suzanne weren't ready:** Confidential source.

38   **Edward and Suzanne's relationship created tension:** Confidential sources; Kelly Pullen, "The Man Who Would Be King: Inside the ruthless battle for control of the $34-billion Rogers empire," *Toronto Life*, October 16, 2014, https://torontolife.com/from-the-archives/edward-rogers-the-man-who-would-be-king/.

38   **Melinda organized a christening:** Melinda's written answers.

38   **It was Canada Day, 1998:** Lind and Brehl, *Right Hand Man*, pp. 1–9, 222–34.

40   **"bigger jerk than before":** Ibid., p. 224.

40   The younger Tory had known: Interview with John Tory for Loretta's obituary.

40   Tory married Barbara Hackett: Jude Ephson, "John's other half: Who is John Tory's wife Barbara Hackett?", *The U.S. Sun,* February 11, 2023, https://www.the-sun.com/news/7369032/who-is-john-torys-wife-barbara-hackett/.

41   "She had a mind like a steel trap": Interview with Dr. Bernie Gosevitz for Loretta's obituary.

41   sober second thought: Interview with John Tory for Loretta's obituary.

41   Nobody was quite sure: Interview with Melinda Rogers-Hixon for Loretta's obituary.

41   their father encouraged them: Melinda's written answers.

41   One summer: McLean and Robertson, "Out of the shadow."

41   business development analyst: Lisa's bio on the Rogers Communications website, https://investors.rogers.com/corporate-governance/board-of-directors/.

41   Around 2005: Melinda's written answers.

41   She loved nature: Martha's written answers.

42   doctor of naturopathic medicine designation: Martha's bio on the Rogers Communications website, https://investors.rogers.com/corporate-governance/board-of-directors/.

42   "Poor girl": Rogers and Brehl, *Relentless,* p. 221.

42   "Ted in a skirt": Van Hasselt, *High Wire Act,* p. 445.

42   Asked about the nickname: Author interview with Melinda for the *Globe and Mail,* November 2021.

42   "Edward the Accountant": McLean and Robertson, "Out of the shadow."

42   Melinda shared Ted's: Melinda's written answers.

43      $4 billion worth of cable assets: John Daly, "The Bigger Picture," *Report on Business,* April 28, 2000, https://www.theglobeandmail.com/report-on-business/rob-magazine/the-bigger-picture/article4163070/.

43   felt otherwise: Lind and Brehl, *Right Hand Man,* pp. 277–8.

43   Ted and Edward met JR Shaw's eldest child: Van Hasselt, *High Wire Act,* pp. 377–8.

43   different management styles: Kirstie McLellan Day, *Above and Beyond: The JR Shaw Family History in Life and Business* (Calgary: Shaw Communications, 2005), p. 338.

43   he once showed Jim a report: Pitts, *Kings of Convergence,* p. 27.

44   "I like the guy": Ibid, p. 27.

44   lower their voices: Confidential source.

Three   The wireless wiz

45   "the frying pan": Lind and Brehl, *Right Hand Man,* p. 73.

45   when Nadir Mohamed walked: Rogers and Brehl, *Relentless,* pp. 228–9.

45   Mohamed, who was terrified of dogs: Van Hasselt, *High Wire Act,* pp. 378–81.

45   golden retrievers: Van Hasselt's book describes the dogs as Labrador retrievers, while in *Relentless* they are referred to as golden retrievers. Seeing as they were Ted's dogs, I have gone with his account.

47   Gemmell knew Chagnon well: Author interview with Robert Gemmell.
47   After weeks of intense negotiations: Rogers and Brehl, *Relentless*, p. 227.
47   Rogers would pay $5.6 billion: Van Hasselt, *High Wire Act*, pp. 372–4.
47   less than 20 per cent: There are some discrepancies between various
        characterizations of the size of the Caisse's stake, with reported figures
        ranging from 17 to 18.8 per cent.
47   a shareholder agreement stipulated: Nicolas Van Praet, "The Notorious
        PKP: How Pierre Karl Péladeau is doubling down on fortress Quebec,"
        Report on Business, October 19, 2018, https://www.theglobeandmail.com
        /business/rob-magazine/article-the-notorious-pkp/.
47   "Quebec Inc.": Van Hasselt, *High Wire Act*, pp. 375–6.
48   the son of a lumber merchant: Jorge Niosi and Ayoub Moustakbal,
        "Pierre Péladeau," *The Canadian Encyclopedia*, last modified February 17,
        2023, https://www.thecanadianencyclopedia.ca/en/article/pierre-peladeau.
48   His ability to parlay: Van Praet, "The Notorious PKP."
48   Pierre Karl Péladeau was thirty-eight: Van Praet, "The Notorious
        PKP."
48   handed out leaflets: Pitts, *Kings of Convergence*, p. 88.
49   "catastrophe for workers": Van Praet, "The Notorious PKP."
49   one former Quebec premier: Van Hasselt, *High Wire Act*, pp. 375–414.
49   Ted was eager: Ibid, p. 376; Rogers and Brehl, *Relentless*, p. 228.
49   worth US$112 million: Ibid., p. 230.
50   as he flew back to Toronto: Interview with Dr. Bernie Gosevitz for
        Loretta's obituary.
50   "We've lost money": Rogers and Brehl, *Relentless*, pp. 232–7.
52   Tensions began to build: Confidential sources.
52   "I'd like to have a shot": Van Hasselt, *High Wire Act*, p. 445.
52   some executives began to sense: Melinda declined to comment on her
        relationship with Edward during that time.
52   Ted lauded his daughter: Van Hasselt, *High Wire Act*, pp. 445–6.
52   In his final television interview: See https://www.youtube.com
        /watch?v=9B-hlNXKYZo.
53   nor had she ever told: Melinda's written answers.
53   while Melinda was pregnant: Confidential sources.
53   They were set up: Author interview with Melinda for the *Globe and Mail*,
        November 2021.
54   Ted had always made it clear: Confidential source.
54   Ted had been planning: Gayle MacDonald, "JR," *Report on Business*,
        February 28, 2003, https://www.theglobeandmail.com/report-on-business
        /rob-magazine/jr/article18284617/.
54   During an emotional conversation: Confidential source.
55   he likened his son: Van Hasselt, *High Wire Act*, p. 437.
55   too financially conservative: Ibid., 443–5.
55   In May 2005: Ibid., p. 396.
55   Ted invited Mohamed's wife: Rogers and Brehl, *Relentless*, p. 230.

Four   Rule from the grave

56   heated family dispute: Van Hasselt, *High Wire Act*, pp. 441–2.
56   A defibrillator roughly: Rogers and Brehl, *Relentless*, p. 242.

56   Ted had implemented a dual-class: Van Hasselt, *High Wire Act*, pp. 428–30.

57   He had arrived at the figure: Confidential source.

57   Founders speak of their firms: Gordon Pitts, *In the Blood: Battles to Succeed in Canada's Family Businesses* (Toronto: Doubleday Canada, 2000), pp. 5–16.

58   Canada's Bronfman family: Graham D. Taylor, "'From Shirtsleeves to Shirtless': The Bronfman Dynasty and the Seagram Empire," *Business and Economic History On-Line*, vol. 4 (Business History Conference, 2006), https://thebhc.org/sites/default/files/taylor_0.pdf; Howard Green, "When billionaires battle: The fall of Seagram sheds light on the role blood plays in family-controlled firms," *Toronto Star*, November 13, 2021, https://www.thestar.com/business/opinion/2021/11/13/when-billionaires-battle-the-fall-of-seagram-sheds-light-on-the-role-of-blood-in-family-controlled-firms.html.

58   New Brunswick's McCain family: Paul Waldie, *A House Divided: The Untold Story of the McCain Family* (Toronto, Viking, 1996), pp. 1–8.

58   When the last remaining heir: Pitts, *In the Blood*, p. 5.

58   "for as many generations": Memorandum of Wishes to the trustees and advisory committee, Exhibit B to affidavit of Loretta Anne Rogers, *Rogers v. Rogers Communications Inc.*, File No.: S219325, October 29, 2021 (hereafter referred to as Ted's memorandum of wishes).

59   dividend payments: Van Hasselt, *High Wire Act*, p. 428.

59   His past experiences: Control Trust Will, Exhibit A to affidavit of Loretta Anne Rogers, *Rogers v. Rogers Communications Inc.*, File No.: S219325, October 29, 2021 (hereafter referred to as the control trust will).

59   The advisory committee's composition: It is unclear whether all of the advisers originally contemplated served on the advisory committee.

60   The ranking was based: Confidential source.

60   Ted compared the system: Rogers and Brehl, Relentless, p. 245.

61   "You can't rule from the grave": Van Hasselt, *High Wire Act*, p. 431.

61   "My father is buried there": Ted's memorandum of wishes, p. 24.

61–2   Edward urged him: Confidential source.

62   He postponed his target: Van Hasselt, *High Wire Act*, p. 428.

62   He never had an honest conversation: Confidential sources.

62   on multiple occasions: Van Hasselt, High Wire Act, p. 442.

62   he made no secret: Melinda's written answers.

62   Ted's funeral: "Ted Rogers: The funeral of a Canadian icon," *Maclean's*, December 9, 2008, https://macleans.ca/economy/business/ted-rogers/; Pullen, "The Man Who Would Be King."

63   sat stoically: Confidential source.

63   installed a cable car: Confidential source.

63   the company announced: "Ted Rogers admitted to hospital for heart condition," The Canadian Press, October 31, 2008, https://www.cbc.ca/news/canada/ted-rogers-admitted-to-hospital-for-heart-condition-1.738088.

63   The night before he died: Confidential source.

63   "young at heart": Pullen, "The Man Who Would Be King."

64   Edward recounted: Pullen, "The Man Who Would Be King."

64   The funeral was followed: Interviews with Melinda Rogers-Hixon and others for Loretta's obituary.

65   He'd worked hard: Confidential source.

65   **dinners with portfolio managers:** The meetings, as well as the contro-
        versy that resulted from them, were described to me by three confidential
        sources. A fourth source close to the company disputed that the meetings
        resulted in conflict.

66   **an event space:** "The History of the Carlu," accessed July 16, 2023,
        https://www.thecarlu.com/about/.

66   **custom handmade silk:** "Write Style," Bella Invites (blog), December 1,
        2009, http://bellainvites.blogspot.com/2009/12/write-style.html.

66   **wore a strapless dress:** Pullen, "The Man Who Would Be King."

66   **Both Melinda and Martha:** Melinda's written answers.

66   **The contract that he negotiated:** Pullen, "The Man Who Would Be
        King."

Five   Tony

68   **Rob Bruce:** See https://www.linkedin.com/in/robertwbruce/, accessed on
        Aug. 24, 2023.

68   **Furlong's legacy:** Terry Glavin, "The allegations against John Furlong
        have become just one more chapter in his inspiring story," *National Post*,
        March 1, 2017, https://nationalpost.com/opinion/terry-glavin-the
        -allegations-against-john-furlong-have-become-just-one-more-chapter-in
        -his-inspiring-story.

68   **Bell was encroaching:** Christine Dobby, "Inside an outsider's fall: How
        CEO Guy Laurence fought the Rogers family and lost," *Report on Business*,
        May 24, 2017, https://www.theglobeandmail.com/report-on-business/rob
        -magazine/robmaghow-ceo-guy-laurence-fought-the-rogers-familyand
        -lost/article35063144/.

69   **when Bell and Telus launched:** Brian Jackson, "Bell, Telus launch HSPA
        wireless service," IT World Canada, November 4, 2009, https://www
        .itworldcanada.com/article/bell-telus-launch-hspa-wireless-service/40064.

69   **He told colleagues:** Confidential source.

69   **Staffieri grew up:** Staffieri's biographical information was provided by
        Rogers Communications.

71   **Once at Rogers:** Confidential sources.

72   **Shortly after he came on board:** "Rogers Communications Announces
        Chief Financial Officer Transition," Rogers Communications Inc. press
        release, October 26, 2011, https://about.rogers.com/news-ideas/rogers
        -communications-announces-chief-financial-officer-transition/.

72   **shedding more than 300 jobs:** Josh O'Kane, "Facing cost pressures,
        Rogers axes 375 jobs," *Globe and Mail*, June 26, 2012, Globe and Mail
        Archival Search.

72   **The sale dragged on:** David Shoalts, *Hockey Fight in Canada: The Big
        Media Faceoff over the NHL* (Madeira Park, B.C.: Douglas and McIntyre,
        2018), pp. 26–7.

72   **Edward and Melinda were disappointed:** Pullen, "The Man Who
        Would Be King."

73   **Martha and Loretta had begun:** Melinda's written answers.

73   **Rogers Venture Partners:** Yuliya Chernova, "Rogers Venture Partners
        Shuts Down," WSJ Pro Venture Capital, October 10, 2018, https://www
        .wsj.com/articles/rogers-venture-partners-shuts-down-1539206281.

73   already had a house: Interview with Melinda for the *Globe and Mail*, November 2021.

73   sowing confusion: Pullen, "The Man Who Would Be King."

74   "absolutely categorically my choice": Steve Ladurantaye and Rita Trichur, "Rogers CEO Nadir Mohamed exiting, analyst sees 'constructive transition,'" *Globe and Mail*, February 14, 2013, https://www.theglobeandmail.com/report-on-business/rogers-ceo-nadir-mohamed-exiting-analyst-sees-constructive-transition/article8710887/.

74   retirement package: Rita Trichur, "Outgoing Rogers CEO entitled to $18.51-million retirement package," *Globe and Mail*, March 28, 2013, https://www.theglobeandmail.com/globe-investor/outgoing-rogers-ceo-entitled-to-1851-million-retirement-package/article10539079/.

Six   Rogers 3.0

75   cavernous arena: Dobby, "Inside an outsider's fall."

75   black leather motorcycle jacket: Ibid.

76   At one point during the town hall: This memorable anecdote was relayed to me by multiple employees who were present at the event but declined to be named.

77   Edward, who was spearheading: Confidential source.

77   dining at their home: Pullen, "The Man Who Would Be King."

77   During an interview at Spencer Stuart's: Melinda's written answers.

77   He liked to tell people: Dobby, "Inside an outsider's fall."

77   In one speech: See https://www.youtube.com/watch?v=r4UklkbHLDI, accessed August 24, 2023.

78   Shortly after he was hired: Interview with Dr. Bernie Gosevitz for Loretta's obituary.

78   Laurence spent his first three months: Pullen, "The Man Who Would Be King."

78   He even went undercover: Christine Dobby, "Rogers CEO admits will take 'some time' to improve service after stint as field technician," *Financial Post*, April 22, 2014, https://financialpost.com/technology/guy-laurence-undercover-boss-rogers-ceo-admits-will-take-some-time-to-improve-service-after-stint-as-field-technician.

78   For instance, he wrote about: Dobby, "Inside an outsider's fall."

78   It's not unusual: Elaine Pofeldt, "Many Firms Don't Survive After Owners Die," *Forbes*, February 26, 2013, https://www.forbes.com/sites/elainepofeldt/2013/02/26/many-firms-dont-bounce-back-after-owners-die/.

79   "Rogers 3.0": "Rogers 3.0: Accelerating growth and overhauling the customer experience," Rogers Communications Inc. press release, May 23, 2014, https://about.rogers.com/news-ideas/rogers-3-0-accelerating-growth-and-overhauling-the-customer-experience/.

79   its practice of scrambling: Dobby, "Inside an outsider's fall."

79   Charles Sirois: Interview with Melinda for the *Globe and Mail*, November 2021.

79   Edward, meanwhile, had agreed: Confidential source.

79   Memos went out announcing: Pullen, "The Man Who Would Be King."

79   He installed Deutsche Telekom: Dobby, "Inside an outsider's fall."

80   the acquisition of struggling wireless: Christine Dobby, "Court
        approves Mobilicity sale to Rogers for $465-million," *Globe and Mail*,
        June 23, 2015, https://www.theglobeandmail.com/report-on-business
        /rogers-to-buy-mobilicity-sources-say/article25081410/.
80   cancelled after just three years: "Rogers terminates Vice partnership
        just over three years after launch," BNN Bloomberg, January 22, 2018,
        https://www.bnnbloomberg.ca/rogers-terminates-vice-media-partnership
        -just-over-3-years-after-launch-1.975030.
80   as was one with Spotify: Gary Ng, "Rogers to Axe Spotify, NHL Live as
        Free Perks with Wireless Plans on July 30," iPhone in Canada, July 6,
        2018, https://www.iphoneincanada.ca/2018/07/06/rogers-axe-spotify-nhl/.
80   aimed to boost: Christine Dobby, "Rogers CEO hopes Spotify partner-
        ship will increase mobile data usage," *Globe and Mail*, September 14,
        2015, https://www.theglobeandmail.com/report-on-business/rogers-ceo
        -hopes-spotify-partnership-will-increase-mobile-data-usage
        /article26361464/.
80   he sometimes met opposition: Dobby, "Inside an outsider's fall."
80   Initially, Edward and Melinda: Confidential sources.
81   By the time the company's: Dobby, "Inside an outsider's fall";
        Confidential source.
81   He publicly called: Christine Dobby, "Rogers CEO Laurence shows his
        stripes, calls out competitors," *Globe and Mail*, October 23, 2014, https://
        www.theglobeandmail.com/report-on-business/rogers-ceo-laurence-shows
        -his-stripes-calls-out-competitors/article21278142/.
81–2   some analysts believed: Two industry analysts speaking on background.
82   larger-than-expected bonus: Dobby, "Inside an outsider's fall."

Seven   Joe

83   invited a friend's husband: Confidential source.
83   Natale grew up: Confidential sources.
84   His grandmother, who lived: Christine Dobby, "Darren Entwistle: A
        man obsessed with Telus," *Report on Business*, June 27, 2018, https://www
        .theglobeandmail.com/business/rob-magazine/article-will-telus-ceo
        -darren-entwistle-ever-let-go/.
85   Top Forty Under 40: Matthew McKinnon, "Top Forty Under 40," *Report
        on Business*, April 26, 2002, https://www.theglobeandmail.com/report-on
        -business/rob-magazine/top-forty-under-40/article1022863/.
85   Telus was little more: Dobby, "Darren Entwistle"; Eric Reguly, "Perfectly
        unhappy," *Globe and Mail*, October 27, 2006, https://www.theglobeandmail
        .com/report-on-business/perfectly-unhappy/article1107895/.
86   His first interview: Confidential source.
87   After landing the job: Confidential sources.
87   They bonded over: Confidential sources.
88   When Monty Carter: Author interview with Monty Carter for the *Globe
        and Mail*, March 2021.
89   Canfield, along with: Confidential sources.
89   The issue came to a head: Confidential source.
89   period of three years: Telus 2015 information circular, p. 47.
90   he promised to move: Confidential sources.

90 Executive chairs were frowned upon: Rita Trichur, "New chair, same boss at Telus," *Globe and Mail*, March 31, 2014, https://www .theglobeandmail.com/report-on-business/entwistle-to-step-down-as-telus -chief-in-may/article17735298/.

90 Natale was taken aback: Confidential source.

90 role delineation agreement: Telus 2014 information circular, pp. 95–6.

91 The members of Team Darren: Three confidential sources.

91 Team Joe felt differently: Four confidential sources.

92 Natale tried to trim: Confidential source.

93 the edicts: "Our strategy and values," Telus Corp., accessed on July 16, 2023, https://www.telus.com/en/about/leadership-team/strategy-and -values.

93 a report about the CEO's performance: "Confidential Briefing for the Lead Director," internal Telus report provided to me and verified by multiple confidential sources.

95 the *Nova Spirit*: Amanda Lang, "Cruise director," *Report on Business*, October 27, 2006, https://www.theglobeandmail.com/report-on-business /rob-magazine/cruise-director/article18175156/; Peter, "NOVA SPIRIT Yacht: Jim Pattison $25M Superyacht" SuperYachtFan, accessed August 13, 2023, https://www.superyachtfan.com/yacht/nova-spirit/.

95 Natale was feeling positive: Confidential source.

95 During such a session: Confidential source.

96 In July, the two men: Confidential sources.

97 Natale would take home: Telus 2016 information circular, p. 76.

97 The vote to oust Natale: Confidential sources.

97 Telus's second-quarter results: "Telus Reports Strong Results for Second Quarter 2015," Marketwired, August 7, 2015, https://finance.yahoo .com/news/telus-reports-strong-results-second-19700594.html.

97 an "impressive" achievement: Christina Pellegrini, "Telus Corp. second-quarter income narrowly tops analyst estimates," *Financial Post*, August 7, 2015, https://financialpost.com/technology/telus-corp-profit -takes-hit-from-blacks-closure-operating-revenue-up-5-1.

97 McIntosh, the head of human resources: Confidential sources.

97 Telus announced the news: "TELUS Announces Leadership Changes," Marketwired, August 10, 2015, https://www.yahoo.com/lifestyle/s/telus -announces-leadership-changes-110000859.html.

98 According to several industry analysts: Multiple industry analysts speaking on background.

98 slashing 1,500 jobs: Christine Dobby, "Telus to cut 1,500 jobs in bid to trim costs," *Globe and Mail*, November 5, 2015, https://www .theglobeandmail.com/report-on-business/telus-to-cut-workforce-by-1500 -positions-in-bid-to-reduce-costs/article27114207/.

99 In a press release: "Announced Layoffs by Profitable Telus, Regrettable and Unnecessary," United Steelworkers (USW) press release, November 5, 2015, https://www.newswire.ca/news-releases/announced-layoffs-by -profitable-telus-regrettable-and-unnecessary-541203001.html.

99 the telecom had just reported: "Telus Reports Results for Third Quarter 2015," Marketwired, November 5, 2015, https://finance.yahoo.com/news /telus-reports-results-third-quarter-110000721.html.

99 Amid the refined: Confidential sources.

99   **Melinda was particularly impressed:** Interview with Melinda for the *Globe and Mail*, November 2021, and Melinda's written answers.

100   **But John MacDonald:** MacDonald's affidavit.

101   **"anomalously large":** Christine Dobby, "$24.1-million: Telus pays the price for swapping CEOs," *Globe and Mail*, April 4, 2016, https://www.theglobeandmail.com/report-on-business/telus-pays-co-ceos-a-total-of-241-million-in-2015/article29516536/.

101   **the more valuable:** Confidential source.

101   **On Thanksgiving Day weekend:** Confidential sources.

101   **Laurence disagreed:** Confidential source.

101   **His departure:** "Rogers Communications announces CEO transition," Rogers Communications Inc. press release, October 17, 2016, https://www.newswire.ca/news-releases/rogers-communications-announces-ceo-transition-597282701.html.

102   **separation payments:** Christine Dobby, "Rogers paid outgoing CEO $42.6-million over three years," *Globe and Mail*, March 20, 2017, https://www.theglobeandmail.com/report-on-business/rogers-paid-outgoing-ceo-426-million-over-three-years/article34357427/.

102   **entered into arbitration:** The arbitration process was described to me by multiple confidential sources. Telus's allegations about Natale are outlined in a May 10, 2017 presentation to the company's board.

102   **reached a deal:** Christine Dobby and James Bradshaw, "Joe Natale to take Rogers helm early after deal with Telus," *Globe and Mail*, April 13, 2017, https://www.theglobeandmail.com/report-on-business/joe-natale-to-take-rogers-helm-early-after-deal-with-telus/article34695327/.

103   **When Joe [Natale] became:** Theresa Tedesco and Emily Jackson, "Rogers tried to get Telus to release Joseph Natale from his non-compete agreement, sources say," *Financial Post*, October 18, 2016, https://financialpost.com/news/rogers-tried-to-get-telus-to-release-joseph-natale-from-his-non-compete-agreement-sources-say.

103   **"exactly the person":** Lind and Brehl, *Right Hand Man*, p. 337.

103   **One day in mid-November 2016:** Multiple confidential sources.

Eight Care Nation

105   **Eric Agius found himself:** Jim Reid, *Leading to Greatness: 5 Principles to Transform Your Leadership and Build Great Teams* (Vancouver: Figure 1 Publishing, 2022), pp. 129–46.

106   **On April 19, 2017:** Rogers Annual General Meeting of Shareholders, April 19, 2017.

106   **Drucker once had this to say:** Peter F. Drucker, "Drucker on Management: How to Save the Family Business," *Wall Street Journal*, November 19, 2009 (originally published August 19, 1994), https://www.wsj.com/articles/SB10001424052748704204304574544260451524596.

107   **Agius learned just how much:** Reid, *Leading to Greatness*, pp. 129–46.

108   **Rogers had pared back:** Christine Dobby, "Rogers to hike spending on wireless network," *Globe and Mail*, December 3, 2017, https://www.theglobeandmail.com/report-on-business/rogers-to-hike-spending-on-wireless-network/article37173377/.

109   **sales representatives were stunned:** Confidential source.

109   **By the end of 2017:** Rogers 2017 Annual Report, p. 26.

109   **frequent leadership changes:** Reid, *Leading to Greatness*, pp. 114–24.

110   **Melinda, in particular:** Author interview with Melinda for the *Globe and Mail*, November 2021.

110   **consistently outperformed:** "National Bank of Canada unveils The Family Advantage Spring 2022 Report," National Bank, June 20, 2022, https://www.nbc.ca/about-us/news-media/press-release/2022/20220620 -rapport-avantage-familial-2022.html.

110   **a dark side:** Descriptions of the corporate culture at Rogers during the time in question, as well as of Edward's continued interference with management, come from interviews with multiple former employees across various levels of the organization, as well as the following article: Dobby, "Inside an outsider's fall."

111   **Several former executives:** Descriptions of the company's financial controls and Staffieri's role come from discussions with five former employees.

112   **mediating disputes:** Confidential source.

113   **"One of my goals":** Christine Dobby, "Joe Natale: hitting reset at Rogers," *Globe and Mail*, December 3, 2017, https://www.theglobeandmail .com/report-on-business/joe-natale-hitting-reset-at-rogers -communications/article37173515/.

113   **"He has tremendous value":** Author interview with Robert Gemmell.

113   **On December 7:** "Rogers Communications announces changes to Board of Directors," Rogers Communications Inc. press release, December 7, 2017, https://www.prnewswire.com/news-releases/rogers-communications -announces-changes-to-board-of-directors-662618883.html.

114   **"Cocktail Joe":** Confidential sources.

114   **Natale had tapped Banks:** Susan Krashinsky Robertson and Andrew Willis, "Hockey, baseball and buzzwords: Can Rogers Media's new boss solve some old media problems?" *Globe and Mail*, October 11, 2019, https:// www.theglobeandmail.com/business/article-hockey-baseball-and -buzzwords-can-rogers-medias-new-boss-solve-some/.

114   **But Edward didn't think:** Written statement from Robert Gemmell.

114   **He had someone else in mind:** Confidential sources.

114   **According to Gemmell, Natale:** Written statement from Robert Gemmell.

114   **Natale confided in several directors:** Confidential sources.

115   **overage fees represented:** Tim Shufelt, "Rogers stock drops as unlimited wireless plans hurt revenue," *Globe and Mail*, October 23, 2019, https:// www.theglobeandmail.com/business/article-rogers-stock-drops-as -unlimited-wireless-plans-hit-overage-fees/.

116   **Rogers announced the launch:** "Rogers Introduces Infinite Wireless Data Plans With No Overage Charges," Rogers Communications Inc. press release, June 12, 2019, https://about.rogers.com/news-ideas/rogers -introduces-infinite-wireless-data-plans-no-overage-charges.

116   **advertised the new plans heavily:** Two industry analysts speaking on background.

117   **During the company's:** Rogers 2019 Q3 earnings call transcript

117   **To stop the revolving door:** Reid, *Leading to Greatness*, pp. 134–46, and a confidential source.

118   **the changes started to bear fruit:** Reid, *Leading to Greatness*, p. 140.

118   **Employee engagement improved:** Ibid., pp. 122–4.

119   In late November 2019: Details of the Mason Capital incident that pre-
        ceded Burgess's departure were shared with me by five confidential
        sources and confirmed by Robert Gemmell, although not everyone agreed
        on all of the details or the event's significance. Mason did not return
        repeated phone calls requesting comment.

119   the Rogers Control Trust announced: "Rogers Control Trust Acquires
        an Additional 5.7 Million Class A Voting Shares of Rogers
        Communications Inc.," Rogers Control Trust press release, December 18,
        2019, https://www.newswire.ca/news-releases/rogers-control-trust-acquires
        -an-additional-5-7-million-class-a-voting-shares-of-rogers
        -communications-inc--816139486.html.

120   "generally happy": Confidential source.

120   But to Burgess: Three confidential sources.

120   he told a class of MBA students: Confidential source.

Nine   "Beans about cable"

122   BCE Inc.'s president: "Bell pays tribute to Canadian telecom pioneer JR
        Shaw," Bell Canada, March 24, 2020, https://www.newswire.ca/news
        -releases/bell-pays-tribute-to-canadian-telecom-pioneer-jr-shaw
        -854780734.html.

122   Telus's Entwistle praised: "Statement from Telus on the passing of JR
        Shaw," Telus Corp., March 25, 2020, https://www.globenewswire.com
        /news-release/2020/03/25/2006319/0/en/Statement-from-TELUS-on-the
        -passing-of-JR-Shaw.html.

122   Edward offered condolences: "Statement from Edward S. Rogers, Chair
        of Rogers Communications Inc., on the passing of JR Shaw," Rogers
        Communications Inc., March 25, 2020, https://about.rogers.com/news
        -ideas/statement-from-edward-s-rogers-chair-of-rogers-communications
        -inc-on-the-passing-of-jr-shaw/.

122   James Robert Shaw was born: Day, *Above and Beyond*, p. 38 onwards.

124   often bickered: Pitts, *Kings of Convergence*, p. 39.

125   "Young man, cable television": Day, *Above and Beyond*, p. 167.

126   10,000 customers: "JR Shaw Obituary," Legacy.com, https://www.legacy
        .com/ca/obituaries/theglobeandmail/name/jr-shaw-obituary?pid=195871099.

126   the Shaws drove through: Day, *Above and Beyond*, p. 195 onwards.

127   "[JR] was such a wonderfully warm": Author interview with former
        Shaw president Peter Bissonnette for JR's obituary in the *Globe and Mail*,
        which ran on March 27, 2020.

128   Reimer argued that: Pitts, *Kings of Convergence*, p. 49.

128   he lined the walls: Christine Dobby, "Shaw's bid to win back the West,"
        Globe and Mail, February 3, 2017, https://www.theglobeandmail.com
        /report-on-business/shaw-communications-strategy-telecom-wireless
        /article33896160/.

128   Julie would later recall: Author interview with Julie Shaw about the Shaw
        family donation to the Glenbow Museum for the *Globe and Mail*,
        February 2022.

129   As a teenager: Grant Robertson, "Jim Shaw's cowboy act," *Globe and
        Mail*, March 25, 2009, https://www.theglobeandmail.com/report-on
        -business/jim-shaws-cowboy-act/article1150303/.

130   "Tomorrow you will": Day, *Above and Beyond*, pp. 330–1.

130   model Harley-Davidson: Pitts, *Kings of Convergence*, p. 272.

130   Jim was known to speak: Christine Dobby, "Late cable family scion Jim Shaw built a media empire," *Globe and Mail*, January 5, 2018, https://www .theglobeandmail.com/report-on-business/late-cable-family-scion-jim -shaw-built-a-media-empire/article37514733/.

131   he continued to consult: Day, *Above and Beyond*, p. 331.

131   generous compensation: Shaw Communications 2019 proxy circular, pp. 24, 30, 40.

131   Eagle Pointe Lodge: "Eagle Pointe Lodge," CanadianLodges.com, accessed on July 16, 2023, https://canadianlodges.com/british-columbia -fishing-lodges/eagle-pointe-lodge.

131   Felesky admired: Author interview with Brian Felesky for JR's obituary in the *Globe and Mail*, March 2020.

132   "I thought he": Robertson, "Jim Shaw's cowboy act."

132   "fall over dead": Robertson, "Jim Shaw's cowboy act."

132   The situation came to a head: Iain Marlow and Susan Krashinsky Robertson, "Jim Shaw steps down after 'unprofessional' behaviour," *The Globe and Mail*, November 18, 2010, https://www.theglobeandmail.com /globe-investor/jim-shaw-steps-down-after-unprofessional-behaviour /article1319550/.

132   The incident accelerated: Susan Krashinsky Robertson and Iain Marlow, "Brad Shaw: The (New) Cable Guy," *Globe and Mail*, June 4, 2011, https:// www.theglobeandmail.com/globe-investor/brad-shaw-the-new-cable-guy /article583936/.

132   He spoke about: Rita Trichur, "The poker-faced Bradley Shaw pegs his future on WiFi," *Globe and Mail*, April 11, 2014, https://www .theglobeandmail.com/report-on-business/careers/management/the-poker -faced-bradley-shaw-pegs-his-future-on-wifi/article17934689/.

133   Brad and his wife: Krashinsky Robertson and Marlow, "Brad Shaw."

133   a rough patch: Day, *Above and Beyond*, p. 237 onwards.

133    $9.5 billion: Dobby, "Shaw's bid to win back the West."

134   between 2011 and 2015: My own calculation based on Shaw's publicly disclosed figures.

134   after conducting a strategic review: Christine Dobby, "Shaw to buy Wind Mobile for $1.6-billion," *Globe and Mail,* December 16, 2015, https:// www.theglobeandmail.com/report-on-business/shaw-buying-wind-mobile -for-16-billion/article27791628/.

134   The move left: Trichur, "The poker-faced Bradley Shaw pegs his future on WiFi."

135   He was in Halifax: Dobby, "Shaw's bid to win back the West."

136   Public Mobile was bought: "Telus buys Public Mobile in surprise move," The Canadian Press, October 23, 2013, https://www.thestar.com/business /tech_news/2013/10/23/telus_gets_federal_blessing_to_acquire_new_player _public_mobile.html.

136   while Mobilicity: Christina Pellegrini, "The inside story of how Rogers Communications Inc acquired Mobilicity: 'Everybody won but Telus,'" *Financial Post*, July 10, 2015, https://financialpost.com/technology/how -rogers-blindsided-telus-by-acquiring-mobilicity.

136   Wind was founded: Anthony Lacavera and Kate Fillion, *How We Can Win:*

And What Happens to Us and Our Country If We Don't (Toronto: Random House Canada, 2017), pp. 1–44.

137   **In October 2009:** Susan Taylor and John McCrank, "Canada opens mobile market to Globalive," Reuters, December 11, 2009, https://www .reuters.com/article/ctech-us-globalive-licence -idCATRE5BA1UB20091211.

137   **Globalive Communications Corp.:** "Globalive and Canada's wireless market: The players, the numbers, the rules," *Globe and Mail*, September 18, 2009, https://www.theglobeandmail.com/report-on-business/globalive -and-canadas-wireless-market-the-players-the-numbers-the-rules /article4216226/.

137   **wild rollercoaster ride:** Author interview with Anthony Lacavera for "Freedom Mobile may be up for sale again, and founder Anthony Lacavera wants to buy it," the *Globe and Mail*, December 18, 2021, https://www .theglobeandmail.com/business/article-freedom-mobile-may-be-up-for -sale-again-and-founder-anthony-lacavera/.

138   **a group that included:** Pete Evans, "Tony Lacavera and West Face buy Wind Mobile from VimpelCom," CBC News, September 16, 2014, https:// www.cbc.ca/news/business/tony-lacavera-and-west-face-buy-wind-mobile -from-vimpelcom-1.2767532.

138   **"I would have never sold":** Trevor Cole, "Broken telephone," *Report on Business*, September 27, 2017, https://www.theglobeandmail.com/news /wind-mobile-founder-anthony-lacavera-on-why-canada-treats-its -entrepreneurs-sopoorly/article36396928/.

138   **close to a million subscribers:** "Shaw Communications Inc. to Acquire WIND Mobile Corp.," Shaw Communications Inc. and Wind Mobile Corp. press release, December 16, 2015, https://www.globenewswire.com /news-release/2015/12/16/1284557/0/en/Shaw-Communications-Inc-to -Acquire-WIND-Mobile-Corp.html.

139   **scores of Shaw employees:** Howard Levitt, "He was unconventional, but Jim Shaw could teach us all something about integrity in the workplace," *Financial Post*, January 17, 2018, https://financialpost.com/executive/0117 -biz-hl-levitt-new-wkpl.

139   **cans of beans:** Day, *Above and Beyond*, p. 310.

139   **in lieu of steak:** Pitts, *Kings of Convergence*, p. 280.

140   **brief illness:** Stephanie Babych, "Shaw Communications announces the death of founder JR Shaw," *Calgary Herald*, March 24, 2020, https:// calgaryherald.com/business/local-business/shaw-communications -announces-the-death-of-founder-jr-shaw.

140   **like a big brother:** Confidential source.

Ten   Rogers v. Cogeco

141   **dinner at Centini:** Confidential source.

142   **two decades:** Rogers first acquired a stake in Cogeco in 2000 as part of its cable swap with Shaw.

143   **roughly half a dozen:** Confidential sources.

144   **three occasions:** Affidavit of Edward Rogers, *Rogers v. Rogers Communications Inc.*, File No.: S219325, October 26, 2021 (hereafter referred to as Edward's affidavit).

144   he was worried that Bell: Confidential source.

144   However, according to Gemmell: Interview with Robert Gemmell.

145   The Montreal-based cable company: Bertrand Marotte, "Cogeco founder Henri Audet dead at 94," *Globe and Mail,* November 5, 2012, https://www.theglobeandmail.com/report-on-business/cogeco-founder -henri-audet-dead-at-94/article4915038/.

145   Over the years: "History," Cogeco, accessed July 16, 2023, https://corpo .cogeco.com/cgo/en/company-overview/history/.

145   passed the reins: "Biography – Louis Audet," *Le Cercle canadien,* accessed July 16, 2023, https://www.cerclecanadien-montreal.ca/en/biography-louis -audet.

145   Louis served as chief executive: "Louis Audet named Officer of the Ordre national du Québec for 2021," Cogeco Inc. press release, June 21, 2022, https://corpo.cogeco.com/cgo/en/press-room/press-releases/louis -audet-named-officer-ordre-national-du-quebec-2021/.

146   They felt that owning: Interview with Robert Gemmell.

146   Buying the ninth-largest: "Altice USA, Inc. Presents Offer to Acquire Cogeco in Order to Own Atlantic Broadband," Business Wire, September 2, 2020, https://www.businesswire.com/news/home /20200902005626/en/Altice-USA-Inc.-Presents-Offer-to-Acquire-Cogeco -in-Order-to-Own-Atlantic-Broadband.

146   in January of that year: "Gestion Audem Sells a Small Block of Subordinate Voting Shares by Way of Private Placement," Cogeco Inc. press release, January 21, 2020, https://www.newswire.ca/news-releases /gestion-audem-sells-a-small-block-of-subordinate-voting-shares-by-way -of-private-placement-853774411.html.

146   69 per cent: Louis Audet, "Gestion Audem Rejects The Unsolicited Non-Binding Proposal From Altice And Rogers," Cogeco press release, September 2, 2020, https://corpo.cogeco.com/cgo/en/press-room/press -releases/gestion-audem-rejects-unsolicited-non-binding-proposal-altice -and-rogers/.

146   Natale saw the play: Natale's thinking on the unsolicited bid comes from his and Dexter Goei's public statements, as well as from a confidential source briefed on Natale's position.

147   several months away: Confidential sources.

147   a combined $10.3 billion: "Altice USA, Inc. Presents Offer to Acquire Cogeco in Order to Own Atlantic Broadband."

147   Rogers shelling out: "Rogers Communications confirms agreement with Altice USA to purchase Canadian assets of Cogeco," Rogers Communications Inc. press release, September 2, 2020, https://about .rogers.com/news-ideas/rogers-communications-confirms-agreement-with -altice-usa-to-purchase-canadian-assets-of-cogeco/.

148   Cogeco was not for sale: "Gestion Audem Rejects the Unsolicited Non-Binding Proposal from Altice and Rogers," Gestion Audem press release, September 2 2020, https://www.newswire.ca/news-releases/gestion-audem -rejects-the-unsolicited-non-binding-proposal-from-altice-and-rogers -865811082.html.

148   Louis had two brothers: "Henri Audet," *Montreal Gazette,* November 7, 2012, https://montrealgazette.remembering.ca/obituary/henri-audet -1066082274.

148   Cogeco's independent directors: "Cogeco and Cogeco Communications
        Boards of Directors Reject Unsolicited Non-Binding Takeover Proposal
        From Altice and Rogers," Cogeco Inc. press release, September 2, 2020,
        https://www.newswire.ca/news-releases/cogeco-and-cogeco
        -communications-boards-of-directors-reject-unsolicited-non-binding
        -takeover-proposal-from-altice-and-rogers-813028998.html.

148   not a negotiating tactic: "Cogeco and Cogeco Communications Send
        Letter to Rogers Communications Inc. and Altice USA Inc.," Cogeco Inc.
        press release, September 16, 2020, https://www.newswire.ca/news-releases
        /cogeco-and-cogeco-communications-send-letter-to-rogers
        -communications-inc-and-altice-usa-inc--841173585.html.

148   tabled a motion: "Cogeco de glace face à la nouvelle proposition de
        Rogers," QMI Agency, September 25, 2020, https://www.tvanouvelles.ca
        /2020/09/25/cogeco-de-glace-face-a-la-nouvelle-proposition-de-rogers-1.

148   dual mandate: Andrew Willis, "Quebec's Caisse gets comfortable with
        dual investment mandate," *Globe and Mail*, July 14, 2017, https://www
        .theglobeandmail.com/report-on-business/streetwise/quebecs-caisse-gets
        -comfortable-with-dual-investment-mandate/article35697902/.

149   Ani Castonguay said in an interview: Andrew Willis spoke to Ani
        Castonguay for the *Globe and Mail* in September 2020.

149   Rogers promised: "Rogers commits to expanding its already strong
        Quebec presence," Rogers Communications Inc. press release,
        September 4, 2020, https://about.rogers.com/news-ideas/rogers-commits
        -to-expanding-its-already-strong-quebec-presence/.

149   Both men were ardent supporters: Confidential sources.

149   Gemmell saw it differently: Interview with Robert Gemmell.

150   He cited health reasons: "Robert Dépatie quitte Québecor pour des
        raisons de santé," *Les Affaires*, April 28, 2014, https://www.lesaffaires.com
        /secteurs-d-activite/medias-et-telecommunications/robert-depatie-quitte
        -quebecor-pour-des-raisons-de-sante/568421.

150   a prominent businesswoman: "Isabelle Marcoux," Transcontinental
        Inc., accessed on July 16, 2023, https://tctranscontinental.com/fr-ca/propos
        /gouvernance/conseil-dadministration-et-comites/isabelle-marcoux-cm.

150   "People scrutinize your moves": James Bradshaw, "A true believer in
        print," *Globe and Mail*, June 30, 2016, https://www.theglobeandmail.com
        /report-on-business/careers/careers-leadership/the-lunch-isabelle-marcoux
        /article30702120/.

150   Marcoux argued against: Confidential sources.

151   "As you know": Ouimet's remarks to the Bank of Montreal's virtual media
        and telecom conference, which I covered for the *Globe and Mail*.

151   Natale and Goei fired off a letter: Dexter Goei and Joe Natale, email,
        September 15, 2020.

151   Cherry wrote back: "Cogeco and Cogeco Communications Send Letter
        to Rogers Communications Inc. and Altice USA Inc.," Cogeco Inc. press
        release, September 16, 2020, https://www.newswire.ca/news-releases
        /cogeco-and-cogeco-communications-send-letter-to-rogers
        -communications-inc-and-altice-usa-inc--841173585.html.

152   "marathon, not a sprint": Goei's remarks to the Bank of America Merrill
        Lynch's virtual conference on September 9, 2020.

152   becoming increasingly concerned: Confidential source.

152   **Natale vowed to invest:** Andrew Willis and Nicolas Van Praet, "Rogers vows $3-billion for Quebec in Cogeco push," *Globe and Mail,* September 25, 2020, https://www.theglobeandmail.com/business/article -rogers-campaign-for-cogeco-includes-3-billion-investment-in-quebec/.

152   **In an interview:** Author interview with Philippe Jetté for the *Globe and Mail* in September 2020.

153   **boosting their offer:** Andrew Willis and James Bradshaw, "Altice, Rogers increase bid for Cogeco to $11.1-billion," *Globe and Mail,* October 18, 2020, https://www.theglobeandmail.com/business/article-altice-rogers -increase-bid-for-cogeco-to-111-billion/.

153   **At least one shareholder:** Author interview with Julian Klymochko.

154   **It was acquiring DERYtelecom:** "Cogeco Communications Announces the Acquisition of DERYtelecom," Cogeco Communications Inc. press release, October 21, 2020, https://www.prnewswire.com/news-releases /cogeco-communications-announces-the-acquisition-of-derytelecom -301156959.html.

154   **"This relatively small acquisition":** Vince Valentini, "Cogeco Announces an Acquisition in Quebec," *TD Securities Inc. Flash Note,* October 21, 2020.

154   **"I think it's fair":** Goei speaking to analysts during a conference call to discuss Altice's third-quarter results on October 29, 2020.

155   **"terrific offer":** Natale's remarks during an RBC Capital Markets virtual conference on November 18, 2020.

155   **He and Edward spoke on the phone:** Three confidential sources aware of the discussions confirmed that they took place, although only two of them recalled Louis Audet's specific comment to Edward.

Eleven   Hell or high water

156   **In total, including the $1.6 billion:** Trevor's English's testimony at the Competition Tribunal, Case No. CT-2022-002 (hereafter referred to as English's testimony).

157   **While Shaw lost:** Shaw 2020 annual report, p. 65.

157   **Telus picked up:** Telus 2020 annual report, p. 7.

157   **Telus's had roughly doubled:** English's testimony.

157   **Brad and English met with the bankers:** Shaw management information circular with respect to a proposed plan of arrangement involving Shaw Communications Inc. and Rogers Communications Inc., April 14, 2021 (hereafter referred to as the takeover circular).

157   **it was humbling:** Andrew Willis's interview with Brad Shaw for the *Globe and Mail,* October 2022.

158   **Bibic had heard rumours:** Confidential source.

158   **Bibic was born:** Bibic's biographical details were provided to the author by various interviewees for a *Globe and Mail* profile that ran in early 2020 when he took over as CEO of BCE.

160   **roughly a dozen:** "Rogers and Shaw to come together in $26 billion trans-action, creating new jobs and investment in Western Canada and acceler-ating Canada's 5G rollout," Rogers Communications Inc. press release, March 15, 2021, https://www.globenewswire.com/news-release/2021/03 /15/2192622/0/en/Rogers-and-Shaw-to-come-together-in-26-billion

-transaction-creating-new-jobs-and-investment-in-Western-Canada-and
-accelerating-Canada-s-5G-rollout.html.

160   **The difference was significant:** Tim Kiladze, "Shaw family to receive
Rogers stock in takeover of Shaw Communications, unlike other shareholders," *Globe and Mail,* March 15, 2021, https://www.theglobeandmail
.com/business/article-shaw-family-to-receive-rogers-stock-in-takeover-of
-shaw-communications/.

161   **They even came up with potential buyers:** Confidential source.

163   **Bell was advocating:** Confidential source.

163   **Rogers announced in a press release:** "Rogers and Shaw to come
together in $26 billion transaction."

164   **according to an analysis:** Yigit provided his analysis to the author for a
Globe and Mail story, "Rogers, Shaw likely to face regulatory hurdles as
deal upends Ottawa's focus on new wireless entrants," March 15, 2021,
https://www.theglobeandmail.com/business/article-rogers-shaw-could-be
-forced-to-divest-wireless-assets-in-deal-expected/.

164   **Clappison had joined the board:** Van Hasselt, *High Wire Act,* p. 438.

165   **Clappison had the unenviable task:** Descriptions of the dynamic
between Clappison and Edward come from multiple confidential sources
as well as MacDonald's affidavit.

165   **fallen by about 20 per cent:** Confidential sources in Edward's camp.

165   **In 2019, the year after:** Three confidential sources.

166   **The independent directors had lined up:** Confidential sources.

167   **Clappison told John MacDonald:** MacDonald's affidavit.

167   **Edward wanted Robert Gemmell:** Confidential sources.

167   **seasoned telecom executive:** MacDonald's bio was removed from the
Rogers website when he ceased to be a director of the company in November
of 2021. I accessed it prior to that date and saved a copy of the text.

168   **Isabelle Marcoux sometimes found:** Confidential sources.

Twelve   A special way to end the night!

170   **From 2008 to 2014:** Wall Communications Inc., "Price Comparisons of
Wireline, Wireless and Internet Services in Canada and with Foreign
Jurisdictions: 2020 Edition," January 15, 2021, https://ised-isde.canada.ca
/site/strategic-policy-sector/en/telecommunications-policy/price
-comparisons-wireline-wireless-and-internet-services-canada-and-foreign
-jurisdictions-2020.

170   **by several studies:** "Is Canada the most expensive wireless market in the
world?" Rewheel, April 2021, https://research.rewheel.fi/downloads
/Canada_most_expensive_wireless_market_world_PUBLIC_VERSION
.pdf; Wall Communications Inc., "Price Comparisons of Wireline,
Wireless and Internet Services in Canada and with Foreign Jurisdictions,"
November 7, 2019, https://www.ic.gc.ca/eic/site/693.nsf/vwapj/2019
_Pricing_Study_Report_EN.pdf/$FILE/2019_Pricing_Study_Report_EN
.pdf, 8.

171   **three-player oligopoly:** Lindsey Keene, "Canada Has a Cell Service
Problem. It's Time to Fix It," Kroeger Policy Review, March 29, 2021,
https://www.kroegerpolicyreview.com/post/canada-has-a-cell-service
-problem-it-s-time-to-fix-it.

171   **Canadians also paid:** Andrew Coyne, "Corporate Canada has been protected from competition for too long. It's time to put consumers first," *Globe and Mail*, January 20, 2023, https://www.theglobeandmail.com /opinion/article-corporate-canada-has-been-protected-from-competition -for-too-long-its/.

172   **wireless prices were 35 to 40 per cent lower:** Competition Bureau, "Review of Mobile Wireless Services," May 15, 2019, https://ised-isde .canada.ca/site/competition-bureau-canada/en/how-we-foster-competition /promotion-and-advocacy/regulatory-adviceinterventions-competition -bureau/review-mobile-wireless-services.

172   **On a bright day:** Author interview with Anthony Lacavera.

173   **he too had phoned Edward:** Confidential source.

173   **That view was shared:** Author interview with Robert Gemmell.

173   **"History shows that":** Quotes from the committee hearing are from my own recordings.

174   **By early April:** This account of Bell and Telus's attempts to lobby the federal government to exclude Shaw from the auction draws from my own previous reporting on this topic for the *Globe and Mail*.

175   **nearly twenty-two hours:** Following a second nationwide outage on July 8, 2022, Rogers Communications Inc. received a letter containing Requests for Information (RFIs) from the CRTC. Rogers responded to those requests on July 22, 2022 with a 26-page document (hereafter referred to as Response to RFIs).

176   **"We're not just going to":** Rogers Q1 earnings call, April 21, 2021.

177   **"Canada's fashion fairy godmother":** Delap, "How Suzanne Rogers became Canada's fashion fairy godmother."

177   **raised more than $3.7 million:** Suzanne Rogers, "Suzanne Rogers Presents," accessed on July 16, 2023, https://suzannerogerspresents.com /suzanne-rogers/.

177   **A second gift followed:** "Ryerson University receives a second gift for The Suzanne Rogers Fashion Institute," The Suzanne Rogers Fashion Institute, Ryerson University press release, November 18, 2020, https:// www.newswire.ca/news-releases/ryerson-university-receives-a-second-gift -for-the-suzanne-rogers-fashion-institute-828564810.html.

178   **"bejewelled pageant queen":** "Suzanne Rogers, celebrity look-alike: the photographic evidence," *Toronto Life*, September 30, 2010, https://toronto-life.com/style/suzanne-rogers-celebrity-look-alike-the-photographic -evidence/.

178   **On the left of the shot:** The photograph in question was posted to Suzanne's Instagram account on May 1, 2021.

178   **posted a selfie:** A screenshot from Edward's Instagram account was shared with me.

179   **"Dinner last night":** Lauren O'Neil, "Some of Toronto's wealthiest families were in Mar-a-Lago with Trump this weekend," BlogTO, May 3, 2021, https://www.blogto.com/city/2021/05/toronto-mar-a-lago-trump/.

179   **Two members of the advisory group:** Sabrina Jonas, "Controversy erupts for Suzanne Rogers after philanthropist posts photo with Trump," CBC News, May 3, 2021, https://www.cbc.ca/news/canada/toronto/toronto -philanthropist-suzanne-rogers-ryerson-university-slammed-1.6011239.

180   "billionaire failson": Andrew Stoeten, "Jesus Christ, Edward Rogers,"
       The Batflip (blog), May 1, 2021, https://stoeten.substack.com/p/jesus
       -christ-edward-rogers.
180   "low income, Black": Jonas, "Controversy erupts for Suzanne Rogers."
180   having donated: "Suzanne Rogers puts Fashion Forward with Gift to
       FCAD," Toronto Metropolitan University, November 3, 2016, https://www
       .torontomu.ca/giving/celebrating-generosity/your-gifts-at-work/news/2016
       /11/suzanne-rogers-puts-fashion-forward-with-gift-to-fcad/.
180   alumni criticized the university: Joe Friesen, "Ryerson students in
       uproar over erasing of message critical of donor's photo with Trump,"
       Globe and Mail, May 3, 2021, https://www.theglobeandmail.com/canada
       /article-ryerson-students-in-uproar-over-erasing-of-message-critical-of
       -donors/.
181   Suzanne issued a statement: Suzanne Rogers posted the statement to her
       Instagram account on May 4, 2021.
181   Natale's leadership team: Confidential sources.
182   "total lack of judgement": Internal company memo from Edward Rogers
       obtained by the author.

Thirteen   The "butt dial"

183   pushed his bike: Confidential sources.
183   tiny hamlet: "Terra Cotta," NeighbourhoodGuide.com, accessed on
       July 16, 2023, https://www.neighbourhoodguide.com/peel/caledon/terra
       -cotta/.
184   bought in 2016: GeoWarehouse Property Report, generated on October 4,
       2021 by Stephanie Chambers.
184   tucked inside his suit jacket pocket: Confidential source.
184   Natale attempted futilely: Confidential source.
185   detailed plan: Two confidential sources confirmed the details of Staffieri's
       supposed plan. A third confidential source confirmed that Staffieri and
       Miller met, but said they did not discuss such a plan.
186   they had rated him as outperforming: Statement of claim, *Joseph Natale
       and Natale Industries Inc. v. Rogers Communications Inc.*, File No.: CV-23-
       00704578-0000, August 17, 2023 (hereafter referred to as Natale's state-
       ment of claim).
186   first reported the existence: Alexandra Posadzki, "Rogers CEO Joe Natale
       learned of Edward Rogers's plan to oust him through butt-dial from CFO,"
       Globe and Mail, October 21, 2021, https://www.theglobeandmail.com
       /business/article-rogers-ceo-joe-natale-learned-of-edward-rogerss-plan-to
       -oust-him/.
186   "butt dial in spirit": Christine Dobby and Richard Warnica, "How
       Rogers came undone: Inside the strangest business battle in Canadian
       history," *Toronto Star*, November 19, 2021, https://www.thestar.com
       /business/2021/11/19/how-60-days-in-autumn-divided-the-rogers-family
       -and-threw-an-empire-into-chaos.html.
187   After Natale had learned: Statement of defence and counterclaim, Joseph
       Natale and Natale Industries Inc. v. Rogers Communications Inc., File
       No.: CV-23-00704578-0000, September 5, 2023.

187   "There was no call to Joe": Richard Warnica, "Who's really in charge at Rogers? On the cusp of the Shaw merger, CEO Tony Staffieri speaks out on the massive outage and the infamous 'butt dial,'" *Toronto Star*, February 4, 2023, https://www.thestar.com/business/2023/02/04/rogers-tony-staffieri.html.

188   By his own admission: Edward's affidavit.

189   Edward was impressed: Confidential source.

190   On September 11: Loretta's affidavit.

190   he had raised concerns: Edward's affidavit.

190   "anything but ordinary": MacDonald's affidavit.

191   Edward depicted the: Edward's affidavit.

192   But MacDonald said there: MacDonald's affidavit.

192   Melinda was particularly happy: Author interview with Melinda for the *Globe and Mail*, November 2021.

192   memorandum to the board: Ted's memorandum of wishes.

192   MacDonald then called Peterson: The account of how MacDonald, Peterson and the other directors reacted after Edward's phone call with MacDonald comes from MacDonald's affidavit as well as multiple confidential sources.

193   although Staffieri's name remained: Rob Gemmell said in a written statement that in September 2021, as part of the company's emergency planning, Natale reported to the board's human resources committee that Staffieri was ready to take over as CEO should Natale unexpectedly leave. "Joe's recommendation cannot be reconciled with his subsequent criticisms of Tony," Gemmell says.

193   Natale had begun: Confidential sources.

193   That was precisely: MacDonald and Loretta's affidavits, confidential sources.

194   "most of the details": MacDonald's affidavit.

194   MacDonald urged Edward: MacDonald and Loretta's affidavits.

194   MacDonald showed up at: The account of the meeting comes from MacDonald and Edward's affidavits, as well as multiple confidential sources.

196   Several of the independent directors: Confidential sources.

196   Edward told the board: MacDonald's affidavit.

196   draft of the meeting minutes: The draft meeting minutes from the September 22, 2021 board meeting are included as Exhibit H to Edward's affidavit.

196   "At no time": Written statement from Rob Gemmell.

197   According to the final version: A portion of the final minutes was provided to the author.

197   Natale would later argue: Reply and defence to counterclaim, Joseph Natale and Natale Industries Inc. v. Rogers Communications Inc., File No.: CV-23-00704578-0000, October 5, 2023.

197   gloomy slides: The presentation is included as Exhibit F to Edward's affidavit.

197   Loretta read out the statement: "Loretta Rogers message," Exhibit G to Edward's affidavit.

198   furious with Edward: Confidential sources.

198   prepared to resign: MacDonald's affidavit.

198   the director group was worried: Confidential sources.

198   **During the meeting:** The arguments put forward by the independent
       directors at the September 22 meeting have been reconstructed based on
       MacDonald's affidavit, draft minutes from the September 22 board meet-
       ing as well interviews with confidential sources.
199   **The terms that he:** Statement of defence and counterclaim, Joseph Natale
       and Natale Industries Inc. v. Rogers Communications Inc., File No.:
       CV-23-00704578-0000, September 5, 2023.
200   **They continued to feel:** MacDonald's affidavit, confidential sources.
200   **He was livid:** Peterson's speech, as well as Melinda's reaction to his resig-
       nation, were described by multiple sources.

Fourteen   Dill pickle martini

201   **according to Melinda:** Melinda's written answers.
202   **Having allowed:** CANADALAND on Twitter, October 28, 2021, https://
       twitter.com/CANADALAND/status/1453774699524198404.
202   **increasingly concerned:** Confidential sources.
203   **"more complete and unbiased":** Loretta's affidavit.
203   **That afternoon, Melinda's:** Confidential sources.
204   **That day, Natale informed:** Edward's affidavit as well as a confidential
       source.
204   **According to Edward's account:** Edward's affidavit.
204   **"incredible work ethic":** Edward's affidavit, Exhibit K.
205   **Horn was especially outraged:** Confidential sources.
206   **crammed into a friend's float plane:** Confidential sources.
206   **resolving the impasse:** Edward's affidavit.
206   **He felt deeply betrayed:** Confidential sources.
207   **one-sentence email:** John MacDonald, email, September 28, 2021,
       Edward's affidavit, Exhibit N.
207   **Bob Reeves:** Loretta's affidavit.
208   **He justified the postponement:** MacDonald's affidavit.
208   **Shortly after 2 p.m.:** John MacDonald, email, September 29, 2021,
       Edward's affidavit, Exhibit O.
208   **backed Edward:** Edward's affidavit.
208–9 **Lisa was particularly vocal:** Confidential source.
209   **Willoughby tried to persuade:** Edward's affidavit.
209   **Loretta spoke about:** The draft meeting minutes from the September 29,
       2021 board meeting are included as Exhibit P to Edward's affidavit.
209   **delivered the news:** Confidential sources.
210   **The press release announcing Staffieri's departure:** "Rogers
       Communications announces CFO transition," Rogers Communications
       Inc. press release, September 29, 2021, https://www.globenewswire.com
       /news-release/2021/09/29/2305840/0/en/Rogers-Communications
       -announces-CFO-transition.html.
210   **Edward wasn't shown:** Edward's affidavit.
210   **via a letter from Willoughby:** Richard Willoughby, email, October 3, 2021,
       Edward's affidavit, Exhibit R.
210   **found this assertion alarming:** Loretta's affidavit.
211   **Braithwaite, the Stikeman lawyer:** William J. Braithwaite, email,
       October 5, 2021, Edward's affidavit, Exhibit S.

211   **written to Lisa Damiani:** David Forrester, email, October 4, 2021,
       Edward's affidavit, Exhibit T.
211   **In early October:** Author interviews with Wojtek Dabrowski and Gareth
       Setlzer for the *Globe and Mail*, November 2021.
212   **act of gamesmanship:** Confidential source.
212   **at least one journalist:** That journalist was me.
213   **published a story online:** Alexandra Posadzki and Andrew Willis,
       "Rogers chairman failed to oust CEO amid power struggle with sister,
       board," *Globe and Mail*, October 8, 2021, https://www.theglobeandmail
       .com/business/article-rogers-chairman-failed-to-oust-ceo-amid-power
       -struggle-with-sister/.
213   **The firm was founded:** "Our History," Torys LLP, accessed July 16, 2023,
       https://www.torys.com/en/about-us/our-history.
213   **Willoughby tried to:** The email exchange that follows was filed in the
       Ontario Superior Court of Justice in connection with *Loretta A. Rogers,
       Martha L. Rogers, Melinda M. Rogers-Hixon v. Torys LLP*, in the matter of
       the estate of Edward Samuel Rogers, Court File No. CV-22-00675419-
       00ES, January 19, 2022.

Fifteen   Schrödinger's board

215   **"William, please do not return":** The email exchanges relating to
       Stransky and the shareholder list are contained within the affidavit of
       Wenny Lai, *Rogers v. Rogers Communications Inc.*, File No.: S219325,
       October 26, 2021 (hereafter referred to as Wenny's affidavit).
217   **That evening, the dissident directors:** The October 19 meeting of the
       Rogers Control Trust has been reconstructed based on the recollections of
       multiple confidential sources who were in attendance.
218   **visibly distraught:** Confidential sources.
218   **she was known:** Pullen, "The Man Who Would Be King."
218   **they butted heads:** Three confidential sources.
219   **The dissident directors waited outside:** Confidential sources.
219   **Edward was convinced:** Confidential source.
219   **served as a director for decades:** Chris Sorensen, "In memoriam: John
       A. Tory," *Maclean's*, April 4, 2011, https://macleans.ca/economy/business
       /in-memoriam-john-a-tory/.
220   **"moral obligation":** Jennifer Pagliaro, "John Tory's ties to Rogers have
       been a source of conflict since he was elected mayor. Now they've
       dragged him into the middle of a bitter family feud," *Toronto Star*,
       October 26, 2021, https://www.thestar.com/news/gta/2021/10/26/john
       -torys-ties-to-rogers-have-been-a-source-of-conflict-since-he-was
       -elected-mayor-now-theyve-dragged-him-into-the-middle-of-a-bitter
       -family-feud.html.
220   **Tory earned $100,000:** Pagliaro, "John Tory's ties to Rogers."
220   **The family owned:** Edward's affidavit.
220   **Tory served as a bridge:** Rogers and Brehl, *Relentless*, p. 244.
220   **Tory did so more frequently:** Pagliaro, "John Tory's ties to Rogers."
220   **close to $5.5 million:** Rogers 2014 proxy circular, p. 18.
220   **Oliver Moore:** Transcript of the scrum provided to the author by Oliver
       Moore.

221   When the board met: Edward and MacDonald's affidavits.

221   emails continued to fly: Edward's affidavit, Exhibit W.

222   Shortly before midnight: I have viewed this email and verified its authenticity.

222   an assertion that Shaw would later deny: Statement provided to the Globe and Mail, https://www.theglobeandmail.com/business/article-shaw -communications-says-it-remains-committed-to-26-billion-takeover/.

223   Rogers reported: "Rogers Communications Reports Third Quarter 2021 Results," Rogers Communications Inc. press release, October 21, 2021, https://www.globenewswire.com/news-release/2021/10/21/2318187/0/en /Rogers-Communications-Reports-Third-Quarter-2021-Results.html.

224   Edward felt that: Edward's position comes from his affidavit as well as confidential sources.

224   The proposals put forward: Confidential sources.

225   To trigger the: Confidential source.

226   Loretta delivered: Loretta's affidavit; confidential source.

226   Only four of them did: Confidential sources.

226   Loretta personally: Loretta's affidavit.

227   MacDonald agreed to: MacDonald's affidavit.

227   cut off a nerve: Confidential source.

227   According to Edward: Edward's position is laid out by his lawyers in documents filed in the B.C. Supreme Court.

228   famed dealmaker: "Jack Cockwell," Forbes profile, accessed on July 16, 2023, https://www.forbes.com/profile/jack-cockwell/?sh=58a937892873.

228   described Kerr: Lind and Brehl, Right Hand Man, pp. 197, 296.

228   The company issued: "A statement on behalf of Rogers Communications Inc.," Rogers Communications Inc. press release, October 22, 2021, https://www.sec.gov/Archives/edgar/data/733099/000119312521305386 /d211037dex992.htm.

228   called for a meeting: Edward's affidavit, Exhibit BB.

229   "Accordingly, the board": Statement provided to the Globe and Mail.

229   That view was shared: Statement provided to the Globe and Mail.

229   "Any assertion that": Statement provided to the Globe and Mail.

229   "Rogers Chairman Fires Board": Matt Levine, "Rogers Chairman Fires Board for Firing Him for Firing CEO," Bloomberg, October 25, 2021, https://www.bloomberg.com/opinion/articles/2021-10-25/rogers-chairman -fires-board-for-firing-him-for-firing-ceo.

230   "If Mr. Natale is": Statement provided to the Globe and Mail.

230   Goodmans denied: David D. Conklin, email, October 25, 2021, Edward's affidavit, Exhibit FF.

230   Martha couldn't sleep: Martha's tweets can be found on her Twitter account: https://twitter.com/MarthaLRogers. Accessed on August 24, 2023. They are hereafter referred to as "Martha's tweets."

231   Edward found the tweets: Confidential source.

231   the King of England: Martha's tweets, October 24, 2021, https://twitter .com/MarthaLRogers/status/1452452208084230152.

231   "No other group of individuals": "A statement on behalf of Loretta Rogers, Melinda Rogers-Hixon, Martha Rogers, John A. MacDonald, John Clappison, David Peterson, Bonnie Brooks, and Ellis Jacob," Rogers Communications Canada Inc. press release, October 24, 2021, https://

www.globenewswire.com/news-release/2021/10/24/2319479/0/en/A
-statement-on-behalf-of-Loretta-Rogers-Melinda-Rogers-Hixon-Martha
-Rogers-John-A-MacDonald-John-Clappison-David-Peterson-Bonnie
-Brooks-and-Ellis-Jacob.html.

231   Gemmell agreed: Author interview with Rob Gemmell.
231   "He should stop immediately": Statement provided to the *Globe and Mail*.
232   mentally sharp: Confidential sources.
232   continued to speak: Multiple confidential sources.
232   put Edward's board on notice: David D. Conklin, email, October 23,
        2021, Edward's affidavit, Exhibit EE.
232   "The unseemly threat": Jonathan Lisus, email, October 24, 2021,
        Edward's affidavit, Exhibit FF.
232   urged the telecom: I have viewed and verified the authenticity of this
        letter, which was reported in the *Globe and Mail*: https://www
        .theglobeandmail.com/business/article-edward-rogerss-lawyers-seek
        -company-rival-board-support-for-expedited/.
233   The B.C. court filing: The documents referred to were filed by both sides
        in connection with *Rogers v. Rogers Communications Inc.*, File No.: S219325.
234   Fuller submitted his own affidavit: Affidavit of David Fuller, *Rogers v.
        Rogers Communications Inc.*, File No.: S219325, October 29, 2021 (hereafter
        referred to as Fuller's affidavit).
235   explosive story: Doug Smith and Christine Dobby, "Edward Rogers
        fought plans to keep Raptors' Masai Ujiri, but was thwarted by MLSE head,
        sources say," *Toronto Star*, October 25, 2021, https://www.thestar.com
        /business/2021/10/25/edward-rogers-fought-plans-to-keep-raptors-masai
        -ujiri-but-was-thwarted-by-mlse-head-sources-say.html.
235   championship rings: Confidential source.
235   "more slapstick than cunning": Cathal Kelly, "Edward Rogers has
        been a pretty good Blue Jays owner, but what could someone new do?"
        Globe and Mail, November 23, 2021, https://www.theglobeandmail.com
        /sports/article-what-might-some-new-owners-do-especially-with-the
        -blue-jays/.
235   without realizing: Bob Elliott, "The inside story on how Rogers tried to
        replace Blue Jays president Paul Beeston," *Toronto Sun*, January 23, 2015,
        https://torontosun.com/2015/01/23/the-inside-story-on-how-rogers-tried-to
        -replace-blue-jays-president-paul-beeston.
235   Vidéotron sued Rogers: Nicolas Van Praet, "Network pact between
        Rogers, Quebecor crumbles with Videotron compensation lawsuit," *Globe
        and Mail*, October 31, 2021, https://www.theglobeandmail.com/business
        /article-network-pact-between-rogers-quebecor-crumbles-with-videotron/.
236   Martha continued her onslaught: Martha's tweets.
236   "baseless": Statement provided to the author.
236   "strong voice for governance": Eamon Hoey, Twitter, November 6, 2021,
        https://twitter.com/EamonHoey/status/1457019620620124170.
237   Brehl's article: Robert Brehl, "How Ted Rogers planned for family con-
        flict and set up rules to resolve it," *Financial Post*, October 25, 2021, https://
        financialpost.com/opinion/robert-brehl-how-ted-rogers-planned-for
        -family-conflict-and-set-up-a-system-for-turfing-edward.

Sixteen   Rogers v. Rogers

238   **The high-tech and high-security courtroom:** Terri Theodore, "Four high-profile trials clog B.C. courts," The Canadian Press, April 19, 2012, https://www.theglobeandmail.com/news/british-columbia/four-high-profile-trials-clog-bc-courts/article4101259/.

238   **As far as anyone was aware:** Including the judge presiding over the case and several of the key lawyers.

239   **"You may have bought into":** McCall's remarks are from an event called "The Rogers boardroom tussle," hosted by the CFA Society Calgary on February 23, 2022.

239   **"I'm sympathetic":** Author interview with Kevin Thomas, October 2022.

239   **Those on the other side:** Irene Galea, "Investors call for limits on dual-class shares in light of Rogers battle," Globe and Mail, November 3, 2021, https://www.theglobeandmail.com/business/article-investors-call-for-limits-on-dual-class-shares-in-light-of-rogers/.

240   **According to McEwan:** The account of the court proceedings draws from my own reporting for the Globe and Mail, as well as the observations of my colleague, Brent Jang, who physically attended the trial while me and Susan Krashinsky Robertson dialled in via phone.

242   **Ted asked Emerson:** Van Hasselt, High Wire Act, pp. 433–8.

242   **Ted called it "simplistic":** Rogers and Brehl, Relentless, p. 204.

242   **urging the regulator:** "Request for Adjournment of the Oral Public Hearing due to due to uncertainty regarding corporate control of the Applicant," Public Interest Advocacy Centre (PIAC) and the National Pensioners Federation (NPF), November 1, 2021.

243   **Bell expressed support:** "Response to Public Interest Advocacy Centre and the National Pensioners Federation," BCE Inc., November 1, 2021.

243   **Telus echoed:** "Procedural request by PIAC to adjourn the public hearing due to uncertainty regarding corporate control of the Applicant," Telus Corp., November 2, 2021.

243   **disingenuous and driven:** "Shaw Response to Procedural Requests," Shaw Communications Inc., November 3, 2021.

243   **There was no dispute:** "Response to Request for Adjournment," Rogers Communications Inc., November 2, 2021.

244   **ruled in Soliman's favour:** Reasons for decision, Soliman v. Bordman, File No.: CV-20-00636658-0000, October 21, 2021.

244   **briefly stepped outside:** Confidential source.

244   **Lisus and Soliman:** Confidential sources.

245   **Justice Fitzpatrick had reviewed:** Reasons for judgment, Rogers v. Rogers Communications Inc., File No.: S219325, November 5, 2021.

247   **"black eye for good governance":** Statement provided to the Globe and Mail.

247   **"Mr. Natale remains":** "A Statement from Edward Rogers," Rogers Communications Canada Inc. press release, November 5, 2021, https://www.newswire.ca/news-releases/a-statement-from-edward-rogers-873907046.html.

Seventeen   Pinky swear

248   eluding him: Confidential sources.

249   Around 7 p.m.: Brad Shaw, email, November 6, 2021.

249   armed with a document: The contents of this document, hereafter referred to as Joe's principles, were shared with me by multiple confidential sources.

251   Lisus had written: Jonathan Lisus, email, November 7, 2021.

251   one-line statement: "A statement on behalf of Rogers Communications Inc.," Rogers Communications Inc. press release, November 7, 2021, https://www.globenewswire.com/en/news-release/2021/11/08/2328856/0/en/A-statement-on-behalf-of-Rogers-Communications-Inc.html.

251   Hotel X: The offsite was described to me by several confidential sources who were in attendance.

252   Martha Rogers walked out: Martha's written answers.

253   passed away in 2016: "Ann Calderisi Obituary," Toronto Star/Legacy.com, October 16–23, 2016, https://www.legacy.com/ca/obituaries/thestar/name/ann-calderisi-obituary?id=40270341.

253   "We will fight for you!" Martha's tweets, November 10, 2021, https://twitter.com/MarthaLRogers/status/1458557904945131522.

253   A week after their initial meeting: Confidential sources and Edward's memo to the board, which was described in detail to the author by a confidential source.

254   "with alacrity": Jonathan Lisus, email, November 15, 2021.

254   Lastman agreed: Dale Lastman, email, November 15, 2021.

254   the firm advised: Edward's report to the board.

254   Lisus received an email: David Conklin, email, November 16, 2021.

255   When Natale addressed: The board meeting has been reconstructed based on accounts provided by multiple sources.

256   "Real life Succession": Holly Honderich, "Real life Succession battle plagues Canada's top wireless firm," *BBC News*, November 1, 2021, https://www.bbc.com/news/world-us-canada-59054146.

256   "Succession-style feud": Leyland Cecco, "Succession-style feud gripping Canada settled as court sides with Edward Rogers," *Guardian*, November 6, 2021. https://www.theguardian.com/world/2021/nov/05/canada-succession-rogers-communications-feud-saga.

257   "Succession? Please": Martha's tweets, October 23, 2021, https://twitter.com/MarthaLRogers/status/1451816279355109385.

257   "nineteen-second video clip": A copy of this video was shared with me, although it could also be viewed on Cameo.com.

Eighteen   Project Mars

259   Tony Staffieri spent: This account draws from discussions with confidential sources as well as Warnica, "Who's really in charge at Rogers?"

259   a public hearing: The hearing, which was streamed online, has been reconstructed based on my own observations notes and recordings, as well as transcripts provided publicly by the CRTC.

260   Telus had pushed: "Procedural request by PIAC-NPF to adjourn the public hearing due to uncertainty regarding corporate control of the Applicant," Telus Corp., November 8, 2021.

260   The regulator reviewed the matter: Claude Doucet, email, November 12, 2021.

261   On a rainy day: I reconstructed this scene based on my own observations, notes and recordings from my interview with Melinda.

263   three Rogers women filed an application: *Loretta A. Rogers, Martha L. Rogers, Melinda M. Rogers-Hixon v. Torys LLP*, in the matter of the estate of Edward Samuel Rogers, Court File No. CV-22-00675419-00ES, January 19, 2022.

263   Torys' position: Torys did not respond to a request to comment on the withdrawn lawsuit for this book.

264   standstill agreement: The existence of the agreement, as well as its purpose and nature, was confirmed by confidential sources.

264   "practical joke": Statement to the *Globe and Mail*.

264   allegedly sent it around: Natale's statement of claim.

264   not amused: Natale's statement of claim.

265   "maximize stability": David Barden, "Mr. Rogers focused on Shaw deal and stability after CEO change," *BofA Global Research*, November 18, 2021.

267   By the end of 2021: Rogers 2021 annual report, p. 14.

267   by the end of 2022: Rogers 2022 annual report, p. 14.

267   "We have the people": Author interview with Staffieri for the *Globe and Mail*, February 2, 2023.

267   the federal government had: Confidential sources.

268   on March 3, 2022: "Minister of Innovation, Science and Industry reaffirms that competitiveness is central to a vibrant telecommunications sector," Innovation, Science and Economic Development Canada press release, March 3, 2022, https://www.newswire.ca/news-releases/minister -of-innovation-science-and-industry-reaffirms-that-competitiveness-is -central-to-a-vibrant-telecommunications-sector-865496347.html.

268   part of the consortium: Christine Dobby, "Who's who in the Wind Mobile deal," *Globe and Mail*, September 16, 2014, https://www .theglobeandmail.com/report-on-business/whos-who-in-the-wind-mobile -deal/article20627068/.

268   "Freedom Mobile may be": Alexandra Posadzki, "Freedom Mobile may be up for sale again, and founder Anthony Lacavera wants to buy it," *Globe and Mail*, December 18, 2021, https://www.theglobeandmail.com/business /article-freedom-mobile-may-be-up-for-sale-again-and-founder-anthony -lacavera/.

269   icy reception: Lacavera outlines, in detail, his attempts to contact the company and its various advisors for the purpose of making a bid for Freedom in a letter to Industry Minister François-Philippe Champagne, Competition Commissioner Matthew Boswell, and the Prime Minister's Office, dated March 24, 2022, hereafter referred to as Lacavera's letter.

269   the company alleged: Van Praet, "Network pact between Rogers, Quebecor crumbles with Videotron compensation lawsuit."

270   media interviews: Péladeau made this argument multiple times, including in an interview with the author and Andrew Willlis for a June 10, 2022 *Globe and Mail* story.

270   lobbied their contacts: Confidential sources.

270   continued to press: Lacavera's letter.

270   Lacavera later claimed in a letter: Lacavera's letter.

271   Staffieri told Péladeau: Commissioner of Competition's Memorandum of Fact and Law, *Commissioner of Competition v. Rogers Communications Inc., Shaw Communications Inc. and Videotron Ltd.*, Federal Court of Appeal, Case File No.: A-286-22, January 13, 2023.

271   Vidéotron and Distributel also refused: Confidential sources.

272   In his memoir: Lind and Brehl, *Right Hand Man*, p. 296.

272   federal government's perspective: Confidential government source.

272   When he was six years old: Lacavera and Kate Fillion, *How We Can Win*, p. 22.

273   published an open letter: Anthony Lacavera, April 6, 2022, https://anthonylacavera.com/wireless/.

273   In a separate letter: Lacavera's letter.

273   becoming impatient: Notice of application for interim order volume 7, Commissioner of Competition v. Rogers Communications Inc. and Shaw Communications Inc., CT-2022-002, May 9, 2022, pp. 210-217.

273   Rogers was pressing: Senior government source.

274   put out a press release: "Rogers and Shaw Remain Committed to Merger Following Notification by the Commissioner of Competition," press release, May 7, 2022, https://about.rogers.com/news-ideas/rogers-and-shaw-remain-committed-to-merger-following-notification-by-the-commissioner-of-competition/.

274   The Competition Bureau argued: Notice of application, *Commissioner of Competition v. Rogers Communications Inc. and Shaw Communications Inc.*, CT-2022-002, May 9, 2022.

275   "I am hopeful": Author interview with Lacavera for the *Globe and Mail* story, "Globalive strengthens bid for Freedom Mobile with Telus deal," which ran on May 19, 2022, https://www.theglobeandmail.com/business/article-globalive-strengthens-bid-for-freedom-mobile-with-telus-deal/.

275   In early June: Author's reporting for a June 2, 2022 *Globe and Mail* story, https://www.theglobeandmail.com/business/article-globalive-bypasses-rogers-takes-freedom-bid-straight-to-shaw/.

275   Finally, on June 17: "Rogers, Shaw and Quebecor announce agreement for sale of Freedom Mobile," Quebecor Inc. press release, June 17, 2022, https://www.newswire.ca/news-releases/rogers-shaw-and-quebecor-announce-agreement-for-sale-of-freedom-mobile-811448865.html.

275   Lacavera was unconvinced: Lacavera's position has been summarized based on his many public statements, social media posts and interviews on the topic, including the author's interviews with him.

276   It took the bureau's staff: Costs submissions of Rogers Communications Inc., Shaw Communications Inc. and Videotron Ltd., *Commissioner of Competition v. Rogers Communications Inc. and Shaw Communications Inc.*, CT-2022-002, December 30, 2022.

Nineteen   Canada's Most Reliable Network

277   **The twenty-year-old aviation student:** Verdier's experience of the
       Rogers outage is outlined in the proposed class action lawsuit, *Arnaud
       Verdier v. Rogers Communications Canada Inc.*, File No.: 500-06-001192-224,
       July 11, 2022. Additional colour comes from the author's interview with
       Verdier.

278   **engineers assembled:** The details of the outage are disclosed in the
       Response to RFIs.

279   **His news apps:** The section that contains an account of Staffieri's reaction
       to the outage is described in Warnica, "Who's really in charge at Rogers?"
       and also pulls from a discussion with a source as well as the Response to RFIs.

280   **vacationing in his native Portugal:** Three confidential sources con-
       firmed this, which has also been reported by Richard Dufour, "Le chef
       techno de Rogers brillait par son absence," *La Presse*, July 16, 2022, https://
       www.lapresse.ca/affaires/entreprises/2022-07-16/panne-du-8-juillet/le-chef
       -techno-de-rogers-brillait-par-son-absence.php.

280   **Fernandes was notified:** Staffieri's comments to the House of Commons
       Standing Committee on Industry and Technology, July 25, 2022.

281   **went into lockdown:** "2 people dead, likely including suspect, after
       'shooting incident' in Langham, Sask.: police," CBC News, July 8, 2022,
       https://www.cbc.ca/news/canada/saskatchewan/emergency-alert-shooting
       -langham-1.6514526.

282   **contacted Rogers:** Response to RFIs.

282   **string of four tornadoes:** Theresa Kliem, "Tornado that damaged farm
       among 4 that hit Saskatchewan on Friday: Environment Canada," CBC
       News, July 9, 2022, https://www.cbc.ca/news/canada/saskatchewan
       /tornado-saskatchewan-friday-july-8-2022-1.6516001.

282   **A Montreal bail hearing:** "Montreal bail hearing on sex charge for Peter
       Nygard delayed by Rogers outage," The Canadian Press, July 8, 2022,
       https://www.theglobeandmail.com/canada/article-montreal-bail-hearing
       -on-sex-charge-for-peter-nygard-delayed-by-rogers/.

282   **the tour-opening concert:** Brad Wheeler, "Why was the Weeknd's con-
       cert called off in Toronto? The doors to Rogers Centre wouldn't open,"
       Globe and Mail, July 14, 2022, https://www.theglobeandmail.com/arts
       /music/article-why-was-the-weeknds-concert-called-off-the-doors-to
       -rogers-centre/.

282   **sent an email to all Rogers stores:** *Verdier v. Rogers*.

283   **In Hamilton, Gregg Eby:** Bobby Hristova, "Hamilton man was unable to
       call 911 during Rogers outage as sister was dying," CBC News, Jul 12, 2022,
       https://www.cbc.ca/news/canada/hamilton/rogers-outage-911-call-1
       .6516958.

284   **The drive from:** *Verdier v. Rogers*, author interview with Verdier.

285   **apology from Staffieri:** "A message from Tony Staffieri, President and
       CEO at Rogers," July 8, 2022, https://about.rogers.com/news-ideas/a
       -message-from-tony-staffieri-president-and-ceo-at-rogers/.

285   **second open letter:** "A Message from Rogers President and CEO," July 9,
       2022, https://about.rogers.com/news-ideas/a-message-from-rogers
       -president-and-ceo/.

286   On the last night: Confidential source.

286   with stops in Tokyo: "Minister Champagne concludes business visit to
       Japan," Innovation, Science and Economic Development Canada press
       release, July 8, 2022, https://www.canada.ca/en/innovation-science
       -economic-development/news/2022/07/minister-champagne-concludes
       -business-visit-to-japan.html.

287   Champagne had spent: Marie-Danielle Smith, "The smiley, friendly,
       cunning François-Philippe Champagne," Maclean's, May 29, 2020, https://
       macleans.ca/politics/ottawa/the-smiley-friendly-cunning-francois-philippe
       -champagne/.

287   Champagne was baffled: Champagne provided his perspective during his
       appearance before the House of Commons Standing Committee on
       Industry and Technology on July 25, 2022.

288   undergoing a medical procedure: Confidential sources.

289   posted online: "General Information - Rogers - Service Outage: 8000-
       C12-202203868," CRTC, https://crtc.gc.ca/otf/eng/2022/8000/c12
       -202203868.htm.

290   At the annual Calgary Stampede: "Opposition to Rogers-Shaw buyout
       surges in Alberta after nationwide outage," OpenMedia, July 11, 2022,
       https://openmedia.org/press/item/opposition-to-rogers-shaw-buyout
       -surges-in-alberta-after-nationwide-outage.

291   "This is certainly": "Industry minister suggests Rogers outage could
       weigh on $26B Shaw deal, Canadian Press, July 15, 2022, https://toronto
       .citynews.ca/2022/07/15/industry-minister-rogers-outage-shaw-deal/.

291   Rogers reported its second-quarter results: "Rogers Communications
       reports second quarter 2022 results," Rogers Communications Inc. press
       release, July 27, 2022, https://about.rogers.com/wp-content/uploads
       /Rogers-Q2-2022-Press-Release.pdf.

291   "Since the outage": Rogers Q2 2022 earnings call.

291   "Now it's clear": BCE Q2 2022 earnings call.

293   criticized the telecom: The committee hearing was broadcast online.
       Quotes and observations are from my own notes and recordings. In some
       places, dialogue has been condensed for brevity.

Twenty   Monolithic Wireless

295   subject of conversation: Confidential sources.

295   ski injury: Author interview with Péladeau for a Globe and Mail story in
       early April 2023.

295-6 bitter divorce and child custody battle: Van Praet, "The Notorious PKP."

296   a temper so legendary: Tu Thanh Ha, "The polarizing Péladeau: Five
       examples of his temper," Globe and Mail, May 5, 2015, https://www
       .theglobeandmail.com/news/national/the-polarizing-peladeau-five
       -examples-of-his-temper/article24255646/.

296   feeling hopeful: Confidential sources.

296   "I want to make": "Statement from Minister Champagne on competitive-
       ness in the telecommunications sector," Innovation, Science and Economic
       Development Canada, October 25, 2022, https://www.canada.ca/en/innovation
       -science-economic-development/news/2022/10/statement-from-minister
       -champagne-on-competitiveness-in-the-telecommunications-sector.html.

296   **Some critics:** Author interview with Klass for the *Globe and Mail.*

296   **Freedom's pricing:** Freedom's cheapest offering for a "bring your own phone" with ten gigabytes of data was $35, while Videotron charged $45 and included only six gigs of data.

297   **Rogers was proposing:** Confidential sources.

297   **Inside the tribunal's offices:** The mediation session has been reconstructed based on interviews with multiple confidential sources.

298   **"close to zero":** Jérome Dubreuil, "Mediation with Competition Bureau fails—lawyer up (again)," *Desjardins,* October 27, 2022.

299   **From a young age:** Author interview with Matthew Boswell, February 2023.

300   **commissioned a report:** Compete to Win, *Government of Canada,* June 2008, https://publications.gc.ca/collections/collection_2008/ic/Iu173-1 -2008E.pdf.

300   **Boswell jotted the quote down:** Joe Castaldo, "Competition commissioner says reform needed to shake up Canada's 'concentrated economy,' oligopolies," *Globe and Mail,* December 22, 2022, https://www .theglobeandmail.com/business/article-competition-bureau-commissioner -matthew-boswell/.

300   **"holy battle":** Jake Edmiston, "'Holy battle': Competition Bureau chief readies for fight to shake up merger laws," *Financial Post,* November 12, 2021, https://financialpost.com/news/economy/boswell.

301   **Jennifer Quaid:** Irene Galea and Alexandra Posadzki, "What happens next in the Rogers-Shaw merger hearing," November 5, 2022, https://www .theglobeandmail.com/business/article-rogers-shaw-merger-hearing/.

301   **virtual hearing:** The virtual hearing has been reconstructed based on my own notes and observations, having covered it for the *Globe and Mail.*

301   **Crampton had been appointed:** "The Honourable Paul Crampton," Federal Court, accessed on July 17, 2023, https://www.fct-cf.gc.ca/en /pages/about-the-court/members-of-the-court/judges/the-honourable-paul -crampton.

302   **pay its bond holders:** Jameson Berkow, "Rogers takeover of Shaw generates substantial fees for lawyers, financial advisers," *Globe and Mail,* April 3, 2023, https://www.theglobeandmail.com/business/article-rogers -shaw-deal-historic-windfall-advisers/.

305   **The institution was created:** "History," Competition Tribunal, accessed on July 17, 2023, https://www.ct-tc.gc.ca/en/tribunal/history.html.

306   **nearly 8,000 people:** Witness statement of Denis Albert, *Commissioner of Competition and Rogers Communications Inc. and Shaw Communications Inc. and Attorney General of Alberta and Videotron Ltd.,* File No.: CT-2022-002, September 26, 2022.

307   **Some mused:** Michael Osborne, a competition lawyer at law firm Cozen O'Connor, in comments provided to the *Globe*'s Irene Galea.

307   **"Rogers-Shaw hearings":** Alexandra Posadzki and Irene Galea, "Rogers-Shaw hearings not so public despite tribunal's pledge to hold open process," *Globe and Mail,* November 11, 2022, https://www.theglobeandmail .com/business/article-rogers-shaw-competition-transparency/.

308   **One bullet point:** Under a bullet point titled "ISED": "Telus advocacy highlights danger of PKP as remedy partner; requests Minister not transfer spectrum licenses."

308   accused of spreading misinformation: "Canada Proud is Spreading Misleading Propaganda Claiming COVID-19 Vaccines Will Be Distributed According to 'Skin Colour,'" PressProgress, March 4, 2021, https://press-progress.ca/canada-proud-is-spreading-misleading-propaganda-claiming-covid-19-vaccines-will-be-distributed-according-to-skin-colour/.

309   "worthy of Netflix": Terence Corcoran, "The Rogers-Shaw hearings: Courtroom melodrama worthy of Netflix," *Financial Post*, December 6, 2022, https://financialpost.com/opinion/terence-corcoran-rogers-shaw-hearings-courtroom-netflix.

309   Dr. Osberg characterized: Witness statement of Lars Spencer Osberg, PhD, *Commissioner of Competition and Rogers Communications Inc. and Shaw Communications Inc. and Attorney General of Alberta and Videotron Ltd.*, File No.: CT-2022-002, September 26, 2022.

309   "the roughly $2.3 billion": The Shaw family was to receive a combination of cash and roughly 23 million Rogers shares, worth a total of about $2.3 billion if Rogers shares were valued at $60.

311   trump card: Tim Kiladze, "The takeover law that has Bay Street rattled, complicating the Rogers-Shaw merger and HSBC Canada's auction," *Globe and Mail*, October 29, 2022, https://www.theglobeandmail.com/business/article-the-takeover-law-that-has-bay-street-rattled-complicating-the-rogers/.

Twenty-One   Pinocchio and Geppetto

314   a document landed: Gregory Ko, "Application for a Municipal Conflict of Interest Act Inquiry," *Adam Chaleff v. John Tory*, July 22, 2022.

314   at one point had served on the board: See https://www.linkedin.com/in/adamkcf/, accessed on August 24, 2023.

315   "As a sports organization": Shapiro's letter is Exhibit C to Chaleff's application.

315   When Shapiro received: Ben Spurr, "Integrity commissioner to probe Mayor John Tory's ties to Rogers," *Toronto Star*, July 29, 2022, https://www.thestar.com/news/gta/2022/07/29/integrity-commissioner-to-probe-mayor-john-torys-ties-to-rogers.html.

315   Chaleff had never been a supporter: Interview with Adam Chaleff.

315   on dozens of occasions: At least thirty occasions over the three years since 2019.

316   Batty responded to Chaleff's request: Jonathan Batty, email, July 27, 2022.

316   the potential penalties ranged: Spurr, "Integrity commissioner to probe Mayor John Tory's ties to Rogers."

316   the clock had run out: Ben Spurr, "Integrity commissioner's probe of John Tory's ties to Rogers runs out of time," *Toronto Star*, August 17, 2022, https://www.thestar.com/news/gta/2022/08/17/integrity-commissioners-probe-of-john-torys-ties-to-rogers-runs-out-of-time.html.

316   emails to reporters: Statement provided to the *Globe and Mail*.

316   "It's tough to tell": Martha's tweets, October 11, 2022, https://twitter.com/MarthaLRogers/status/1579829450879143936.

317   Martha had hugged Tory: I personally witnessed this.

317   **The Beaverton took a shot:** Luke Gordon Field, "Rogers exec keeps side
       hustle," The Beaverton, October 25, 2022, https://www.thebeaverton.com
       /2022/10/rogers-exec-keeps-side-hustle/.

317   **Batty finally completed:** "Report on Mayor John Tory, the Toronto Blue
       Jays and ActiveTO," Jonathan Batty, Integrity Commissioner,
       December 20, 2022, https://www.toronto.ca/wp-content/uploads/2022/12
       /8d73-2022-12-20-Report-on-Mayor-John-Tory-the-Toronto-Blue-Jays
       -and-ActiveTO.pdf.

317   **Chaleff, meanwhile, was disappointed:** Interview with Chaleff.

318   **one lawyer characterized:** Jonathan Hood, case management conference,
       January 3, 2023.

318   **The cable companies responded:** "Rogers and Shaw Issue Statement on
       Commissioner of Competition's Application for an Injunction and Appeal
       of the Tribunal Decision," Rogers Communications Canada Inc. press
       release, December 30, 2022, https://www.globenewswire.com/news-release
       /2022/12/30/2581310/0/en/Rogers-and-Shaw-Issue-Statement-on
       -Commissioner-of-Competition-s-Application-for-an-Injunction-and
       -Appeal-of-the-Tribunal-Decision.html.

318   **The commissioner had been intransigent:** Costs submissions of Rogers
       Communications Inc., Shaw Communications Inc. and Videotron Ltd.,
       *Commissioner of Competition v. Rogers Communications Inc. and Shaw
       Communications Inc.*, CT-2022-002, December 30, 2022.

319   **"unseemly rush":** "Rogers-Shaw Merger Approval Signals Decade of
       Competitive Winter for Consumers," *Public Interest Advocacy Centre*,
       December 30, 2022, https://www.piac.ca/2022/12/30/rogers-shaw-merger
       -approval-signals-decade-of-competitive-winter-for-consumers/.

319   **The rapidity of the decision:** Notice of Appeal, *Commissioner of
       Competition v. Rogers Communications Inc., Shaw Communications Inc.*,
       Federal Court of Appeal, File No.: A-286-22, December 30, 2022.

319   **prior to the Rogers-Shaw case:** Before that, the quickest decision from
       the Competition Tribunal had come thirty years earlier, in 1992, in the
       matter of *Director of Investigation and Research v Hillsdown Holdings
       (Canada) Limited et al.*, which took just under three months.

319   **wait for clarity:** "Decision on Rogers-Shaw takeover to come after clarity
       in legal battle, says Minister Champagne," *Canadian Press*, December 31,
       2022, https://www.theglobeandmail.com/business/article-decision-on
       -rogers-shaw-takeover-to-come-after-clarity-in-legal-battle/.

320   **In letters to the court:** The back-and-forth between the two sides is
       contained with correspondence filed as part of *Commissioner of Competition
       v. Rogers Communications Inc., Shaw Communications Inc. and Videotron
       Ltd.*, Federal Court of Appeal, File No.: A-286-22.

320   **The 88-page document:** "Reasons for order and order," Competition
       Tribunal, *Canada (Commissioner of Competition) v. Rogers Communications Inc.
       and Shaw Communications Inc.*, File No.: CT-2022-002, December 31, 2022.

321   **"It is now clear":** "Shaw Communications Statement on Decision by
       Competition Tribunal," Shaw Communications Inc. press release,
       January 2, 2023, https://www.globenewswire.com/en/news-release/2023/01
       /03/2581782/0/en/Shaw-Communications-Statement-on-Decision-by
       -Competition-Tribunal.html.

321   **added two more:** Amended Notice of Appeal, *Commissioner of Competition v. Rogers Communications Inc., Shaw Communications Inc. and Videotron Ltd.*, Federal Court of Appeal, File No.: A-286-22, January 6, 2023.

322   **"This appeal is":** Virtual case management conference was attended by the author.

323   **Alexander Gay approached:** Virtual hearing was attended by the author.

324   **"a foray into fiction and fantasy":** Reasons for Judgment of the Court, *Commissioner of Competition v. Rogers Communications Inc., Shaw Communications Inc. and Videotron Ltd.*, January 24, 2023, https://www.lolg .ca/docs/default-source/default-document-library/federal-court-of-appeal ---reasons-(public)f19e3f826168616da574ff000044313a .pdf?sfvrsn=6ff65ed5_0.

325   **"We brought a strong":** "Statement from the Commissioner of Competition on the Federal Court of Appeal's decision regarding the Rogers-Shaw merger," Competition Bureau press release, January 24, 2023, https://www.newswire.ca/news-releases/statement-from-the -commissioner-of-competition-on-the-federal-court-of-appeal-s-decision -regarding-the-rogers-shaw-merger-817211464.html.

325   **Sitting behind:** Descriptions and dialogue from the hearing in front of the INDU committee, which was streamed online, are based on the author's notes and recordings.

325   **recommended against the deal:** Joël Lightbound, "Proposed acquisition of Shaw Communications by Rogers Communications: Better Together?" Report of the Standing Committee on Industry and Technology, March 2022.

328   **huge profits:** Maiya Keidan and Nell Mackenzie, "Dozen hedge funds eye bonanza as Rogers-Shaw deal nears close," Reuters, January 27, 2023, https://www.reuters.com/markets/deals/dozen-hedge-funds-eye-bonanza -rogers-shaw-deal-nears-close-2023-01-27/.

328   **"due course":** Alexandra Posadzki, "Rogers, Shaw and Videotron extend takeover deadline again pending final approval from Ottawa, "*Globe and Mail*, February 17, 2023, https://www.theglobeandmail.com/business /article-rogers-shaw-videotron-takeover-deadline-extends/.

329   **published an open letter:** Rick Perkins, Ryan Williams, Brad Vis and Bernard Généreux, January 27, 2023, https://twitter.com/RickPerkinsMP /status/1619007195777236992.

329   **In February, federal NDP leader:** "Singh calls on Champagne to reject Rogers-Shaw merger," NDP, February 13, 2023, https://www.ndp.ca/news /singh-calls-champagne-reject-rogers-shaw-merger/.

330   **"strong suit":** Alexandra Posadzki, "Rogers profit jumps 25 per cent as wireless gains fuel revenue growth," *Globe and Mail*, February 2, 2023, https://www.theglobeandmail.com/business/article-rogers-q4-earnings-2022/.

330   **higher fourth-quarter revenue and profit:** Rogers Communications Reports Fourth Quarter and Full-Year 2022 Results; Announces 2023 Financial Guidance," Rogers Communications Inc. press release, February 2, 2023, https://www.globenewswire.com/en/news-release/2023 /02/02/2600332/0/en/Rogers-Communications-Reports-Fourth-Quarter -and-Full-Year-2022-Results-Announces-2023-Financial-Guidance.html.

330   **The improvements were at least partly:** Analysts speaking on background.

331   **Roughly twenty:** Author interview with Tony Staffieri.

331   reported in the media: Bloomberg News first broke the news that
       Champagne planned to approve the transfer; the *Globe and Mail* followed
       soon after.

332   "massacre of layoffs": Anthony Lacavera in an interview with BNN
       Bloomberg, April 3, 2023, https://www.bnnbloomberg.ca/rogers-shaw-sale
       -means-massacre-of-layoffs-coming-anthony-lacavera-1.1903843.

332   "I'm a lawyer": Quotes from the press conference are from the author's
       notes and recordings.

332   relief washed over Staffieri: Tony Staffieri in conversation with Andrew
       Willis at the Canadian Club Toronto event, held at the Fairmont Royal
       York in Toronto on April 12, 2023.

Epilogue

334   Martha's heavy breathing: This scene is reconstructed based on my own
       notes and observations from attending Loretta's funeral at the Cathedral
       Church of St. James in Toronto on June 21, 2022.

335    $14.1 million severance payment: Rogers 2022 management information
       circular, pp. 41–2.

336   Melinda had organized: Confidential sources.

337   After studying: "Our Story," Scarlett Gasque, accessed August 21, 2023,
       https://www.scarlettgasque.com/pages/our-story.

337   Eventually, the advisory committee did: Alexandra Posadzki and
       Andrew Willis, "Rogers executive Thomas Turner joins advisory commit-
       tee of Rogers Control Trust, sources say," Globe and Mail, September 18,
       2023, https//www.theglobeandmail.com/business/article-rogers-executive
       -thomas-turner-joins-advisory-committee-of-rogers/.

338   Toronto's 68-year-old mayor resigned: David Rider, Ben Spurr, and
       Alyshah Hasham, "Mayor John Tory steps down from office after admit-
       ting he had relationship with staffer," *Toronto Star*, February 10, 2023,
       https://www.thestar.com/news/gta/2023/02/10/a-serious-error-of
       -judgement-mayor-john-tory-had-relationship-with-staffer.html.

338   Rogers parted ways: "Rogers Announces Executive Leadership Appoint-
       ments," Rogers Communications Canada Inc. press release, April 20, 2023,
       https://www.globenewswire.com/en/news-release/2023/04/20/2651612/0/en
       /Rogers-Announces-Executive-Leadership-Appointments.html.

338   stoked controversy: Anja Karadeglija, "'Incredibly concerning': Rogers'
       hiring of former Liberal industry minister slammed by opposition,"
       National Post, April 21, 2023, https://nationalpost.com/news/politics/rogers
       -hires-former-liberal-industry-minister.

338   The announcement prompted: Ashee Pamma, "House of Commons
       committee puts appointment of Navdeep Bains to Rogers' exec team under
       scrutiny," IT World Canada, June 21, 2023, https://www.itworldcanada
       .com/article/house-of-commons-committee-puts-appointment-of-navdeep
       -bains-to-rogers-exec-team-under-scrutiny/541408.

338   sued his former employer: Statement of claim, *Woodhead v. Rogers
       Communications Canada Inc.*, File No.: CV-23-00702148-0000, July 4, 2023.

338   Another executive: Statement of claim, *Singh v. Rogers Communications
       Inc. and Rogers Communications Canada Inc.*, File No.: CV-23-
       00697830-0000, April 12, 2023.

338   The company denied: Statement of defence, *Singh v. Rogers Communications Inc. and Rogers Communications Canada Inc.*, File No.: CV-23-00697830-0000, June 20, 2023.

338   In its response: Statement of defence, *Woodhead v. Rogers Communications Canada Inc.*, File No.: CV-23-00702148-0000, July 27, 2023.

339   Natale sued: Natale's statement of claim.

339   Rogers countered: Statement to the *Globe and Mail*.

339   The investigation: Confidential sources.

339   statement of defence and counterclaim: Statement of defence and counterclaim, Joseph Natale and Natale Industries Inc. v. Rogers Communications Inc., File No.: CV-23-00704578-0000, September 5, 2023.

340   the company announced: Tony Staffieri, email, Sept. 11, 2023.

340   written document outlining: "Reasons for order and order," Competition Tribunal, Canada (Commissioner of Competition) v. Rogers Communications Inc. and Shaw Communications Inc., File No.: CT-2022-002, August 28, 2023.

341   expressed disappointment: Alexandra Posadzki, "Merger court awards Rogers millions over Competition Bureau's attempt to block Shaw merger," Globe and Mail, August 29, 2023, https//www.theglobeandmail.com/business/article-merger-court-awards-rogers-millions-over-competition-bureaus-attempt/.

341   "legal smackdown": Andrew Willis, "Competition Bureau needs to move back to real world after Rogers fiasco," Globe and Mail, September 5, 2023, https//www.theglobeandmail.com/business/commentary/article-competition-bureau-needs-to-move-back-to-real-world-after-rogers/.

341   "worrying": Jennifer Quaid, "Despite legal costs awarded to Rogers-Shaw, the competition commissioner's challenge to the telecom merger was not a waste of taxpayer money," The Conversation Canada, September 15, 2023, https//theconversation.com/despite-legal-costs-awarded-to-rogers-shaw-the-competition-commissioners-challenge-to-the-telecom-merger-was-not-a-waste-of-taxpayer-money-213053.

342   proxy advisers Glass Lewis: David Milstead, "Agnico Eagle disappears a director—but what does it mean for Rogers?", *Globe and Mail*, May 2, 2023, https://www.theglobeandmail.com/business/commentary/article-agnico-eagle-disappears-a-director-but-what-does-it-mean-for-rogers/.

342   Glass Lewis cited: "RCI.A April 26, 2023 Annual Meeting," Glass, Lewis & Co., March 31, 2023.

342   Staffieri had received: Rogers 2023 management information circular, p. 40.

342   The one filed: "Class action request over Rogers outage should be heard in June, lawyer says," *Montreal Gazette*, March 31, 2023, https://montreal-gazette.com/news/local-news/class-action-request-over-rogers-outage-should-be-heard-in-june-lawyer-says.

342   "Although both Cockwell": Cockwell left the board in May, while Kerr departed in August. They were not immediately replaced, and the company did not issue a press release announcing their departures, which were brought to the public's attention via an article that I penned for the Globe and Mail. Alexandra Posadzki, "Rogers boardroom undergoes another shakeup with two recent departures," *Globe and Mail*, September 27, 2023,

https//www.theglobeandmail.com/business/article-rogers-boardroom
-undergoes-another-shakeup-with-two-recent-departures/.

343   seeing that the early votes: Interview with Robert Gemmell.

343   on top of $400 million: David Milstead, "There's no way to track the last
of the Shaw mystery millions," *Globe and Mail,* April 4, 2023, https://www
.theglobeandmail.com/business/commentary/article-rogers-shaw-deal
-severance-payments/.

INDEX